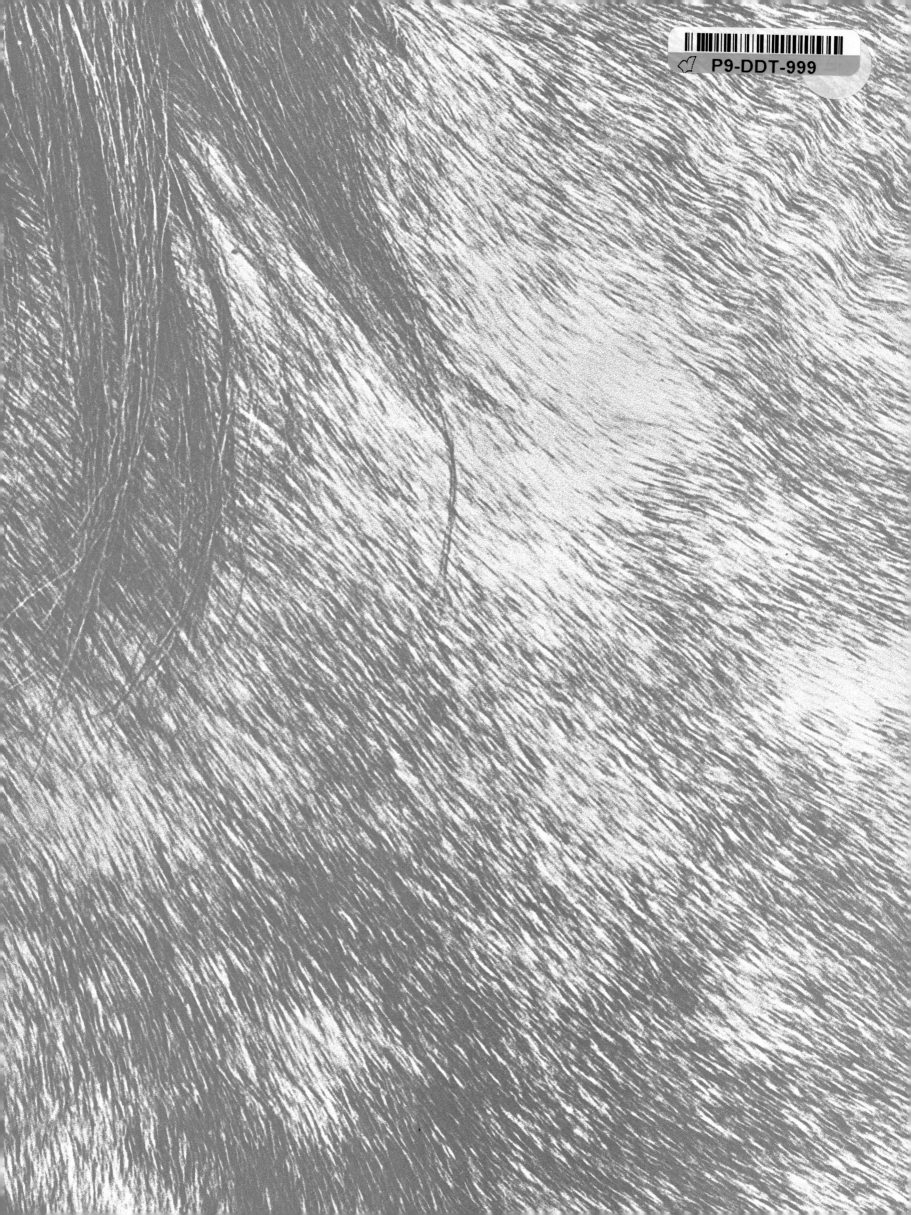

Foreword by
H.R.H. The Duke of Edinburgh, K.G., K.T.

The
NOBLE

MONIQUE AND
HANS D. DOSSENBACH

HORSE

BARNES
&NOBLE
BOOKS
NEW YORK

ACKNOWLEDGEMENTS

We would like to express our warmest thanks to the many individuals and institutions, including those whose names are not mentioned here, without whose assistance this book could never have been written.

We are especially grateful to Dr Kurt Weibel, Hallwag's Managing Director, for his invaluable assistance, for being so sympathetic and understanding, for placing his trust in us and for showing such keen interest in our work.

We are most grateful that Michael White and David Bateman of David Bateman Limited accepted the challenge of publishing this English language edition.

We would also like to thank Margaret Whale Sutton, who has so ably translated our original German manuscript, and Margaret Forde, the editor of the English language version.

Our thanks also to Claude Kuhn-Klein who produced the graphic designs, often under very difficult conditions.

H.D.D.

1

3

This edition published by Barnes & Noble Inc. by arrangement with David Bateman Ltd.

1997 Barnes & Noble Books

©1983 Hallwag AG, Bern.
©1985 English Language David Bateman Ltd.

ISBN 0-7607-0591-7

M 10 9 8 7 6 5 4 3 2 1

Produced by David Bateman Ltd.,
30 Tarndale Grove
Albany Business Park
Auckland
New Zealand

Printed in Hong Kong by
Everbest Printing Co., Ltd.

4

5

9

10

14

15

Since coins were first minted many different nations have chosen to decorate them with horse motifs as a tribute to the horse for the valuable role it played in their lives.

1. Celtic gold coin from Jura, 22 mm.
2. Gold coin of the Marger, 15 mm.
3. Philip II of Macedon in war chariot, 18 mm.
4. Coin of the Armorican Veneti.
5. Marger gold coin.
6. Coin of the Parisii.
7. Coin of the Osismii.
8. Silver coin of the Elusates, 18 mm.
9. Philip 11 of Macedon silver coin, 23 mm.
10. Coin attributed to the Atrebates.
11. Celtic coin.
12. Coin attributed to the Baiocasses.
13. Celtic coin.
14. Gold coin of the Parisii, 20 mm.
15. Gold coin of the Unelli.
16. Gold coin of the Redones, 20 mm.
17. Celtic coin.
18. Gold coin of the Marger.

2

6

7

8

11

12

13

16

17

18

CONTENTS

PART 1

THE NATURAL HISTORY
OF THE HORSE

PART 2

THE HISTORICAL
RELATIONSHIP
OF HORSE AND MAN

PART 3

HORSE AND MAN TODAY

Horses and dogs have been man's most intimate
and faithful companions since the dawn of history,
but the horse has certainly been the most useful.
In sport, agriculture, transport and warfare, the
horse has contributed more to human pleasure,
ambition and progress than any other animal.

Mechanisation has changed all that, except for
sport. Paradoxically there are probably more horses
being used by man to day than ever before. The equestrian
sports have enjoyed a most remarkable expansion during
the last 20 years. There is a greater variety of
equestrian sports, more national and international
competitions and more people taking part than in the
days when horses were indispensable to civilised human
existence.

It is not really surprising therefore, that popular
interest in horses is greater than it has ever been. The
value of this splendid book is that it traces the long
and intimate relationship between man and the horse from
the very earliest records to the present day. It explains
many things and it answers many questions but, perhaps
even better, it contains some of the best horse pictures
and photographs ever put together in one collection.

President
Federation Equestre Internationale

1985

PART 1

THE
NATURAL HISTORY
OF THE HORSE

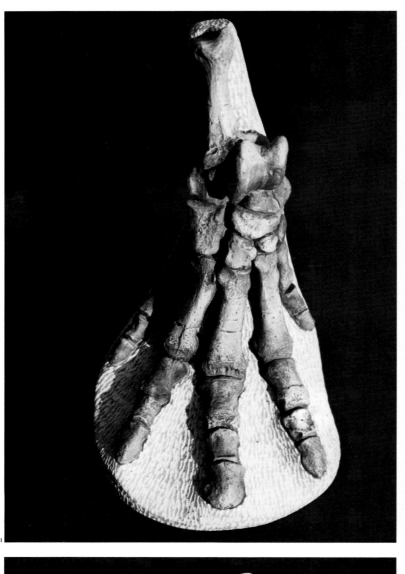

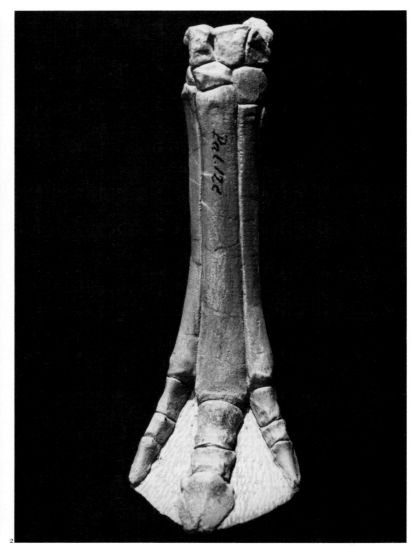

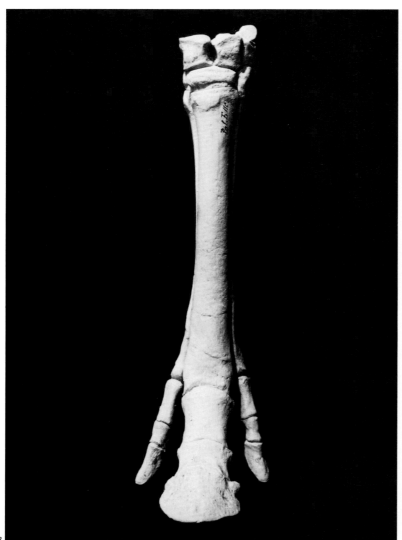

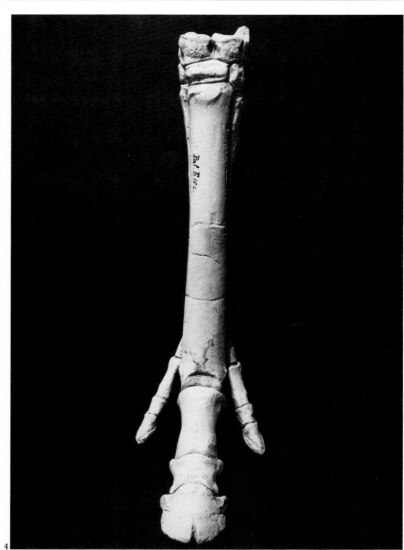

The horse and its relatives are unique among mammals, for in no other species is the theory of evolution so well substantiated by archaeological finds. Some particularly striking examples are shown here of the fossil chain which stretches back in an almost unbroken line to the Eocene period, to that famous several-toed creature, which was no bigger than a hare, named Hyracotherium *or* Eohippus.

1 Hind foot of Condylarthren phenacodus, *found in Wyoming. Condylarthren were very numerous during the early Eocene period (65 to 50 million years ago).* Hyracotherium *developed from one of the species of* Condylarthren *during the Eocene period (about 50 to 35 million years ago). Its more common name is Eohippus and it is the most primitive form of the horse that is known today.*

2 Fore foot of Mesohippus, *found in South Dakota. It dates from the Oligocene period (35 to 25 million years ago).*

3 Fore foot of Merychippus *from the Miocene period (25 to 10 million years ago). It was found in Colorado.*

4 Fore foot of Hypohippus *which lived in the Miocene period (25 to 10 million years ago) and also in the early Pliocene period (10 to 7 million years ago). Found in Colorado.*

5 Skull and parts of the jaw of Hyracotherium *the famous 'Dawn Horse', found in England. It lived in the Eocene period (50 to 35 million years ago).*

6 Skull of Mesohippus *dating from the Oligocene period. Found in South Dakota.*

7 Molars from the left half of the upper jaw of Hyracotherium, Mesohippus, Anchitherium, Hipparion *and* Equus.

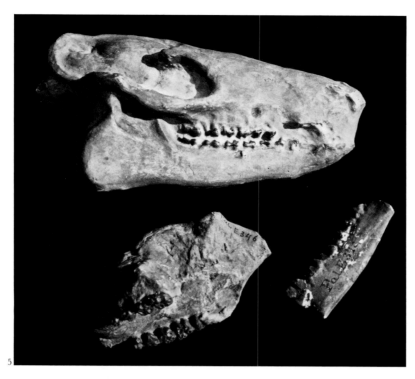

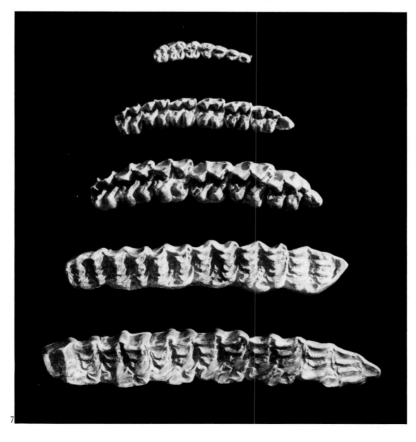

EVOLUTION

On 1 July 1858, Charles Darwin addressed a congress of scientists in London on the evolution of life, and in his lecture propounded a theory that placed the accepted view of the world in doubt. The reaction of the public was surprising — almost complete silence. Yet it seems that his theory of evolution did evoke some interest, for when, one year after Darwin's lecture, a book appeared that combined the results of over twenty years of his research — *On the origin of species: by means of natural selection, or, the preservation of favoured races in the struggle for life —* the first printing of 1250 copies sold out overnight, and its publication created worldwide shock. Darwin was bitterly denounced by both the church and the scientific community.

Acceptance of his theory was, however, only a matter of time. No lasting arguments succeeded in contesting a theory that finally even the Vatican was forced to accept about a century later. Reputable scientists have long ceased to doubt the validity of Darwin's theory, which, ultimately, explains the evolution of man.

Since that time palaeontologists have measured and classified countless bones of extinct animals. Reconstructed skeletons, or parts of skeletons, enable us to identify the species or families of various types of animals, and reveal their evolution over the course of millions of years from their primitive to present forms.

The horse is an exemplary model of the theory of evolution. Its ancestral chain can be traced back in unbroken links for something like fifty million years to the famous *Hyracotherium* or Eohippus of the Eocene period, an animal no bigger than a hare, with many toes.

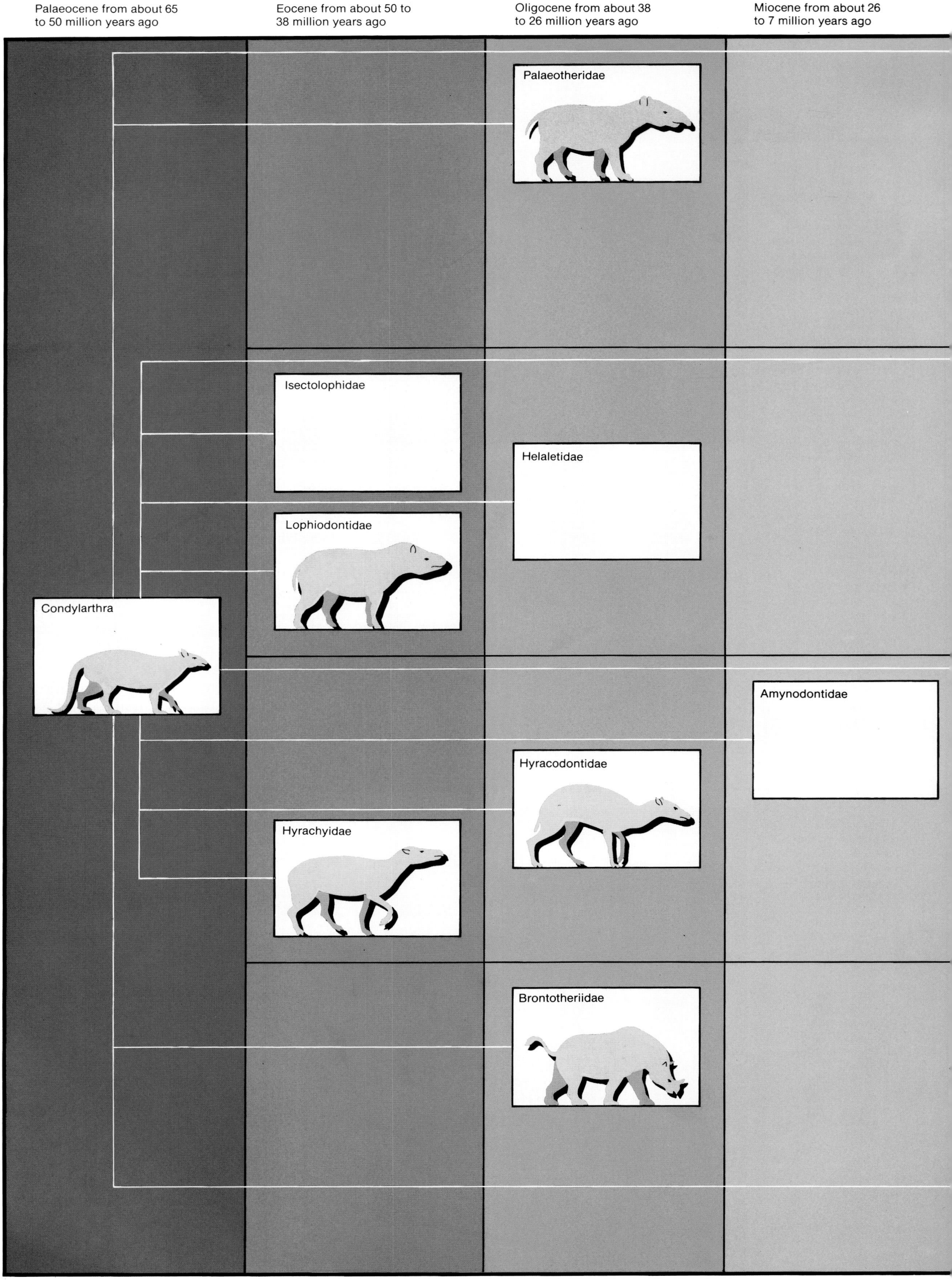

Palaeocene from about 65
to 50 million years ago

Eocene from about 50 to
38 million years ago

Oligocene from about 38
to 26 million years ago

Miocene from about 26
to 7 million years ago

Palaeotheridae

Isectolophidae

Helaletidae

Lophiodontidae

Condylarthra

Amynodontidae

Hyracodontidae

Hyrachyidae

Brontotheriidae

14

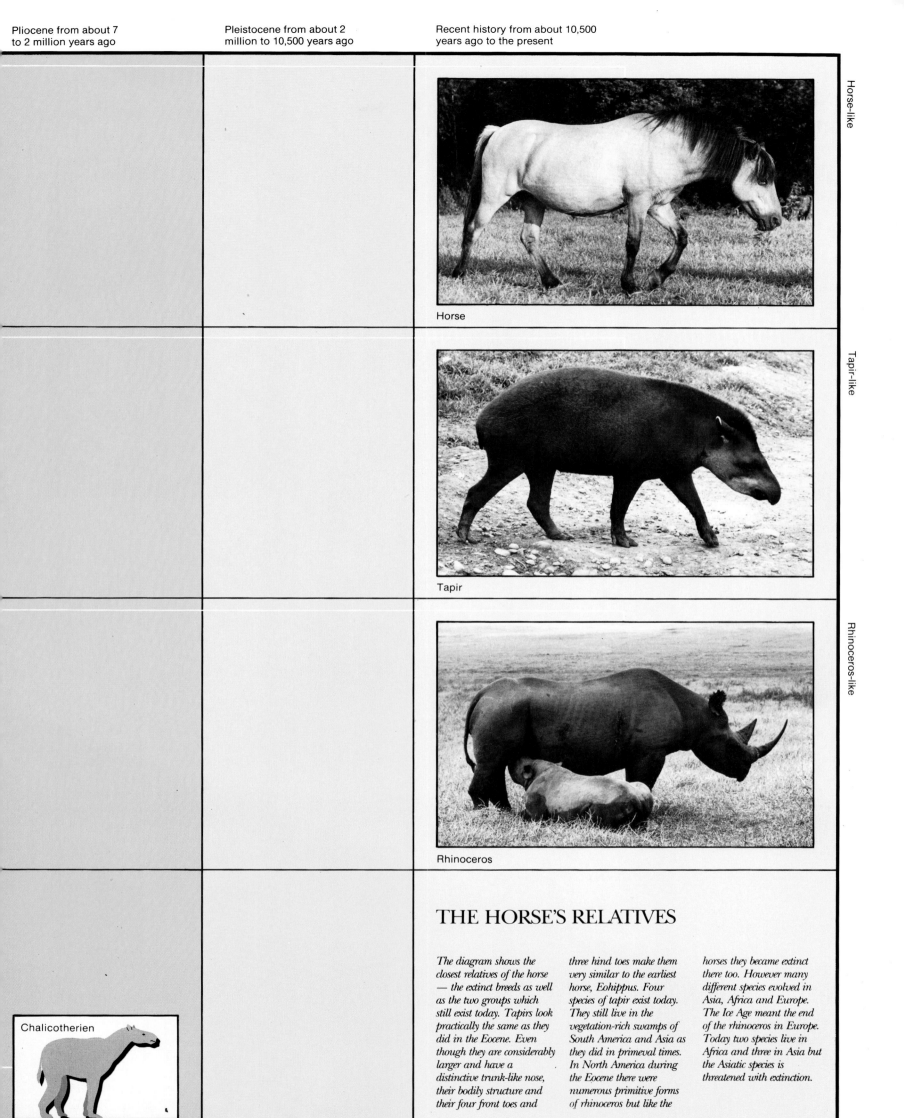

Horse-like

Horse

Tapir-like

Tapir

Rhinoceros-like

Rhinoceros

Chalicotherien

THE HORSE'S RELATIVES

The diagram shows the closest relatives of the horse — the extinct breeds as well as the two groups which still exist today. Tapirs look practically the same as they did in the Eocene. Even though they are considerably larger and have a distinctive trunk-like nose, their bodily structure and their four front toes and three hind toes make them very similar to the earliest horse, Eohippus. Four species of tapir exist today. They still live in the vegetation-rich swamps of South America and Asia as they did in primeval times. In North America during the Eocene there were numerous primitive forms of rhinoceros but like the horses they became extinct there too. However many different species evolved in Asia, Africa and Europe. The Ice Age meant the end of the rhinoceros in Europe. Today two species live in Africa and three in Asia but the Asiatic species is threatened with extinction.

PALAEONTOLOGISTS AND THE PRIMITIVE HORSE

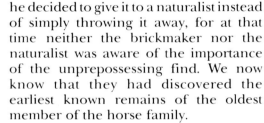

There is something miraculous about the discovery of the remains of an animal which lived millions of years ago. The fate of almost every animal when it dies it to lie where it falls, to be torn apart by scavengers, decomposed by saprophytic bacteria and for its weathered bones to crumble to dust. But on rare occasions it can happen that a dying animal sinks into the mud and its skeleton is preserved there for whole geological eras. It is an even more rare occurrence when such a fossilized bone structure is found by someone who is not completely ignorant of the importance of such a discovery. Small wonder that there are such large gaps in the fossil records of many animal species and that many researchers in this field are forced to rely on conjecture. It is a singularly happy circumstance that the lineage of the horse family can be substantiated by a chain of fossils more complete than that of any other species of mammal. Thanks to the passion for collecting — and the good fortune — of numerous researchers, the evolution of the horse can be traced back for about fifty million years.

In 1838, one William Colchester, when he was digging clay to make bricks, found a tooth on the banks of the river Deben in Suffolk, England. No one knows why he decided to give it to a naturalist instead of simply throwing it away, for at that time neither the brickmaker nor the naturalist was aware of the importance of the unprepossessing find. We now know that they had discovered the earliest known remains of the oldest member of the horse family.

In Kent a year later the naturalist William Richardson discovered a much better preserved skull among some fossilized plants. Richard Owen, who investigated the find, named the animal to which it must have belonged, *Hyracotherium*, i.e., the hyrax-like beast. (Hyraxes or dassies are mammals, eight species of which are distributed throughout Africa and the Near East; they have much in common with the marmots but actually belong to the Hyracoidea order Paenungulata and are more closely related to the elephant.) Owen cannot be blamed for making this assumption as the skull was little bigger than that of a hare and the teeth which remained in it were small and uneven and bore no resemblance to the large grinders of the horse. At that time it would have seemed absurd to call this animal an ancestor of the horse. In the first place far too few examples of later types of horse had been found for any recognizable connection to be made between the small leaf-eater and the present-day horse, and secondly the theory of evolution was uppermost in the minds of only a few naturalists, if they were aware of it at all. The majority of scientists dismissed it as absurd nonsense. Yet it was only twenty years later that Charles Darwin published his work on the origin

7 8 9

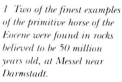

10

1 Two of the finest examples of the primitive horse of the Eocene were found in rocks believed to be 50 million years old, at Messel near Darmstadt.

2 In 1859 Charles Darwin (1809 to 1882) published his most important work on the origin of species. Using the results of twenty years' research he was able to convince almost all reputable naturalists of the validity of his theory of evolution.

3 Thomas Henry Huxley (1825 to 1895) was Darwin's closest friend. By putting Darwin's theories into practice he was able to arrange four different fossil types into a sequence of ancestors.

4 Wladimir Kowalewsky (1842 to 1883), a Russian palaeontologist, researched in depth the links between various European fossils.

5 In 1869 the American Joseph Leidy (1823 to 1891) published a book on fossils which became a classic. In it he described numerous extinct fossil forms.

6 Othniel Charles Marsh (1831 to 1899) did some of the most brilliant research on fossilized horses. In 1879 he had already put the horse's ancestors into a geological sequence which present-day research has proven to be basically correct.

7 Edward Drinker Cope (1840 to 1897) was considered to be Marsh's greatest rival. His achievements were less spectacular but one of his most important contributions was the discovery that Hyracotherium which was found in Europe and was the most primitive form of horse, was identical to the American Eohippus.

8 Henry Fairfield Osborn (1857 to 1935) was curator at the American Museum of Natural History in New York, where he directed the assembling of the best series of fossil horses in the world.

9 William Diller Matthew (1871 to 1930) using Osborn's collection as a basis described the evolution of the horse with such accuracy that since then only a few details have had to be modified.

10 William Berryman Scott (1858 to 1947), a professor at Princeton University, made a name for himself through his comprehensive works on the extinct mammals of America.

of species and thereby effectively demolished the then accepted view of the world. His arguments were so compelling that in a comparatively short time he was able to convince most naturalists of the validity of his theory but it took almost two decades before *Hyracotherium*, discovered in England, was acknowledged as the 'Dawn Horse', i.e., as the most primitive ancestor of the present-day horse. Before that conclusion was reached hundreds of collectors and researchers had first to salvage and thoroughly investigate thousands of fossil bones.

Thomas Henry Huxley, another Englishman, was the first to notice the connections between the various fossilized horses. (As well as being the most famous defender of Darwin's theory, he was the grandfather of both Julian Huxley, the famous zoologist who died in 1975, and Aldous Huxley, the author.) Taking four of the fossilized animals which had been found in Europe, namely *Palaeotherium* from the Palaeocene and Eocene, *Anchitherium* from the Oligocene and Miocene, *Hipparion* from the Pliocene and an extinct *Equus* from the Pleistocene, he placed them in their chronological order.

This interpretation prompted Wladimir Kowalewsky, the Russian palaeontologist, to devote several years to intensive research on the fossilized bones of mammals. Although he did not put it in its correct place at the beginning of the series, he was the first to note that the small *Hyracotherium* was related to the horse.

There were still large gaps in the series which Huxley had pieced together and Kowalewsky had confirmed. Soon the reasons for these gaps became clear when it was realized that the main branch of the horse family had evolved not in the Old World but in North America. Those ancestors of the horse, up to *Equus*, which had been found in Europe were only side-branches and after a while they had become extinct.

Joseph Leidy was the foremost American naturalist, when, in 1869, he published a classic volume in which he brought together a whole series of fossil horses, but although he was extremely knowledgeable, very industrious and gratifyingly precise in his work he lacked the necessary boldness and the stroke of genius which would have inspired him to place them in their correct order of age.

In the meantime Othniel Charles Marsh, the professor of Palaeontology at Yale University, was wasting no time. As well as employing numerous collectors he made several trips himself to the most important sites in the south-western US. Many of the early forms he found were unknown to Leidy and by 1874 he had already worked out a geological pedigree which he described as follows: 'The line of descent appears to have been direct and the remains now known supply every important form.' This conclusion was a little over-optimistic but it was Marsh himself who was later to add other highly important forms.

In 1871 and 1872 the remains of a horse from the early Eocene were found in North America. After Edward Drinker Cope, Marsh's great rival, had examined these fossils he called them Eohippus, but Marsh did not receive the bones until 1876 and only then was he able to put them in their correct place at the beginning of the ancestral series. Some years later Cope realized that his Eohippus was exactly the same animal as *Hyracotherium* which had been discovered forty years before in England. As this animal had already become part of zoological nomenclature as *Hyracotherium*, the name Eohippus (horse of the Eocene) became superfluous but it has remained in popular usage.

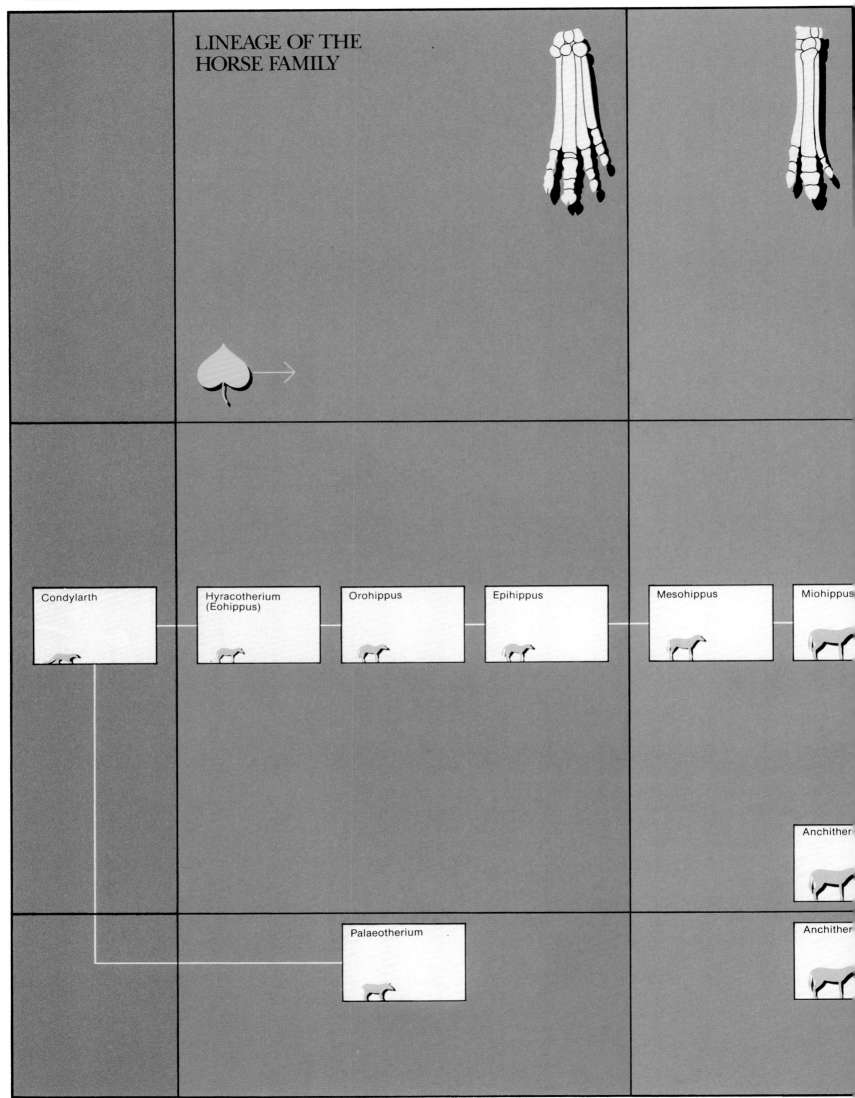

LINEAGE OF THE
HORSE FAMILY

Condylarth

Hyracotherium
(Eohippus)

Orohippus

Epihippus

Mesohippus

Miohippus

Anchither

Palaeotherium

Anchither

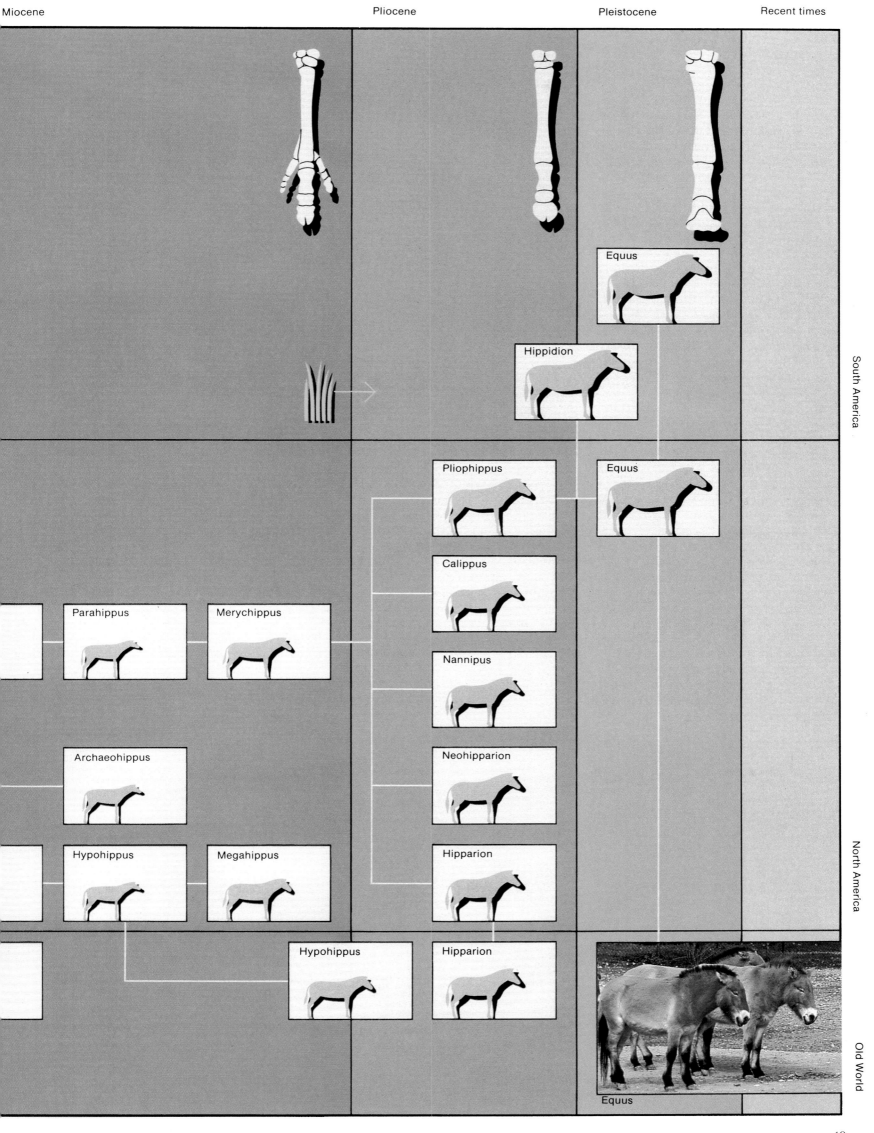

Equus

Hippidion

Pliophippus

Equus

Calippus

Parahippus

Merychippus

Nannipus

Archaeohippus

Neohipparion

Hypohippus

Megahippus

Hipparion

Hypohippus

Hipparion

Equus

South America

North America

Old World

19

THE LIVING WILD EQUIDAE

Although a great deal of detailed information is available and the history of the horse family can be traced as far back as the primeval swamps of the Tertiary period of the Eocene to an equine ancestor named *Hyracotherium*, a solution has still not been found to the riddle of who were the direct forebears of those wild Equidae alive today. Different species of *Plesippus* found in geological layers which date from the Tertiary eolithic period in North America, Europe and Asia, display some similarities with asses, semi-asses and zebras; but not enough to prove conclusively that they are the ancestors of these animals. Among the now extinct breeds of American horse there were animals which showed similarities with semi-asses or Asiatic Wild Asses still extant, but here too it is impossible to prove ancestral links.

Only one fact is certain and that is that the wild Equidae have long since had their heyday. The few varieties of the genus which survived the Ice Age are but a pitiful remnant of what was originally a wealth of breeds.

Six varieties of the single-toed animals or Equidae were able to survive to the present day: these are the wild horse, Grevy's zebra, the plains zebra and the mountain zebra, the African Wild Ass and the Asiatic Wild Ass. In appearance these different breeds are not at all similar and in their behaviour patterns, too, they also differ greatly; yet they are so closely related that they can be crossed at will. Although, because of their different behaviour patterns, such

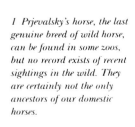

1 Prjevalsky's horse, the last genuine breed of wild horse, can be found in some zoos, but no record exists of recent sightings in the wild. They are certainly not the only ancestors of our domestic horses.

2 Pure-blooded tarpans no longer exist. Although there are horses which look like the now extinct wild tarpan, they are not genuine tarpans but were bred from horses which closely resembled the wild animal. This stallion was photographed in the Popielno Reserve in northern Poland.

crosses would never take place in nature, in captivity horses have been crossed with zebras and zebras with ponies. For thousands of years the donkeys and hinnies, which were the results of these crosses between horses and asses, played an important role as pack animals and in certain regions they are still being bred today. It is not possible to breed from these crosses as they are normally sterile.

The theory almost universally held by authors of books on horses is that Prjevalsky's horse is the original ancestor of our domestic horse. This view cannot be true, but it most probably stems from the fact that in popular language only one geographical or subspecies of the

wild horse is called Prjevalsky's horse, namely the wild horse of the Eastern steppes which is the only breed of wild horse to survive to the present day. In scientific terms, however, *Equus przewalskii* is used to refer to other varieties of wild horse as well as our domestic horse. The primitive ancestor of the pony which was already extinct during the Eocene period was called *Equus przewalskii gracilie*. The forest tarpan which became extinct in the eighteenth century was called *Equus przewalskii silvaticus*; the steppe tarpan is called *Equus przewalskii gmelini*; Prjevalsky's horse is *Equus przewalskii przewalskii* and the domestic horse is referred to as *Equus przewalskii caballus*. Prjevalsky's horse is not the sole ancestor of our modern horse. The tarpan and other earlier wild breeds are certainly also among its ancestry.

Three varieties of genuine wild horses have survived into recent times. The forest tarpan, which is small and particularly lightly built, used to be widely spread throughout the forest regions of Europe, but by the Middle Ages it had already disappeared from Western Europe. In Eastern Europe the last of the free roaming herds was destroyed at the end of the eighteenth century. A Polish Count Zamojski, who was concerned about the preservation of the forest tarpan, kept a number of these animals on his estate. During the winter of 1808, when his supply of hay was running out, he distributed these horses among the farmers in the region, who tamed them and then continued to breed them. Although they were later crossed with the domestic horse, these Polish Konics, which are often only the size of

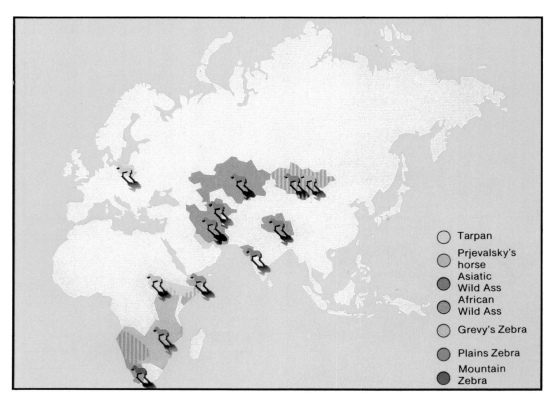

- Tarpan
- Prjevalsky's horse
- Asiatic Wild Ass
- African Wild Ass
- Grevy's Zebra
- Plains Zebra
- Mountain Zebra

3 With a withers height of about 140 cm the finely striped Grevy's zebra is the largest of the wild Equidae still extant.

4 The plains zebra is the only one of the wild Equidae which can still be found in large numbers. Several hundred thousand are still extant.

5 The South African Mountain Zebra was threatened with extinction.

6 The Somali Wild Ass is the only subspecies of the African Wild Ass of which a few hundred still exist. The zebra stripes on its legs are particularly striking.

7 The Onager from northern Iran is threatened with extinction. It belongs to the race of Asiatic Wild Asses which are more like horses.

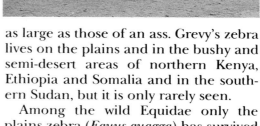

3
4
5
6
7

a pony, have retained their similarity to the tarpan.

In recent times an attempt was made at so-called retrograde breeding. The animals which resulted from this experiment can be seen and marvelled at in various zoos and in two Polish reserves. They are called tarpans but, of course, they are not genuine pure-blooded tarpans.

The larger and more strongly built steppe tarpan inhabited the steppes of southern Russia, but the last one died in the nineteenth century and this breed too has disappeared forever.

Today only one race of wild horses still exists. This is Prjevalsky's horse from the regions of steppe and desert which lie to the east of the Urals. The last free-roaming animals of this breed were seen in the inaccessible regions of the Gobi desert, but it is most likely that by now they will have disappeared there too. In order to save these animals from extinction a breeding herd was established and an international stud book was begun. Now the total number of Prjevalsky's horses has risen from about 50 to about 250 animals, all in zoos. The largest living representative of the wild Equidae is Grevy's zebra (*Equus grevyi*), easily distinguished from the other kinds of zebra by the much finer pattern of its stripes and by its ears which are almost as large as those of an ass. Grevy's zebra lives on the plains and in the bushy and semi-desert areas of northern Kenya, Ethiopia and Somalia and in the southern Sudan, but it is only rarely seen.

Among the wild Equidae only the plains zebra (*Equus quagga*) has survived in large numbers. Giant herds still exist in West Africa, and on the Serengeti plains alone there are about 180,000 animals. Two subspecies became extinct about the turn of the century.

The mountain zebra (*Equus zebra*) lives in the mountainous regions of western South Africa. Two subspecies have been identified, but both are very rare, and of one only a few dozen animals are known to remain.

The African Wild Ass (*Equus asinus*), the ancestor of all the breeds of wild ass, is also in danger of extinction. Wild asses were domesticated much earlier than wild horses, i.e., about 6000 years ago, probably in the Lower Valley of the Nile. A distinction is drawn between three subspecies. The North African Wild Ass which was the first to become extinct; the Nubian Wild Ass which has not been seen for decades and therefore must also be considered to be extinct; and the Somali Wild Ass of which only a few hundred still exist.

Because the Asiatic Wild Ass (*Equus hemionus*) has characteristics of both the horse and the ass it is called a semi-ass or horse ass. One of the seven subspecies has long been extinct and those remaining are all threatened with extinction.

Most historical researchers believe that the Asiatic Wild Ass was domesticated by an early civilized race which lived in Mesopotamia, and drawings have been found of animals in harness which do look similar to asses. But even after being bred in zoos for several generations, Asiatic Wild Asses, in contrast to the African species, are still so wild and unruly that it is impossible to put them in harness or use them as pack animals.

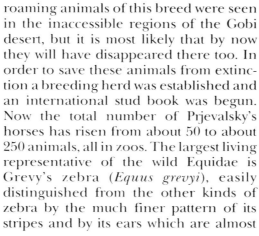

8
9

8 Mules (horse mare) or hinnies (ass mare) are obtained by crossing horses or ponies with asses. These offspring are normally sterile. There are exceptions: the mare leading a foal is a cross between an ass and a pony.

9 Sterile zebroids can also be obtained by crossing zebras and horses. This animal is the result of a cross between a Grevy's zebra and a Welsh pony.

Below: Migratory paths of prehistoric horses from North America to Asia, Europe and Africa. Different geographical breeds or subspecies of horse evolved wherever individual populations were isolated for long periods of time. The map is partly conjecture but by and large it is based on authenticated finds.

The native habitat of both the small primitive pony and the massive ancestors of the cold-blood breeds was the glacial landscapes, moors and heaths of the northern tundra.

The forest type was less specialized. It survived into the eighteenth century in the shape of the European forest tarpan and had considerable influence on the breeding of warm-blood horses.

ANCIENT BREEDS OF HORSE

Over millions of years primitive breeds of horse migrated from their North American homeland to the Old World across the Bering land-bridge which used to connect Alaska and Siberia where the Bering Sea is now. The last single-toed representatives of the genus *Equus* also took this path and while their relatives in North America mysteriously died out about 10,000 years ago they themselves spread out over Asia, Europe and Africa and evolved into the familiar shapes of the present-day zebras, donkeys and wild horses.

Among the wild Equidae, the original horses had probably the largest area of distribution. During the Ice Age they were able to survive under the most diverse living conditions on moor and

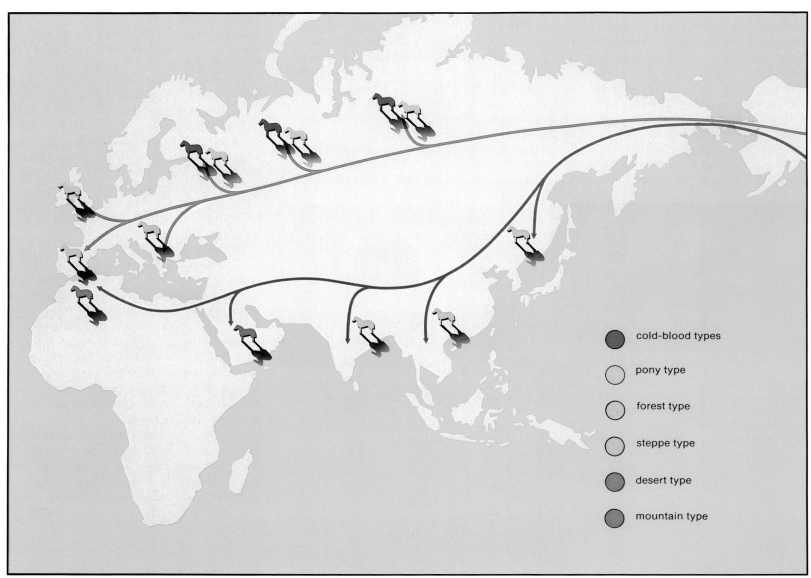

- cold-blood types
- pony type
- forest type
- steppe type
- desert type
- mountain type

A very light long-legged horse with a striking ram-like head lived in the bleak mountainous regions of North Africa. It became the 'father' of the majestic parade horses of the Baroque.

In the desert areas of south-west Asia a more finely-limbed type built for speed evolved. It is called either the primitive pure-bred or the primitive Arab.

Although life in the steppe region did not demand any high degree of specialization, several different breeds of steppe horse did nevertheless evolve. There was, for example, the grey small-headed, very lightly built steppe tarpan and the yellowish-brown heavier-headed Prjevalsky's horse (picture) or Eastern steppe wild tarpan.

tundra, in forests, mountains, steppes and desert-like regions. Both their bodily structure and their natures were shaped by the climate, vegetation, and condition of the ground. In the course of several generations different breeds of geographical subspecies of horse evolved from having to adapt to these varying conditions, particularly where the isolated living conditions of individual populations prevented any further exchange of genes.

There were at least four main types as well as numerous hybrids. On the moors and glacial landscapes of the northern tundra a tough sturdy little horse eked out a bleak existence. This primitive pony had a broad rump which allowed plenty of room for the robust digestive organs, long teeth specially designed to cope with being constantly worn down by grinding, and strong masticatory organs which enabled it to feed on tough stringy plants, lichen and even the bark of trees. Doubtless it also had a coarse fatty coat and a luxuriant mane and tail. The northern ponies are descended from this type which the naturalist called *Equus przewalskii gracilis*. Most of the domestic breeds of pony retained their essential characteristics despite being cross-bred with other breeds, but only the Exmoor pony of south-western England has remained pure-blooded since the Ice Age.

A large massive horse with a heavy head also lived in the north alongside this small agile pony. It too could survive on large quantities of poor food, and certain subspecies reached a withers height of about 180 centimetres. This was *Equus przewalskii robustus*, said to be the founding father of all the cold-blood breeds, even though these too have been cross-bred with other domestic breeds of

horse including Arabs. The Norwegian fjord horse has retained most of the qualities of the original colouring.

In the mountainous regions of north west Africa a comparatively large but very lightly built horse evolved. Its tapering head with swelling muzzle and the unusual distance between the eyes and the nostrils give it a very striking appearance. These Barb horses characterized by their amazing stamina and sure-footedness have been cross-bred with Arabs, but basically they trace their descent from the desert mountains breed. The Islamic conquerors took the horses with them to south-west Europe and used them as the basis for breeding the noble Andalusian horse which in the Baroque period was much prized throughout the whole of Europe. On the stud farms belonging to the nobility the Andalusian was then used as the basis for developing such famous breeds as the Neapolitan, Lipizzaner, Frederiks-borger, Knabstruppper and Klanruber. The American Mustang and, through them, the Western breeds of horse are also descended from these Andalusians.

Finally a fourth basic type, a small graceful finely-boned almost gazelle-like horse evolved on the bleak expanses of the deserts of south-west Asia. As the grasses which thrived in their native habitat were not very lush, though they were nourishing, this breed of horse did not need either particularly large or long teeth or very capacious digestive organs. There were no hiding places on that open terrain, so a quick escape was always the best protection from hostile predators. With a fiery temperament which guaranteed a lightning reaction to danger and a broad thorax allowing plenty of room for efficient lungs and a strong heart, more than any other

breed of horse this desert type was built for speed. The Arabs inherited this legacy and it is an indisputable fact that the breeding of warm-blood horses throughout the world would be unthinkable without their contribution.

Hybrid animals which were spread over much larger areas and were less highly specialized, not having had to adapt to such extremes of living conditions, were naturally domesticated much more frequently than any of the four main types. Thus Prjevalsky's horse, a steppe type, which fits in somewhere between the cold-blood breeds and the desert type, was the origin of numerous Asiatic breeds of horse.

Mongolian ponies, for example, have retained many of its qualities. However this, the last of the wild horses, is definitely not, as is often claimed, the founding father of all domestic horses. In addition to other breeds of primitive horse, the tarpan, which was spread over Central and Eastern Europe, played a particularly important role in the development of the domestic horse. These forest and steppe horses provided the basis for the breeding of warm-bloods in Europe and it is very likely that they were the first horses to be domesticated.

PONIES

Most Europeans would define a pony as a small sturdy horse with a luxuriant mane and tail. What they are in fact describing is a Shetland pony, and were they to come face to face with Connemara or Macedonian ponies they would then have to ask themselves whether these were perhaps small horses or even overgrown ponies which looked like horses. Most people, for example, consider a Haflinger to be a small horse, which is exactly what it is. According to international ruling every horse with a withers height of less than 148 cm is considered to be a pony and as far as sporting activities are concerned the problem is solved, but the question of what really are the characteristics of a pony remains unanswered. Haflinger and Fjord ponies are the right size for ponies, but if they are classified according to their types they are cold-blood horses. Macedonians, Camargue horses, Mustangs and many others are warm-blood horses but because of their small stature they are also classified as ponies. Many genuine desert Arabs do not grow larger than 148 cm, yet they could not possibly be called ponies. Many cowboys and polo players refer to their mounts as ponies when undoubtedly they are horses; and many devotees of the Icelandic breed speak of Iceland horses, yet these animals are typical ponies.

The pony is a distinct zoological type which traces its descent from the primitive pony of the Ice Age. Only the English Exmoor pony and the so-called northern breeds have remained almost pure-blooded. Genuine ponies have an ample girth plus very efficient digestive organs, which enable them to deal with a food supply both meagre and difficult

to digest. Their molars are also specially designed to cope with being constantly worn down by grinding. The rough coat, with its subcutaneous fat, provides protection against the damp weather and grows in autumn into a winter coat which is almost as thick as a bear's. The legs are strong but comparatively short, intended not for high speeds but rather to enable the animal to keep going at an easy pace even in difficult country.

Until some time after World War Two there were comparatively few ponies in Central Europe. These were mainly Shetlands. It was only about twenty years ago that larger ponies first began to be more widely used, mainly as trekking animals for adult riders. Since then this alternative to the classical European custom of riding only large horses has gradually become more wide-spread. Icelandic ponies are much favoured and initially they dominated the scene. Two breeds which were used mainly as pack animals were the dun-coloured Fjord pony from Norway and the blond-maned Haflinger from the Tyrol. The British Isles are described as the traditional land of the pony. Of all the native breeds the Welsh ponies are by far the most popular internationally, for as well as being particularly beautiful animals they are also remarkably even-tempered.

Normally, ponies are noticeably hardier and less demanding than large horses. Their upkeep costs only a third to a fifth that of a horse. In addition they make ideal trekking animals because they have an even temperament, are very sure-footed, and have plenty of stamina and robust health.

Acchetta (1)
There have been native ponies on Sardinia for at least 2000 years since it was settled by the Numidians. The animals, which are about 120 to 130 cm tall and wirily built, are really more like horses than ponies. They are extremely tough, undemanding and easy to handle, yet despite these qualities are not well known outside their native country. Besides the small Acchetta, Sardinia also has the Acchettone, similar in type but taller (about 150 cm). This pony was particularly popular as a cavalry mount for the Italian army.

Ariège pony (2)
For a very long time an interesting but little known breed of mountain pony has been extant in the southern French department of Ariège on the northern slope of the Pyrenees. These lively, placid black ponies are used mainly as pack and draught animals, though they are equally suitable for riding. The breeding animals live in half-wild herds. While the origin of the breed is unknown many zoologists believe it is closely related to the Shetland pony. Pure breeding of these Ariège ponies has been carried on for some time and, for over thirty years they have been recorded in a breeding register.

Assateague pony (3)
The wreck of a Spanish ship from the sixteenth or seventeenth century was found near the island of Assateague off the coast of Virginia in the US. As most Spanish ships which went to America in those days also carried horses on board it is probable that this one was no exception, and that a number of these animals were able to save themselves and reach the nearby island. Today there are about 120 wild ponies there. Every year the surplus young stallions are caught and made to swim across the channel to the neighbouring island of Chincoteague, where they are sold by public auction.

Bosnian ponies (4)
There are about a million horses in Yugoslavia today, almost half of which are Bosnian mountain ponies. They are highly regarded both by the mountain farmers and by the army who put them to work as tough sure-footed pack

animals. In recent years a few thousand of them reached Western Europe. With their good nature, liveliness and robust health, they have proved excellent animals for sporting activities.

Camargue pony (5)
Like all horses which have lived in the wild for countless generations, the famous greys of the swamps of the Rhone delta have over the years become smaller and thereby hardier. Although they are probably descended from the North African Barb they are nowadays only about 130 to 145 cm tall and are regarded as ponies. They make excellent mounts for the local cattle herders, provide the tourist with riding pleasure, and are sold as excellent saddle horses for leisure time activities.

China pony (6)
There are a large number of pony breeds, types and stock in China but not many of them are pure-bred. For the most part their origins can be traced back to the ignoble, wiry Mongolian ponies and through them to Prjevalsky's horse. Few could be described as beautiful but as they are kept outdoors all the time they are very tough, robustly healthy and of an undemanding nature.

Connemara pony (7)
Ireland has produced not only first-class show horses but also ponies of the highest quality. Most of these ponies thrive in a half-wild state in barren Connemara in the north-west of the country. They trace their origins, not to the British moorland ponies, but rather to the riding animals of the Celts who settled in the British Isles in the fourth century BC. Connemara ponies, which are about 130 to 140 cm high, are distinguished by their gentle natures, the fact that they make excellent saddle horses, and especially by an amazing aptitude for jumping.

Costeno (8)
In the course of many generations a robust breed of pony developed from the Spanish horses which were taken to Peru in the sixteenth and seventeenth centuries. These animals, used for herding and as pack animals by the Indians who live in the Andes at

1

7

2

8

3

9

4

10

5

11

6

12

heights of 3000 to 4000 metres, are noted for their tremendous stamina, their sure-footedness and astonishing ability to carry heavy burdens. Because of the extremely harsh conditions in which they live these Costenos also became smaller and now are usually only about 130 cm high.

Dales pony

The English Dales pony is little known outside its native habitat. About 140 to 148 cm tall, usually black in colour, they have distinct cold-blood characteristics which means that they do not look like ponies at all. At present the breeding complement of about a hundred animals is restricted almost exclusively to northern England. Dales ponies used to be more widely spread and were used both for transporting lead ore and as adaptable undemanding cavalry mounts.

Dartmoor pony (9)

Most Dartmoor ponies still live in a semi-wild state on the bleak moors of Devon in south-west England. Years ago, when used for work in the mines, they were often crossed with the smaller Shetlands to obtain ponies which, while retaining their strength, were as small as possible. Dartmoor ponies today are on average about 120 cm tall. Because they are so good-natured they are considered by many experts to be the most suitable mounts for children. Every year foals are taken from the herds and sold by auction.

Dülmen pony (10)

Since 1850 a herd of about 200 half-wild ponies has lived in the Merfelder Bruch of North Rhine Westphalia under the protection of the Counts of Croy. These Dülmen ponies are about 120 to 135 cm tall. To improve the bloodstock, several stallions from breeds which had similar characteristics to these wild ponies were introduced to the herd, including, for example, English Exmoor ponies, Polish Konics, Huzules from the Carpathian mountains and ponies from the Pyrenees. Most of the Dülmen ponies today look rather like Exmoor ponies or like the Konics which in turn resemble the tarpans. The young stallions are auctioned annually in May.

Exmoor pony (11)

The Exmoor pony apparently traces its descent in a direct line from the primitive pony of the Ice Age. Because they lead an almost completely isolated life on the wild moors of Devon and Somerset in south-west England they have been able to retain nearly all their pure-blooded qualities. They are therefore considered to be the most primitive of all the breeds of domestic horses. Their agility and excellent natures make them good saddle ponies for children. Adults often use them for hunting on their native moors even though they are only about 122 cm tall.

Falabella pony (12)

A century ago, on the ranch of the Falabella family in Argentina, the world's smallest breed of horse was developed as the result of a careful selective breeding programme based on Shetland ponies. As most Falabella ponies are barely 65 cm tall they cannot even be used as saddle horses by children. They are now bred in many countries but purely as a hobby as they have no practical value.

Fell pony

Black Fell ponies are similar to the Dales pony. They are the same size and have many excellent qualities, but have become very rare and barely 400 breeding animals remain. Formerly they were bred extensively and used as work horses, their main task being to carry baskets of iron ore, each one weighing about 100 kg, from the mines to the industrial towns about 400 km away on the coast of northern England. Their origins are debatable. According to their type they are not Moor ponies, nor is it likely that they are descended from the Celtic ponies, as are the Welsh and Connemara breeds, for in appearance they are like diminutive Friesian horses.

Fjord pony (13)
Like the Icelandic breed, the Norwegian Fjord ponies are also descended from the ponies of the Vikings. From these the Norwegian farmers have since bred a small compact muscled horse with distinctive cold-blood qualities. It weighs from 400 to 500 kg, is 130 to 145 cm tall, and is admirably suited for all farm work. The dun colour and the short upright mane are characteristics of the breed. During the last twenty years a lighter weight breed has been developed.

Fjord-Huzule pony (14)
For some years attempts have been made in Czechoslovakia to produce a new breed of pony by crossing Huzule ponies from the Carpathians with Norwegian Fjord ponies. The result is a pony with excellent qualities, larger and stronger than the original mountain pony, lighter and more agile than the Fjord pony.

Galiceno
Though the origins of this Mexican pony are said to go back to the horses of Iberian Galicia, it is more likely that Spanish horses were the founding parents. They are about 135 to 145 cm tall, not very well-proportioned, but lively, amazingly fast and very good-natured. For about thirty years they have also been bred in the US, where efforts are being made to improve its external appearance by concentrating on pure breeding and by strict selection.

Garrano pony
There are about 40,000 of these ponies (also called Minhos), but although they have excellent qualities and would be inexpensive to buy, the breed is little known outside its native Portugal. About 115 to 135 cm tall, they live in a half-wild state in the northern part of the country. They are used as saddle, draught and pack animals and because of their hardiness and stamina are also very popular with the army.

Gotland pony (15)
A population of wild ponies which became extinct elsewhere was able to survive on the forest-covered island of Gotland in Sweden. This 'Skogruss' pony, which is 112 to 132 cm tall, is now bred throughout Sweden and used for sporting

purposes. Intelligent and lively, it has a long-striding action, and is considered one of the best ponies for children. It is now being bred extensively in the US, as well as in several other countries.

Haflinger (16)
For centuries there have been small mountain horses in the Alps of the Tyrol. They were sometimes crossed with the heavy Noriker stallions but the decisive influence was an Arab stallion which was introduced about 1873. The result was the modern Haflinger which is both hardy and high-spirited and although it belongs to the cold-blood breeds is fairly lightweight and very agile. One of the most popular ponies for leisure time pursuits, it is bred in twenty countries. It is chestnut-coloured with light, almost white-coloured mane and tail.

Highland pony
The Scottish Highland pony or Garron is thought to be of Celtic descent, but for about 500 years it was cross-bred with Clydesdales, Arabs and other breeds. It is the biggest and strongest of all the British ponies, weighing up to about 450 kg and with a withers height of 145 cm. It is very sure-footed and easily able to carry heavy loads — such as the stalker and his stag booty — through the wild countryside. A smaller breed, about 10 cm less in height, lives on the islands to the west of Scotland.

Huzule pony (17)
Just as the Icelandic pony was so important to the Icelanders, this hardy tireless mountain pony has played a prominent part in the lives of the Carpathian people. It grows to about 130 cm tall and is indispensable in many regions for use as a saddle horse, as a pack animal and to draw carts. The main breeding region is in Rumania but there are other studs in Poland, Czechoslovakia and Austria, and in other countries, including England, even though that country has such a wealth of indigenous breeds of its own.

Indian pony (18)
The ponies of the North American Indians are descendants of the horses which the Spaniards brought to America in the sixteenth and seventeenth

centuries. Like their close relatives, the Mustangs, these ponies are hardy and tenacious, have amazing speed and stamina and are very undemanding. They are on average about 135 cm tall and frequently dappled or spotted, the result of the Indians' particular liking for colourful horses.

Icelandic pony (19)
At least a thousand years ago Norwegian Vikings settled the distant island of Iceland and took their sheep, cattle and ponies with them on their open ships. The extremely hardy ponies are still the most important means of transport in the rugged volcanic and glacial interior of the island. Since no fresh stock was allowed to be brought in, as a protective measure against disease, they remained pure-blooded for over a thousand years. Today these self-willed but lovable ponies are highly sought after for leisure time pursuits.

Macedonian (20)
The main characteristics of this little-known small horse from Yugoslavia are sure-footedness, tremendous stamina, robust health and a friendly nature. Many experts trace the origins of this pony back to the Thessalian horse of Greek antiquity. The Oriental influence is unmistakable. To keep this breed going, for it is dying out in its native homeland, a number of Macedonians were introduced into Switzerland where they are now being bred.

New Forest pony (21)
There were wild ponies in the New Forest, a large forested area to the south of London, when King William Rufus hunted there over a thousand years ago. These ponies, originally very similar to the Exmoor pony, have been influenced by many different breeds, but particularly by Arabs and English Thoroughbreds. Although they have remained pure-bred for some decades now, they still differ a great deal in size and type, but one trait they all have in common is an excellent nature.

POA (22 and 23)
The Americans have produced in the POA, the 'Pony of the Americas', a riding animal suitable for children and young people

which is to be envied, and not only for its unusual colouring. Following the example of the Nez Percé Indians in Idaho, who used spotted Spanish horses as a basis and produced the Appaloosa breed which has proved to be extremely popular and now has over 150,000 animals, the Americans attempted to breed a pony of the same type which would be suitable for children. They were completely successful. They used Appaloosa horses and finely limbed American Shetland ponies and the result was a dainty yet very strong pony. About 130 cm tall, it is described as undemanding, hardy, very willing and devoted, with plenty of stamina and with a long-striding action in all gaits. They are bred in seven distinct Appaloosa-like patterns of spots. Here two examples of the 'spotted blanket' pattern are shown: on a grey (22) and on a black (23) pony.

Shetland pony (24, 25 and introductory picture)
For over two thousand years there have been small ponies on the bleak, storm-lashed Shetland Isles. The local farmers found their help invaluable. About fifty years ago they first became popular as children's ponies and have been in great demand ever since. These 'Shelties' are intelligent, hardy and amazingly agile animals and despite being very self-willed are extremely lovable. Unfortunately, because of their small stature, only about 100 cm at the withers, they are often pampered, but they should be made to spend the whole year outside in the fresh air if they are to retain their robust health. The Shetland's typical colouring is shown in (24); occasionally they are bred in a leopard-spotted pattern (25).

Leopard-spotted pony (26)
Ponies with a distinctive leopard-spotted pattern on their coats have been bred in England for many years. Nowadays they are bred in other countries as well. In contrast to the American POA, which is a small horse if classified according to its type, the leopard-spotted is a typical pony.

Welsh ponies (27 to 29)
Together with the Shelties and the Icelandic ponies, the

13

14

15

16

17

18

19

25

20

26

21

27

22

28

23

29

24

30

Welsh ponies are among the most popular breeds worldwide. They trace their origins back to the fast, strong, wiry ponies of the Celts, who settled in the green hill country of Wales. The ponies were often crossed with other breeds, but it is the Arab influence which is most clearly seen in many Welsh ponies. They can be as small as 100 cm tall, but also as large as a horse and are therefore divided into different categories or sections. Section A (27) has remained closest to the original mountain pony. It grows up to 122 cm tall, is strong but finely limbed, and has a fine Arabian head. The pony of Section B (28) is the same type but grows to 137 cm. Section C pony is the same height but much larger and stronger. The Welsh Cob which grows up to 158 cm is, if classified according to its type, a strong compactly built small horse. It is classed as Section D. Finally Section K animals (29) are those which can prove from their pedigree papers that they have Arab blood, up to a maximum of seventy-five per cent. These ponies also frequently grow to over 148 cm and therefore often have to be classified as horses.

Hackney pony (30)
The Hackney is an ancient breed of horse with a special aptitude as a carriage horse. The Hackney pony, which was developed by crossing a Hackney stallion with a distantly related pony mare, is about 130 cm tall and is used almost exclusively as a flamboyant show pony in front of a light carriage.

COLD-BLOOD BREEDS

The term cold-blood, which is not a very apt description, for the body temperature of these breeds is the same as that of the warm-blood breeds, is more a reference to the typically quiet, calm, phlegmatic temperament. The breed is further characterized by the medium to very heavy body, the strong legs with large hooves which are often covered with long hair or 'feathered', the short muscled neck, the head which despite its heavy bulky appearance, is frequently very expressive, and the bifurcated croup which is 'dipped' along its length.

France was undeniably the most important country in the history of the breeding of cold-bloods, and several first class breeds such as the Percheron, Boulonnais, Ardennais, Breton, etc., originated there. The powerful Belgian Heavy Draught was also much sought after worldwide and has been used for improving many other breeds. It played, for example, an important role in the development of the thriving Russian cold-blood breeding industry. The English Shire Horses are also extremely popular. They are the largest of all the horses and the stallions can have a height at the withers of more than two metres.

Up until a few decades ago the cold-blood ruled the horse-breeding scene, and in many countries they made up about eighty per cent of the total equine population. With the massive increase in mechanisation after World War Two, however, they became superfluous in most of the civilized world and now relatively few remain.

Ardennais (1)
Most of the cold-blood breeds which originated in France have been used extensively in the breeding of cold-bloods throughout the world. They all have excellent qualities but this breed from the Ardennes is one of the foremost. It weights about 800 kg and is therefore classified as a medium-heavy breed.

Belgian Heavy Draught (2)
This is one of the most powerful horses of all, used for pulling the heaviest loads. It weighs over 1000 kg and has a height at the withers of about 175 cm. Mostly chestnut-coloured or red roans but occasionally also dun-coloured.

Boulonnais
This very ancient medium-heavy breed originated in the region around Boulogne. It is bred in two types. One is a heavy draught horse which weighs about 800 kg and is 170 cm tall, the other is smaller and more agile, weighs about 600 kg and is 160 cm tall.

Breton (3)
Three types of a versatile robust cold-blood breed come from Brittany. The first is a large heavy draught horse which weighs over 550 kg and is over 160 cm tall; the second is a somewhat lighter mountain type which grows to about 150 cm; and the third is the Postier, also about 150 cm tall, which became livelier and achieved a good active trot as the result of being crossed with the Norfolk Trotter.

Clydesdale (4 and introductory picture)
This is an impressive, immensely strong, but never clumsy cold-blood breed which often grows to around 170 cm. It originated in Scotland in the eighteenth century and is still very popular, particularly in the US, Australia, New Zealand and South Africa.

Comtois
The Comtois, a comparatively light draught horse of about 150 to 160 cm in height, is a typical mountain cold-blood breed. It is well-proportioned and has a characteristic head. Unfortunately the breeding of these animals has almost completely ceased.

Døle Trotter
This small light draught horse is today an indispensable part of Norway's forest and farming economy and accounts for over half the total Norwegian complement of horses.

Freiberger (5)
A very light draught horse, with a height at the withers of 153 to 162 cm, from the Jura mountains region of Switzerland. It has proved a good cavalry mount, but attempts to improve its riding qualities by crossing it with Arabs — as was done with the Haflingers — have up till now not had the desired results.

Jutland (6)
This very ancient breed from southern Denmark is powerfully and strongly built. The typical colouring is a dark chestnut with light coloured mane and tail.

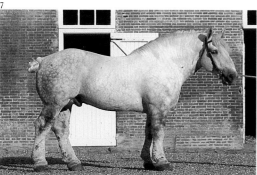

7

13

8

14

9

10

11

12

particularly for forestry in the high-lying regions of the Black Forest. It is chestnut-coloured with lighter coloured mane and tail.

Swedish Ardennes (11)
This excellent medium-heavy draught horse was developed about a hundred years ago by cross-breeding with the Belgian Ardennes. Today it makes up about half of the total Swedish horse population and deserves to be described as the most widely spread of all the cold-blood breeds.

Shire Horse (12)
These horses were formerly used to carry heavily armoured knights into battle. They are the world's biggest breed of horse, weighing up to 1300 kg and usually having a withers height of between 170 and 180 cm, though occasionally it can exceed two metres. Despite their strength they are far from clumsy horses.

Soviet Heavy Draught (13)
This heavy medium-sized breed originated about forty years ago and stallions of various Western breeds played a major role in its development. Today it is used extensively for heavy agricultural work.

Suffolk Punch (14)
This is a striking chestnut-coloured, short-legged, immensely strong and compact horse from the English county of Suffolk. In contrast to the Shire Horse it is noted for its ability to thrive on meagre rations.

Trait du Nord
This breed originated in northern France and is very similar to the Belgian Heavy Draught Horse. It may weigh over 900 kg and is very strong and hardy.

West Friesian
This exclusively black horse has been bred in Friesland for a long time. In appearance it is very like a powerful warm-blood and only shows its cold-blood characteristics on closer examination. As well as being a saddle horse it is frequently used to pull two-wheeled carts.

Woronesh
Like the West Friesian this breed, which was developed about 200 years ago in Russia, also looks very like a warm-blood. It weighs only about 500 kg and has a height at the withers of 150 to 165 cm.

Mulassier
For centuries this very lethargic and not very beautiful breed has been used mainly for the breeding of mules. About three-quarters of the mares are mated with large Poitevin jackasses. The resultant offspring are very strong and much sought after.

Dutch Draught
In this century a standardized breed was developed from the ancient Dutch cold-blood breeds by crossing with other breeds, in particular with Belgian Heavy Draught stallions. Dutch Draughts weigh up to about 1000 kg and have a withers height of about 160 cm.

North Swedish
As the result of discriminating breeding a comparatively light and agile cold-blood breed was developed from the ancient Swedish draught horse. These are very undemanding horses with a kind temperament and long-striding action.

Noriker (7)
Depending on where it is bred, this breed is also called Pinzgauer, Oberländer or South German cold-blood. These well-built medium-heavy horses trace their origins to the ancient work-horses of the Roman state of Noricum. Today they are found frequently in the mountain regions of Bavaria, Württemberg and Austria.

Percheron (8)
The powerfully built, usually grey-coloured Percheron weighs up to 1000 kg. Its small fine head and the fact that, in relation to its size, it moves very freely, betray its Arab ancestry.

Rhineland Heavy Draught
This ancient breed used to be inferior to the French and Belgian cold-blood breeds, but towards the end of the last century it was greatly improved by systematic crossing with Belgian stallions.

Russian Heavy Draught (9)
These small stocky undemanding animals have a withers height of 143 to 152 cm. They are capable of pulling very heavy loads and were developed about a century ago in the Ukraine by crossing Ardennais, Belgian Heavy Draught and Orlov Trotters. This breed is very popular in the Eastern bloc where work-horses still have an important role to play.

Schleswig Heavy Draught
This is basically the same breed as its southern Danish neighbours, the Jutlands. It is very similar in appearance and is suited to the same sort of work.

Schwarzwälder (10)
This horse probably traces its origins to the ancient Norike breed, but it is smaller and more agile. It is still used for agricultural work,

WARM-BLOOD BREEDS

It is now an accepted fact that the more than 300 breeds of domestic horse are not descended from one single breed of horse, i.e., Prjevalsky's, as had been assumed for so long, and that the origins of the domestic horse can be traced to at least four distinct different geographical breeds of the animal as well as various hybrids. These could be defined as a primitive pony, a primitive cold-blood, a primitive pure-bred and various primitive warm-bloods. Domestication has, of course, changed all these basic types, which have been affected, not only by the different methods of breeding and training, but also by the fact that they have been crossed with each other countless times.

It is particularly difficult to define the term warm-blood, as warm-bloods belong to numerous types and breeds, apart of course from ponies and cold-blood breeds. The so-called halfbreds, i.e., horses of which one parent, usually the sire, is an English or Arab pure-bred, are also warm-bloods. The offspring of a cross between an English and an Arab pure-bred is not a pure-bred but a warm-blood. Many ponies have been so strongly influenced by the larger horse breeds, above all by Arabs and English Thoroughbreds, that if they are classified according to their type they fall into the warm-blood category rather than the pony — but in this case the international ruling on the limit of height at the withers is the determining factor.

Nowadays the term warm-blood also covers a horse which has been nobly bred — a quite definite type of horse, and one which to a greater or lesser degree has inherited the qualities of the English Thoroughbred and therefore fulfils the requirements of modern horse racing. This has been the chief aim of much of the breeding industry from Sweden to Italy and Spain to Russia, and over the past decades a breed of horse has been developed which could be called the European warm-blood. Even a specialist now finds it difficult, if not impossible, to differentiate between, e.g., a French Anglo-Norman, and a Hessian, Swedish, or Hungarian warm-blood.

Germany has been particularly successful in the breeding of modern warm-bloods. The Hanoverian and the closely related Holstein are both large, relatively heavy, but still essentially noble breeds which distinguish themselves by a tremendous aptitude for jumping. The noble Württemberg warm-blood is versatile, very attractive in appearance and reminiscent of the Trakehner. The French Anglo-Norman which is bred in Switzerland among other countries has also been extremely successful in top international sporting events. The Swedish warm-blood is also very talented, though specially suited to dressage. In Germany the Irish Hunter is often described, tongue-in-cheek, as a horse of no particular breed. This is actually quite true, for it is nearly always the result of the crossing of a Draught or Hunter mare with a Thoroughbred stallion and therefore a halfbreed, or to put it more bluntly, a bastard. This fact, however, has not prevented the Irish Hunter from becoming the world's most successful jumper.

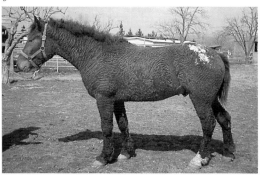

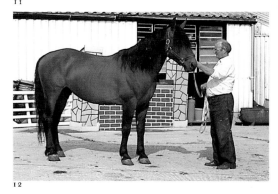

7

13

8

14

9

15

10

16

11

17

12

18

Akhal-Teké (1)
Very noble, very fast saddle horse from Turkmenistan, with tremendous stamina, often a striking metallic sheen to its coat.

Albino (2)
Not a breed but a type of colouring. In contrast to greys, albinos are born white.

Altèr-Real (3)
A beautiful Portuguese horse with particular aptitude for advanced dressage.

American Saddle Horse (4)
Former utility riding horse, today a show horse, which is taught unnatural show gaits.

American Standard Trotter (5)
The fastest trotting breed. Bred as Normal (Diagonal) and as Pace trotters.

Andalusian (6)
A breed, once the most prized in Europe, strongly influenced by Barbs and Arabians.

Anglo-Arab (7)
A breed which was developed in France, Poland and Hungary as the result of crossing English Thoroughbreds and Arabs.

Anglo-Argentine
A fast saddle horse bred from Argentinian Criollos and English Thoroughbreds.

Anglo-Norman (8)
A cross between Norman and English horses. Bred for sporting purposes and as a working horse.

Appaloosa (9)
Saddle horse of great stamina, originally bred by American Indians, with distinctive spotted patterns on the coat.

Bavarian
Riding horse at present in great demand for sporting activities.

Bashkir Curly (10)
American breed of unknown origins with a striking curly coat.

Barb
Elegant fast riding horse from North Africa with tremendous stamina.

Brandenburg
Modern saddle horse similar to the Hanoverian.

Buckskin (11)
A type of colouring of the American Western horse considered to be very hardy (original wild horse colour).

Budyonny
Modern versatile saddle horse from the Soviet Union.

Cleveland Bay (12)
An English breed in great demand as a carriage horse.

Criollo (13)
Small hardy breed from South America, descended from Spanish and Portuguese horses.

Don (14)
The hardy mounts of the Don Cossacks.

Einsiedler
These horses which have been bred for about a thousand years in the Stud of the monastery at Einsiedel, Switzerland, are today of the modern Anglo-Norman breed.

European Trotter (15)
A trotting breed developed from French, American, and Russian trotters.

Finnish Hack
Excellent small versatile horse from Finland.

French Trotter
An excellent trotting breed developed mainly from Norman and English Thoroughbreds.

Frederiksborg (16)
Formerly Baroque parade horses, today mostly modern saddle horses.

Furioso-North Star (17)
Noble Hungarian breed with two English Thoroughbreds as the foundation sires.

Gelderland
A light horse from Holland similar to the cold-blood breeds; an excellent carriage horse.

Gidran (18)
Hungarian Anglo-Arab breed.

Groningen
Originally a carriage horse, today a saddle horse from the Netherlands.

Hackney (19)
Flamboyant carriage horse with high-stepping knee action unfortunately often 'improved' by the use of cruel methods.

Hanoverian (20)
Large, strong saddle horse, well known for its tremendous jumping ability.

Hessian
Saddle horse very like the Hanoverian or Trakehner.

Holstein (21)
Modern horse excellent for sporting purposes, world-famous through Granat, the horse ridden by Christine Stückelberger.

Hunter (22)
Riding horses developed in England and Ireland, mostly from warm-blood mares and Thoroughbred stallions, usually first class horses for sporting purposes.

Irish Draught (23)
Strong heavy breed most suitable as a work horse and for the breeding of hunters.

Kabardin (24)
Small, very tough saddle and pack horse from the Caucasus mountains.

Karabakh
Noble fiery saddle horse from the Azerbaijan region of the Caucasus mountains.

Karabair (25)
A breed of three types from the mountains to the south of the Aral Sea, draught horse, all-rounder and saddle.

Kladruber (26)
Noble Baroque carriage horse, of which a few still exist in Czechoslovakia.

Knabstrup (27)
Splendid horse in a leopard-spotted coat, once bred at the Danish Court, rare today.

Kustanai
Originally a steppe breed, ennobled by Arabs and English Thoroughbreds.

Lipizzaner (28)
Parade horses from the Baroque age, made famous by the Spanish Riding School and the circus, mostly greys.

Lokai
Small robust riding and pack animal from the Aral Sea region.

Lusitano
Ancient breed from Portugal, similar to the Andalusian but smaller and more elegant, excellent dressage horse.

Malapolski
The Polish Anglo-Arab.

Mecklenburg
Bred in East Germany, smaller version of the Hanoverian.

Missouri Fox Trotter (29)
Small attractive compact horse with a natural aptitude for specialized varieties of gait.

Morgan (30)
Small fast excellent riding horse, has had considerable influence on the American Trotter as well as other breeds.

Mustang (31)
A feral horse of the American West, of Spanish origin.

Novokirghiz
Noble riding horse developed from the crossing of steppe horses with the thoroughbreds of the Don Cossacks.

Dutch Warm-blood
Modern versatile riding horse with excellent qualities.

Nonius (32)
Hungarian breed of two types, a lively saddle horse and a larger animal for agricultural work.

Oldenburg
Originally bred as a superior carriage horse, today a modern riding horse.

Orlov Trotter
A Russian trotting breed developed in the eighteenth century.

East Bulgarian
Noble modern horse excellent for competition work.

East Friesian (33)
Much prized by medieval knights, later an imposing carriage horse, today a versatile riding horse.

19

25

20

26

21

27

22

28

23

29

24

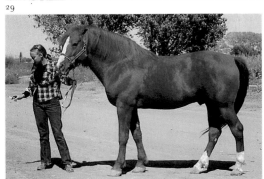

30

31

37

43

32

38

44

33

39

Paint Horse (34)
American horse with variegated coat, always of the Quarter Horse or English Thoroughbred type, not to be confused with the Pinto.

Palomino (35)
A Western horse similar to the Arab, with shining golden coat, and flaxen to silver-white mane and tail.

Paso
Small noble horse bred mainly in Peru and Colombia, with a natural aptitude for the amble.

Pinto (36)
Piebald or skewbald American Western horse of Spanish origins, rather small, hardy, fast, undemanding, with tremendous stamina.

Quarter Horse (37)
Short-legged muscular horse, very fast and agile, popular American breed with over one million animals registered.

Swedish Warm-blood (38)
Noble riding horse and excellent competition horse.

Shagya (39)
Noble breed from Hungary, very closely related to the Arab.

Tennessee Walking Horse (40)
Originally a horse used for work on the plantations, today a show horse; cruel methods are used to make it perform unnatural gaits.

Tersky
A breed of three types from the Soviet Union.

Trakehner (41)
Top-class saddle horse, originated at the Trakehnen Stud in Prussia, today bred in many countries.

Waler
Modern saddle horse from Australia bred largely for military and ranch use.

Welsh Cob (42)
The largest of the Welsh ponies (q.v.), usually grows to over 148 cm therefore classified as a horse.

Westphalian
Nowadays simply a Hanoverian which has been bred in Westphalia.

Wielkopolski (43)
A Polish breed of horse developed from the Trakehner.

Württemberg (44)
First class riding horse, with distinct Trakehner qualities.

Yorkshire Coach Horse
Elegant harness and riding horse, with a large proportion of Thoroughbred blood, has been used to improve many other breeds.

Zweibrücker
Saddle horse developed from English cross-breeds and Anglo-Normans with addition of some Arab blood.

34

40

35

41

36

42

THE PURE-BRED ARAB

Most people consider the Arab to be the embodiment of the perfect horse, and it is indisputable that the breeding of warm-blood horses throughout the world would be unthinkable without its contribution. Over the centuries, to a greater or lesser degree, most of the warm-blood breeds and many pony and even cold-blood breeds were improved by being crossed with Arabs, and, as a result, these animals had more stamina, became swifter and livelier, more amiable and, last but not least, more beautiful creatures. Oriental horses also played a major role in the development of the English Thoroughbred, and in doing so provided the impetus which sent the breeding of racehorses along its modern path.

The Arab is the most important horse in the history of the breeding of horses. It is a happy coincidence that it is also the most beautiful horse of all. For many centuries the Bedouins of Nedj in the Arabian high country were the sole masters of this marvellous breed and they could certainly not afford to breed for beauty. They placed the greatest emphasis on the animal's performance and therefore concentrated on stamina, soundness, speed, amiability and loyalty up to the point of exhaustion. To maintain the unique performance of their animals, the Bedouins were not only ruthlessly selective in their breeding programmes, but also paid fanatical attention to keeping the blood line pure. A breeder was quite prepared to ride his

mare for days on end so that she could be mated with the right stallion. And every breeder knew the pedigree of all his horses by heart.

The origins of the Arab breed are unclear. It is known from many descriptions that the Assyrians, the Persians, and above all the Egyptians of the Age of the Pharaohs (see the historical section, pages 90-93) possessed graceful, noble horses with very delicate limbs. It can certainly be assumed, too, that this lightly built, swift breed of horse did not originally develop in this way while living under human protection, but evolved as a geographical breed of wild horse because of the extremely harsh conditions of its life in this desert-like region. The different breeds and races which are known collectively today as Orientals developed from such horses as these. The noblest and best representatives of these Orientals were always to be found in the breed which lived in the wild high country of the Arabian peninsula.

An often-repeated legend affirms that all pure-blooded Arabs can be traced back to the seven or perhaps five favourite mares of Mohammed, but it remains only a legend. The Prophet was, however, extraordinarily far-sighted and made some decisive changes in the breeding of Arabs for which he instigated strict laws, some of them laid down in the Koran (see Mohammed, pages 114-115). The spread of the Islamic faith carried with it the Arab horse, along the long trail across the whole of North Africa to south-western Europe.

In later centuries dealers from throughout the world sought, bought and

exported Arab horses. Nowadays there are stud farms on every continent. In the US alone there are over 50,000 horses of the Arab breed, most of which can trace their ancestry back in a direct line to the desert Arabs, and are therefore entitled to call themselves pure-bred Arabs.

The pure-bred Arab is divided into three so-called Bio-types : the Kuhaylan is virile and strong with incredible stamina; the Saqlawi is gentle, feminine and finely built; and the Muniqi, which is the type bred mainly for flat racing, is long-boned, somewhat angular and very fast. A large number of pedigrees and families are combined in these three types. There are, for example, 105 breeding families of the Kuhaylan type alone.

For beauty, nobility and generally distinctive qualities no horse comes anywhere near a first class pure-bred Arab, and no other breed is such a perfect combination of fire and gentleness, stamina, affection and loyalty.

THE ENGLISH THOROUGHBRED

Only one breed of horse is comparable to the Arab: the English Thoroughbred. This breed owes its superlative characteristics not, as does the Arab, to the demands of its surroundings and its owners, but rather to that passion for sports and immense talent for raising domestic animals which are characteristic of the British.

Horse racing in England is an ancient pastime. At least 700 years ago and perhaps even earlier, the Britons began mating those pony stallions and mares which had been successful in racing. The aim was to breed for speed. From about the fifteenth century on, more and more frequently Oriental horses were brought to the British Isles and crossed with the native ponies. A number of mares — of which probably the majority had more Oriental horse blood than British pony blood in them — formed the female basis for the actual breeding of Thoroughbreds which began about 1700. The founding sires of the breed were three Oriental stallions: Godolphin Barb, also called Godolphin Arabian, a Barb from Tunisia; Byerley Turk, an Oriental, probably a genuine Arab from Turkey; and Darley Arabian, probably a pure-bred desert Arab of the finest blood line. All existing pure-bred English Thoroughbreds (and there could be around 700,000 of them) are descended from a few dozen original mares and the three Oriental stallions. By far the greatest number are descendants of

Darley Arabian. In almost every country those Thoroughbreds registered in the Stud Registers must be able to prove an uninterrupted line of descent in the *General Stud Book*, which was first published in England in 1793 and since then has appeared at irregular intervals. (The history of the breeding of Thoroughbreds which is directly connected with the development of modern horse racing will be dealt with in more detail in the chapter on racing page 188ff.)

From that time on the quality of the horses selected for breeding was always determined by their racing performance. Apart from a few rare exceptions, every horse must have attained a certain level of performance on the racecourse before it is used for breeding. The exceptions are those horses which for some reason cannot compete at racing, although their ancestors distinguished themselves on the course. This selective breeding has naturally left its imprint on the build and temperament of these horses.

As with the Arabs, English Thoroughbreds also were not bred for beauty, but they too are exceptionally beautiful horses. With their long, delicate limbs and slender, elegant bodies the total impression is one of harmony and aristocratic nobility. The head is usually rather small but fine and strikingly chiselled. The eyes are large, observant, and full of expression. The profile of the nose is straight or somewhat dished, but not as strongly dished as it is in Arabs. The neck is long, slender but muscular. The shoulder is very sloped, allowing the front legs to step out freely and widely. The chest is broad and very deep to give

the breathing and circulatory organs plenty of room. The back is fairly long and ends in a strongly muscled, long sloping croup, in contrast to the straight, very short croup of the Arab with its high-set tail. The legs are lean and extraordinarily strong in spite of their comparatively short bones. The coat, which is silky and fine, is mostly brown or dark brown in colour. Occasionally it may be a different colour but never dappled.

In temperament the horse can be both exuberant and explosive and normally demands a good to very experienced rider. There are Thoroughbreds, however, which are particularly gentle and tractable and could be safely ridden by a child.

The English Thoroughbred is the racehorse *par excellence* and unbeatable over middle distances. It is also a first class performer as a jumper and as a cavalry horse. Its greatest achievement, however, is that for many centuries its blood has been an ennobling factor when it has been crossed with other breeds. The versatile modern warm-blood horse owes a great many of its qualities to the Thoroughbred.

THE BODY OF THE HORSE

Probably no horse could truly be described as ugly, and one could claim that very few people remain completely unmoved by the sight of a horse. It may be that only the confirmed horse enthusiast waxes rhapsodic when describing the nobility of the horse's head, the sublime curve of the neck or the clarity of its form, but the sight of a healthy horse in movement touches the aesthetic sensibility of the layman as well.

It is not only the fiery pure-breds and stately warm-bloods which deserve the designation beautiful; the monumental presence of cold-bloods and the unique charm of sturdy ponies are equally worthy of admiration.

Horses are ugly only when man has interfered with nature — by means of so-called 'cosmetic surgery', such as the senseless shearing of mane and tail hair so that the dock stands upright, the use of cruel training methods to teach certain gaits, and many other distasteful practices.

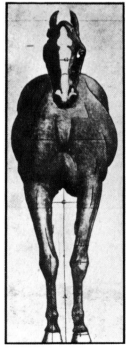

Eclipse: the epitome of speed and stamina. When this horse, the most marvellous of all English Thoroughbreds, died in

1789, Charles Vials de St Bel, the anatomist, measured its body and used the measurements to produce this drawing.

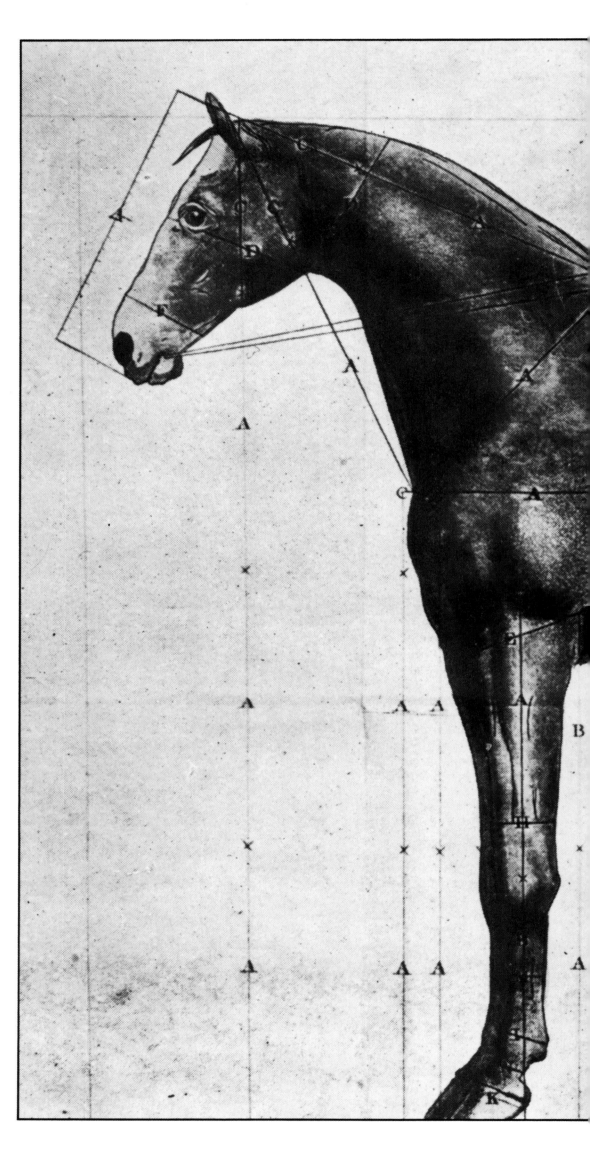

36

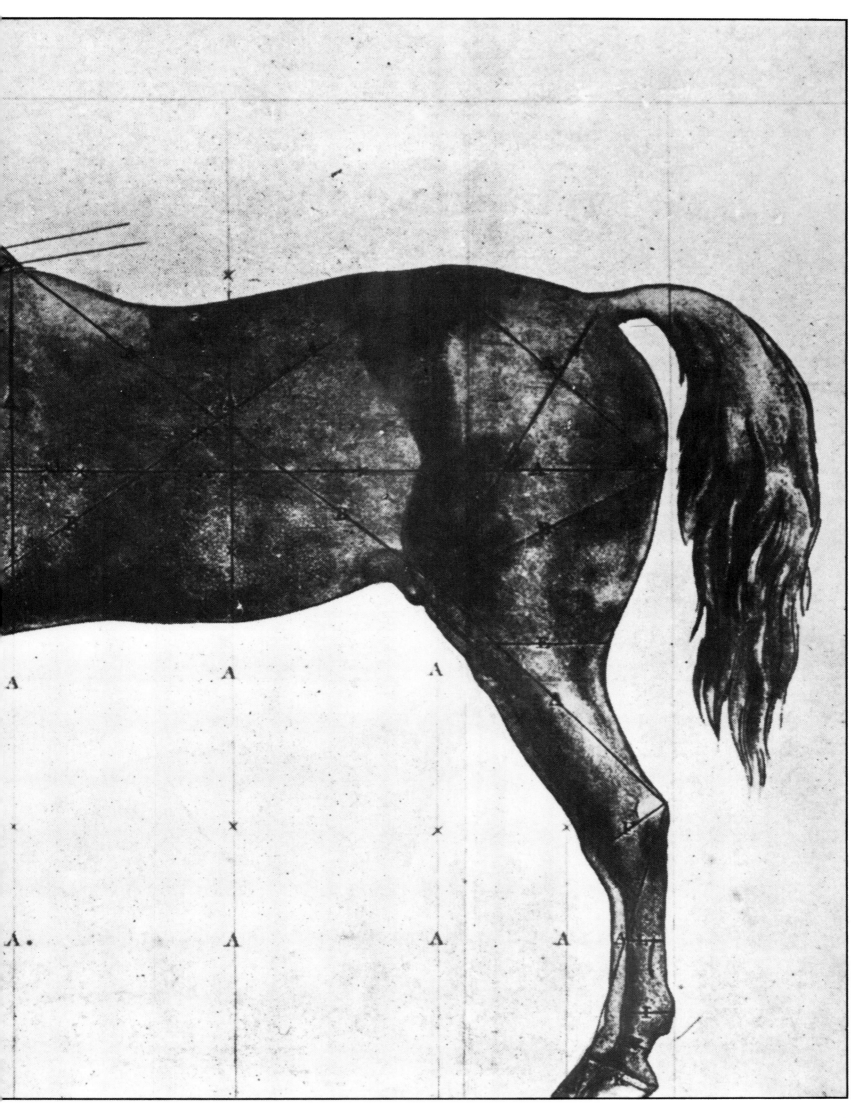

EXTERIOR, MUSCULAR SYSTEM, INTERNAL ORGANS AND SKELETON

The body of every animal has largely adapted to the prevailing living conditions: to its method of locomotion, to the kind of food that is available, to the structure of the landscape and to the climate.

The method of locomotion moulds a body's structure quite specifically, particularly in an animal which is predominantly a migratory creature dependent on speed to escape from danger. In all those breeds which are descended from the primitive horses of the plains and deserts, the locomotory mechanism is designed for speed down to the smallest detail. The long slender limbs are sinewy and have small hard hooves with very little supporting surface. The strong and correspondingly heavy muscles are densely packed on the rump. From there the energy is transferred to the limbs by tendons. The head is long and comparatively fine, the neck extended and well adapted to maintaining the animal's balance provided it is not restricted in any way. The rump is very slender since the horse's food of nourishing grasses does not require a large digestive system. The chest is deep and wide and provides plenty of room for the powerful lungs and the highly efficient heart.

In contrast the breeds which are descended from the primitive ponies and horses of the northern tundra are not designed for speed at all. As a rule they are more compactly built and therefore much better able to withstand cold. The rump is distinctly roomier and contains capacious digestive organs which enable the animal to digest its fibre-rich but meagre food supply. The head appears heavy, but probably only because the teeth are very large. The legs with their medium to large hooves are shorter and sturdier, but have tremendous stamina and are ideally suited to carrying the heavy body at an easy pace.

As herbivores, horses have a digestive system which is larger and more efficient than that of the carnivores. In a domestic horse the average length of the intestines is almost forty metres. In herbivores the appendix, almost superfluous in humans, has an essential function to fulfil and it measures about a metre. The colon, which is joined to the appendix, is particularly large, with an average capacity of about 80 litres, occasionally as much as 130 litres.

When fleeing from a predator an immense strain is put, not only on the muscular system and the skeleton, but on the heart and lungs as well. The heart of an average-sized warm-blood gelding weighs about three kilograms, that of a stallion somewhat more, that of a mare somewhat less.

The lungs have to be able to supply the body with sufficient oxygen, particularly at times of great stress. To enable them to exchange gases as efficiently as possible they are equipped with an immense surface area, about 2500 square metres. By comparison the alveolar surface in cattle is only about 650, and in humans 90 to 150 square metres.

While the eyes of the horse are much better than those of a dog, they play a less important role than in the human body and are designed mainly for perceiving movement at great distances. Because they are set on the side of the horse's head their three-dimensional vision is somewhat limited, but this is compensated for by enabling the horse to scan the whole horizon without having to turn its head. The horse relies on its hearing more than it does on its sight, but most important is the sense of smell.

EXTERIOR

The expert can gain much useful information about a horse's potential, both as a performer and a worker, from its external appearance.

1 ear
2 poll
3 neck
4 crest and mane
5 withers (a horse's height is measured at this point, usually with a measuring stick, occasionally along the curve of the body with a tape)
6 back
7 loins
8 croup
9 base of the tail
10 dock
11 tail
12 hindquarters
13 knee
14 gaskin
15 point of hock and point of heelbone or calcaneum
16 cannon (the size of the cannon bone indicates how robust the legs are)
17 pastern
18 fetlock with 'feathers' (in cold-blood breeds this area is often covered with luxuriant hair)
19 coronary bone and coronet
20 hoof
21 belly
22 girth line (the chest is measured here)
23 cannon bone
24 wrist (often wrongly described as the knee)
25 forearm
26 point of elbow
27 breast
28 shoulder (length and angle of the shoulder blade are co-determinants of the forward movement and therefore of the horse's galloping ability)
29 lower jaw or cheek
30 chin groove
31 chin
32 under lip
33 upper lip
34 nostril
35 nose
36 eye
37 forehead and forelock

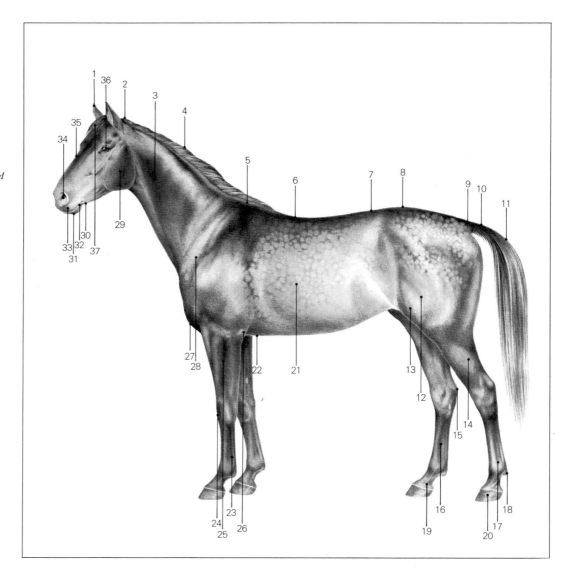

THE MUSCULAR SYSTEM

When the skin and the muscular system belonging to it are removed, the superficial muscular system of the skeleton becomes visible. In the horse this is very powerful, particularly around the limbs. The sole purpose of whole groups of muscles is to provide passive support for the weight of the horse, usually about 500 kg, though in certain cold-blood breeds it can be over a tonne. Considerably more muscle power is required, of course, to enable the animal to reach speeds of from forty-five to over sixty kilometres an hour and to maintain a tempo only slightly slower for long distances at a time.

1 ear depressor
2 splenius muscle
3 neck section of serratus ventralis muscle
4 neck section of trapezius muscle
5 chest section of trapezius muscle
6 latissimus dorsi
7 outer intercostal muscle
8 upper serratus muscle
9 tensor fasciae latae muscle
10 great gluteal muscle
11 superficial gluteal muscle
12 biceps femoris muscle
13 semitendinosus muscle
14 common digital extensor tendon
15 lateral digital extensor
16 Achilles tendon
17 superficial flexor tendon
18 deep flexor tendon
19 tendon of hallucis longus muscle
20 common digital extensor tendon
21 external oblique abdominal muscle
22 tendon of hallucis longus muscle
23 deep flexor tendon
24 superficial flexor tendon
25 radial carpal flexor muscle
26 ulnar carpal flexor muscle
27 lateral digital extensor tendon
28 common digital extensor tendon
29 lateral digital extensor
30 ulnaris lateralis muscle
31 common digital extensor
32 radial carpal extensor muscle
33 arm muscle
34 superficial pectoral muscle
35 supraspinatus
36 cervical muscle
37 sternocephalic muscle
38 brachiocephalic muscle
39 shoulder-hyoid bone muscle
40 exterior masseter muscle
41 cheek muscle
42 arcus zygomaticum
43 upper lip depressor
44 nose-jawbone muscle
45 upper lip levator
46 nostrils levator
47 temporalis muscle
48 deltoid muscle

INTERNAL ORGANS

The two most striking features of the horse's internal structure are the capacious digestive tract of the herbivore, and the broad chest which provides plenty of room for the large heart and the two equally large lungs. When compared with the ruminants, horses have a small stomach since the process of fermentation, which breaks down the raw fibrous food, does not take place there. Instead it takes place in the large intestine which consists of the caecum, the large colon and the small colon. The diagram shows a mare's internal organs from the left hand side.

1 brain
2 pharynx
3 left lobe of liver
4 stomach
5 spleen
6 left kidney
7 small colon
8 left horn of the uterus with ovary
9 rectum
10 bladder
11 vagina
12 small intestine
13 left ventral colon
14 left dorsal colon
15 transverse dorsal colon
16 diaphragm
17 left ventricle
18 right ventricle
19 trachea
20 oesophagus
21 larynx

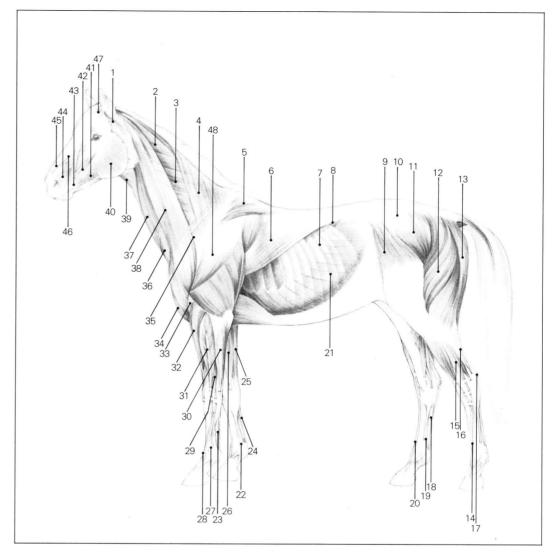

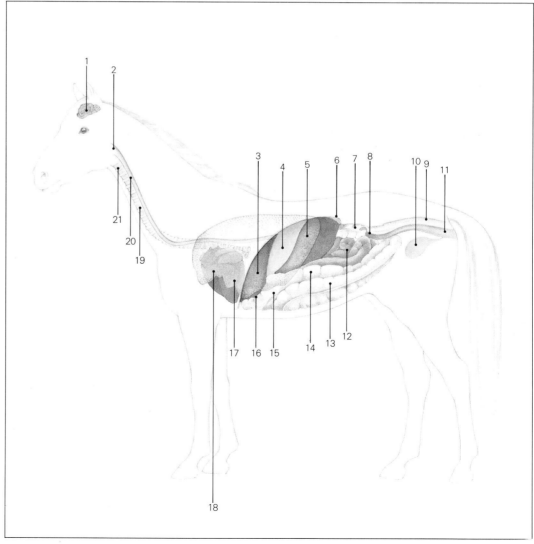

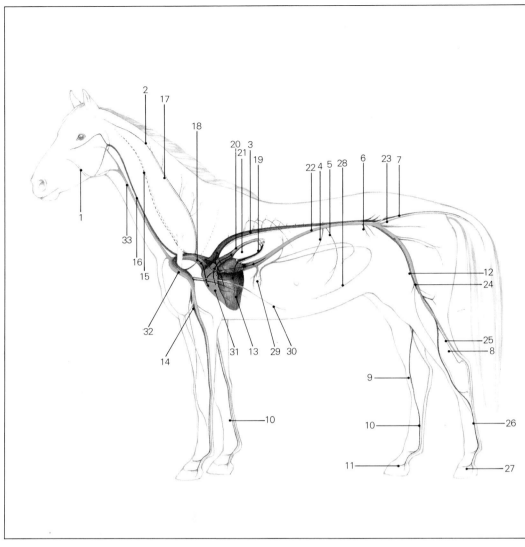

THE MOST IMPORTANT BLOOD VESSELS

Even under extreme constant pressure the highly efficient heart is able to keep up a continuous supply of blood to the body. On average it weighs about 2.85 kg, but in Thoroughbred horses it can weigh more than 5 kg. The arteries (1 to 16) are coloured in red, the veins (17 to 33) in blue.

ARTERIES

1 facial artery
2 neck artery
3 aorta
4 abdominal artery for spleen, stomach, and liver
5 anterior mesenteric artery for small and anterior large intestines
6 posterior mesenteric artery for posterior large intestine
7 coccygica artery
8 posterior tibial artery
9 anterior tibial artery
10 saphena artery
11 pedis artery
12 femoral artery
13 left ventricle
14 subclavian artery
15 cervical artery
16 carotid artery

VEINS

17 neck vein
18 anterior vena cava
19 pulmonary vein (rich in oxygen)
20 pulmonary artery (poor in oxygen)
21 pulmonary circulation
22 posterior vena cava
23 iliac vein
24 femoral vein
25 saphena vein
26 saphena vein
27 pedis vein
28 mesenteric vein
29 portal vein
30 pectoral vein
31 right ventricle
32 subclavian vein
33 jugular vein

evolution all the remaining toes have completely atrophied, so that the horse's foot now has a very small supporting surface. This has helped in the development of the horse as one of the fastest land mammals.

1 cranium
2 1st cervical vertebra
3 7th cervical vertebra
4 1st dorsal vertebra
5 scapula
6 18th thoracic vertebra
7 1st lumbar vertebra
8 18th rib
9 point of hip
10 6th lumbar vertebra
11 ilium
12 sacrum
13 hip joint
14 1st coccygeal vertebra
15 point of ischium
16 femur
17 patella
18 stifle joint
19 fibula
20 tibia
21 heel bone
22 point of the hock
23 outer splint bone
24 cannon bone
25 point of hock
26 pisiform bone
27 lateral tarsal bone
28 cannon bone
29 sesamoid bone
30 coronary joint
31 navicular bone
32 coffin joint
33 coffin bone
34 coronary bone
35 pastern bone
36 fetlock joint
37 inner splint bone
38 carpal bone
39 carpal joint
40 forearm
41 radius
42 ulna
43 elbow joint
44 sternum
45 humerus
46 point of the shoulder
47 1st rib
48 lower jaw or mandible
49 facial skull and upper jaw

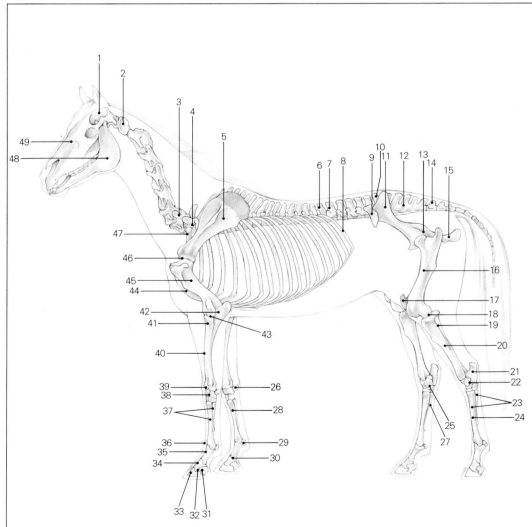

THE SKELETON

The most obvious aspects of the horse's skeleton are the size of the skull which provides space for the teeth and their roots, the length of the neck, and the strength of the back, shoulder and hip sections. The hind legs are angled so that when the horse is galloping, they have the necessary strength and mobility to throw the whole weight of the body forwards. The forelegs and the shoulder are equipped to absorb the shock and to project the movement forwards. The foot's skeleton has become uniquely specialised and only the middle toe still touches the ground. In the course of

TEETH

Eohippus obviously lived on a diet of leaves, tender herbage, fruit and probably on various small animals as well, because the small primitive horse of the Eocene had teeth which were perfectly equipped to cope with just such a diet. The front part of the skull, or facial skull, was comparatively short, the incisors were still very large and the molars, which were clearly not designed to cope with constant wear, were uneven and small.

The change in diet from this easily digested food to fibrous grasses and coarse stringy herbage required the development of a much more efficient dental mechanism. The two most striking features of the horse's skull are that the upper part or cranium is tiny compared to the size of the facial skull, and that the lower jaw, to which the masticatory muscles are attached, seems to be disproportionately large. Each half of the jaw has six fully formed molars embedded in deep root cavities. In the upper jaw in front of these teeth there is also occasionally a tiny vestigial wolf tooth, called an anterior molar or premolar, No 1, P 1 for short. The next three cheek teeth are the premolars 2 to 4. The remaining back teeth are called molars 1 to 3. There are no molars in the temporary milk teeth.

The powerful molars have depressions, folds or wrinkles in their enamel. The edges of these are particularly hard and produce a rough rasp-like grinding surface which can finely crush even very

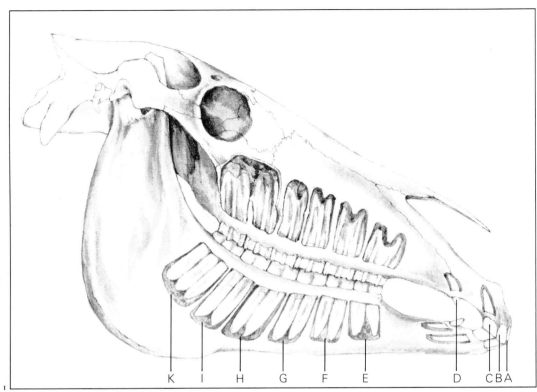

K I H G F E D C B A

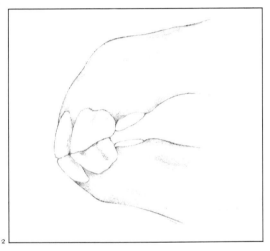

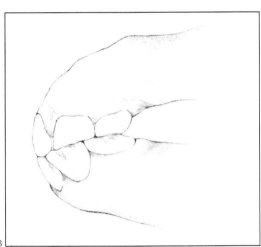

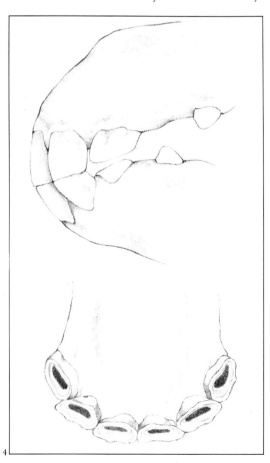

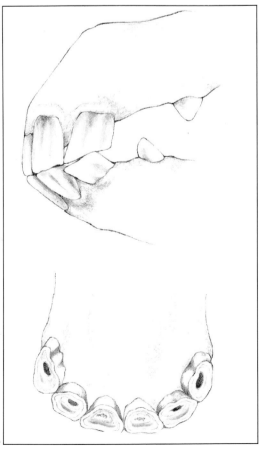

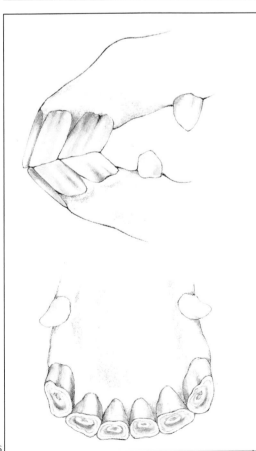

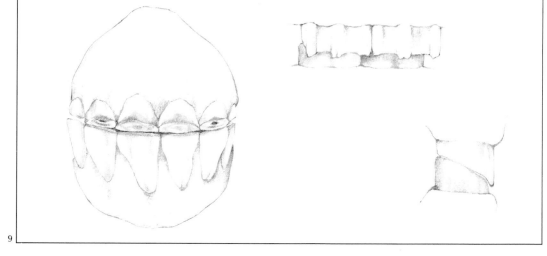

1 The striking feature of the skeleton of the horse's head is the contrast between the massive dental mechanism and the tiny cranium. On the diagram the bone has been cut away to show the enormous size of the molars. A to C are the cutting teeth or incisors: A is the central, B the lateral, and C the corner incisor; D is the canine or tush which is tiny and hardly visible in mares but grows much larger in male horses; E to G are the front or premolars, H to K the molars.

2 The incisor teeth of the milk or temporary teeth of a foal, aged about 8 months.

3 Incisor teeth in a foal, aged about 16 months. Complete set of milk teeth.

4 The incisors and the canine teeth (stallion or gelding) and, below, the incisors (mare) at 4 to 5 years. The teeth form a vertical straight line, the tables are flat and oval, the cups which are visible as

darker depressions in the table, are long and small.

5 At 7 to 8 years the table is wide and oval, and the cups are distinctly shorter. (Above in a stallion, below in a mare.)

6 At about 12 years the table has become rounded, the cups are oval (stallion).

7 At about 17 years the table is triangular and the marks are rounded. (Above in a stallion, below in a mare.)

8 At about 20 years the incisor teeth are again oval-shaped, as they were at 8 years, but when seen from the side, they now form an angle of about 90° (stallion).

9 A number of teeth defects can occur, e.g. incisors which fit badly on top of each other and affect the horse's ability to eat. On the left is a 'parrot mouth'; the two diagrams on the right depict 'sharp teeth'.

stringy food. Once formed, the teeth do not continue to grow, but instead are gradually filled in from below by a bony substance. Normally they are worn down evenly, and are filled in at about the same rate as they are worn down.

There is a toothless space next to the molars where the bar of the horse's bit is placed. The next tooth is the tush or Caninus (D). In mares this tooth is very small and usually does not even break through the gums, but in male horses it grows large and conical-shaped. In front of the canine tooth there are three chisel-like teeth or incisors in each half of the jaw. The foremost one is called the central incisor or I 1, the second is the lateral incisor or I 2, and the outer one is called the corner incisor or I 3. Each half of each jaw contains therefore a set of teeth consisting of 10 permanent teeth (occasionally 11 in the upper jaw) making a total of 40 or 42 respectively.

The horse's teeth have three main functions. After the animal's large mobile lips have enfolded bunches of grass, the incisor teeth have the task of pulling them up and cutting them off. The horse also uses its teeth to groom its own coat and for the social grooming of the coats of other horses. Horses often indulge in mutual grooming and nibble each other's coats, particularly in the withers region and on the croup. Finally teeth are used as weapons, though they are far less effective than hooves.

It is possible to deduce the approximate age of a horse from the condition of its teeth, though only an experienced specialist can do so with certainty. Many who open a horse's mouth with an apparently practised grip will gain no benefit from it at all except perhaps a psychological one — for such a gesture will prove unsettling to an unscrupulous horse-trader who has altered the horse's teeth.

In a normal 'bite' the incisors fit exactly on top of each other and wear down evenly. In the younger horse the biting surface or table is elliptical and narrow from back to front, but with increasing age it becomes wider and finally triangular. There is also a blackened depression on the table known as the mark or cup, which is clearly visible. These marks too, change their shape at certain regularly defined intervals. In younger horses the incisors form a vertical straight line, but with age they project more and more towards the front.

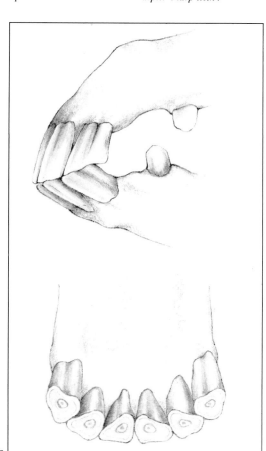

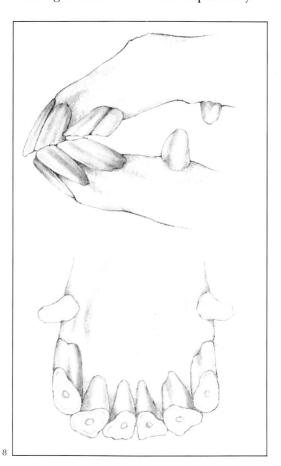

LIMBS

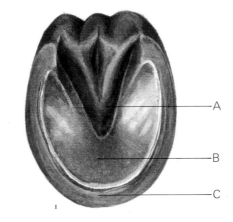

Horses have extremely robust limbs and even when fleeing from danger over rough stony ground they seldom do themselves any serious harm. Even a slight injury to the leg can put a horse temporarily out of action and as they are dependent on speed to escape, this would greatly reduce their chances of survival in the wild. Any predator would immediately recognise such an animal as easy prey.

When domestic horses are being selected for breeding purposes, therefore, a great deal of emphasis is placed on strong correctly aligned limbs. Riding and carriage horses frequently have to be destroyed while still young because of leg injuries. There are several reasons.

Because of selective breeding practices and 'favourable' rearing conditions domestic horses are on average about thirty to forty centimetres taller than wild horses. Their legs are therefore considerably longer, which enables them to take longer strides with a livelier and more energetic action. It also gives them a more elegant appearance. However, because of the way their leverage mechanism is adjusted, longer legs also expose the animal to greater stresses and make it more susceptible to injury. It is significant that the horses ridden by cowboys or gauchos, despite the great demands put on them, seldom suffer leg

injuries. These animals are usually only about 135 to 145 cm tall, therefore much shorter in the leg, and, unlike those warm-bloods and Thoroughbreds which take part in competitive sporting events, are not required to jump.

Jumping makes very heavy demands on any animal, and especially on one already made more susceptible to injury. With the added burden of a rider the horse is most at risk when landing after a jump, particularly so when the point of landing is below the level of the take-off point. The legs of dressage horses are also subject to injuries and infections more frequently than is often assumed. Classical dressage often consists of very strongly collected gaits which place a greater burden on joints and tendons than even an extended cross-country ride. Long stretches on hard street surfaces, particularly if these are covered

at the trot, can cause lameness and lead to chronic infections, injuries to which carriage horses are very susceptible.

When buying a horse and, even more to the point, when selecting one for breeding purposes, it is very important to make sure that its legs are as correctly positioned as possible, for they will then be less prone to infections and injuries. When seen from the side the foreleg should stand absolutely vertical, that is, it should be possible to draw a vertical line from the middle of the elbow joint through the middle of the under-arm, through the hock (often wrongly called the knee), the cannon bone and the fetlock joint to the ground just behind the hoof. In the hind leg the vertical line should run from the hip joint through the hock and again end up directly behind the hoof while the stifle joint, because of the angle made by the upper thigh and the gaskin, lies further forward. Seen from the front and from the rear the legs should be vertically parallel to each other and the fetlocks and the hooves should face directly towards the front. If there is any departure from these guidelines then a greater pressure is put on certain joints or tendons, making them more liable to injury. All positional defects are, however, not of equal importance and the extent of the defect also plays a role. Besides, many faults only become crucial under competitive conditions. A cow-hocked position of the hind legs, for example, is not really a

1A frog
B hoof sole
C white line

2A coronet
B hoof wall
C coronary cushion

3A common digital extensor
B superficial flexor tendon
C deep flexor tendon
D suspensory ligament
E ball and plantar cushion
F coffin bone

4A cannon bone
B sesamoid bone
C pastern bone
D coronary bone
E plantar cushion
F navicular bone

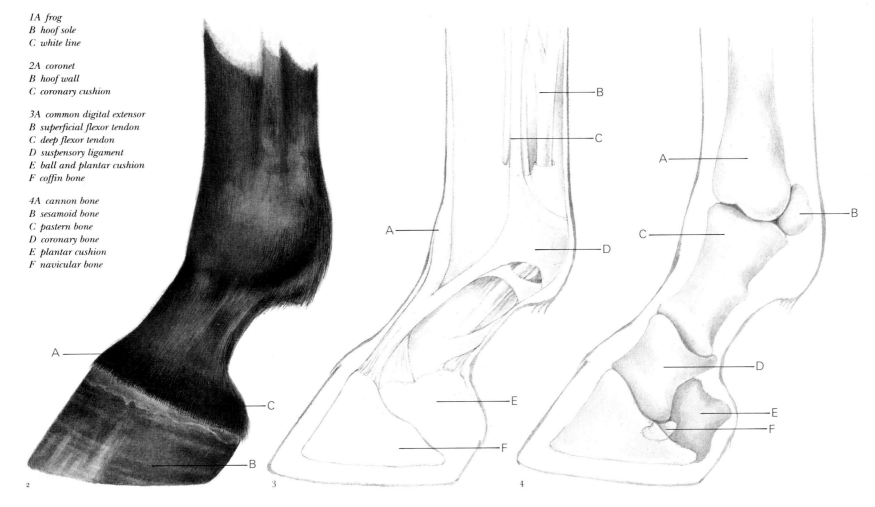

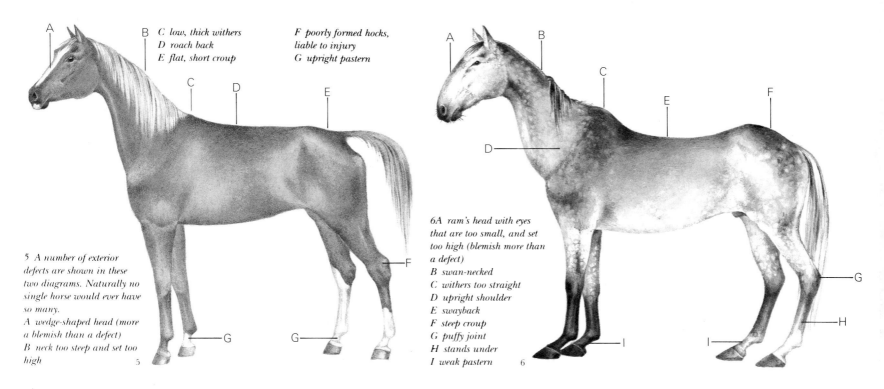

A
B
C low, thick withers
D roach back
E flat, short croup
F poorly formed hocks, liable to injury
G upright pastern

5 A number of exterior defects are shown in these two diagrams. Naturally no single horse would ever have so many.
A wedge-shaped head (more a blemish than a defect)
B neck too steep and set too high

6A ram's head with eyes that are too small, and set too high (blemish more than a defect)
B swan-necked
C withers too straight
D upright shoulder
E swayback
F steep croup
G puffy joint
H stands under
I weak pastern

disadvantage so long as these horses are not required to take part in competitive sports. This position occurs frequently in mountain and northern ponies, and there are specialists who maintain that cow-hocked ponies are more sure-footed, although it is more likely that this can be ascribed to the hereditary soundness of the breed and the individual animal.

The limbs are liable to infection and injury for many reasons, for example, ganglion or puffy bones, which can develop as the result of periostitis.

Depending on where they occur they can simply mar the horse's beauty, or can lead to a serious reduction in its efficiency. Bone spavin is the name given to the appearance of ossification on the hock, which is then extremely tender. This condition occurs most frequently in dressage horses and trotters. Bone fractures in horses are not, as is so often assumed, incurable, but their treatment is so difficult that usually it is not considered practicable. The healing process normally takes at least four

months and is only successful if the leg is kept absolutely still, a process which is not only extremely difficult technically, but a torment for a naturally active animal.

Damage to the tendons, the digital flexor tendon in particular, occurs much more frequently than bone infections. After being overloaded for several days, or even hours, the tendons become overstretched, a condition which only becomes apparent some time later when the tendon swells or becomes inflamed. Usually the damage can be fully repaired, however, and there is much more difficulty involved in curing a pulled tendon. This can result from a sudden overloading of the tendon and can lead to immediate lameness. A torn tendon is often incurable. It, too, can be the result of a sudden overloading of the tendon.

Finally, the hoof also can be afflicted by a number of injuries and infections. Unprofessional shoeing or careless cutting of the hoof in unshod horses can have serious after effects, allowing foreign bodies to get into the hoof. Other infections may develop as the result of insufficient care. Hereditary hoof defects can also cause temporary or permanent lameness.

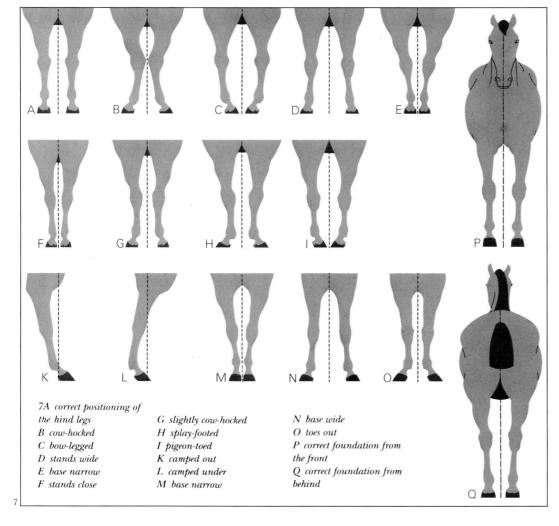

7A correct positioning of the hind legs
B cow-hocked
C bow-legged
D stands wide
E base narrow
F stands close
G slightly cow-hocked
H splay-footed
I pigeon-toed
K camped out
L camped under
M base narrow
N base wide
O toes out
P correct foundation from the front
Q correct foundation from behind

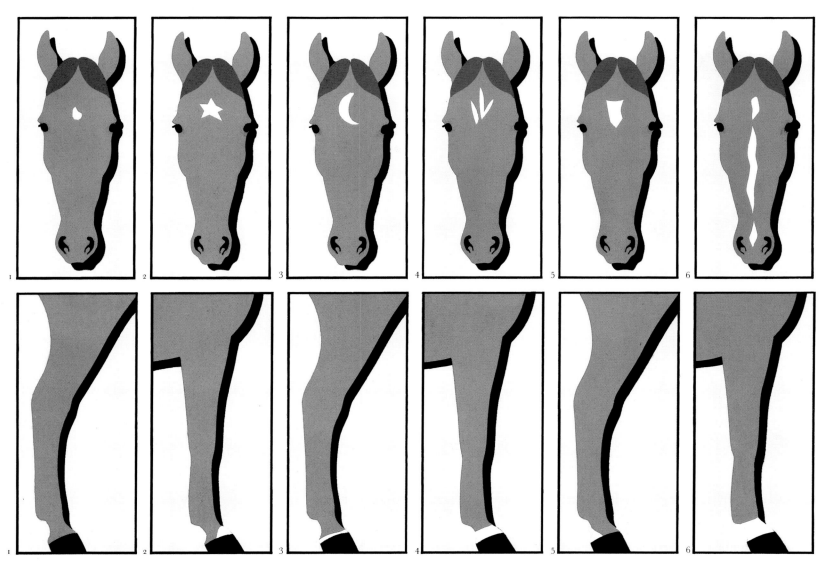

DISTINGUISHING MARKS

Markings are defined as those white patches of hair which are found on the horse's head and legs, and sometimes on other parts of the body. Being both innate and permanent, they are useful for identification purposes and are therefore entered on the horse's birth certificate, passport, pedigree, etc. As two horses of the same colour will seldom have an identical combination of markings one horse is rarely mistaken for another.

Many horses, however, have no markings at all, and brand marks, numbered ones in particular, are then used for identification. Most horses are branded on the loins, neck, saddle area or fore and hind quarters, but in America thoroughbreds are often branded with numbers on the inside of the lower lip.

Some horses, the powerful Clydesdales from Scotland for example, have markings along their rumps, particularly on their bellies. If the markings are widely distributed then they are described, not as markings but as a spotted pattern.

White hairs often grow on the scars of wounds or saddle sores — generally the result of a saddle which does not conform to the shape of the horse's back. These often form permanent white spots, but they do not, of course, constitute markings.

Horses which are coloured black, dark brown, brown, chestnut, or roan, as well as some palomino breeds (such as the Shire), may all have markings. There are some breeds where practically every animal has markings, and there are others where only a few do. A few breeds — e.g., the Suffolk Punch — never have any markings at all.

Both markings and spotted patterns are, however, a sure sign that a horse either belongs to a domestic breed or has been crossed with a domestic breed. Wild horses are never spotted, nor do they have markings but instead are always a camouflage colour. Prjevalsky's horse, the only surviving genuine breed of wild horse, ranges in colour from a

1 This Scottish Clydesdale has the characteristic unusual markings on its belly as well as markings on its head and legs.

2 Larger spots which are distributed over the whole body are described, not as markings, but as a spotted pattern. While this occurs frequently in some breeds, in others it is rare, e.g., in Anglo-Arabs. This horse from the Polish stud of Janow Podlaski is just such an exception.

46

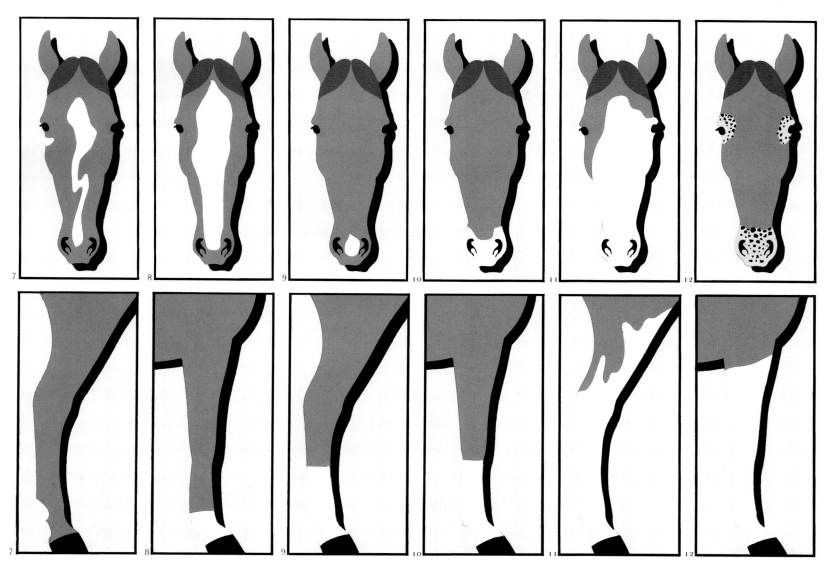

light yellowish-brown to a greyish-yellow. It usually has a dark eel-stripe along its back, and its short upright mane, tail and the lower parts of its legs are almost black. A light-coloured, almost white muzzle is also a characteristic trait.

Wild horses, and dun-coloured domestic ones, often have faint 'zebra stripes' running crosswise over the upper part of their legs.

The extinct tarpan was a mouse-dun colour and its close relatives, which are still extant, have retained that colour. They have the distinctive eel-stripe on the back, a mouse-grey coat, black mane and tail, and black stockings.

The northern primitive ponies must have been brown, for their closest

relatives, the English Exmoor ponies, which have remained pure-blooded, have a brown coat with black mane and tail, and black stockings. They also have the characteristic 'sand-colour' around the mouth, the eyes and on the inner side of the legs.

In south-western Europe, Stone Age cave-drawings have been found depicting horses liberally sprinkled with dark spots. Most likely the animals which were the models for these drawings were not leopard-spotted, that is, white with spots, but brown horses with a somewhat darker spotted pattern, that is, dappled.

Unfortunately nothing is known of the coat colours of those wild horses which lived in the semi-desert and desert areas

Top row: The markings on the horse's head vary a great deal in size and shape. These are some of the more common ones (they are often given different names).
1 fleck, 2 star, 3 moon, 4 flower, 5 large fleck, 6 small irregular stripe, 8 blaze, 9 snip, 10 white muzzle, 11 white face, 12 toad face with irregularly pigmented rings around the eyes.

Bottom row: A selection of white leg markings.
1 without markings, 2 white crown, 3 white band, 4 half-white pastern, 5 white heel, 6 white pastern, 7 white fetlock, 8 white sock, 9 half-stocking, 10 white stocking, 11 irregular white stocking, 12 white leg. In cases where the markings cover most of the legs the hooves are often unpigmented, making them a light horn colour.

and from which the Oriental horses and the Arabs are descended. Apparently they were the source of the domestic horse's coloured coat. Nor is it known whether in their wild state these horses were already inclined to be grey and to have spots. Grey Arabs, often with markings, have certainly existed for a long time. Many experts assume that white markings, spotted patterns and a grey colour in the domestic horse breeds date from the time when they were first crossed with Arabs. They believe in fact that the Orientals 'invented' markings.

3 The term markings is not used to describe a leopard-spotted pattern. This is a Danish Knabstrup stallion with a foal. The spotted pattern is one of the basic characteristics of the breed.

HAIR COLOURS

Napoleon rode only greys. Mohammed recommended dark chestnuts for particularly difficult tasks. Many cowboys swore that duns were the hardiest and had the greatest stamina and were therefore the most suitable horses for working with cattle. Up to a point they may be right, but the truth is not, however, that dun-coloured horses are naturally better workers than horses of another colour. Cowboys naturally bred their horses for performance, and because they preferred dun-coloured horses to other coloured horses of probably equal performance, their breeding programme produced dun-coloured horses of a high quality.

Colour is never an indication of quality. A grey can be just as fine a horse as a black or a bay. The most that colour can do is reveal that a horse is not pure-blooded — for example, Cleveland Bays are always bay, Suffolk Punches are always chestnut, and Ariège ponies are always black. If a horse of one of these breeds is another colour then it is not a pure-bred. Most breeds only produce spotted offspring when they are crossed with an animal of another breed. A spotted 'Thoroughbred' is therefore not a pure-bred Thoroughbred (and naturally therefore not a Thoroughbred but a halfbred), but this does not, of course, automatically change the quality of the animal.

More and more breeders are now breeding horses or ponies for specific colours. It is often possible, after some generations, to obtain animals which continue to breed true for colour, such as the bay Cleveland Bays or the dun-coloured Fjord ponies, but it is not always possible to obtain consistent results with some other colours. Some greys breed true and others have foals of which one in four will be a different colour. While Fjord ponies breed true, most of the other dun-coloured ponies do not. Most chestnuts, bays and cream-coloured albinos are consistent but many white albinos are not. I know of a chestnut stallion from an American stud which always sires spotted foals regardless of the colour of their respective dams.

Every horse, and every other animal (including humans), receives two sets of determiners of heredity or genes. During mating, the foal is given one set by each parent, and therefore inherits characteristics both from its sire and from its dam. All these hereditary traits will reappear in succeeding generations and according to Mendel's Law the ratio of genetic inheritance can be calculated in advance. Some genes are 'dominant', which means they will reappear in the first generation, while others are 'recessive' and will not

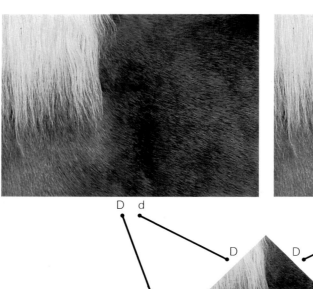

recur until later generations. If two animals, each with a dominant gene for determining colour, mate, then the foal will be the same colour as its parents. It will then breed true for colour and will pass on the dominant colour-determining gene to its offspring, which will in turn continue to breed true for colour. If the colour-determining gene is a recessive one then it will appear only in the second or third generation or even later.

Although every knowledgeable breeder is well versed in these laws, attempts to breed consistently true for colour are not always successful. Palomino breeders, for example, have been racking their brains for decades over the problem of how to make the horse's marvellous colour into a dominant gene. It seems they will never succeed. Palominos have a coat the colour of a

Left: If a cream-coloured horse is mated with a chestnut, then the result is the highly prized palomino colour.
Below: The mating of palomino with palomino produces foals of which fifty per cent will be palomino, twenty-five per cent will be cream-coloured albinos and twenty-five per cent will be chestnut.

'polished gold coin' and flaxen to silver-white mane and tail, but apparently every horse of this colour possesses one gene which dilutes the basic colour and another which does not have that effect. In breeding this means that, on average,

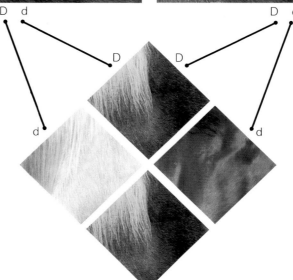

half the foals of palomino parents are palominos, that a quarter are affected by the lightening gene and are cream-coloured albinos, and the remaining quarter receive no lightening gene and are chestnut coloured. The schematic diagram should clarify this phenomenon. (While I am writing this I am eagerly waiting for my palomino mare to foal. She was covered last year by a palomino stallion and I am most interested to see what colour the foal will be.)

The breeding of spotted horses is also complicated. The spotted pattern is itself a gene, and not, as is often assumed, the result of the crossing of two different

48

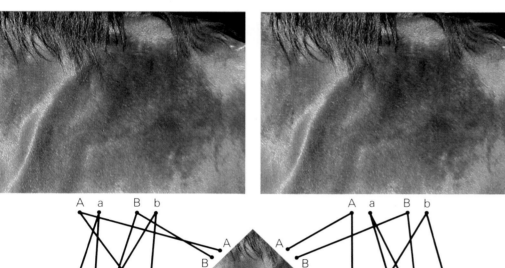

A A B B   A A B B

A A B B

Right: There are bay horses, Cleveland Bays for example, which always breed true for colour.
Below: In breeds which are bred in various colours, two bay-coloured parents will produce a calculable ratio of bay, chestnut, and black foals.

genes. If a grey is crossed with a horse of another colour, the result may be a spotted foal, but only if spotted horses are already present in its ancestry, and most spotted foals have at least one spotted parent. When two spotted horses are mated, they will produce spotted foals, but will also occasionally produce foals of only one colour.

Colourful horses occurred frequently among horses of Spanish descent. During the Baroque period they were much sought after in Europe but went out of fashion later when it was considered vulgar to ride on such a showy horse. Today, however, different coloured horses are becoming increasingly popular.

The Spaniards took many spotted horses with them to the New World. The Indians were particularly fond of these animals but so far as is known, only one tribe tried to breed them systematically. This was the Nez Percé tribe in Idaho and Oregon who created the Appaloosa breed. As fishermen they were more settled than the other tribes, but when they were forced to renounce their rights their horses were dispersed in all directions and almost disappeared for ever. Fortunately the few horses which survived were sufficient to start a new breeding programme, and the Appaloosa breed is now the third largest in North America and has about 200,000 registered animals.

The Appaloosa is bred in seven distinctive spotted patterns. The leopard pattern is an all-over spotted pattern consisting of round black or brown spots, about two to eight centimetres across, on a white background. In another variation, only the loins are spotted and the rest of the body is white. The lesser spotted leopard pattern has only a few dark spots on a white background and ideally has a dark mane and tail, dark ears with white tips, and dark patches on the leg joints. The blanket pattern consists of white quarters and loins on an otherwise dark coat — ranging from black to chestnut or grey — on which leopard spots are desirable but not essential. In the latter case the pattern is called white blanket. The marble roan pattern is a roan with dark leopard spots, often shadow spots as well, over the whole body except for the head. The rare snowflake pattern consists of white spots, sometimes sharply defined, sometimes not, on a dark background. The frost pattern, or spotted hip, has a dark background with an indistinct frosty white pattern or white flecks all over the loins.

The 'Ponies of the Americas' (POA) are bred in the same spotted patterns (see Ponies, page 27).

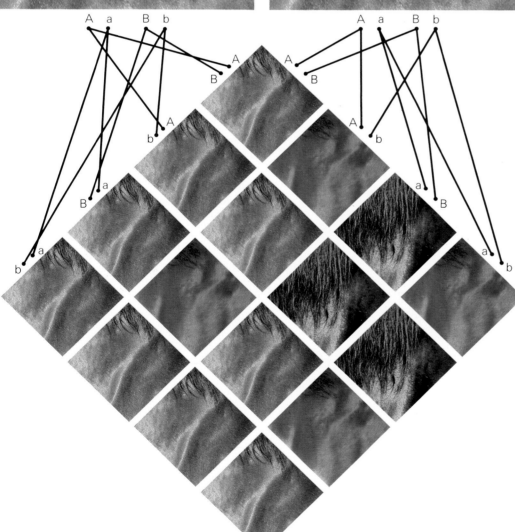

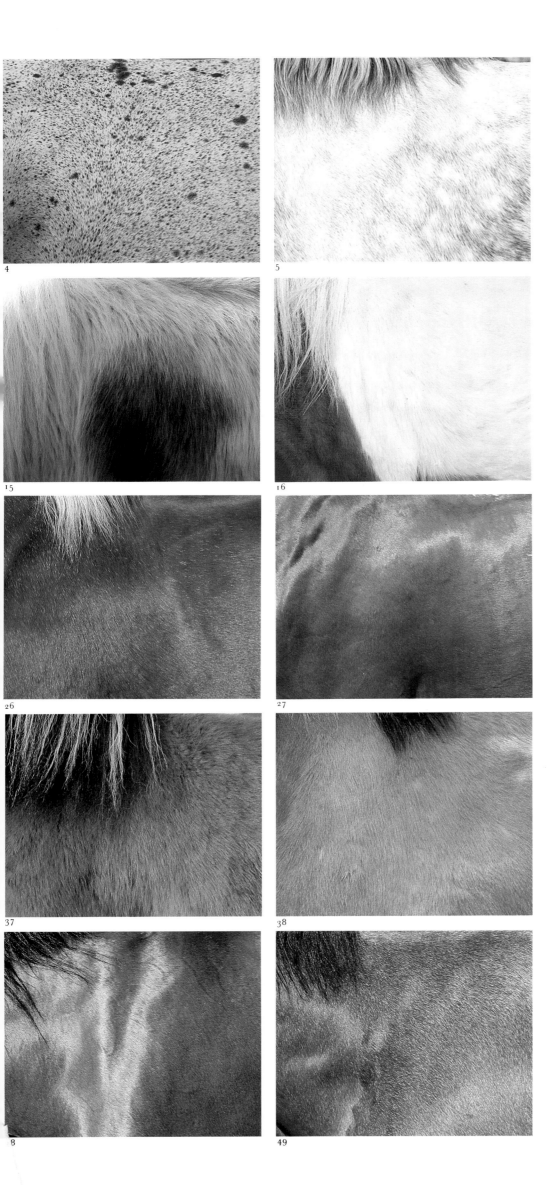

4
5
15
16
26
27
37
38
8
49

COLOUR CHART

Although there can be no precise classification of all horse colours, because there is an almost endless range between black and white, both of colour shadings and of patterns, there are a number of standardized colours and patterns.

Albinos are horses which are born white or almost white. Genuine albinos produce no colour pigments at all and have white hair, a pinkish-red skin and red eyes. They occur in most animal species, but not in horses, and those horses which are known as albinos are not genuine albinos as they have brown, light brown or blue eyes ('glass eyes'). *Greys* are born black or dark brown. White hairs begin to appear as the animals become older and they may eventually become pure white. *Roans* have a uniform sprinkling of individual white hairs on a brown, reddish or black coat. *Duns* vary in colour from yellowish-brown to mouse-grey (mouse-dun), have a black mane and tail, black stockings and a dark eel-stripe along the back. *Chestnuts* are reddish to golden-brown or pure brown. The mane and tail are always the same colour as the coat, though sometimes in a lighter tone. *Bays* can have varying shades of brown in their coats, but are also distinguished by their black mane and tail and black stockings. *Browns* are completely black except for the cinnamon colouring around the muzzle and the eyes, and on the belly and inner side of the legs. *Blacks* are, as their name indicates, generally black. *Spotteds* have their spots over a large area and leopard-spotteds are spotted in tufts. These horses are said to have a *blanket pattern* if they are spotted all over, but have a brown or black head and neck. They are said to have a *snowflake pattern* if they are dark brown or black with white spots over the loins. A *marble pattern* describes bay roan horses which have occasional white spots.

1 Albino
2 Grey
3 and 4 Fleabitten grey
5 and 6 Dapple-grey
7 and 8 Grey
9 to 11 Roan
12 Leopard spotted
13 Leopard spotted in a
   blanket pattern
14 Marble roan

15 to 18 Spotted
19 Cream-coloured albino
20 Isabella or palomino-
   coloured
21 to 35 Various shades of
   chestnut
36 to 40 Dun
41 to 52 Bay
53 to 55 Black

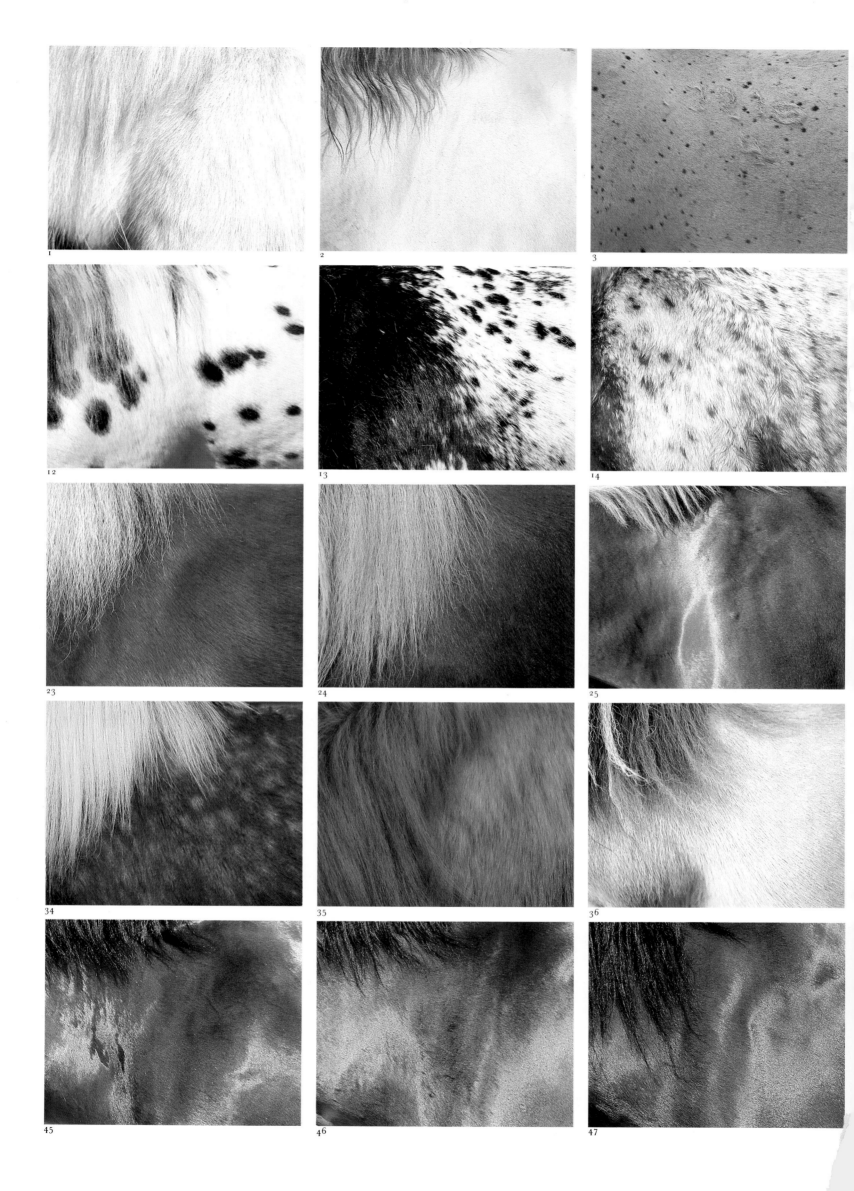

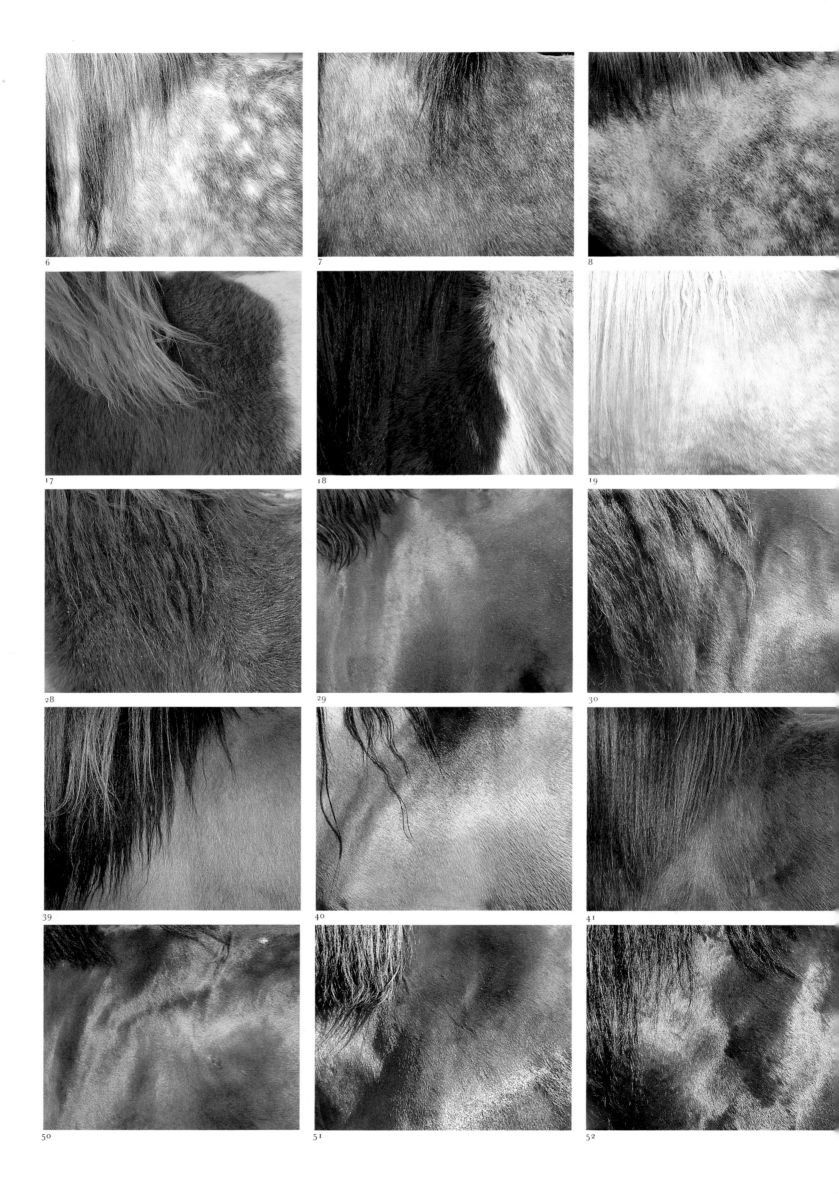

6

7

8

17

18

19

28

29

30

39

40

41

50

51

52

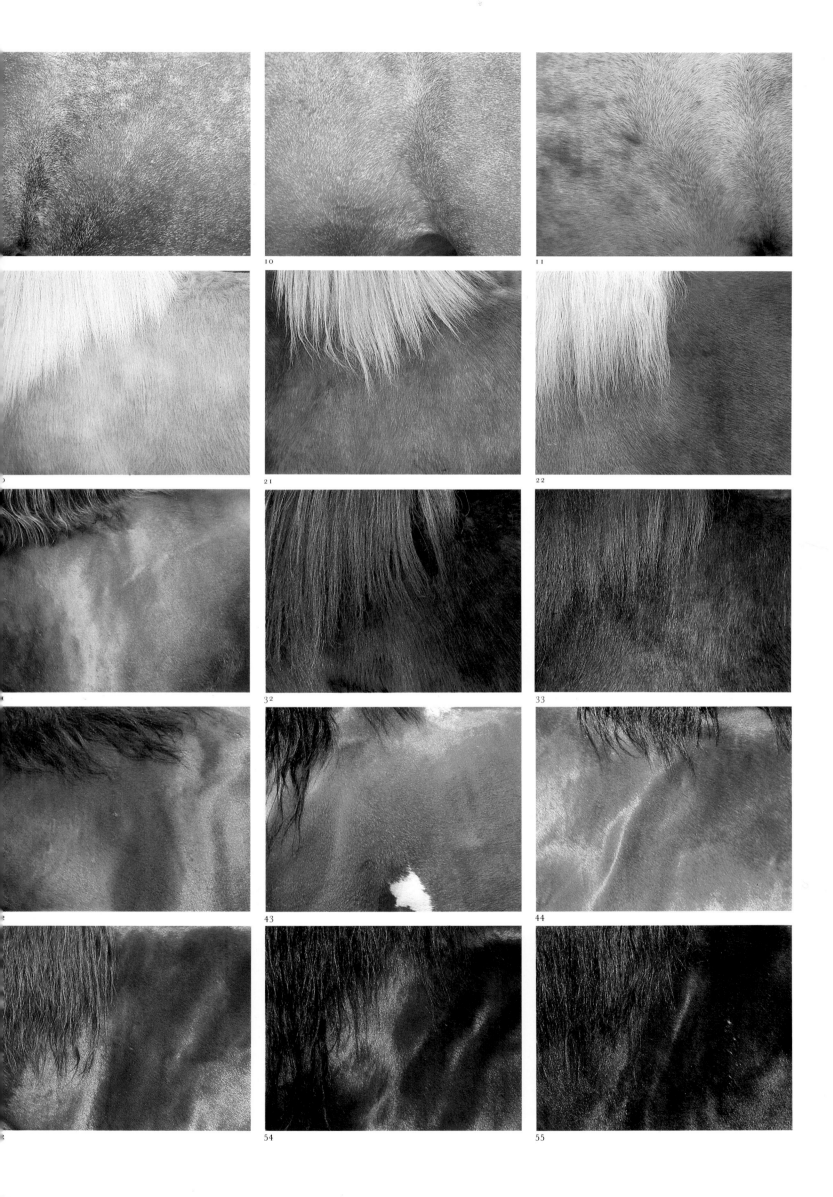

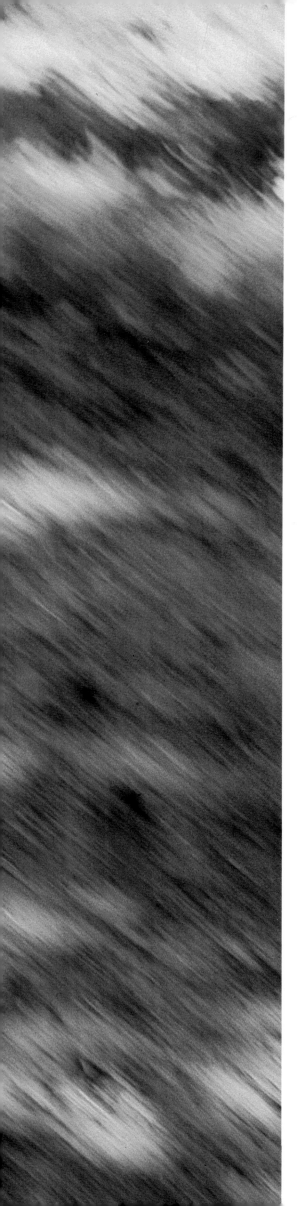

HOW THE HORSE MOVES

The very essence of the horse is expressed in the way it moves. When motionless it is simply a beautiful statue; only in movement does it display its incomparable nobility, elemental strength and dancing grace.

After the horse abandoned its primitive browsing existence, millions of years ago, and left the protection of the luxuriant vegetation of the primeval swamp, its survival depended on a high level of mobility. It became a migratory creature with a seemingly innate need to be on the move, and wandered from its North American homeland to Asia, Europe and Africa. Depending on speed for its safety, the horse never developed any effective weapons with which to defend itself, although it can use its teeth to grab hold of an adversary and, if lucky, can put one out of action with well-aimed blows from its hooves.

The whole of the horse family's evolutionary development — which culminated in the gazelle-like progenitor of the Arab breed — has had the purpose of improving the animal's speed.

The horse's mobility has, in fact, moulded its entire anatomical structure. From the nostrils to the tip of the tail its bodily proportions are perfectly balanced, allowing it to move freely while maintaining its equilibrium. Powerful muscles, which provide the animal with immense propulsive energy, are concentrated in densely packed pockets on its body. A huge thorax allows plenty of room for the large lungs, enabling them to supply the blood with the amount of oxygen the animal requires to maintain a high level of performance. Finally four long sinewy legs and hooves, each with a very small supporting surface, complete the picture of the fast runner.

We humans are two-legged creatures and have only one basic gait, putting one foot down in front of the other in a simple left-right-left-right sequence. The only difference between walking and running is that, as the tempo increases, both feet remain momentarily suspended in the air after each step.

The horse, however, has four feet, and as it can vary the sequence in which it raises and puts them down it has several possible gaits. Although some specialists maintain that the horse has at least twelve gaits, in actual fact it has only four basic ones — walk, trot, gallop and pace. All the others are variations on these four, whether they are called tölt, amble, rack, running walk, stepping pace, broken amble, single foot, fox-trot or whatever. The four basic gaits are described on the following four pages. In addition there are descriptions of the tölt, the jog and the lope. The tölt is a very rapid walk which has been made more widely known by the use of Icelandic ponies for riding, and the jog and the lope are the customary gaits used when riding Western style. These two variations were developed by people who did not have to cover long distances on horseback. In tempo they correspond to a trot and are much more comfortable for the rider.

The remaining gaits, particularly those variations which have been developed in North America, are show gaits with little or no practical purpose. Horses have to be taught these gaits and not only is the learning process difficult and laborious, but highly dubious teaching methods are used, some of them extremely cruel. The Tennessee Walking Horse, for example, is required to have a 'knee action' which is as high as possible. This means that at every step the horse has to lift its bent foreleg extremely high, and, to make it do this, its forelegs are weighted down with thick blocks of wood, and a loose chain fastened around the fetlock which hits the horse on the coronet of the hoof and makes every step painful. Similarly brutal methods are used to train Hackneys, Saddle Horses and others. It is a matter of opinion whether such show gaits can be described as beautiful — certainly they have nothing in common with the harmonious picture presented by a horse moving freely around.

WALK

The walk is the horse's slowest gait and the one it uses most frequently. It is the normal gait of the heavy cold-bloods, which are aptly called 'cart-horses', and is the ideal gait for pulling carts.

The walk is a four-beat gait with equal intervals between the beats. The sequence of foot-falls is right-fore, left-hind,

TROT

The trot is a medium fast gait which the horse uses for covering long distances at a brisk tempo. The sequence of foot-falls is fore-right and hind-left, fore-left and hind-right, etc, and the two diagonal feet are brought to the ground so quickly one after the other that in fact there is only one audible foot-fall or beat.

In rare cases the feet are brought down simultaneously.

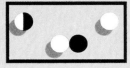 

GALLOP

The gallop is the horse's fastest gait, and feral horses will gallop only when threatened by imminent danger or during courtship rituals. Those horses which originated in the northern tundra, moorlands and icy plains have a less pronounced galloping ability than their relatives from the southern regions of steppe and desert.

The gallop has a three-beat cadence — three beats in a

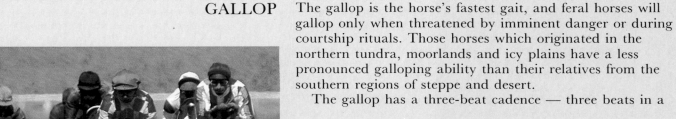

left-fore, right-hind, etc. In the normal walk two or three feet are always on the ground at the same time.

In addition a dressage horse has to perform a 'collected walk' in which the hind feet touch the ground behind the footprints of the forefeet; the 'medium walk' in which the hind feet touch the ground slightly in front of the footprints of the forefeet; and the much more relaxing 'extended walk' in which the hind feet should touch the ground clearly in front of the footprints of the forefeet.

Christine Stückelberger who won the Gold Medal for Dressage at the 1976 Olympics and was also World Champion in Dressage in 1978 kindly put herself at our disposal so that each phase of these gaits could be photographed.

After each foot-fall there is an interval when all four feet are off the ground for an instant — a moment of suspension.

Various breeds of horse have a natural aptitude for long-striding trotting movements, and only as the tempo increases do they break into a gallop. The English Norfolk and the Dutch Harddraver are trotting breeds, and such horses formed the basis for the different breeds of trotters which now compete in trotting races. Occasionally they are ridden but more often they are harnessed in front of the sulky.

In dressage a distinction is drawn between the 'collected trot', the somewhat more energetic 'working trot', the elastic 'medium trot' and the 'extended trot'.

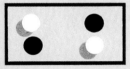   

regular sequence followed by a short pause (the moment of suspension) when all four feet are off the ground.

The gallop differs from the other gaits in not being symmetrical on the two sides, so may be led either on one side or the other. In the left lead, the horse strides out first with the left foot, and in the right lead, with the right foot.

When running freely the horse can change quickly and effortlessly from left to right lead. When ridden it needs the co-operation of the rider, who must adjust his weight accordingly.

For the left lead the sequence of foot-falls is fore-left, hind-right, hind-left and fore-right almost together.

 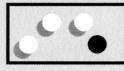  

59

PACE

Various animal species — camels, for example — are natural pacers. Their sequence of foot-falls, instead of diagonal, is left-fore and left-hind, right-fore and right-hind, etc.

The pace is a natural gait in certain breeds of horses and also in some individual animals. Most of these horses have,

TÖLT

In the Middle Ages and in the Baroque period the tölt was very popular and the palfreys which perfected it were much esteemed.

Between then and now it fell into disuse in most countries, but was retained in Iceland and in some other places because it is wonderfully comfortable for the rider.

JOG AND LOPE

The cowboys of the American West often had to cover great distances on horseback. Because the normal trotting tempo was too uncomfortable, and the distances were too great to be ridden at a proper gallop, they tried to devise an ideal 'working gait'. The result was the jog and the lope.

The jog (picture sequence) is a slow trot which has a

however, a normal walk, i.e., one with a diagonal sequence of foot-falls, and break into the pace only at the trotting tempo. At walking tempo the pace has the same four-beat rhythm because here, as in the trot, two feet, namely left-fore and left-hind, and then right-fore and right-hind, hit the ground almost simultaneously. As in the trot there is also a moment of suspension in between the two beats. The

stepping pace — the one depicted in the photographs — is a gait which lies between the walking pace and the trotting pace.

The Peruvian Paso (colour photo) is a trotting breed. One of its natural gaits is a very fast broken (stepping) pace. The American trotting breed (Standardbred) is divided into two groups : Trotters and Pacers.

In recent years this gait has once again become more widely known, mainly as the result of the increasing popularity of Icelandic ponies for riding.

Horses with an aptitude for the pace also have an aptitude for the tölt. To put it simply, the tölt is a gait which lies between the normal walk and the pace. One characteristic is that the neck is carried very high so that its

lower part often appears to be curved forwards. As a result the back is completely relaxed and hardly sways at all as the fore and hind legs move.

The tölt provides the rider with a very comfortable ride, but is much more strenuous for the horse than a trot or gallop.

slight break in its rhythm. The diagonal pair of feet are not set down at the same time as in a normal trot. Instead one foot hits the ground slightly before the other, so that instead of a two-beat, an irregular four-beat can be heard.

The lope is a very slow gallop, distinguished from a normal gallop by the fact that the third and fourth feet are put down distinctly one after the other. This changes an

irregular three-beat rhythm into a four-beat one with a pause after the fourth beat.

Both variations have to be taught to the horse, but once it has learnt them it is so relaxed that the rider can remain comfortably seated, and they do not tire the animal even over long periods.

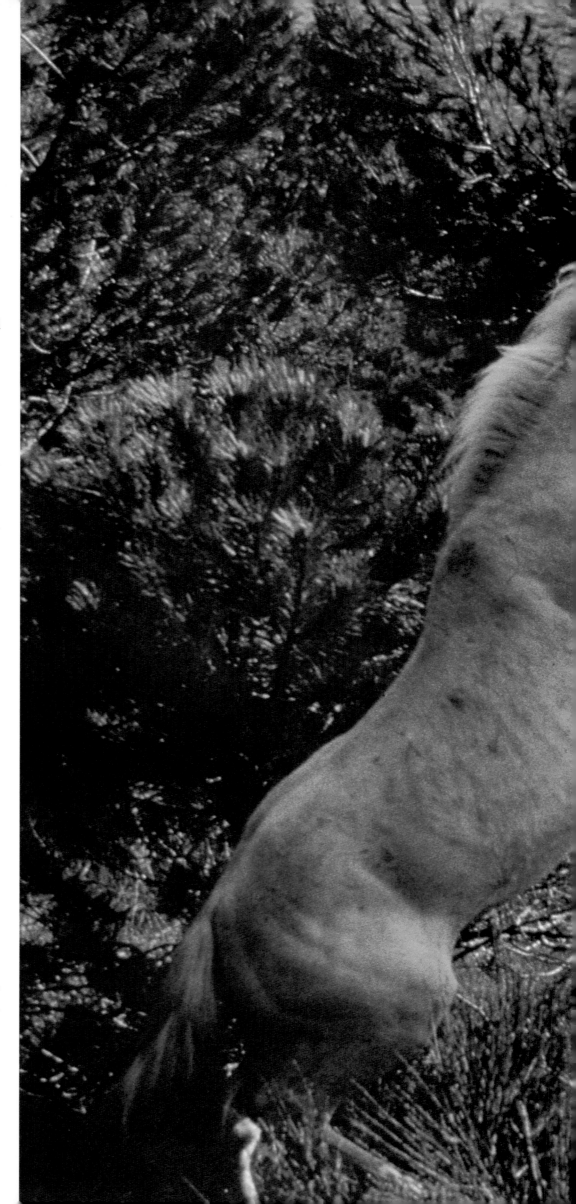

HOW THE HORSE BEHAVES

Fifty million years ago the animal which was eventually to evolve into the horse was an inhabitant of humid regions with luxuriant vegetation. It lived alone or in small family groups and led a secretive life.

As the climatic conditions changed, the immense swamp regions of North America, Europe and Asia gradually dried out and became savannahs, prairies, tundra or deserts. The primitive horse could have followed the example of its close relative, the tapir, and withdrawn into the tropical and sub-tropical swamps of southern Asia or Central and South America, but Eohippus possessed latent aptitudes of a different nature. The migratory urge was strong and the horse needed to extend its living space. The ability to adapt to changing conditions eventually enabled it to live successfully in open country, but first the animal had to adapt its bodily structure, from the teeth to the tips of its toes, to fit the requirements of its new way of life, and then make significant changes in its behaviour patterns. If it had continued to live a solitary life, its chances of survival in the open landscape would have been slim despite the fact that it was becoming a very much faster runner. In a herd there would always be some animals on the alert and ready to give the alarm at the first sign of potential danger. The communal life, however, demanded the development of a unique social behaviour which in turn produced the horse's distinctive qualities, and it is on the knowledge of these behaviour patterns that man has been able to build a successful working relationship with the horse.

Fights between stallions play an important role in ensuring the preservation of a healthy species by guaranteeing that only strong stallions dominate and cover the mares.

BEHAVIOUR PATTERNS

Is there a rider who has not at some stage had difficulty trying to take one particular horse away from its stable? And has not everyone been through the experience of finding, after a long strenuous ride, that on the homeward journey his horse suddenly shows no more signs of being tired but on the contrary needs to be forcibly restrained from galloping madly home? This behaviour is described as the 'homing instinct', and can be observed not only in horses which are housed with others of their own kind but also in animals which are kept in a stable on their own. This could easily lead one to the conclusion that the horse loves its stable, but in reality the stable is nothing more than a substitute — and an imperfect one at that — for the herd.

The herd instinct is deep-rooted in the horse, and when left alone it feels defenceless and afraid. In the wild, without continually alert companions, it would have fallen victim to predators, and the need to be with others of its kind is irresistible.

Experience teaches the stabled horse that its box or stall offers protection. There are few unusual sounds or unpleasant surprises there, but the world outside the stable is full of unexpected and

1 The 'laughing' horse is in reality a yawning horse. Incidentally yawning is just as 'catching' in horses as it is in humans.

2 Horses can sleep standing up. Among horses living in the wild only the younger ones lie down for any length of time; the older ones seldom or never do.

3 In each herd the 'pecking order' has to be continually confirmed. This involves nipping those of lower rank on the shoulder, neck, croup or dock.

frightening events. Fear bordering on panic can be aroused by the noise of traffic, by a rustling in the foliage, by the sight of a deer fleeing past or a piece of paper being blown up into the air. The horse therefore feels safe and secure in its stable, though this does not necessarily also mean that it is happy there.

A horse kept on its own — particularly if it has nothing to do for several hours a day — becomes dull and listless. Out of boredom it often begins to gnaw at pieces of wood, to paw and scrape the ground, to swallow air — for this it develops a particular technique referred to as cribbing — and to sway its head backwards and forwards. It may also become an aggressive biter or kicker. Ignorance, or arrogance, labels such behaviour 'vices', and the unfortunate animal, which has been adversely

64

4 In young stallions the curling back of the upper lip is a threat-face often used in play.

5 This expression is called the flehmen response. Stallions, mares and foals all use it to investigate interesting smells.

6 A very common social activity: mutual nibbling of the coat.

7 A definitely threatening facial expression: ears pinned back, eyes, nostrils and edges of the mouth pressed tightly together. head and neck stretched out.

4

5

6

7

affected by its environment, is branded a 'criminal'. No society, even a herd of horses, can exist without a certain order, and a horse needs to live in the company of its own kind in order to preserve its 'spiritual balance'. When a herd of horses living in the wild is observed, it soon becomes obvious that it is a society with precise rules and customs and not a disorderly jumble. There is a lead mare. She leads the herd. Not one of the other members of the herd dares to challenge her authority. She is the highest-ranking animal and always at the front when the group moves from its grazing grounds to the watering or resting places along the same well-worn paths at the same time each day and always in single file. She is the first to drink at the watering place and selects the choicest feeding area unopposed. On the other hand she is always extremely alert and instinctively aware of possible dangers, and she guarantees that her companions will be well protected.

There is also a strict 'pecking order' within the herd, a hierarchical structure which is based on the self-confidence of each individual horse as much as on its bodily strength. Squabbles about rank rarely develop into a fight. Usually an aggressive manner is sufficient, and, there is no need for a bite or kick.

This 'pecking order' has played a crucial role in the history of the rela-

tionship between man and horse, for if it were simply the product of acts of force then the horse could never have been made into a useful domestic animal. To a certain extent the tame horse regards a human as one of its own kind, i.e., as a member of the herd, and by being self-confident and, if necessary, aggressive we may play the role of the highest ranking 'horse'. This is a clue to the correct handling of a horse.

Every experienced rider knows that horses can have very different natures, and, in this, characteristics of certain breeds play an important part. Many ponies can be extraordinarily self-willed and need far more tactful handling than most of the large horses. Arabs on the other hand, despite having very pronounced personalities and being one of the most intelligent breeds of all, are usually very willing and obedient. The

breed is, however, not the sole determiner of character. An individual which would have had a high ranking place in the herd does not easily allow itself to be dominated and controlled, but once such a horse has accepted its rider as the higher in rank then it will go through thick and thin for him. A horse which would naturally have been a lower ranked individual is usually very impressionable and presents no problems though it is sometimes inclined to be more easily frightened.

If the 'pecking order' is to be maintained there must also be a means of communication, a 'language'. This consists of a number of facial and acoustic expressions, some used to reject, others to attract. They can be full of nuances. Whinnying, for example, can express a whole range of emotions from joyful excitement to deepest confusion. As well there are sounds which are intended to soothe or comfort, to allure, reject, terrify or to express aggression. The inventory of facial expressions is even more important than the acoustic ones. These range from the friendly 'greeting face' through conceited display behaviour to threatening expressions which if necessary are reinforced with bites and blows.

HOW THE HORSE BREEDS

The mating season is a stormy time for horses living in the wild. For weeks the stallion has little peace, as he trots continually around his little herd of five to ten mares, the young animals from the previous year and the new-born foals. Not only does he have to protect the herd from predators, but he must keep the mares together and drive off other stallions attracted by the mares, which are ready for mating about ten days after foaling. The stallion also has to determine exactly when each of his mares is at the optimum moment for conception, for when the mare is in oestrus, conception is possible only within a very short time-span. Having established that the mare will be receptive — for this he relies on instinct aided by his acute sense of smell — the stallion then performs a beautiful courtship ritual. He tempts her with loud insistent whinnying. Then, with neck curved high and nostrils flared, he approaches her at a jaunty cadenced trot. He dances around her, bites and nibbles her, then finally he mounts her.

Most of this ritual is never seen on studs where horses are bred under human care. Usually the stallion is kept separated from the mares, and it is the breeder who decides the right moment for mating. The mare is held still, quite often with her hind legs hobbled and her upper lip held in a twitch. The stallion, too, is held on a long rein throughout. The pair are given no time to get to know each other, although this is an important part of their natural behaviour. Mating becomes just a mechanical process, and the wedding with all its ceremonial has become a rape, resulting in horses with disturbed behaviour patterns and a conception ratio of only fifty to sixty per cent. Horses living free in the herd may choose their partners and court and mate without human interference, with the result that over ninety-five per cent of the mares become pregnant.

MATING

Horses naturally mate in spring. In Europe the ideal time is from about the beginning of May, through June which is the optimum month, till the end of July. In wild studs, i.e., those in large reserves where the herds of mares can run freely with the stallion, all matings take place at this time. It is logical, for it means that when the foals are born a good eleven months later there is an abundance of fresh grass rich in protein, and the foals' first months of life coincide with what is climatically the most pleasant time of the year.

The pituitary gland or hypophisis is a small gland situated directly under the brain, which ensures that under natural conditions mating takes place at the right time of year. This gland reacts to light absorbed through the eyes. The light first affects a particular part of the brain which in turn works on the pituitary gland. In the spring the amount of sunlight increases, causing the gland to produce and release increasing quantities of a hormone known as FSH (follicle stimulating hormone). This hormone reaches the mare's ovaries through the bloodstream, and stimulates some microscopically small eggs to grow. Some days later another hormone called LH (luteinizing hormone) causes the egg to detach itself from the ovary. This process is called ovulation, and it is immediately after this that the mare is able to conceive.

In spring the stallion's pituitary gland also produces these two hormones in increasing quantities. In the stallion the FSH stimulates the formation and growth of sperm cells, and LH plus an additional hormone awakens the sexual drive.

The production of hormones is also affected by other factors, such as the rise in temperature and the higher protein content of the food supply. The sex hormone is produced throughout the year, not just during spring, but during the spring months the quantities are increased. Throughout the year, too, the eggs continue to develop in the mare's ovaries and detach themselves normally about every twenty-one days. The mare could conceive even in December, when she is still receptive to the stallion and can arouse his sexual urge by emitting her special scent. Outside the natural mating time, though, the development of the eggs is often irregular. Ovulation, and therefore conception, can cease for prolonged intervals of time. The stallion also produces fewer sperm and displays a diminished sexual drive.

The production of hormones can be influenced artificially, something which was already being done even before anything was known about hormones. Canaries and laying hens were probably the first animals to be treated in this way. In England the breeding of racehorses is controlled in similar fashion. Because the natural foaling time coincided with the flat-racing season, the English Jockey Club has, since 1823, moved it to the beginning of January. So that high conception ratios can still be achieved, the horses' stalls are heated, electric light used to lengthen the days artificially, and the feed supplemented with high protein additives to simulate the quality of spring grass. The extremely successful results confirm the superior technical know-how of English horse breeders. Around seventy per cent of the mares become pregnant. Admittedly this rate is lower than that of horses living in the wild or kept on wild studs, but it is higher than that obtained in most countries by conventional breeding methods, where mating is usually carried out in the spring.

The impressive courtship ritual is part of a horse's natural mating behaviour. When horses are allowed to run freely the stallion begins to woo the favours of the mare several days before the optimum conception time. Swaggering display behaviour is part of the ritual. Similar displays can often be observed when two stallions meet. Demonstrations of tenderness, however, also play a role. Many mares remain completely passive throughout; others are decidedly importunate.

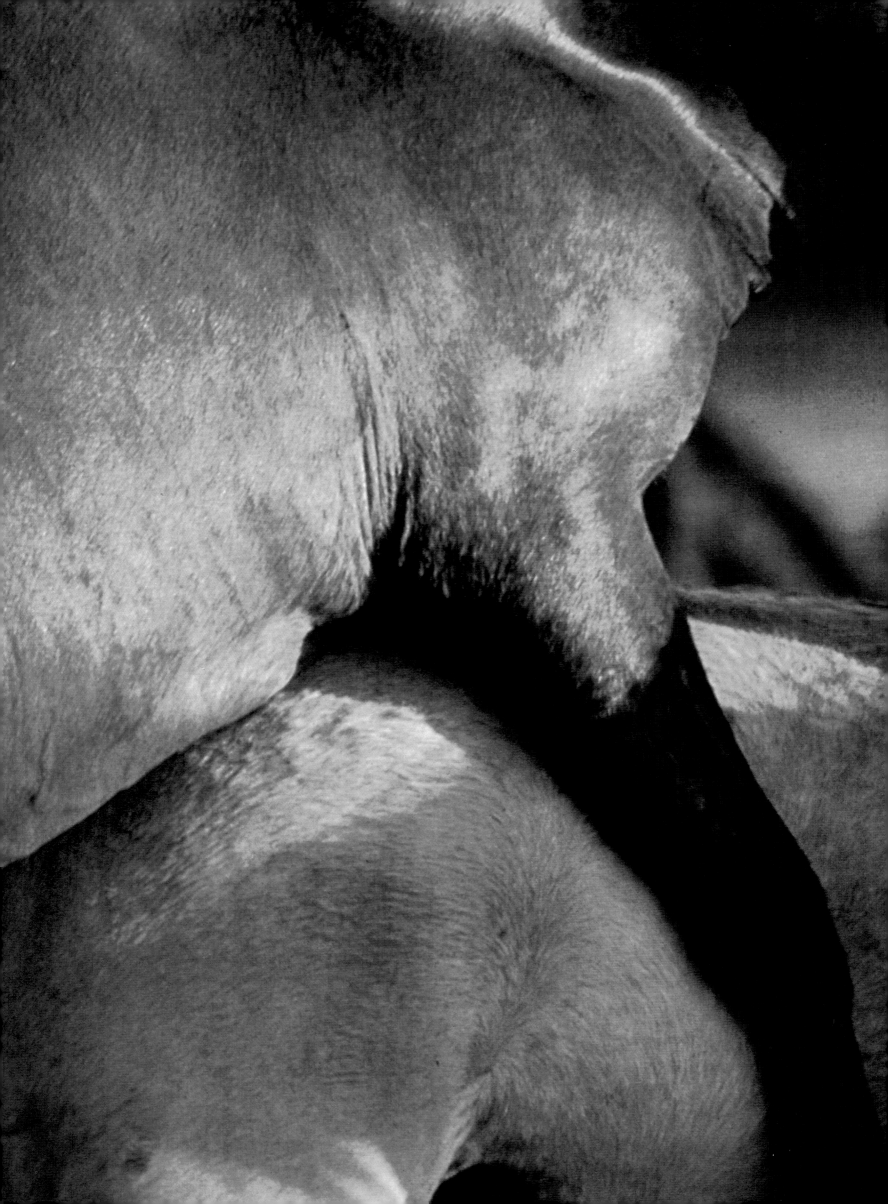

THE PREGNANT MARE

If the mare does not come back into season again three weeks after mating, then it is assumed that she has 'held' to the service, i.e., that an egg cell was fertilized and the embryo is developing. Some mares may show no signs of heat even though they are not pregnant, usually because, although an egg has been fertilized, the embryo has died, and its remains in her womb will prevent her coming into season again. Other mares may be pregnant and yet still come on heat again. This is described as a 'false' heat, and although these mares display all the external signs of being in season, as a rule they decline the stallion's advances.

The breeder naturally wants to know as soon as possible whether or not a mare is pregnant, so that if necessary he can have her covered again. By observing changes in the mare's behaviour, an experienced person has little difficulty in determining whether she is pregnant. Pregnant mares often become very aloof, both towards other horses as well as humans. They become more wary, very lazy, and jealous and possessive about food, with a noticeable increase in their appetites. But it requires very keen observation to recognise these signs.

The veterinary surgeon has a choice of several methods for determining pregnancy. At four to five weeks, sometimes as early as three weeks after mating, he can make a rectal examination, and from the state of the uterus deduce whether an embryo is present.

Between the fortieth and hundredth day after mating considerable quantities of a hormone known as PMSG — pregnant mare's serum (gonadotropin) — are found in the mare's blood. At this stage a blood sample is usually taken and sent to the laboratory for examination by the well known 'mouse-test', which has now been in use for several years. Some drops of the mare's blood are injected into an immature female mouse, and two days later the mouse is killed and dissected. If the mare is pregnant there will be visible changes in the mouse's internal sex organs. It is not necessary to use mice, however, as the so-called immunological process can be applied to prove the presence of PMSG in the blood. After the hundredth day, the urine test can be carried out, as from this time on there is a noticeable increase in the amount of a particular hormone similar to oestrogen in the urine of pregnant mares.

After about six months the opinion of a veterinary surgeon is no longer needed, for by putting a hand on the mare's stomach one can feel the foal moving. The foal is particularly lively after its

Normally about seven months after mating the rounding of the mare's stomach indicates that she is pregnant. This condition is not obvious in some mares (ponies in particular) even after eleven months, i.e., shortly before the birth. More than one pony owner had no inkling that a mare was pregnant until one morning he found a foal standing beside her.

mother has been drinking cold water. About a month later the mare's bodily circumference gradually begins to increase, though mares which have borne several foals already have larger bellies and sometimes even at this stage the pregnancy is not really noticeable. Many pony mares have such rounded 'grass bellies' that their size can be very deceptive, and the surprised buyer of a pony can be faced with the unexpected sight of a foal standing beside its mother one morning.

Horse breeders, riders and veterinary surgeons are not in complete agreement about what is a reasonable workload for a pregnant mare. Farmers, of course, have never thought of this as a problem. They needed their horses to work on the land. A farmer's mare, pregnant or not, had to work until just before she foaled, and was expected to pull the harvest cart in summer, the plough in autumn and the tree trunks in winter. Shortly after giving birth in spring she had to help prepare the fields, though this was comparatively light work. Usually she suffered no ill-effects at all.

It is nevertheless sensible to take some precautions. A pregnant mare should not be used for racing, for competing in strenuous distance rides or in show-jumping competitions, though she may be ridden daily or put in harness, and as long as the horse is not overtaxed this can only be beneficial. It is undoubtedly preferable to allow the mare freedom of movement in an open stall, and to let her exercise in the open air even in winter, rather than to keep her tied up in a warm stable. The cold will not harm her nor her foal, provided she has access to a dry shelter out of the wind.

If horses are well cared for the danger of a 'miscarriage' or an 'abortion' is slim, though not out of the question. Mares probably expel over ten per cent of all embryos or foetuses before the 300th day of pregnancy. Usually they are already dead, but, even if they are alive and quite

well-grown and their hearts beating strongly, they have no chance of survival as their lungs are under-developed. It is not possible to obtain an exact figure for all abortions as some of them occur before the fortieth day of pregnancy, that is, before a pregnancy can be diagnosed with certainty. At that stage, too, the rejected embryo is so small that it would be easily overlooked in the straw or in the paddock.

Foals born between the 300th and 325th day of pregnancy are considered to be premature births, and with the right care they usually survive.

An abortion can be caused by an unlucky fall, a hefty blow to the stomach, or even colic, but more frequently the cause is a bacterial infection such as one caused by staphylococci, bacillus coli, or streptococci. Most abortions can be traced back to virus infections — to the Equid Herpesvirus I in particular. Formerly called Equine viral Rhinopneumonitis, this causes an infection of the respiratory organs. Fortunately this 'viral abortion' can be prevented by inoculation.

Quite often a twin pregnancy is the cause of a miscarriage. In approximately one out of a hundred matings two eggs are fertilized and begin to develop, but the uterus of a female horse is apparently too small to carry two foetuses to term. Twins usually die about half-way through the pregnancy and are then expelled.

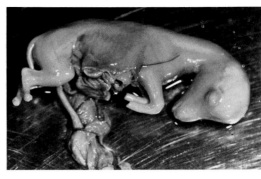

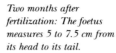
Two months

Two months after
fertilization: The foetus
measures 5 to 7.5 cm from
its head to its tail.

After four months: Length
12 to 22 cm. First hairs on
upper and lower lips.

After six months: Length 35
to 60 cm. Small hairs on
lips, nostrils, eyebrows and
eyelashes.

After seven months: Length
35 to 70 cm. First hairs on
tip of tail.

After eight months: Length
50 to 80 cm. Hair beginning
to grow on mane, external
ear, back and extremities of
limbs.

After nine months: Length
60 to 90 cm. Short thin hair
covers body except for
abdomen and inner thighs.

From the extent of the body
hair an expert can tell the
age of foals which have been
miscarried or born
prematurely.

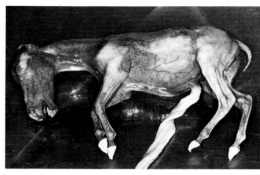

Four months

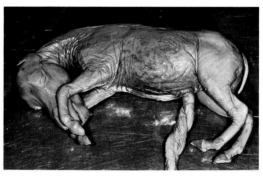

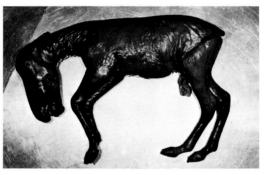

Six months

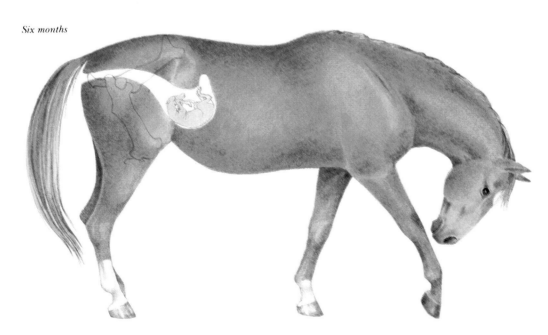

HOW A FOAL DEVELOPS

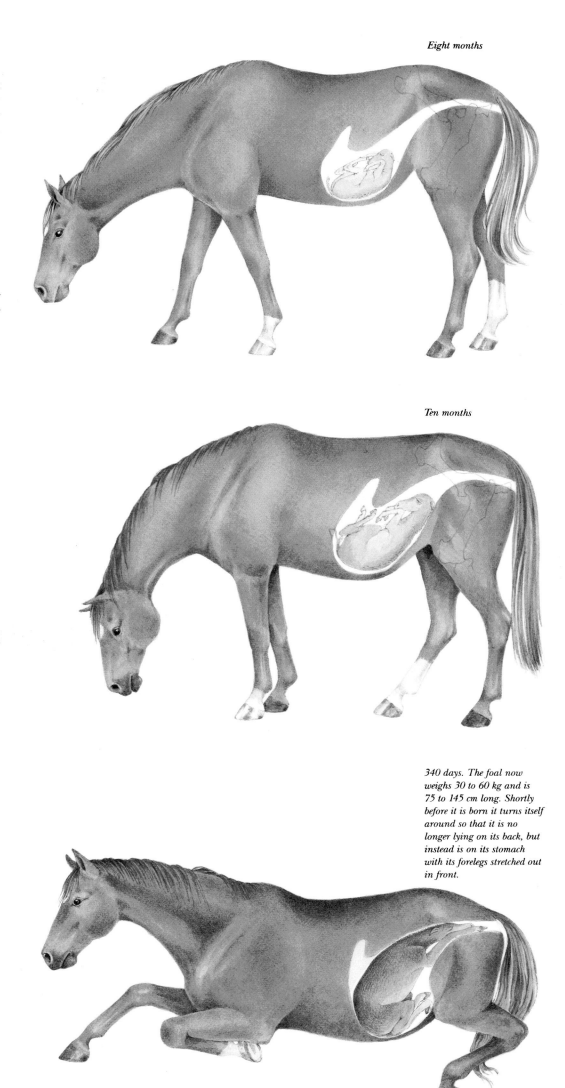

Eight months

Ten months

After mating, the most wonderful event takes place hidden from our eyes in the warm interior of the mare's body : a new life begins to develop. Out of the billions of sperm, a single one has fertilized the egg cell, which now begins to divide. In rapid succession the single cell becomes first two cells, then four, then eight, sixteen, thirty-two and so on. These cells become more and more numerous and gradually assume the shape of the future foal. Only twenty days after fertilization a living creature, barely two centimetres long, already exists. It is a foetus, the name used to describe the embryo of every mammal. It consists of millions of cells and has four tiny legs and a large head.

The future foal needs nourishment and life-sustaining oxygen if it is to stay alive and grow. To supply this, a special organ, the placenta, develops in the mare's uterus. It is connected to the foetus by the umbilical cord, which is composed of three blood vessels along which the blood flows to and fro. The placenta itself is firmly fixed to the wall of the uterus, from where numerous small blood vessels link it to the mare's bloodstream. Maternal blood reaches the foetus through the placenta and umbilical cord and then travels back into the mare's bloodstream. In this way the foetus receives nourishment and oxygen, and waste products (such as urine and carbon dioxide) are carried back to the mare for disposal.

By the second month of pregnancy the foetus is already recognizable as a tiny horse. By the third month, when the embryo has reached a length of seven to fourteen centimetres, the hooves and even the nipples can be clearly seen. By the fourth month the first small hairs are growing on the lips, and the external sexual characteristics are visible. In the meantime the placenta has developed rapidly and begun to attach itself to the wall of the uterus. From the sixth month on various internal organs assume their final shape.

On average the foal is ready to be born 340 days after conception.

340 days. The foal now weighs 30 to 60 kg and is 75 to 145 cm long. Shortly before it is born it turns itself around so that it is no longer lying on its back, but instead is on its stomach with its forelegs stretched out in front.

BIRTH OF A FOAL

Towards the end of the gestation period thick yellowish globules of wax appear on the mare's nipples. This is the signal that the foal will be born within twenty-four hours. The birth pains start some hours before the great moment, and the mare begins to pace around. She breaks out in a sweat, particularly over the region where the kidneys are, and is obviously uncomfortable. Often she licks her coat — a sign that her instinct to lick the newborn foal is already awakened. As a final sign that the birth is imminent the 'waters break': there is a sudden gush of water from the vagina.

During the first stage of labour her womb starts to contract. The contractions become increasingly stronger and finally cause the membranes of the water-bag to burst and some of the allantoic fluid held within escapes. Now the actual birth phase begins. This normally lasts about twenty minutes, but in a mare which gives birth easily it can take only five minutes. It should never last longer than an hour. Shortly after the waters break the mare lies down. Almost all mares foal lying on their sides. As the second stage begins, uterine contractions increase and the abdominal muscles also start to contract. The foal is pushed from behind into the birth canal and finally out of its mother's body. First the forelegs appear encased in whitish membranes. Then, lying along the forelegs, the foal's head emerges. The most difficult part is now over. Shoulders and chest slide much more easily though the narrow opening, and after a few moments the rest of the foal arrives.

Even as the chest is beginning to emerge the foal begins to gasp for air, and about a minute later it starts to breathe more regularly. The oxygen content of its blood increases rapidly and gives the little creature the energy it needs to enter this new phase of its life.

Ninety per cent of all foals are born at night between 7 p.m. and 7 a.m. — the majority of them between 9 p.m. and 2 a.m.

FROM FOAL TO ADULT HORSE

Foals are typical of defenceless animals which rely on speed for survival in open country. By the time they are born they are already highly developed, for horses living in the wild must be able to follow the herd soon after birth, and if necessary flee quickly from danger. Despite thousands of years of domestication these abilities have been retained.

Two or three minutes after it is born a healthy foal will lift its head for the first time, push itself up on to its chest and pull its hindlegs under its body. At the same time the eyes and ears begin to function and it can whinny quietly. Soon it makes its first attempts to stand. First it stretches out its forelegs and pushes itself up, then raises itself on its hindlegs — and usually collapses back on to the ground. In no time at all, however, it becomes steadier on its feet and after an hour is able to remain standing. Any foal which, an hour after birth, still cannot get up is either sick or weak and underdeveloped.

As soon as the foal can stand — usually within the first two hours — it starts to explore its mother's body. Usually beginning at her forelegs, it sniffs and nudges its way along her flank until finally it finds her udder.

It is very important that the foal takes the mare's first milk or colostrum as soon as possible, for this contains not only nourishment but also antibodies which give the foal continuing protection against a variety of infectious diseases.

Within twenty-four hours a healthy foal becomes completely adjusted to the new demands of life outside its mother's body. The newborn must maintain its body temperature at about 37.6°C., even when the external temperature sinks to freezing point or below. After the hasty breathing of its first minutes it soon settles down to a normal frequency of thirty to forty breaths a minute and a pulse rate of about 100. Within at least two days it must expel the meconium,

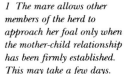

its first dung, which has collected in the foal's intestines up till the moment of birth.

At birth the foal's coat is wet with the amniotic fluid which surrounded it, the smell and taste of which play an important role in enabling the mare to get to know her offspring. Just a few minutes after the mare has licked and smelt the foal for the first time she will no longer accept any other foal, although some mares, often called 'nannies' or foster-mothers, are exceptions to this rule, and can safely be entrusted with the upbringing of orphaned foals.

During the first few days the mare will not allow any other horse near. Although she is still within the herd's protective custody, her behaviour ensures that her companions keep their distance, and only when the foal is thoroughly familiar with its mother's smell and colour, the sound of her voice and her way of moving, does their contact with the herd become closer.

In the meantime an intimate relationship has developed between mare and foal. Even when the foal is at a distance playing with other foals, or when the mother moves away to graze while the little one is sleeping, they need to be reassured of each other's presence by constant contact. If the mother notices any sign of possible danger her high pitched whinnying call will bring the youngster running to her side. If the foal finds itself on its own it calls fearfully and shrilly for its mother, who responds with a deep rumbling call to reassure,

1 The mare allows other members of the herd to approach her foal only when the mother-child relationship has been firmly established. This may take a few days.

2 Within the first two hours a healthy foal will suckle for the first time. For about the next three months its mother's milk is its main source of nourishment. Normally it suckles for almost a year.

3 Early on the foal makes contact with other members of the herd. After some months it normally forms a close friendship with another of its own age.

4 Foals, like adult horses, stand up first on their forelegs then on their hindlegs — cows get up the opposite way.

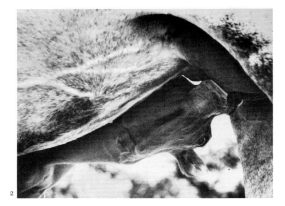

comfort it and show her presence.

Under natural conditions the mother suckles her foal for almost a year. If she does not become pregnant again she will continue into the second and even the third year. During its first weeks of life the foal will drink large quantities of milk. Depending on the size of the breed, it can range from about eight to twenty litres a day. This is divided into small frequent portions, as horses have comparatively small stomachs, and a young

5 to 8 In the wild a group of young stallions will form their own herd, and on studs they are usually raised in separate groups, where they spend their time preparing for the battles which lie in front of them when they will have to win mares and found their own harems. Stallion fights are often very bitter but they seldom result in serious wounds.

foal will drink from its mother about forty to fifty times over a period of twenty-four hours.

The rate at which the young animal grows in its first few weeks is amazing. Even during its first days it will start to nibble at grasses, and after barely two months it has doubled its birth weight. After about three months its mother's udder is no longer its main source of food. Later the rate of growth decreases noticeably. In the first three months its withers height increases about as much as it does in the following nine months. After a year it has reached about eighty per cent of its final body height. After three years it grows very little, although its bones are not completely developed until its fifth year, or even later in breeds which take longer to mature, e.g., northern ponies.

Shortly before the mare gives birth to a new foal she 'rejects' the yearling and drives him away from her. Because their relationship has gradually become much less intense, he does not find it too difficult to accept this, and normally by this time, too, the foal has formed a close friendship with another youngster of the same age.

Conventional breeding methods all too often ignore natural behaviour patterns. On most studs, foals are 'weaned' at six months, and it is true that they no longer need their mother's milk, though they often continue to suckle, and as domestic animals they can also manage without their mother's protection. Psychologically, however, they are not ready to be separated, and enforced separation is always an emotional torment for both mare and foal.

THE HISTORICAL
RELATIONSHIP
OF HORSE AND MAN

c. 20,000 BC:
Cro-Magnon man, an
early biological stage
on the road to
modern man,
distinguishes himself
from earlier
prehistoric man by,
among other
characteristics, his
distinctly developed
chin and the shape of
his frontal sinus. He
inhabited large areas
of Europe and North
Africa.

He used horn, ivory,
and various kinds of
stones to produce a
wide selection of
weapons and tools
such as knives, axes,
tips for arrows, spears
and harpoons,
scrapers, needles and
gouges.

Early beginnings of
pottery. Early
beginnings of plant
cultivation. A
fisherman and plant
collector as well as a
hunter.

20,000 to 10,000 BC:

THE HORSE AND THE HUNTERS OF THE ICE AGE

Since man first awoke from the dreamtime existence and became aware of his mortality, the horse has been his companion. In his first attempts to express himself creatively modern man drew pictures of horses — along with drawings of other animals such as reindeer, aurochs, mammoths and bears, all game animals which he hunted for food.

As recently as two hundred years ago archaeologists believed the history of man began with the Greeks and the Romans. About a century ago they became better acquainted with the much more ancient civilizations of Egypt, but it was not until 1900 that excavations proved there were civilized people living in Mesopotamia 9000 years ago.

In France in the middle of the last century two spelaeologists, Edouard Lartet and Edouard Piette, excavated a large number of sculptures and carvings on bones and stones. At that time no one guessed that these were art works from the Ice Age which had been produced between 20,000 and 10,000 BC.

The French had been excavating for fifteen years when in 1879 Marcellino de Sautuola found the first coloured cave

1 A horse's head in the caves of Asturias in Spain. The hindlegs of a horse with distinct zebra stripes can be seen at top left. This marking is found in wild horses of the steppes and also in many dun-coloured domestic breeds.

2 Horse and other game animals, dated from 20,000 to 15,000 BC in the cave of Lascaux in the Dordogne. This cave, first discovered in 1940, contains the most superb cave drawings ever found.

drawings in Altamira in northern Spain. With amazing intuition he described them as prehistoric paintings. In 1880, however, at an International Congress for prehistorians held in London, those present unanimously declared their opinion that the paintings of Altamira were not of prehistoric origin.

During the next twenty years archaeologists, digging for stone tools, found more cave paintings in southern France, but they dared

3

3 This drawing of a horse is also from Lascaux.

4 This picture of a horse, found in the 'Salon Noir' in Niaux, Ariège, in 1906 is 20,000 to 15,000 years old. The fact that it is of a different breed from the animals shown in pictures 2 and 3 implies that the Ice Age hunters knew of several breeds.

5 Outline of a horse's head from Asturias, Spain. Almost all the 130 or so places where Ice Age works of art have been found are in Spain and France. Only a few isolated finds were made in Portugal, Italy, Germany and the Soviet Union.

Overleaf: a drawing from Pech Merle, 15,000 to 10,000 years old.

Between 15,000 and 10,000 BC

The wolf was the first animal to be domesticated. As well as caves, holes with roofs over them and simple huts served as dwellings. Baked clay is used to produce lamps which burn oil or fat. Cro-Magnon man continues to evolve and spreads further across Europe as far as the Near East.

not publicize their findings for fear of being made to look foolish in the eyes of the scientific pundits.

It was not until 1902 that two Frenchmen, Emile Cartailhac and Henri Breuil, were able to prove that these cave paintings were over 10,000 years old. After they had examined several caves in France they remembered Altamira, and there they discovered the most extensive collection of cave drawings ever found.

4

5

In the meantime hundreds of archaeologists from all over the world were at work. Although not always successful, they did make discoveries at about 130 sites, almost all in France and Spain. About 4000 cave drawings and a similar number of small works of art from the Ice Age are known to exist today. Among them there are some marvellous artefacts, of which the numerous pictures of horses are some of the most beautiful.

For thousands of years, therefore, man had not only produced weapons and tools, but had also painted pictures. The discovery of this latter activity prompted the inevitable question of its purpose, and the natural answer seemed to be that these drawings were intended to decorate living areas. But man had never inhabited the caves which contained the paintings. There were no remains of fireplaces or sleeping quarters. These caves must have been places of worship where supplications were made to the gods for, unlike the inhabited caves, these were often situated in hidden inaccessible places. These pictures may well be the first evidence of an incipient religion.

The men of that time survived by hunting. Because their quarry was usually much faster than they were, and usually well able to defend itself the hunters relied on

instinct and experience as well as on weapons. But they also needed luck — and it is probably safe to assume that they connected the concept of luck with a god, probably a being who ruled over the animal world and to whom they could appeal for help. It is understandable that the spiritual concerns of these men should revolve almost exclusively around hunting.

Whoever traces the development of art through the millennia will find again and again that it has a religious content. Art has a cult basis whether in Egypt, in the advanced Indian civilization of Middle and South America, in early China or in Greece. *L'art pour l'art*, art for its own sake, is a modern phenomenon.

Arrowheads made of deer antlers.

Development of an agricultural civilization brings a greater degree of permanence. Barley, wheat and millet are the first cereal crops grown.

This drawing found in the Vallorta ravine in eastern Spain depicts a group of hunters. Pictures like this, intended to bring success in the hunt, also show definite artistic talent.

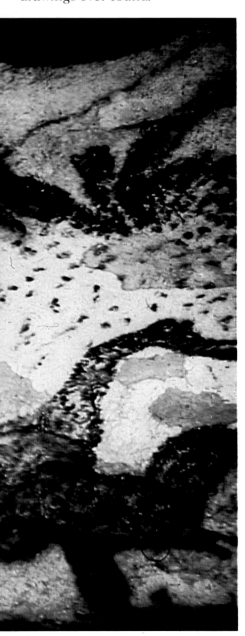

3000 to 2500 BC:
South-eastern and
later Central Europe
are culturally under
the influence of Egypt
and Mesopotamia.
Pictorial writing is
invented. Early
Minoan pottery is
produced on Crete. At
Giza the pyramid of
Cheops is begun
(c.2850 BC). The first
flowering of the
dynasty of the
Egyptian Pharaohs.

c. 2500 BC:
Nomadic tribes from
the Urals invade
south-eastern Europe.
Under King Onnos
the Pharaoh dynasty
begins to decline.

c. 2400 BC:
The Sumerians
conquer Babylon and
Elam. The wheel is
improved by the
addition of spokes.

Papyrus drawing of
the annual rebirth of
Osiris the god of
vegetation.

c. 2000 BC:
During the Middle
Minoan period on
Crete linear writing is
invented. Crete
exports wine, oil and
cereals and imports
goods from Egypt.

Left: A nomad camp in the Afghan mountains. The camps of the Eurasian horsemen who were the first to domesticate the horse probably looked just like this 4000 years ago.

Below: Sumerian clay tablets with writing scratched on them, tell the story of the first horse peoples who, with their war chariots, erupted out of the steppes and overran neighbouring races.

The Sphinx was built at Giza. In the background is the Pyramid of Cheops which is at least 800 years older.

c. 1760 BC:
Another period of decline in Egypt.

c. 1550 BC:
Beginning of the 'New Kingdom' in Egypt.

c. 1500 BC:
In northern Europe the Germanic tribes create bronze artefacts. Greece adopts from Egypt the use of the war chariot harnessed with horses.

c. 1400 BC:
End of Cretan civilization. Numerous artistic elements are adapted into Mycenaean art on the Greek mainland. Chinese art flourishing.

c. 1300 BC:
Zenith of temple-building in Egypt.

c. 1270 BC:
The Israelites forced to leave Egypt and are led by Moses and Aaron through the desert.

c. 1200 BC:
The Trojan War between the Trojans and Achaeans.

3000 to 1000 BC

THE FIRST HORSE PEOPLES

Wolves, sheep, goats and llamas were the first animals to be domesticated, and it was not until some time between 3000 and 2000 BC that horses were first tamed and bred in captivity. It is impossible to pinpoint exactly when this happened, but the first horse peoples were almost certainly one of the nomadic groups of the Eurasian steppes — the enormous grasslands which lie to the north of the Caucasus mountains. They belonged to the Indo-Germanic language family and are known to have been cattle herders for a considerable period.

Originally horses were probably kept to provide milk and meat. It seems quite possible that these migrating tribes loaded their luggage, and then themselves, on to their horses, but as the wheel had already been invented in Mesopotamia and cattle were often harnessed to carts, hippologists continue to dispute the question of whether horses were first ridden or put in harness.

It is known that around 1800 BC these nomads harnessed horses to their war chariots and thereby obtained a new and enormously effective weapon.

c. 3000 BC
End of the Stone Age
and beginning of the
Metal Ages in Europe.
In Greece aristocratic
and military leaders
force the agricultural
lower classes to accept
their dominance.
Copper is being
worked in the Near
East.

Cave painting
probably with an
underlying cult
significance. Southern
Rhodesia.

c. 2800 BC
Memphis becomes
the capital of the
Egyptian realm. Cities
are built and
hieroglyphic writing is
developed in
Mesopotamia.

Bas-reliefs on the
gateway of the temple
of Philae in Egypt.

Cultivation of figs,
olives and wine on
Crete. Production of
stone urns similar to
those of the
Egyptians. In Egypt
the cult of the dead
leads to the building
of colossal
monuments.

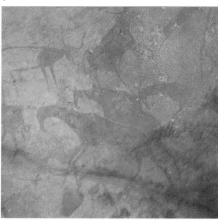

*1 Drawing of a
charioteer in a chariot
with four-spoked wheels
drawn by two horses.
Found in the Grotte de
Peinture in Wadi Djérat
in Algeria.*

*2 Pictures of cattle and
a horse painted in red
ochre from Jabbaren,
Tassili n'Ajjer, Algeria.*

*3 This cart with four-
spoked wheels and a
basket-like structure for
the charioteer was found
at Tadrart Acacous,
Teshuinat, in the Libyan
desert.*

3000 to 1000 BC

NEOLITHIC MAN IN THE SAHARA

Prehistorians and hippologists are
still mystified by a number of cave
paintings found in the Sahara.
These are unmistakably drawings
of charioteers, and the intriguing
fact is that the two-wheeled carts
have horses harnessed in front of
them. According to archaeologists
they date from the New Stone Age,
which began about 4000 BC and
ended around 1600 BC, but, apart
from these drawings, no evidence
has been found to support the
theory that horse-drawn vehicles
existed in the Sahara at such an
early period; not even the tiniest
scrap of iron from such a cart has
been found. Yet these paintings
contain details which would seem
to indicate that their artists were
not simply painting carts from
hearsay. Almost certainly, too,
these harness animals were horses
and not asses.

But how did those carts get
there? When were they there? Why
did they disappear again? No one
has yet been able to provide a
satisfactory answer to these
questions.

There are grounds for assuming
that immigrants from Egypt
brought horses and carts with
them, and there is undoubtedly a
close ethnological relationship
between the neolithic men who
inhabited the Sahara and the
people of Egypt.

It is also known that during the
New Stone Age the Sahara was
much more fertile than it is today
and was well able to support both
hunters and cattle herders. About
3000 BC or perhaps one or two
thousand years earlier, many
different cultural groups migrated
from the areas along the perimeter
of the Sahara into the interior
where they settled. It seems that
the earliest inhabitants were
almost exclusively hunters, but
were also acquainted with
different varieties of useful plants.
Some of these they used for food,
some for medicine and dyes.
Fishermen constructed boats from
bundles of reeds, and used fishing
rods made of ivory and wood, as
well as harpoons to catch their
prey. Later some of the tribes also
bred zebus. It has been possible to
deduce all these facts from utensils
and weapons which have been
excavated, as well as from a wealth
of cave drawings and engravings.
From all the evidence it seems very
unlikely, however, that neolithic
man ever cultivated crops in the
Sahara. No utensils have been
found which could have been used
for working the soil and there are
no drawings of men digging the
soil, though in contemporary
Egyptian iconography this was a
recurring motif. This would seem
to contradict the theory that the
horses which apparently existed in
the Sahara were brought from
Egypt, for if they had been the
agricultural techniques would have
been introduced with them. The
riddle seems to be insoluble.

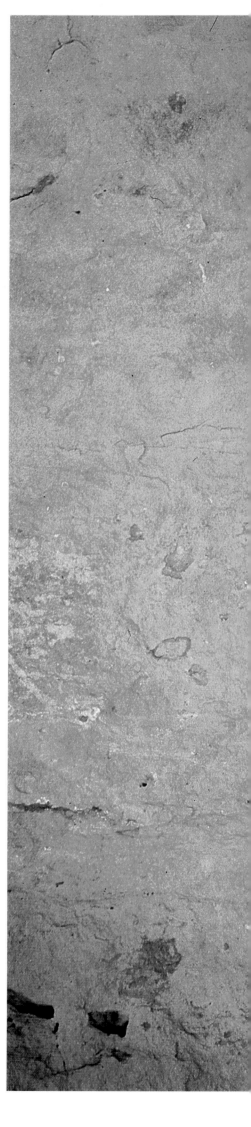

c. *2600 BC:*
Beginnings of use of
bronze on Crete.

c. *2300 BC:*
Beginning of the
Shun dynasty in
China. Cattle herding
and farming become
more widespread,
particularly the
cultivation of rice.
Cuneiform script
found on clay tablets
of the Akkadian
dynasty.

c. *2000 BC:*
Age of the great
kingdoms in India.
Settlements of the so-
called 'long houses'
on the Lower Rhine.

c. *1800 BC:*
Huge cyclopean walls
built around the cities
of Mycenae and
Tiryns in Greece.
Trade along the so-
called 'Amber Road'
from Greece to
northern Europe.
Stone houses are
being built in Europe.

The daughter of
Payouzem with a
drawing of a snake
found in an Egyptian
Royal tomb. Papyrus
of Heuttowe.

c. *1400 BC:*
Two giant sculptures
of King Amenophis
III built at Thebes in
Egypt — the colossi of
Memnon.

Cultural zenith of the
Shang dynasty in
China (1500 — 1100
BC).

The middle Minoan
Age begins on Crete.
The Hittites emerge
from the region
around the Black Sea
and spread across
Anatolia.

c. 1800 BC:
In Greece immense
walls are built around
some towns
(cyclopean masonry).

Stonehenge, focal
point of a mysterious
cult, is built in
England.
Mediterranean ideas
and beliefs probably
lay behind its
construction.

c. 1750 BC:
On Crete the King's
palace at Knossos is
decorated with
spectacular wall-
paintings.

c. 1550 BC:
Knossos is rebuilt
after a devastating
earthquake. Cultural
zenith of the Late
Minoan Age.

c. 1520 BC:
Military tactics using
the war chariot are
adopted by the Greeks
from the Egyptians.

1500 to 1100 BC:
Shang dynasty in
China. Symbolic
writing using symbols,
manufacture of silk,
bronze artefacts are
all evidence of a
highly cultured
society.

c. 1450 BC:
Middle Mycenaean
Age in Greece.
Subjugation of the
Minoan realm and
destruction of
Knossos.

2000 to 1000 BC:

THE EGYPTIANS

The most ancient of all advanced civilizations originated around the year 3000 BC with the founding of the kingdoms of Upper and Lower Egypt. These were united under the Kings of the Thinite period. The 'Old Kingdom' lasted from about 2635 to 2135 BC, and was a period of tremendous cultural growth, as the Great Pyramids testify. It was, however, followed by a period of economic and cultural decline. About 2040 BC a new upsurge began with the establishment of the 'Middle Kingdom', and once again colossal monuments were constructed. These necropoli, dedicated to the gods and the dead, were decorated with magnificent paintings and relief sculptures — all of which had an underlying cult significance. The basis of the Egyptians' wealth was their land's immense fertility. Their rich grain fields were the envy of their neighbours, but for centuries the Egyptian army was invincible — until the arrival of the horse.

Then the legions of the Hyksos with their horse-drawn war chariots overran Syria and Palestine, driving any opposition like chaff before them. In 1650 BC they conquered Egypt, and their army leaders appointed themselves kings over the conquered territory. It was a hundred years before the Egyptians were able to expel them, and they hit back at the usurpers with the same weapon that had been their own undoing — the horse-drawn war chariot.

From this time on, the horse was

1 Sculptural relief of an Egyptian King from the temple at Karnak. The largest of the ancient Egyptian temple complexes, it was connected to the Temple of Amon at Luxor by a now famous avenue lined with stone statues of rams.

2 Tutankhamen in his war chariot. These two fine, very noble looking horses are richly adorned. Tutankhamen was King from about 1347 to 1336 BC. Over the past few decades his name has become known worldwide because of the marvellous works of art found in his tomb which in 1922 was discovered almost completely intact in the Valley of the Kings.

3 Wall painting from a burial chamber c.1400 BC. This relief from the tomb of Horemhab is considered to be the most ancient drawing of a horse. In earlier drawings the animals being ridden cannot clearly be identified as horses, or else they are unmistakably Asiatic wild asses.

to play an increasingly important role. Soon it began to appear in reliefs and paintings, these drawings indicating that to the Egyptians the horse had become one of the noblest of animals.

As yet no form of bridle or headstall was used. When horses were harnessed in front of the chariots, a kind of frill was put around the middle of their neck

and reins fastened to it, which when pulled, increased the pressure on the animal's neck and made it slow down or stop. This method was commonly used for controlling Asiatic wild asses. It has been suggested that the Hyksos used a simple bit made of a straight piece of metal, but this seems very unlikely, for if they had possessed such a device the

4 In Egypt kings were mummified when they died as were some animals, including horses. These mummified remains of a horse date from around 1500 BC.

5 The battle of Kadesch, on a temple dedicated to Rameses II.

Egyptians would certainly have adopted it. The early Egyptian charioteers first used a bridle with a low slung noseband. This pressed on the cartilage of the animal's nose and restricted its ability to breathe; not a particularly refined method but very effective.

Bits made out of a single rod

4

did, however, exist in Egypt about the fourteenth century BC, and a little later jointed mouthpieces were also in use. The jointed bit enabled a greater degree of control, and was fitted with a longish cheek piece on each side to prevent it from slipping through the horse's mouth if pulled too hard. These cheek pieces often had barbs which could be made to poke in to the horse's cheek, and in rough hands must have been instruments of torture. It is a moot question whether the Egyptians invented the jointed bit, for exactly the same type of bit was being used by their contemporaries, the Scythians, and also in Luristan and in India.

5

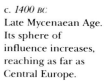

c. 1400 BC:
Late Mycenaean Age. Its sphere of influence increases, reaching as far as Central Europe.

c. 1360 BC:
The Assyrian monarchy makes its first appearance under Assurballidh.

1290 to 1223 BC:
Pharaoh Rameses II.

c. 1270 BC:
The Assyrian King Shalmaneser I conquers Mesopotamia. Israelites driven out of Egypt and, led by Moses and Aaron, wander through the desert. On Mt Sinai Moses receives the Ten Commandments.

c. 1250 BC:
Mounted warriors gradually replace war chariots as a military tactic.

c. 1180 BC:
Painted bas-relief of Libyans taken captive by the Egyptians illustrates the success of Rameses III's defensive campaign.

c. 1100 BC:
The original nucleus of the city of Rome is formed by groups of huts protected by a circular wall. The Germanic tribes spread out from Scandinavia to Central Europe. Beginning of the Iron Age in Europe.

THE ASSYRIANS

c. 900 BC:
Athens becomes the capital of Attica.

c. 800 BC:
The Hittites create giant stone sculptures and enjoy a cultural revival.

The legendary blind poet Homer probably composed the great Greek epics, the *Iliad* and the *Odyssey* at this time.

776 BC:
First Olympiad is held in Greece. From this time on this event is held every four years.

c. 750 BC:
The Celts and Illyrians in Central Europe now enter the La Tène Age or Late Iron Age.

683 BC:
The monarchy is abolished in Athens and a democracy founded in its place. At about the same time the Greeks are beginning to develop a Geometric style in art.

Five thousand years ago Assyria was a fertile flourishing country between the Tigris and the mountainous country around Ararat. It was inhabited mainly by Semites. About 2300 BC it was conquered by Akkad, later by Ur and finally by Babylon under King Hammurabi. The Assyrian people freed themselves from the last invaders and became independent, and by the thirteenth century BC had themselves become a military power and overrun neighbouring Babylon. They reached the zenith of their power during the reigns of Shalmaneser III (858 to 824 BC), Tiglath-Pileser (745 to 727 BC) and Assurbanipal (669 to about 627 BC). Then the borders of the realm extended from the Taunus mountains to Palestine and for a time stretched from the Mediterranean to the Persian Gulf and included part of Egypt as well.

The Assyrians were extremely brutal conquerors who refined a particularly heartless system for destroying the independent spirit of the peoples they subjugated. They deported to the farthest corners of the realm those who carried any political or social

1 *Assyrian warriors grooming their horses. Clay tablets giving detailed instructions on the care and training of war horses existed as early as the reign of Shalmaneser III.*

2 *Assyrians capturing wild single-toed animals. These are unlikely to have been horses; probably they were wild asses. Neither have very long ears but, unlike horses, asses have brushlike tails, similar to the tails on the animals shown here.*

3 *The Assyrians were the first military power to deploy both mounted archers and war chariots in battle.*

weight, and left only the peasants in their native homeland. The country was then divided into numerous provinces, each one governed by Assyrian officials.

Like earlier great powers, the Assyrians, too, owed their military superiority to the horse, and in

particular to a completely new military tactic: they 'invented' the cavalry.

However, it seems that they were rather slow to realise the strategical importance of the horse. At the time of their quarrels with Hammurabi they had neither

4

mounted soldiers nor war chariots, even though the horse-drawn war chariot had been invented at least five hundred years earlier. Yet they already possessed tame Asiatic wild asses or semi-asses and possibly were also breeding mules, which had been in existence for a few hundred years.

From a hippological point of view the Assyrians become interesting only in 900 BC when troops of mounted warriors are first mentioned in history in the report of a battle fought by the gruesome King Assurnazirpal II against the King of Nairi near Lake Van. During the following

5

epochs mounted warriors and hunters were depicted in many famous reliefs and drawings.

The Assyrians had, however, not developed any high degree of horsemanship, as pictures from the time of Shalmaneser III show. The riders sit as if on donkeys — at the back, on the animal's croup. Their legs are acutely angled and they cling firmly to the horse's sides with their calves and feet. In addition the horse of every archer is led by a mounted companion — understandably so, for besides the difficulty, with such a seat, of guiding a horse by changing weight position or using thigh aids, the archers needed both hands for shooting. But despite such obvious defects mounted troops were more mobile than large groups of war chariots, especially as the art of driving had also not yet been perfected.

By the time of Tiglath-Pileser III radical changes had been made in

the 'cavalry'. True, the rider still sat too far back, but now he had achieved the correct 'deep' seat, and with his legs almost stretched out he could use his thighs to guide the animal. Many horsemen rode bareback; others rode on decorated covers held firmly in place by straps tied around the horse's chest and tail.

The horses on the Assyrian reliefs bear little resemblance to the wild horses of the eastern steppes or to Prjevalsky's horse. They are more slender and have a much nobler, more harmonious appearance. They are similar to the Egyptians' horses but already appear to be larger, probably about 140 cm.

For centuries the Assyrians kept their neighbours in a state of fear and awe, but finally they lost their monopoly on mounted warriors and war chariots, and were no longer the only people capable of breeding fine fast horses. By the time of Assurnipal II, the Chaldaeans, the Arabs, Egyptians, Elamites and Medes had all become much more aggressive opponents. With Assurbanipal's death the fate of the Assyrian realm was finally sealed. In 615 BC the capital city Assur was destroyed and in 612 Nineveh was sacked.

4 Riders from the time of Assurnipal II on a lion hunt. By this time the Assyrians had developed a good deep seat which enabled them to grip their horses tightly with their thighs.

5 Tiglath-Pileser III in his war chariot.

6

6 and 7 Charioteers and archers from the time of Shalmaneser III. The art of riding was apparently still in its infancy, for riders sat almost on the horse's croup and gripped its sides tightly with calves and heels.

7

c. 650 BC:
The migrating Celts with their horses and cattle reach northern France and the shores of the Atlantic.

Scythians erupt out of Asia Minor into southern Russia.

Greek instrumental music is refined by the addition of the cithara and the Lydian flute.

The goddess Neith from the late Egyptian Age.

c. 600 BC:
The Greek poetess Sappho writes lyrical love poetry.

In Rome the Capitol (the central fortress) was being built along with the Forum, the Servian Wall which enclosed the city and a giant underground water conduit system.

93

CONTEMPORARY
EVENTS
c. 2000 BC
In China and Egypt
there is an upsurge in
scientific and
philosophical thought
(Medicine,
Mathematics and
Theology).

c. 1800 BC
Classical Age of Art in
Egypt. Tombs are now
built in cliffs and
building of pyramids
gradually stops.

c. 1700 BC
The Hyksos conquer
Lower Egypt and take
over state
administration and
the artistic and
cultural life of the
Egyptians.

c. 1580 BC
Amosis I drives the
Hyksos out of Egypt
with the help of
Greek and
Mycenaean soldiers.

c. 1550 BC
Beginning of the
'New Kingdom' in
Egypt. This lasts till
1085 BC.

Under Tutankhamen
the ancient belief in
gods is revived about
1330 BC.

c. 1300 BC
Temple building
reaches its zenith in
Egypt.

c. 1150 BC
Tiglath-Pileser I
expands the Assyrian
realm to the Black Sea
and then to the
Mediterranean. He
builds his palace in
Assur.

c. 1030 BC
After the Age of the
Judges in Israel the
Age of the Kings
begins with King Saul.

c. 1000 BC
David, the second
Israelite King, defeats
the Philistines,
captures Jerusalem
and conquers the
land east of Jordan.

c. 950 BC
King Solomon,
David's son, lays the
basis for a state
founded on law and
order. In Italy the
Etruscans are
beginning to expand.

THE GREEKS

About 1700 BC Aryan tribes, known collectively as Achaeans, migrated into Greece. Between 1400 and 1300 BC they founded settlements on Crete, Rhodes and Cyprus. An artistic people, highly skilled in arts and crafts, their culture was to have a far-reaching influence.

Around 700 BC they took the first step along the road to greatness when they abolished the monarchical system and established the first 'democracies'. These gave equal rights to all citizens, except those such as the numerous slaves and immigrants, who were stateless.

The great Greek epics date from this period : the *Iliad*, the narrative of the Trojan War; and the *Odyssey*, the story of Odysseus' adventurous journey from Troy to his home in Ithaca. Although Homer, the blind poet, is generally thought to have been the author of both, it is possible that they date from an earlier period, and he may merely have been the first to write them down.

According to other theories, such a person as Homer may never have existed at all. Men like Heraclitus, Thales and Anaximander, however, were genuine historical figures. They were the first philosophers, that is, the first to enquire into the meaning of man's existence.

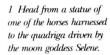

1 *Head from a statue of one of the horses harnessed to the quadriga driven by the moon goddess Selene.*

2 *This bronze statuette from Olympia was probably an offering made to the gods.*

3 *This beautiful piece of terracotta is about 2900 years old. Three horses are harnessed side by side on top of a pyxis made in the Geometric style.*

After Greece became a Roman province in 27 BC, it experienced another period of cultural and artistic growth, but finally lost its influential position when it was absorbed into the Byzantine realm in AD 395.

The horse-drawn war chariot was introduced into Greece *c.* 1500 BC, but never played a decisive role. Chariots were just as impractical a means of transport on the mountainous mainland as they had been on the islands of the Aegean Sea.

The Greeks had no cavalry force of any note until about 700 BC when the cities of Chalcis and Eretria fought for possession of the fertile Letantine plain.

Two hundred years later they apparently still considered a cavalry force to be of little value, though fighting a fierce war against the Persians, who bred outstanding horses and were themselves intrepid horsemen. The Persians were finally defeated and driven back to their ships after they had attempted to land on the coast of Marathon. For some

strange reason the Greeks then chose an infantry soldier, not a mounted one, to carry the news of the victory to Athens, over forty kilometres away. This 'marathon run' has since become a competitive sporting event.

The Greek cavalry did not become a really decisive force until Alexander the Great (pages 116-117).

Yet the horse played a much greater role in the cultural life of the Greeks than it had in any other earlier civilization. Its privileged position is reflected in the many ways it is depicted, both in art and in myth. The Sun god Helios in his four-horsed chariot rises up in the eastern sky; Eos, goddess of the Dawn, is pulled from there by the two horses, Lampos and Phaeton; horses are harnessed to the chariot of her sister, the moon goddess Selene; Pegasus, the winged horse, drags around the lightning and thunder belonging to the all-powerful god Zeus; the chariot of Ares, the god of war, is driven by his sons Phobos (Terror) and Deimos (Fear); Pluto uses a horse-drawn chariot to carry Persephone off to Hades; and when Heracles takes the town of Elis he rides the immortal stallion, Arion, the son of Poseidon.

Bibulous gods, however, such as Bacchus and Hephaestus, are depicted riding donkeys or mules.

In many countries mules were highly prized and even the nobility often preferred them as riding animals, but in Greece they were only bred to carry out those

3

4

5

6

7

menial tasks considered to be beneath a horse's dignity. Individual races for mules, harnessed either in pairs or in fours, were actually included in the Olympic Games at one stage.

Since men first learnt to drive horses they have enjoyed betting on horse races, but the Greeks first organized these on a grand scale

and built hippodromes expressly to accommodate them.

Chariot racing is discussed at length in the *Iliad*. The tactical advice which Nestor gives to Antilochus, for example, shows that he is well acquainted with the sport.

It was just as important to be *au fait* with driving techniques and

tricks of the trade as it was to have a fast horse with excellent powers of endurance.

Horse racing had long existed in different regions of Greece, but it was not until the twenty-fifth of the series of games held in the temple complex at Olympia (one of the two great religious centres) that chariot races for quadrigas (four horses harnessed to a two-wheeled chariot) were included along with the gymnastic events.

4 On this red-figured amphora a maiden is pouring a drink of wine for a rider before a race.

5 Bigas, or carts drawn by horses harnessed two abreast, on a pitcher in Geometric style from the middle of the eighth century BC.

6 Bowl made in Attica about 570 BC. A masterpiece of the black-figured style, it is 66 cm high, richly decorated with miniature-like pictures and was used for mixing wine and water.

7 Fragment from a relief on a Cycladian amphora from the seventh century BC depicts the legendary Trojan Horse.

8 Geometric terracotta votive sculpture representing a horse and rider. It was made in the seventh century BC on Cyprus.

8

c. 880 BC
Beautiful bas-relief sculptures depict King Assurnazirpal II of Assyria both as warrior and lion hunter in a horse-drawn chariot.

c. 800 BC
Founding of Carthage.

c. 776 BC
First Olympiad in Greece.

c. 753 BC
Legendary founding of Rome by Romulus and Remus. (Rome had already been in existence as a settlement for some time.)

c. 750 BC
Celts in Europe enter the Early Iron Age.

c. 740 BC
King Tiglath-Pileser III founds the Assyrian Empire thanks to his well-trained cavalry and heavy war chariots. Assyrian-Babylonian art and culture flourishes once again.

c. 720 BC
Assyrians conquer Israel.

c. 680 BC
The Assyrian King Esarhaddon conquers Egypt and makes a pact with the Scythians. His successor Assurbanipal (669 to about 627 BC) loses Egypt again. The famous clay tablet library along with historical documents and Assyrian and Sumerian literature is assembled in the Assyrian city of Nineveh (about 120,000 inhabitants).

c. 650 BC
The Celts reach Gaul and migrate into Spain where they mix with the Iberians (Celtiberians).

95

In 680 BC a certain Pagondas from Thebes won the race with his team of mares. Though they were not much faster than his opponents' teams of stallions, they were more obedient.

The first flat-races — with the riders riding bareback — were held eight Olympiads or thirty-two years later.

Hippodromes were built at Olympia, Delphi, Corinth and Pylos. The racetracks were rectangular or oval, and marked with turning posts, and a chariot race consisted of twelve rounds of the course. As the oval at Olympia is about 740 metres in circumference, a race there was about nine kilometres in length.

In 396 BC, races over shorter distances were introduced for young stallions, both ridden and harnessed in fours.

Many famous people took part in the Olympic horse races. Historically Philip II of Macedon is perhaps the most well known. It is said that one day during the games held in 356 BC, Philip was congratulated by three separate messengers: one told him that his army had taken Potidaea; the second that his wife had borne him a son (the future Alexander the Great); and the third that his quadriga had won the chariot race. If the historians can be believed, the third piece of news is supposed to have delighted him the most! Alexander never took part in the games. As the reason for this, he is said to have remarked that he only competed against kings.

With the advent of Christianity, when Greece was controlled by the Romans, the games gradually lost their religious significance and

assumed instead the air of a circus performance. The Emperor Nero, who won several races himself, did introduce races for ten-horsed chariots — but he also included competitions for cithara players and storytellers.

In AD 393 under Theodosius I the Olympic Games were banned. They were not reinstated until 1896, that is, 1500 years leater.

Both the classical art of riding and the first books on horses also originated in Greece. It is true that written instructions on the

maintenance, care and feeding of cavalry horses have been found scratched on clay tablets dating from the time of the Assyrians, but these could not be described as comprehensive manuals on the subject.

Simon the Athenian was a professional trainer of horses and riders. His book, written about 400 BC, is not very well known as only fragments of it have survived, but these confirm that Simon was extremely knowledgeable about the horse's anatomy.

5

6

7

8

9

10

11

12

1 Apollo's Quadriga.

5 to 12 Fragments from the Parthenon frieze. During the years 448 to 432 BC a man-made wonder was created in Athens: the Parthenon, designed by the architects Ictinus and Callicrates. The frieze which decorates it is a marvel in itself. The sculptor Phidias and his pupils produced the relief figures, a great many of which are horses, some with riders. They bear witness to the artistic excellence the Greeks had attained and also — of particular interest to hippologists — give a clear

indication that the art of riding was held in high regard in ancient Greece even before the time of the great Xenophon. The horses are collected and standing well. The riders are mostly bareback, sit close behind the withers and 'deep' into the horse. They are perfectly relaxed, their thighs are only slightly angled and their calves hang down loosely. In these drawings it is, however, obvious that the size ratio between the horse and rider is wrong even though the Greeks' horses were certainly much smaller than our present-day warm-blood breeds.

Xenophon, who lived from about 430 to 355 BC, was the most famous of all hippologists, and wrote a number of books on horse-breeding, hunting and the art of riding. *Peri Hippikes* in particular contains all the important guidelines for the correct psychological approach to handling a horse.

Xenophon is also considered to be the creator of classical dressage, an art which lapsed into oblivion when the civilization of Ancient Greece declined, and was not revived until the Renaissance in Italy.

2 to 4 As well as horses, some of them ridden, centaurs are also depicted on the frieze. These legendary mythical beings possibly developed in the imaginations of the early Greeks as the result of their first encounters with the invading horsemen of the steppes. American Indians also thought the first horsemen were godlike beings, half-man, half-horse. Almost the whole of the Parthenon frieze is now in the British Museum, London.

4

c. 300 BC
Outstanding sculptures produced in India often showing Hellenic influence.

218 BC
Hannibal crosses the Pyrenees and moves through Gaul with 50,000 infantry, 9000 mounted soldiers and 37 war elephants. With tremendous losses he crosses the Alps to northern Italy.

c. 210 BC
Great Wall of China is completed.

146 BC
The Romans conquer Carthage.

100 BC to the advent of Christianity
Roman architecture at its zenith (theatres, temples, cities). All have a strong Greek influence.

27 BC
Beginning of the age of the Roman Emperors. The Roman Empire extends from the Red Sea to the Atlantic and to England in the north.

AD 6
Jesus of Nazareth is assumed to have been born.

AD 70 to 90
Building of the colosseum in Rome.

c. AD 200
High point of central American cultures. Huge pyramid temples are built.

c. AD 300
Christianity becomes more widely spread.

AD 375
The Huns break through into Europe and trigger off the migrations of the Germanic tribes.

97

CONTEMPORARY EVENTS

THE PERSIANS

As the Greeks in their cities in southern Italy, Asia Minor and the Balkans reached undreamt-of levels of intellectual and artistic achievement, a realm was coming into existence in Asia which at the height of its power would extend over an area of hitherto unimaginable dimensions. The Medes, who had dealt the death blow to the Assyrian Empire, were united with the Persians under their King Cyrus, who in 539 BC conquered Babylon which then became the main trading centre. Greek cities in Lydia and Asia Minor were taken over, and during the reign of Cyrus' son Cambyses, Egypt was also annexed. Darius I, the third Persian king who reigned from 522 to 486 BC, extended his realm to its greatest limits. At the height of his power he ruled over an area which reached from the Indus to the Balkans and from Armenia to Egypt. The Persian conquerors evolved a very efficient form of government which allowed the subjugated peoples to retain a large proportion of their independence.

Only the Scythians — hordes of horsemen who lived to the north of the realm — continued to make forays into the country. Relying on surprise tactics, they were usually able to escape unscathed with their booty, so King Darius decided to attack them in their southern Russian homeland.

Setting off with a large army, he crossed the Bosporus, then the Danube in Bulgaria and continued to penetrate further northwards, but was never able to force the Scythians into a decisive battle. Repeatedly bands of Scythian horsemen made surprise attacks on his army at its weakest points. After cutting off stragglers or barring the way to an advance

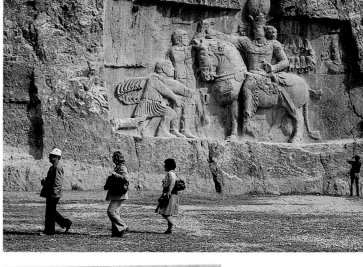

460 BC
Hippocrates the 'father of medicine' is born in Greece.

c. 450 BC
Classical epoch in Greece reaches its highest point. Beginning of the La Tene Age in northern Europe.

The Greek Xenophon founds the art of classical dressage. His guidelines are still basically valid.

399 BC
Death of Socrates, the Greek philosopher.

c. 380 BC
The Celts spread throughout Europe and migrate into Asia Minor. Ireland is first settled about 376 BC.

c. 350 BC
Building of the tomb for Mausolus, King of Caria. One of the Seven Wonders of the Ancient World.

347 BC
Death of Plato, Socrates' pupil.

323 BC
Death of Alexander the Great.

guard, they would butcher them all, then immediately disappear again, their tough hardy horses raising clouds of dust behind them. The foot soldiers were powerless against these horsemen. The small number of Persian cavalry were neither well organized nor sufficiently mobile to make successful counter attacks against the Scythians. Darius was forced to make an inglorious retreat.

Encouraged by his failure, the Greeks of Asia Minor resolved to free themselves from the Persian yoke, and appealed to the Greeks on the European mainland for help. Darius then decided to conquer European Greece as well, took charge of his fleet and successfully captured one island after the other. In 490 BC he mounted the main attack on Athens, but was unexpectedly and thoroughly routed. Ten years later Xerxes, Darius' son and successor, collected the largest army that had ever been seen and determined to conquer Greece, but the Greeks were able to repulse even this superpower.

The Persians continued to be a threat for the following 150 years until Alexander the Great, the Macedonian, set out to conquer

their realm. Well organized and highly skilled in tactics, the cavalry was the decisive weapon in his unprecedented campaign plan.

The Persians should have had a cavalry that was equal, if not superior, to Alexander's. Persian stallions were highly prized everywhere and the Persian army certainly had a plentiful supply of horses, all of an excellent quality,

hardy, very fast and with plenty of stamina. Two hundred years before, when the Persians were at the height of their power, they were extremely skilful at selecting breeding animals and bred horses that were larger and stronger than those of either the Egyptians or the Assyrians. But the art of riding seemed to have made very little progress. The ancient drawings almost without exception depict horses with badly fitting bridles. The mouth pieces of Persian bits from this period had spikes on them or were sharp-edged discs, which would certainly stop a horse from bolting but would hardly teach it to be an obedient riding animal. The Persians when riding normally, sat on top of a pile of saddle cloths, and could not possibly have had such a secure seat as the Greeks who rode with bare legs and naked buttocks, virtually glued to the horse's back.

356 BC:
Philip II conquers
Amphipolis, Pydna
and Potidaea and also
gains control of the
eastern coast of
Macedonia.

355 to 346 BC
Third Sacred
(Phocian) War. The
Phocians seize the
shrine of Delphi and
then wage war on
Thebes. The latter
appeals to Philip for
help. Phocis is
defeated.

347 BC
Death of Plato in
Athens. He was
Socrates' pupil and
the founder of
idealism in
philosophy.

345 BC
The Persians fail in
their attempt to
conquer the kingdom
of Magadha in the
valley of the Indus.

344 BC
Philip expands the
Macedonian realm by
conquering the
Illyrians and Dardani
in the north and
annexing Euboea and
Thessaly in the south.

1 Bust of Alexander the Great. Louvre, Paris.

2 Fragment from the famous mosaic found at Pompeii which depicts Alexander at the battle of Issus. National Museum, Naples.

356 to 323 BC

ALEXANDER THE GREAT

Horses which achieved outstanding successes at the ancient Olympic Games were greatly honoured. Songs were written about them and painters and sculptors immortalized them. Bucephalus, the most famous horse in Greek antiquity, was, however, not a 'sporting horse' at all and apparently never took part in the games. But he was a Thessalian horse (many reports say he had a Berber sire but this is highly unlikely) and those horses which were bred in the fertile Thessalian basin were some of the finest of all. Even for

a Thessalian he was evidently outstanding, for his breeder offered him to the King — his choice of a buyer could not have been more exalted — and then demanded the kingly price of thirteen talents of gold.

Plutarch describes this sale in detail. The black stallion with the white star on its forehead (he is depicted as a grey in some pictures and miniatures, in others as a chestnut-coloured unicorn with a peacock's tail) was led before Philip II, the King of Macedon. A number of experienced riders from the royal

stables tried unsuccessfully to calm the wild stallion and to mount him, so the King ordered the obviously unmanageable black horse to be taken away. His son Alexander, then twelve years old, called out: 'What an excellent horse they lose for want of address and boldness to manage him!' His father was annoyed but allowed the boy to go up to the stallion. Alexander spoke quietly to it, took hold of the reins and then turned the animal to face the sun, for he had noticed that it was afraid of its own shadow. Then he swung himself on to its back and galloped off. He trotted the stallion back and brought it to a halt in front of his father, who is said to have thrown his arms around his son saying: 'O my son, look for a kingdom equal to and worthy of you for Macedonia is too small.'

For eighteen years Bucephalus was Alexander's constant companion and the young king rode him throughout the campaigns which created a realm more extensive than any that had

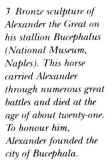

3 Bronze sculpture of Alexander the Great on his stallion Bucephalus (National Museum, Naples). This horse carried Alexander through numerous great battles and died at the age of about twenty-one. To honour him, Alexander founded the city of Bucephala.

4 King Philip II of Macedon, Alexander's father, on a Greek coin. Philip was the first commander to deploy a well-organized cavalry force in the field.

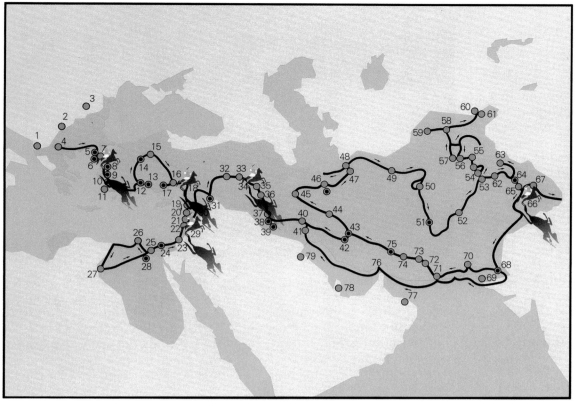

The map shows the campaigns of Alexander the Great. In 334 BC he left Pella, the city where he was born, originally to avenge himself on the Persians for the destruction they had wrought in Greece. In May 334 BC he defeated an army led by Darius III at Granicus. In November 333 BC he defeated a much stronger army at Issus. In 332 he entered Egypt as a liberator and founded Alexandria. In 331 he finally defeated Darius at Gaugamela and entered Babylon as the conqueror of the whole Persian realm. His last campaign took him to India from 327 to 325 BC.

343 to 340 BC
Aristotle, the greatest philosopher of his time, tutors the young Alexander.

342 BC
Indian scholars observe the astronomical zodiac and make great advances in medicine.

c. 340 BC
Celtic La Tene culture spreads throughout western and central Europe.

340 to 338 BC
The Latin cities fight for equal rights with Rome in the Latin War. Rome defeats them at Sinuessa. The Latin League is dissolved and Roman influence is extended.

c. 339 BC
The Indian poet Vyasa composes 100,000 rhyming couplets on the famous sagas of ancient heroes.

c. 337 BC
Hellenic influences can be seen in Indian sculptures.

Present-day names of the cities are written in italics

1 Tiranë
2 Sofia
3 Bucharest
4 Pella
5 Sestos
6 Troy
7 Granicus
8 Sardis
9 Ephesus
10 Miletus
11 Bodrum
12 Aspendus
13 Side
14 Gordium
15 Ankara
16 Tarsus
17 Soli
18 Issus
19 Byblos
20 Beirut
21 Saïda (Sidon)
22 Sur (Tyre)
23 Gaza
24 Pelusium
25 Cairo
26 Alexandria
27 Oasis Siwa
28 Memphis
29 Damascus
30 Homs
31 Thapsacus
32 Nisibis
33 Mosul
34 Gaugamela
35 Erbil (Arbela)
36 Kirkuk
37 Baghdad
38 Opis
39 Babylon
40 Sousse (Susa)
41 Ahwaz
42 Persepolis
43 Pasargadae
44 Isfahan (Aspadana)
45 Hamadan (Ecbatana)
46 Teheran
47 Damghan (Hecatompylos)
48 Gorgan (Zadrakarta)
49 Meshad
50 Herat
51 Prophthasis
52 Candahar (Alexandria Arachoton)
53 Kabul
54 Istalif
55 Kunduz (Drapsaca)
56 Mazar-i-Sharif
57 Balkh (Bactra)
58 Samarkand (Marakanda)
59 Bokhara
60 Leninabad
61 Alexandrea Eschate
62 Jellalabad
63 Dir
64 Taxila
65 Rawalpindi
66 Bucephala
67 Jammu
68 Pattala
69 Karachi
70 Bela
71 Gwadar
72 Sarbaz (Pura)
73 Bampur
74 Basman
75 Alexandria
76 Harmozeia
77 Maskat
78 Doha
79 Kuwait

existed before it. Bucephalus fully deserves to be called history's most eminent horse.

King Philip's ambition was to rule over all Greece. He controlled an army which was better trained than any other. Reorganized on the basis of the phalanx — a military formation consisting of sixteen rows of soldiers packed closely together — his men were armed with 3.5 metre long spears used, not for throwing, but in hand-to-hand fighting. But the mounted soldiers were the most distinctive characteristic of this army. They were trained in offensive tactics and for the first time in history provided a manoeuvrable force.

The decisive battle against the allied Greeks was fought in 338 BC at Chaeronea in central Greece. Numerically superior by about 5000 men, the Greeks attacked the Macedonian phalanx in the early morning, and to their surprise King Philip very quickly gave the order for his troops to withdraw. But the triumphant Greeks were suddenly attacked from the side by his cavalry force of 2000 men. At its head rode Alexander, then only eighteen years old. A few hours later the Greek army was defeated.

Two years later King Philip was assassinated. Within a year Alexander had managed to bring peace and order to his realm which now included the whole of Greece. When he was twenty-one, the young king turned his

attention to the Persians, the old enemy, still powerful and undefeated. This was the beginning of his Asian campaign which was to last twelve years. His army now consisted of 32,000 infantry and a highly trained cavalry force of 5000 men. At the river Granicus he defeated the 20,000 foot and 20,000 horse of the Persians led by Darius III. In the spring of 333 BC at the battle of Issus, Alexander defeated about 500,000 Persian soldiers. In the decisive battle of Gaugamela Darius is said to have pitted a million infantry and 40,000 horse unsuccessfully against Alexander.

In his final great battle on the banks of the river Hydaspes (Jhelum) in 326 BC, Alexander again rode Bucephalus, but the horse died a short while later from its wounds. He was over twenty-one years old.

Three years later Alexander himself fell ill, probably of malaria. He died on the evening of 11 June, 323 BC, at the age of thirty-three years.

Mounted figure made
from clay. Grave-
offering from the time
of the Western Chou
dynasty in China.
Burial objects were
common in most of
the ancient
civilizations.

776 BC:
First Olympic games
in Greece.

c. 750 BC:
Early Iron Age in
central and south-
eastern Europe

c. 740 BC:
Tiglath-Pileser III
overthrows Babylon
and founds the
Assyrian realm. He
achieves military
successes with heavy
war chariots and the
first mounted archers.

c. 625 BC:
In Gaul the Celts
reach the shores of
the Atlantic Ocean
and migrate into the
Iberian peninsula.

c. 600 BC:
Founding of the first
Roman colonies.

551 BC:
Birth of Confucius,
philosopher and
moralist, in China.

c. 530 BC:
Persian realm reaches
from the coasts of
Asia Minor to the
Indus.

Black-figured style in
Greek pottery
becomes more
widespread.

800 to 300 BC:

THE ETRUSCANS

The Etruscans' origins are
shrouded in mystery. About
10,000 inscriptions indicate that
their script was similar to that of
the Greeks, but scholars do not
agree about its origin. Some think
it could be related to the
language of the Hittites. The
Etruscans are assumed to have
migrated from Asia Minor about
3000 years ago into what is now
Tuscany. It is not known for
certain whether they brought
horses with them from their
original homeland though later
on the horses did have a
significant part to play in their
cultural life.

The Etruscans maintained
close connections with central
Europe from an early period,
borrowing many metallurgical
techniques, probably about the
ninth century BC. They were an
immensely creative race and as
their Italian homeland was
extremely fertile and they had
access to a plentiful supply of
copper and tin, their settlements
and cities flourished, and they
evolved a highly cultured
civilization. Their population
increased and at its height the
Etrurian kingdom stretched from
the Po plain in the north to
Campania in the south.

At that time the most southern
part of Italy was a Greek colony.
As early as the eighth century the
Etruscan cities attracted Greek
traders and craftsmen, and from
that time Hellenic art became a
major influence in the Etruscans'
culture. Thousands of amphorae,
drinking bowls and other richly
decorated clay vessels were
brought to Etruria from Greece.

The simple indigenous style of
Etruscan art was very attractive
and contained both Hellenistic
and Oriental elements.

*1 Soldiers returning
from battle are depicted
on this fragment from a
stone sarcophagus.
Museo Archeologico,
Perugia.*

*3 Drawing of a chariot
race, on display in the
Museo Archeologico in
Naples.*

*4 and 5 Wall paintings
from an Etruscan tomb
chamber, Tomba del
Barone in Tarquinia.*

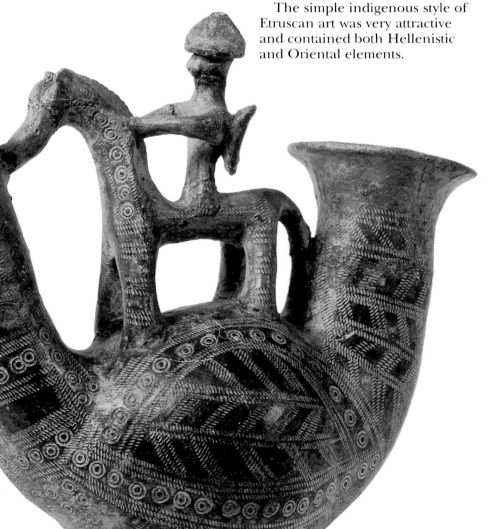

*2 Etruscan art contains
Oriental elements, as
can be seen in this clay
Askos with the head of a
bull and a mounted
figure on top. It was
found in the Benacci
grave at Bologna.
Museo Civico, Bologna.*

The Etruscans may have possessed horses before they came in contact with the Greeks, but if so these animals did not play a significant part in their lives. The breeding of horses and the arts of riding and driving began to thrive in Etruria only as the influence of Greek culture increased. The decisive impulse probably came from the south-eastern coast of Sicily where the Greeks had founded large studs and were breeding high quality horses. Etruscan drawings show these horses as light and finely limbed with short noble heads set on elegant necks. They must have been about 140 cm at the withers, about a hand-breadth taller than the usual riding animals of the Asiatic peoples. There are Etruscan engravings of horses which look very like noble desert Arabs, and even allowing for artist's licence it can still be

assumed that most Etruscan horses were beautiful, high-spirited animals.

The Etruscans also followed the Greeks' example and introduced chariot races. The riders sat on the horse's bare back, right behind its withers, with their legs only slightly angled. They seem to have achieved a good 'deep' seat. About the same time, Oriental horsemen were putting covers on their horses' backs. Although giving the rider a more comfortable seat, they also made it less secure. Meantime, between about 500 and 300 BC, the Scythians in southern Russia had invented the first saddles, consisting of several layers of leather, fastened on with a girth strap. The Scythians also seem to have had the decidedly novel idea of fixing leather loops to the saddle as a primitive form of stirrups.

Although the Etruscan armies included mounted troops, little is known about their tactical deployment, and their role was probably not decisive. In their cultural and artistic life, however, the horse did play a significant part, particularly in connection with the burial customs. Around 700 BC the Etruscans gradually abandoned their custom of ritually burning their dead and began to bury them instead. Burial objects, mainly terracotta figures and paintings, were intended to beautify the after-life. For those who were wealthy, particularly splendid grave-chambers were built in the cliffs, the walls of which were completely covered with pictures, some of them among the most

outstanding of all Etruscan artworks. As the dead were not expected to have to forego any of the delights of their earthly existence, the most popular motifs were dancers and musicians, pictures of hunting, erotic scenes and feasts of all kinds. Horses, with and without riders, feature again and again both in racing scenes and harnessed to war chariots.

There was a thriving trade and a fertile exchange of artistic ideas between Etruscans and Greeks in Italy, but by the fifth century BC, a growing rivalry had developed between these two major powers which inevitably resulted in acts of aggression. At the same time Rome was becoming more powerful and beginning to exert pressure on the Etruscans. In addition bloody disputes along their northern border with the Ligurians, who controlled the Gulf of Genoa, became more and more frequent. They also clashed with the Venetians and the barbaric tribes who lived in the mountains. The power of the Etruscans was broken by the fourth century, and by the third century BC they no longer existed.

c. 500 BC
Sacred monuments built by the Maya in Yucatan.

A religious relief for Aleximachos. An example of late Greek relief art.

490 BC
The Greeks defeat the Persians at the battle of Marathon. A runner from Marathon conveys news of the victory.

Rome takes the she-wolf as its symbol. Etruscans create bronze sculptures.

460 BC
Birth of Hippocrates in Greece. He is known as the 'father of medicine'.

c. 450 BC
Indian society evolves into a system of four castes (or levels).

c. 430 BC
Creation of the Parthenon frieze on the Acropolis at Athens. The relief is 160 m long. On it there are horses performing classical dressage movements: piaffe, levade, passage.

410 BC
Birth of Diogenes, Greek philosopher.

399 BC
Death of Socrates, Greek sage.

c. 390 BC
Potters' wheel and iron tools from the Celtic La Tene culture. Celts move into northern Italy.

323 BC
Death of Alexander the Great.

THE SCYTHIANS

1 A gold wall decoration, measuring about 5 x 5 cm, with a Pegasus motif. An example of Greek handicrafts. Although the Scythians were themselves excellent craftsmen they let the Greeks produce pieces for them.

2 A cart apparently used in ceremonies to honour the dead. The carts used for everyday tasks were more solid and easier to steer. This cart was found in a grave together with the skeletons of four horses.

c. 700 BC
Greeks settle in southern Italy.

683 BC
Beginnings of democracy in Greece.

669 to about 627 BC
Assurbanipal is King of Assyria.

c. 600 BC
Building of the temple to Marduk in Babylon. In the European Hallstatt culture grave mounds consisting of chambers made of stone and wood. These contain weapons, rings, tweezers and razors, all made of bronze. Red and black painted ceramic vessels.

500 BC
Birth of Greek philosopher Pythagoras.

c. 560 BC
Gautama Buddha spreads his religious teachings.

518 BC
Darius founds Persepolis, the Persian capital.

496 BC
Birth of the Greek poet Sophocles.

Because the Scythians had no written language, almost everything known today about this nomadic race from the Eurasian steppes has been learned from their 'educated' neighbours, the Greeks in particular, and from objects found in the graves of their chieftains. These horse peoples spoke Iranian and probably originated in central Asia. In the eighth century BC they migrated to that part of the steppes which lies to the north of the Black Sea, and, about 700 BC, advanced into Asia Minor, later reaching the borders of Greece and even penetrating as far as central Europe. For centuries they maintained trade and cultural links with the Greeks. The Scythian homelands covered a vast area, and in the fifth century BC those tribes who lived in the eastern steppes remained nomads while those in the western part became more settled and began to found cities. From the third century on, they gradually lost their independence, conquered first by the Sarmatians, an ethnologically related people, and later by the Huns and the Goths.

The Scythians spent most of their nomadic lives on horseback, and with their herds of horses were almost constantly on the move. Yet they still managed to produce some outstanding craftsmen. Their chieftains' burial mounds (also known as tumuli or kurgans) which date from the sixth to third century BC, when excavated, were found to contain numerous objects made of gold, silver, bronze, bones, wood and ceramic, all indicating a highly developed artistic style. This has been described as the *Scythian animal style*. This art was undoubtedly closely bound up with their religious customs, for these nomads would certainly never have expended such effort simply for the sake of aesthetic enjoyment.

The Scythians were also skilled at producing practical objects. Although the Persians and some of the Greeks put saddle cloths on the backs of their horses, the Scythians can be credited with inventing the first saddles. They devised a double leather cushion about 60 cm long, firmly stuffed with hair, raised slightly at the back, and held in place by a girth strap around the horse's belly. Even though this object had no firm saddle tree it was certainly a type of saddle, and guaranteed that the rider had a comfortable and secure seat and that his weight was evenly distributed on the horse's back. There are even some indications that the Scythians could have used leather loops fixed on to the saddle strap as stirrups, which would mean that they and not the Huns invented stirrups.

On their campaigns the Scythians carried a short sword, about 60 cm long, but they

preferred to fight with bows and arrows. They were much feared opponents who attacked when least expected, galloping at high speed along the enemy lines, shooting at them from a distance. Their short double-curved bow consisted of several layers of wood and horn and is said to have had a range of over 400 metres.

The Greek historian Herodotus gives a vivid description of the Scythians' burial customs. The belly of the dead chieftain was opened and cleaned, filled with bruised cypress leaves, incense, and parsley and anise seed and then sewn up again. Then the corpse was covered with wax, put on a cart and taken in turn to each tribe, whose members expressed their grief by cutting their hair, and a piece from their ears, and by wounding themselves on the left hand, the arm, the nose and the forehead. When the chieftain was finally laid in his grave, one of his concubines, a cook, a cupbearer, a groom and about a dozen horses were strangled and put in the grave with him, along with golden goblets and other objects. Then a large earth mound was built over

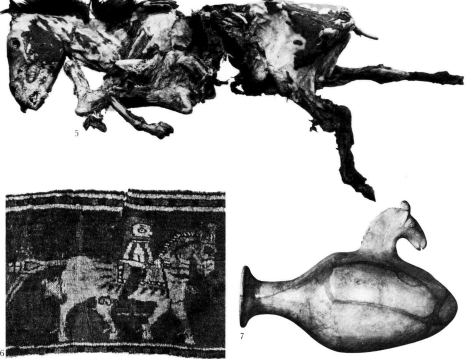

the grave. One year after the chieftain's death a great sacrifice took place. Fifty of his servants and fifty horses were strangled. Spears were thrust lengthwise through the horses' bodies, which were propped upright in a circle around the grave mound and held erect by wooden supports. The dead servants, also supported by spears stuck through their bodies, were then seated on the horses' backs, the dead horses were bridled and the reins bound fast to stakes. These silent riders now kept watch over the dead.

3 Belt-clasp from the eighth to seventh century BC. Found in the Ordos region, China.

4 A golden comb from the fifth century BC. Found near Dnieper. The Scythians possessed a great deal of gold jewellery and utensils. Because they buried these valuable objects with their dead, most of their graves were plundered.

5 Mummy of a Scythian horse from Pazyryk.

6 Piece of a Scythian carpet. The Scythians seem to have invented the specialised knotting technique for which Persian carpets later became famous.

7 A clay vessel, about 30 cm tall, found in the grave of the Scythian leader Mingetschauer. Discovered in 1933 in Azarbaijan.

490 BC
Battle of Marathon between the Persians and the Greeks.

477 BC
Aegean cities form an alliance under the leadership of Athens against the Persians. Known as the Delian Confederacy.

464 BC
Sparta is destroyed by an earthquake.

460 BC
Birth of Hippocrates in Greece. The 'father of medicine'.

c. 450 BC
The classical era is at its height. Construction continues on the Parthenon considered by many authorities to be the epitome of architectural perfection.

c. 410 BC
Birth of Diogenes, Greek philosopher.

c. 380 BC
In Athens Scopas, Praxiteles, and their pupils create sculptural masterpieces.

376 BC
Celts settle in Ireland.

c. 280 BC
La Tene Age produces clay jars and mints coins.

221 to 210 BC
The Great Wall of China is built.

Aphrodite of Cnidus
by the sculptor
Praxiteles, a late
classical masterpiece
of Greek sculpture.

323 BC
After the death of
Alexander the Great
the Athenians drive
out the Macedonians.

c. 320 BC
Greek painting
changes from late
Classical to
Hellenistic style.

The Macedonians are
driven out of India. In
India temple dancers
are included in
religious celebrations.

Indian Gupta Pillar.

c. 315 BC
The Macedonian
ruler Cassander
marries the sister of
Alexander the Great
and founds
Thessaloniki
(Salonika) and
Cassandrea. Later he
has Alexander's
widow and son
executed.

c. 300 BC

THE CELTS

Of all the pre-Christian horse peoples the Celts are probably the closest to the modern world, for their descendants have retained an unusual passion for horses. Today ponies and cobs from Wales and Connemara, and Irish hunters are sought after worldwide.

The history of the Celts can be traced back for about 3000 years. The earliest finds, which are dated about 1000 BC, were made in southern Germany. Although the origins of these horsemen cannot be verified, they belonged to the Indo-Germanic group of races, possibly descended from the nomads of the Eurasian steppes and perhaps even direct descendants of the first horse peoples. These are known to have broken out of their homeland, and with their horse-drawn war chariots overrun their neighbours about 1800 BC.

A Celtic burial ground near Hallstatt in Upper Austria in which over 2000 urn graves and numerous grave offerings were found gave its name to a whole cultural epoch. The Celtic Halstatt culture, which lasted from about 1000 to 500 BC, extended in a broad strip across Europe north of the Alps and continued through into Spain (Celtiberians). In the Danube region the Illyrians also belonged to this cultural group. The Hallstatt era had a characteristic geometric art style and used iron as well as bronze.

The origins of the Celtic horses are also shrouded in mystery. Tall and well built, the Celts generally rode strong mobile horses which

although fast, were little more than 140 cm at the withers. Larger horses simply did not exist at that time. We can assume that when the Celtic tribes first migrated into what is now southern Germany, they rode a breed of horse that was a mixture of Prjevalsky's horse and the steppe tarpan. As they moved through central Europe they probably appropriated pure-bred steppe tarpans, and later forest tarpans as part of their booty, so that by about 300 BC, when the Celts were at the height of their power, their ponies probably looked more like the attractive tarpans and had lost most of the characteristics of Prjevalsky's horse. The descendants which most resemble them today are the Connemara ponies from the extreme north-west of Ireland. Although they have not remained pure-bred and seldom have the mouse-dun colouring of the wild horse, in type and character they are very similar.

The most commonly held view with regard to war horses or saddle horses is — the larger, the better. The Celts completely refute this, however, as do the last remaining horse peoples, from the Mongols to the Gauchos, whose riding animals, too, are not much over 140 cm tall. The Celts were not, of course, weighed down by heavy armour, and usually fought completely naked, though sometimes they wore chain breastplates and bronze helmets; often two men would ride on one pony! The Sicilian-born Greek historian Diodorus told of the Celts on their campaigns in Italy. They took Rome in 387 BC! By

1 Celtic bronze ornamental clasp in the form of a horse's head.

2 Epona, the Celtic goddess of horses. A find from the temple complex at Altbach.

3 and 4 Bronze ornamental clasps, artistically decorated.

5 Mouthpiece with coloured enamel decorations.

then they no longer fought in the same way as did their supposed ancestors, the horsemen of the steppes, but had developed a strategy uniquely their own. First they intimidated their opponents with wild shrieking, much shouting and discordant blowing on their horns, which also unleashed their own war-like aggressiveness. Then riders and infantry would race towards the enemy while the war chariots on their flanks moved forwards. The Celtic chariots had four wheels, unlike those of the steppe warriors, Babylonians, Egyptians, Greeks and Romans which were two-wheeled. Two Celtic warriors would ride together, one to guide the horses while the other threw spears into the ranks of the enemy. When all his spears were thrown the warrior would jump from the chariot and continue to fight with sword or lance, and the driver would turn the chariot around in readiness for an eventual escape. When two warriors rode one pony one would hold the reins while the other threw the spears. Then both jumped off, tethered the horse and continued to fight on foot. According to Diodorus one of the Celtic customs was to decapitate their enemies and then hang the heads over their doorways at home like trophies. Not for nothing did the Romans call them *Furor Celticus!*

It is generally assumed that the Celts invented horseshoes, but there is no proof of this. Although the earliest are called 'Celtic horse-shoes', they were probably made some centuries after the birth of Christ, and most likely not by the Celts. But the Celts did invent the chain bit — a noteworthy innovation. The reins were fastened to the lower end of the side pieces of the snaffle bit and a chain, which fitted into the horse's chin groove, was fastened to the

upper end. When the rider pulled on the reins the grip of the chain made the small rod work on the horse's lower jaw bone not, as previously, on the corners of the horse's mouth, which pushed the head downwards (as with the curb bit) so that the animal was unable to avoid the effect of the reins. The spiked bits which were such instruments of torture thus became superfluous though this did not necessarily mean they were no longer used.

The Celts reached the height of their power around 300 BC, when there were Celtic tribes from Asia Minor to Spain and from Great Britain to Italy. In the following centuries they were either driven to the extremities of their territories or they amalgamated with their conquerors. Only in Brittany, Wales, Scotland and Ireland were they able to retain their identity.

8

6 A skeleton of a Celtic pony from the La Tene era (500 BC to the advent of Christianity) found recently by Lake Neuchâtel in Switzerland. Celtic horses were probably very similar to tarpans. As they were only about 140 cm tall they were really more like ponies.

7 A bronze ritual axe from the burial ground at Hallstatt in Upper Austria.

8 Bronze horse from Obrany in Czechoslovakia.

6

7

c. 300 BC:
A marvellously preserved Celtic kiln which was found in Germany in 1932.

c. 295 BC:
In the third Samnite War the Romans defeat the combined forces of the Samnites, Etruscans and Gauls.

Two clay urns and bronze bracelets from a Celtic grave in Germany.

286 BC:
A bronze statue, 34 m high, of the Sun-god, Helios, is erected at the entrance to the harbour at Rhodes. This Colossus of Rhodes was one of the Seven Wonders of the Ancient World.

Giant basalt head from Tabasco, Mexico.

c. 280 BC:
Coins are minted during the second La Tene era in Central Europe.

THE ROMANS

Alexandria becomes a cultural centre. Scientists and scholars from all fields gather there and a large library is founded.

c. 270 BC
In China the end of the Chou dynasty results in an end to unification.

c. 260 BC
The Gauls conquer northern Italy.

c. 250 BC
The first of the monumental temple complexes to the Buddha are built in India.

c. 220 BC
The Great Wall of China is built.

c. 175 BC
Work starts on Olympia in Athens.

c. 100 BC
Beginning of the third La Tene era.

c. AD 50
Founding of Cologne.

c. AD 70
Paper is invented in China.

A 'mosaic of marine life' from the Roman town of Pompeii. When Vesuvius erupted in AD 79, Pompeii was buried under lava and volcanic ash.

The Roman calendar begins in 753 BC, the year Romulus, son of the war god Mars, was said to have founded the city of Rome. According to the legend Romulus and his twin brother Remus were left as infants on the bank of the Tiber, where a she-wolf found and raised them. The story, however, was the invention of Roman historians in the first century BC. The Roman Empire, once the Carthaginians had been defeated, surrounded the entire Mediterranean, and the chroniclers were united in the belief that such an immense realm could only have been established with the help of the gods. In reality the Italic tribes (who also formed part of the Indo-European language group) migrated into the boot of Italy, settled in the south-west between 1500 and 1000 BC, and in due course Latin settlements grew up around the group of hills on the lower reaches of the Tiber. At that time the Greeks and the Etruscans were the masters of the Italian peninsula. Around 600 BC the latter conquered the Latin villages, proceeded to surround them with a city wall and laid the foundations of the city of Rome. A century later the Romans drove off their oppressors and founded a republic.

Artistically and culturally the Etruscans and the Greeks were far superior to the Romans who were, however, much more practical,

better organizers and possessed of an insatiable will to expand. Soon after the birth of Christ the Roman Empire attained its greatest dimensions. It stretched from Great Britain across the whole of that part of Europe which lies to the south-west of the Rhine and the Danube, across North Africa

and the Near East to the Parthian kingdom (modern Iran).

The collapse of Rome began around AD 260 when the Alemanni invaded northern Italy. The Empire finally fell when in 476 the Germanic tribes deposed the boy-Emperor Romulus Augustus.

Although the Roman cavalry is

1 Pluto abducts Persephone in a quadriga. This famous wall painting is in the Tomba Nasoni on the Via Flaminia near Rome.

2 The equestrian statue of Marcus Aurelius. It was erected around AD 170 and stands in front of the Capitol in Rome.

3 This marble sarcophagus is carved with battle scenes. It dates from the third century and is now in the museum by the Baths in Rome.

4 Metal protective head masks were part of a cavalry horse's armour.

AD 54 to 68
Nero is the Roman
Emperor.

AD 80
The colosseum at
Rome is completed.

c. 114
The Roman Empire
reaches its greatest
dimensions.
Germanic tribes begin
to migrate.

359
Division of the
Roman Empire into
Western and Eastern.

From 360
The battles between
Rome and the
Visigoths and
Alemanni become
more and more bitter.

410
Under Alaric the
Visigoths take Rome.

445
Attila becomes King
of the Huns.

450
The Hunnish hordes
invade India.

475
Fall of the Roman
Empire.

571 to 632
Prophet Mohammed.

711
Arabs storm the
Iberian peninsula and
continue to advance
until stopped in
France and pushed
back over the
Pyrenees by the
Frankish King
Charles Martel (714 to
741).

768 to 814
Charlemagne.

c. 800
Zenith of Arabic
sciences.

*4 and 5 Horse's head
and a Chinese
horseman. Chinese
artists preferred making
clay models of horses,
which were then used as
grave offerings for dead
rulers. Many of these
figures are glazed in
different colours. Those
produced during the
Tang dynasty in
particular testify to a
great deal of skill and a
love of detail.*

*6 The 'flying horse' from
the Han period (202 to
220). This bronze
statuette is considered to
be one of the most
beautiful of all.*

*7 Saddle horses from the
Tang period (618 to
906). Some graves from
this dynasty were found
only recently. The
mausoleum of the Crown
Prince Yide, for example,
which dates from 706
was discovered in 1971.
Numerous figures of*
*horses were found closely
packed together in the
side niches of the 100-
metre long hallway
which leads to the burial
chamber. In one niche
alone there were 119
horses with and without
riders and in various
poses.*

The Chinese learnt the art of riding from their enemies, from whom they also borrowed the saddle, the double-curved bow, and wide riding trousers in place of their own ankle-length robes. It seems, too, that the Huns provided them with stirrups, the most important hippological advance since the invention of the bit.

During this period horse-breeding was also considerably improved. Until then most Chinese horses were descended from the Mongolian ponies, which, although tough, wiry, undemanding animals, were not very fast and lacked fire and nobility. The Chinese had, however, heard of the 'heavenly horses' of the Near East and sent expeditions to Persia to buy stallions and bring them back to China.

This is evidenced by the many paintings and other works of art which depict harmoniously built animals with fine heads and long beautifully curved necks. Much of the horse-breeding industry was transferred from the damp flat country to the dry chalk soil of the north-western steppes, and horses were also fed grain to supplement their green feed.

With its increase in importance the horse became a popular artistic motif, found most frequently in the form of ceramic figures used as grave offerings during the Tang dynasty.

During the Shang and Chou period (about 1450 to 221 BC) people of importance had their possessions, including their servants and animals, buried with them, but by 500 BC the sacrifice of animals and people was less common and instead figures made of wood, clay or bronze were put in the graves with the dead.

During the Tang period the wealth and artistry of these grave offerings reached their high point, and hundreds of figures of horses, both with and without riders, have been found in graves dating from this period.

Statue of the Buddha
in a cave temple in
Kyungjoo.

400 to 900
Classical age of the
Mayan civilization.

c. 500
Judaism moves into
Arabia. The zenith of
architecture in Indo-
China produces
beautiful temples.

Temple on Phnom
hill which gave its
name to the capital of
Cambodia.

c. 590
The Slavs advance
into the Balkans.

c. 600
Monza cathedral is
built.

607
Construction of the
pagoda at Horyuji, the
Buddhist monastery
near Nara in Japan.
Classical Chinese
design.

403 to 553

THE GERMANIC TRIBES

The origins of the Germanic tribes, who belong to the Indo-Germanic group of languages and are closely related to the Celtic and Italic tribes, can be traced back to about 1500 BC when they settled east of the Baltic Sea. Gradually they expanded in all directions and formed new racial groups, for example, the north Germans or Scandinavians, the West Germans including the Angles and Saxons, and the East Germans with the Goths and the Vandals.

Around AD 403 the Germanic tribes began to exercise a decisive influence on the course of history as hordes of Visigoths surged southwards over the Alps and collided with the Roman Empire at its most sensitive point. About 150 years later the collapse of the Ostrogoth hegemony heralded the end of the Germanic tribes' influence in Italy.

Many of these tribes were horse peoples, and a number of place-names testify to their close affinity with the animal.

In the heroic sagas, too, the

horses of the Valkyries played an important role; a role reflected by Brunhilde's stallion Grane in Wagner's *Ring of the Nibelung*.

Little is known of the beginnings of horsemanship among the Germanic tribes, and their horses' origins are also unclear, but these animals are described as small and strong and are probably descendants of the tarpan.

It is interesting that in Nordic mythology all the horses dedicated to the gods are white. The standard of the Germanic tribes also depicts a galloping white horse. As white colouring only occurs in breeds which at some time have been in contact with Oriental horses it suggests that the Germanic horses must have had some Oriental blood in their veins.

The Germanic tribes were aptly described as barbarians. In more ways than one they were made from a different mould than were, for example, the Greeks who made riding into an art and long before the advent of Christianity had developed an advanced school of riding. Nevertheless the Germanic tribes were natural riders, and such excellent ones that they were sought after as mercenaries in the Roman army. For some time, Caesar commanded an elite troop of Germanic horsemen who called themselves *alauda* (larks). It seems that the Germanic tribes were particularly adept at training their horses to be obedient and they are said to have often dismounted during battle to continue fighting on foot while their horses stayed imperturbably in the same spot. As riders only the Celts were more highly valued by Caesar.

The Germans who were in the service of the Romans gradually refined their riding style, probably under the influence of the Carthaginians and the Numidians, both excellent horsemen. They even began to practise artistic equestrian tomfoolery, and were apparently the first to arrange tournaments.

The historian Procopius who accompanied Belisarius, Justinian's great military commander, reports that in 552 Totila, King of the Ostrogoths, performed tricks in front of his army. He made his horse execute dainty turns, threw his spear into the air while galloping at full speed, caught it again and performed circus acrobatics like an artiste in the arena. This kind of display, which was probably practised by many riders among the Gothic tribes, falls somewhere between the classical riding style and the natural, often daring brilliance of riders like the Cossacks or the gauchos.

Not all the Germanic tribes shared this passion for horses. Riding was part of the life style of restless and warlike people like the

1 Lombard relief panel probably from the eighth century.

2 The equestrian stone of Hornhausen from the seventh century. The Saxon Baron's horse depicted in this drawing is about half a metre taller than in real life. The Germanic horses were seldom more than 140 cm tall.

3 The 'chariot of the sun' from Trundholm, Zealand, Denmark is the most famous of all Germanic cult objects. It is said to date from the fourteenth century BC.

4 Rider with two hounds from a picture stone with runic script from Uppland, Sweden.

Vandals, Alans, Goths and Sueves, but they perished during the upheavals of the migratory period and disappeared somewhere in southern Europe or Africa. More settled tribes, for example, the Angles and the Saxons, the Lombards and the Franks, did not possess the same affinity for the horse.

622
Mohammed flees from his opponents from Mecca to Medina.

630
Mohammed marches victorious into Mecca.

632
Mohammed dies. His followers are, however, ready to wage the Holy War.

637
Arabs conquer Jerusalem.

639
Arabs conquer Egypt.

640
Arabs conquer Persia.

668
Arabs conquer North Africa.

c. 700
High point of temple building in India.

The hall of columns in the temple at Dilwara Dschain.

113

MOHAMMED AND THE ARAB HORSE

Although geographically close to where the first advanced civilizations developed, for millennia the Arabian peninsula remained untouched by historical events. The Bedouins of the wild barren deserts bred sheep and used camels as riding and draught animals. Their sheiks had long possessed horses, but little or nothing is known about these animals before the time of Mohammed, and the numerous legends passed down from generation to generation are of little help in our search for the origins of the Arab horse. Around 600 BC though, no one would have suspected that so soon afterwards both Arabs and the Arab horse would have such important roles to play.

An Arabic trader, who on his travels had become acquainted with the beliefs of the Jews and the Christians, felt himself called to be the last and greatest prophet and to reveal Islam to his people, i.e., 'the yielding to the will of God'. At first no one was interested in the teachings of this Mohammed, and in 622 he and his followers were driven from Mecca, his home town. From this date begins the calendar of the Mohammedan Arabs. From Medina Mohammed waged war with the Meccans, and acknowledged with inspired insight that there were two weapons superior to all others: religious fanaticism and excellent horses. He promised his followers that all those killed while fighting for their beliefs in a Holy War would go straight to Heaven. And as he was endowed with a remarkable understanding of horses and horse-breeding, he produced the incomparable Arab pure-bred.

According to legend, Mohammed ordered that a herd of horses be left without water for seven days. When their enclosure

was opened the animals raced towards the watering place. But the prophet then sounded the call to battle. Immediately five mares turned in response and raced back to him without having first quenched their thirst. All pure-bred Arabs are said to be descended from these five mares. There may be a grain of truth in the story, for Mohammed was stringently careful when selecting horses for breeding and demanded that the bloodlines be kept absolutely pure. He made the breeding of horses an integral part of his religious teachings, and in the Koran, the Mohammedans' holy book compiled after his death from his revelations, he set out rules for breeding and training horses. It states, for example, that 'no evil spirit will dare to enter a tent where there is a pure-bred horse', or 'for every barleycorn that is given to a horse Allah will pardon one sin'.

Soon after Mohammed's death in 632 the Arabs were ready to embark on the Holy War to which the prophet had called them. With

1 *Islamic horseman. Around 950 Arabic drawings were produced on papyrus.*

2 to 4 *The presence of the Arabs in Europe had a substantial influence on the breeding of horses. After a great deal of cross-breeding of Arab (2) and Berber horses the* noble Andalusian (3) *was developed in southern Spain and the Neapolitan (4). These two breeds then formed the foundation of all the notable breeds of Baroque horses. These drawings are from a book by Baron von Eisenberg which appeared in 1748.*

horses faster, hardier, and with more stamina than all others, the Arabs' religious fanaticism made them almost invincible, and in an astonishingly short campaign they conquered Syria, Palestine, and Egypt, then part of the Eastern Roman Empire. One single battle was sufficient to cause the fall of the kingdom of the Sassanides. Soon the hooves of the Arabs' horses were thundering across Persia, through Afghanistan, to India, Tibet and Turkestan. The Islamic hordes overran North Africa, overthrew the Berbers, crossed the narrow strait of Gibraltar into Europe and conquered the Visigoth Empire on the Iberian peninsula, an advance not stopped until it reached France. At Tours and Poitiers Charles Martel with his heavily armoured forces was able to bring them to a halt and force them back over the Pyrenees.

For centuries, however, the Arabs remained as rulers in some parts of southern France and in most of Spain. A large number of words added to the European languages give some indication of their cultural attainments: algebra, chemistry, zenith, elixir and alcohol, among others. And they left the inheritance of their marvellous horses whose blood now flows in almost every one of the world's breeds.

5 Mohammed rides to Heaven on Burag. In the Islamic religion saints are not allowed to be given features. Therefore Mohammed is depicted without a face.

680
The Frankish ruler Ebrion is assassinated. Peace is concluded between the Langobards and Byzantium.

688
Pepin II becomes the ruler of the whole of the Frankish Empire.

710
Roderick becomes the last King of the Visigoths.

711
Roderick is defeated at Jerez de la Frontera in Andalusia by the Arabs led by Tarik. End of the Visigoth realm.

714 to 741
Pepin's son Charles Martel becomes King of the Franks.

741
Charles Martel divides the Frankish realm before his death between his sons Carloman and Pepin III.

c. 750
Islam reaches China and brings an end to Christianity there. In China the aristocracy plays polo.
Zenith of Chinese painting.

Pepin III's son Charlemagne becomes King of the Franks and from 771 to 814 is the sole ruler of the Frankish kingdom.

5

115

c. 800
Last of the North
German migrations.
Charlemagne receives
as a present the first
mechanical water-
clock. Heyday of the
Carolingian
illuminated
manuscript.

814
Death of
Charlemagne. His
successor is his son
Louis the Pious.

840
Louis dies.

841
Louis' son Lothar I
wants to rule over the
whole Empire alone
but is defeated at the
battle of Fontenay by
his brothers Charles
(the Bald) and Louis
(the German).

843
By the Partition of
Verdun Lothar, Louis
and Charles agree to
divide the Empire and
thereby lay the
foundations of the
German and French
realms.

c. 850
Chess, a game which
originated among the
Indians and Persians,
is brought to Europe
by the Arabs.

855
Lothar I dies. His
(central) realm is
divided between his
sons Louis II and
Lothar II.

THE VIKINGS

Just as the Arabs possessed a natural aptitude for riding, so the Vikings could be described as born seafarers. Both, however, were enlightened enough to be receptive to new ideas. Not long after the uprising of the Holy War the Arabs already had a fleet. They based it on Cyprus and were then able to control the whole of the Mediterranean, with the exception of the Aegean and Adriatic Seas. With the same kind of adaptability, when the time was ripe, the Vikings, sensing the importance of the horse, soon mastered all the aspects of horsemanship.

The Vikings of northern Germany, later known as Normans, were most famous, however, for their unique ships. So cleverly constructed as to be equally effective on rivers and on the open sea, they were open boats, about twenty metres long and fitted with sails and oars. They provided room for about fifty men, but were also used to transport sheep, cattle, ponies or horses. The Vikings took ponies from Scandinavia with them on their exploratory voyages and warring campaigns — tough, wiry animals about 130 cm tall. Whenever they needed additional riding animals they simply appropriated them as booty.

In 866, for example, the Vikings are said to have plundered all the stables and fields in eastern England.

Like the mounted hordes of Genghis Khan or the Huns under Attila ('the scourge of God'), the Vikings were feared for their cruelty. Around the year 700 they set out on their campaigns of conquest, first occupying the Shetland and Orkney Isles to the north of Britain. A century and a half later they began to plunder England and Ireland, and then moved into the stretches of land along the coast of north-western Europe. They took their boats up the rivers and laid waste larger settlements such as Hamburg, Paris and Rouen. Around AD 1000 they controlled the whole of Ireland, and from 1016 to 1042 the whole of England, in the meantime having completed their conquest of Normandy and settled there.

In the history of the horse two events are of particular interest.

In Norway some 900 large groups of Vikings loaded up their ships and set sail in an effort to escape from their tyrannical King. Some of these emigrants sailed first to Scotland and from there continued to Iceland, while the rest journeyed directly to that northern volcanic island. Whichever way they travelled, they had to cross about 850 kilometres of open sea — a dangerous and

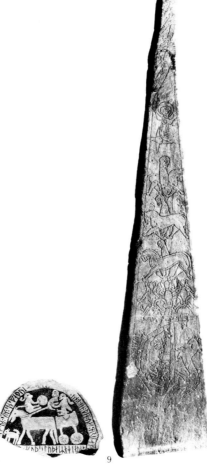

1 to 7 These mounted warriors carved by the Vikings out of walrus ivory were found on the island of Lewis which lies to the north-west of Scotland.

8 to 13 Countless picture-stones show that the Vikings had a relationship bordering on the religious, both with their horses and with their ships.

14 The mounted figure made from baked clay gives some indication of the small stature of the Germanic ponies.

15 and 16 Stirrups and spurs have been found in Scandinavia dating from the time of the great Viking voyages of conquest.

17 The Oseberg ship is one of the greatest known masterpieces of Viking ship-building. It was found in a large burial mound together with the bones of a queen, a servant who had been ritually sacrificed, and various animals.

18 This cart also came from the Oseberg site. Perhaps the most notable discovery of Nordic antiquity, it is elaborately carved with scenes from sagas, and was used for ceremonial purposes.

difficult journey which must have claimed many lives. Although Iceland was extremely barren and little agriculture was possible, the Vikings settled there and started to breed cattle and sheep and catch fish and sea birds.

Thanks to their ponies they were able to travel over the rugged volcanic and glacial terrain, and today the pony is still the only

14

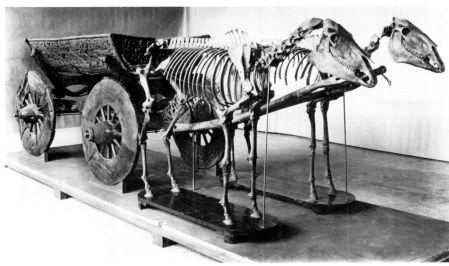

15   16   17

18

means of transport in the interior of the island.

About 930, after the first wave of settlers had arrived, a national assembly, or Althing, was called. Both religious rituals and sporting events formed part of this political gathering, which from that time on was held annually. Stallion fights were a particularly popular sport, even though ponies were often badly injured and sometimes killed. Afterwards, much to the enjoyment of those present, the outraged owners often quarrelled just as bitterly as the ponies.

It is assumed that in addition to their own Germanic ponies the Vikings took native moorland and Celtic ponies from the British Isles

with them to Iceland. Around the year 1000, afraid of an outbreak of horse diseases which would have put the island's inhabitants at risk, the Althing decided to forbid the importing of any more horses or ponies to the island. This law is still in force, and for about a thousand years Icelandic ponies have remained pure-bred. They are such an excellent breed that it would in fact be superfluous to introduce other horses. According to various estimates there are at present between 40,000 and 65,000 ponies on Iceland, an island with a population of only some 200,000 people.

The second event, although more sensational, did not have such a lasting effect. In 986 Vikings, under the leadership of Eric the Red, left Iceland on a new voyage of discovery. They reached Greenland but lost eleven of their twenty-five ships. Four years later part of the fleet sailed further and reached North America, half a millennium before it was 'discovered' by Columbus. Although this has been known for a long time, only recently were some burial places discovered which date from the Viking age and which contained skeletons of both horses and men. Before their conversion to Christianity the Viking often had their horses buried with them. It seems therefore that the Vikings, not the Spaniards, were the first to bring the domestic horse to America, although those horses have apparently disappeared there just as the Vikings themselves did.

The Norwegian King Harald Hardrada tries to conquer England but is killed at Stamford Bridge by the Anglo-Saxons under King Harold.

Gottschalk the oblatory Christian knight is killed by the heathen in Germany.

The bishoprics of Mecklenburg (picture: Neubrandenburger Tor at Mecklenburg), Ratzeburg and Hamburg are destroyed.

1066

THE NORMANS IN ENGLAND

In 1066 the Normans invaded England and defeated the troops of the Saxon King Harold at Hastings, the battle at which William of Normandy himself is said to have killed Harold. The Normans then went on to impose a feudal system on English society.

This event was the inspiration behind a unique work of embroidery — the tapestry that hangs at Bayeux cathedral.

Scenes from the battle, with commentaries written in Latin, are depicted on a strip of linen 70 m long and 50 cm wide. The tapestry has a total of 1515 figures and includes 626 people, 202 horses, 55 dogs, 505 other animals, 37 buildings, 41 ships and 49 trees. The designers of this wall-hanging, produced over 900 years ago, are unknown. It cannot even be said with certainty whether they were English or Norman.

Baghdad becomes the centre of Islamic religion and culture.

The Tower of London is built.

THE AGE OF CHIVALRY

Dancing Shiva, India.

Dancing Apsaras in the Bayou temple in Angkor, Cambodia, from the twelfth century.

Although it is difficult to imagine a knight without a horse, the armoured cavalrymen of the Middle Ages were anything but accomplished riders, at least in the sense of classic horsemanship. As the knight's armour became heavier, his movements became more and more restricted. A knight in the full armour that was characteristic of the later Middle Ages could no longer use delicate thigh equipment to guide his horse, especially since his saddle was a monstrosity weighing approximately twenty-five kilograms. He guided and reined his horse by shifting his weight and with the help of spurs and a curb bit, which worked, in effect, as instruments of torture.

The knights may have lacked riding skills, but a high degree of training was not asked of his

1 A mounted Italian soldier in armour. An amazing example of skilled metal workmanship from the fifteenth century.

2 Tournament scene. A wall picture by H. Schäufelein from Tratzberg in the Tyrol.

Early in the Middle Ages knights were not of the nobility, but simply ordinary soldiers on horseback, and it was only gradually that the professional soldier achieved noble status. Before a squire could

aspire to knighthood he had to prove that he had undergone strict professional training and that he was ready to risk his neck in the tournament lists.

At that time these equestrian games, which had their origin in military exercises organized by the various reigning monarchs, were extremely popular spectacles. Charles II, the Bald, 823 to 877, the King of the West Franks and Roman Emperor as well for the last two years of his life, is said to have frequently held manoeuvres which required large numbers of soldiers to stage mock attacks. Usually two groups would storm towards each other, but before they collided, one group had to turn, divide where possible, and then by skilful riding, attack the opposing faction on the flank.

A few hundred years later these military games had inevitably lost much of their mobility, for the original helmets and chain-mail or leather shirts with pieces of metal sewn on to them had been replaced by heavy suits of full armour. And in place of the light, fast horses on which the Normans, for example, won the Battle of

mount either. The man's armour gradually became larger and heavier, and eventually extended to the unfortunate animal as well, which had to be capable of carrying 150 kg. This required both size and strength, and accordingly the breeding of massive cold-blood horses flourished, especially in France, Flanders and England. Many were undoubtedly imposing horses, but they completely lacked nobility, fire and sensibility — all those qualities which produce a really outstanding riding animal.

3 The 'racecourse' on the horse market held in Frankfurt. The equestrian games which took place here had very little in common with racing even though the most popular of them was called Ritterliche Köpfe Rennen (the Knights' race).

4 and 5 King Louis
XIII as a young man
entering the tournament
and training with his
famous riding teacher
Antoine de Pluvinel at

single combat with the
sword. These beautiful
copper engravings are by
Crispin de Passe (see
also pages 150 to 155).

Hastings (as depicted in the Bayeux tapestry, pages 118-119), there were massive horses, greatly hindered by their cumbersome armour.

The question as to whether the French or the Germans invented the tournament is just as hotly debated as whether a tournament horse was or was not a carefully trained, well-ridden animal.

It was a Frenchman, Geoffroy de Preully, a knight himself, who was killed in a tournament in 1066, who provided the first written tournament rules.

In principle a tournament was defined as follows: two riders rode towards each other on parallel tracks, separated by a waist-high barrier, and, using long lances, tried to lift their opponents out of the saddle. It was, therefore, an advantage to have a deep saddle which provided a more secure seat. It was not necessary to be an adept rider, as the horse quickly learnt to move forward at its heavy gallop, but courage was certainly a prerequisite.

Tournaments were always dangerous affairs, even in de Preully's time when full suits of armour were still unknown. Even a blunt lance could cause a lethal wound, and a fall was equally risky to a rider whose mobility was so restricted.

Many of the various forms of tournaments were exceptionally dangerous. In 1241 at one single tournament, for example, held in Neuss in the Lower Rhine region, no less than sixty knights were killed, a large number said to have 'been asphyxiated in the dust or trampled to death by the horses'.

6 Grey Frederick of
Leiningen. Miniature
from the Manesse
manuscript.

7 Albrecht Dürer's
drawing of a German
knight in full armour, c.
1498.

1147
Work begins on the (leaning) tower of Pisa.

1189
Third Crusade.

1206
Genghis Khan begins the Mongolian campaigns of conquest.

c. 1270
The Venetian, Marco Polo.travels to Asia.

1291
Founding of the Swiss Confederation.

1348 to 1352
The plague kills around a third (25 million) of the European population.

1431 to 1525
Aztec civilization.

1450
Johann Gutenberg invents the printing press.

1452 to 1519
Leonardo da Vinci, artist and scientist of genius.

1471 to 1528
Albrecht Dürer, German painter and graphic artist.

1475 to 1564
Michelangelo Buonarroti, Italian sculptor and painter.

1483
Birth of the reformer, Martin Luther. Raffael Santi, Italian painter is born.

1492
Christopher Columbus discovers America.

1532
Pizarro destroys the Inca civilization.

1555
Birth of Antoine de Pluvinel.

1592
Birth of William Cavendish. Shakespeare writes Richard III.

1203 to 1259

THE MONGOLS

To the north-east of the immense expanse of the Eurasian steppes lived a small group of Turkish nomads. These were the Mongols who suddenly abandoned their more or less peaceful pastoral existence, erupted out of their homelands, and within an unbelievably short time conquered the largest empire in the history of mankind.

By the twelfth century these wanderers had already overthrown a number of neighbouring tribes, but their power really dates from 1203 when Temujin (1162 to 1227) made himself the sole ruler of the Mongol Empire. He became famous under the name of Genghis Khan. After his death three of his successors were able to keep the huge empire together as one unit, but when his grandson Möngkö died in 1259, it began to collapse.

At its zenith the empire of the Mongols stretched from the north-western coast of the Pacific to the Oder and the Adriatic, and from Lake Baykal to Vietnam. China had long been harassed by various nomadic peoples, but only the Mongols succeeded in conquering that giant land.

Without the horse most of their battles and campaigns of conquest would have been unimaginable. Never before had the horse played such a central role, except perhaps in the lives of the Huns. There

1 Chinese clay figure of a Mongolian horseman.

2 This Chinese painting depicts a Mongolian herdsman. His animals are obviously not of Mongolian descent. The leopard spots and the snowflake pattern indicate that they are Chinese horses which in early centuries had been crossed with horses brought from the Near East.

3 In 1203 Temujin made himself the sole ruler

over the Mongolian Empire. He was the first Khan, who became famous under the name of Genghis Khan and was one of the most astonishing conquerors of all.

4 A Chinese silk painting of Genghis Khan hunting with falcons.

5 Mongols catching horses with a lasso on a stick.

were no infantry in the Mongolian army; every soldier was a horseman. During the campaigns the Mongols' horses also provided the greater part of the men's rations. They milked the mares and let the milk thicken to a sour curd cheese in leather skins, to be eaten later just as it was or thinned with water and drunk. Small amounts of blood were regularly taken from the horses in much the same way as the Masai herdsmen now living in East Africa extract blood from their zebus. Finally the horses were slaughtered for their meat. This was soaked in salt water and large pieces were then tenderized by being placed under the saddle and ridden on. The meat was stored in leather

pouches and kept well, though in time it stank abominably.

This method of obtaining food and their custom of frequently changing horses meant that they required a great many riding animals. It is said that each soldier possessed eighteen or twenty horses. At times the Mongolian army consisted of over 200,000 soldiers and an estimated four to five million horses.

Except for those horses taken as booty, the riding animals of the Mongols were wiry, extremely resilient steppe ponies, only about 130 cm tall. Their proverbial toughness and strength were remarkable in proportion to their size, but they tired more quickly than the horses of their

opponents, which were much larger and almost twice their weight. This was not, however, much of a disadvantage, for the Mongols had so many animals that if one showed signs of exhaustion it could easily be exchanged for a fresh mount. In any serious battles they would ride their best ponies which, besides being fast and mobile, were always well rested. Their opponents on the other hand lacked substitute animals and were therefore never able to rest their horses.

Historians often maintain that

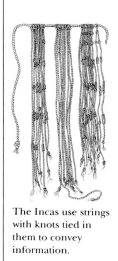

The Incas use strings with knots tied in them to convey information.

A pot from the early Inca period.

1242
The Manesse manuscript consisting of 7000 verses and 138 miniatures is completed.

1248 to 1254
Sixth Crusade.

1256
Founding of the Sorbonne in Paris as a students' hostel.

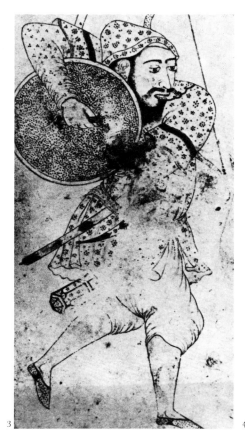

American Indians used the same strategy, but while the Indians usually rode bareback and hugged their animals' backs, the Mongols buckled their stirrups short and during the attack floated high above their saddles, thereby obtaining a greater degree of accuracy.

the Mongols owed their successes to their numerical superiority. This is only partly true. Many of their battles were displays of extraordinary strategical skill. Their attacks may have looked wild, but their troops were far from undisciplined horsemen, and their fighting technique was extremely effective. They rode across the front of the enemy lines, wheeling again and again, able to shoot their arrows into the enemy's ranks while they themselves presented a moving target at which it was difficult to aim. The

THE HORSE IN THE RENAISSANCE

CONTEMPORARY EVENTS

c. 1350
The book trade becomes more widespread.

1370
Founding of Tenochtitlan, the Aztecs' capital city. In 1521 it is completely destroyed by the Spaniards.

1382
The Mongols destroy Moscow.

1386
Work begins on Milan cathedral.

1404
Civil War in France.

c. 1430
Copper engraving (gravure process) begins to supersede wood-cuts.

1450
Completion of St Stephen's Cathedral in Vienna.

1453
End of the Hundred Years' War between England and France.

c. 1475
Under King Huayna Capac the Inca realm reaches its zenith. It extends from Ecuador to Chile.

The term Renaissance refers to that period between the Middle Ages and modern times during which the forgotten cultural and artistic marvels of antiquity were revived. After the gloom of the Middle Ages, the life-affirming style of the Renaissance spread quickly from Italy throughout the greater part of Europe. Artistic expression, which for centuries had been restricted and repressed, now burst forth with renewed vigour, and it is no coincidence that the art of riding also experienced its 'renaissance' during this period.

Xenophon was the first to publish manuals on the subject, and these early works were important in the revival of the classical art of riding in Naples in 1530. By chance, a nobleman named Federico Grisone learned of Xenophon's works, *Peri Hippikes* and *Hipparchikos*, which had only just been rediscovered. He made a thorough study of them and in 1532 opened a riding academy in Naples, where young noblemen, as well as being taught how to handle

1 Hunting scene by Andrea Mantegna (1431 to 1506), one of the leading painters of the Renaissance. As the Court Painter in Mantua he created the first group portrait and with the fresco known as 'Camera degli Sposi' in the castle of Mantua, the first three-dimensional picture.

2 'The journey of the Magi' by Benozzo Gozzoli in the chapel of the Ricardi palace in Florence. This fresco is a brilliant example of the Renaissance love of life.

horses, were tutored in the arts and graces of courtly life. The academy was so successful that within a few years it could number the sons of princes and kings from throughout Europe among its pupils. Grisone crowned his activity with *Ordini di Cavalcare*, published in 1550, which did not, however, fully deserve the success it achieved, for not only had Grisone simply appropriated many riding instructions almost word for word from Xenophon, but he also put forward many ideas which seemed to contradict his basic attitudes. The Greeks' attitude to riding was very enlightened in

trying to understand a horse's natural aptitude and temperament instead of using brute force. Simon, one of Xenophon's predecessors, expressed the concept very succinctly: 'You cannot use a whip and spurs to teach a dancer to dance.' Grisone writes in a similar vein, but then suddenly recommends the use of such forceful measures as 'hitting an unmanageable horse between the ears and on its head while avoiding the eyes.' Such treatment would have ruined even the most good-natured animal. Grisone's work also mentions his invention of several bits which would have been instruments of torture in the mouth of any horse.

Nevertheless Grisone's school did play a very significant role, and it was the means by which the long-neglected classical art of riding then spread from Naples and Rome throughout Europe. Giovanni Pignatelli was one of the most talented of Grisone's pupils, and later taught the Frenchman Antoine de Pluvinel, the most famous of all the riding instructors of that period (see pages 150 to 155).

Horses and riders were a dominant motif in Renaissance painting and sculpture; only in the Baroque period which followed did they play a more important role. Some of the most talented painters in this field were Benozzo Gozzoli, Andrea Mantegna, Paolo Uccello, Francesco Pesellino and Vittore Pisano, and in their work a lively atmosphere filled with light replaces the stiffness of medieval paintings. Riders are no longer awkward, but relaxed and at ease, apparently well versed in the art of horsemanship for they are well balanced and not continually pulling at the animals' mouths.

'Mona Lisa' by Leonardo de Vinci (1452 to 1519).

3 Francis I of France (1494 to 1547) on horseback in a painting by his Court painter Francois Clouet (1522 to 1572). Louvre, Paris.

5 Sketch of a horse-drawn war machine by Leonardo da Vinci (1452 to 1519). Da Vinci was equally talented as a painter, sculptor and architect. He was also far ahead of his time as a scientist and inventor. 3

4 Equestrian statue of Count Eberhard V (1445 to 1496) in the courtyard of the Old Castle of Stuttgart.

4

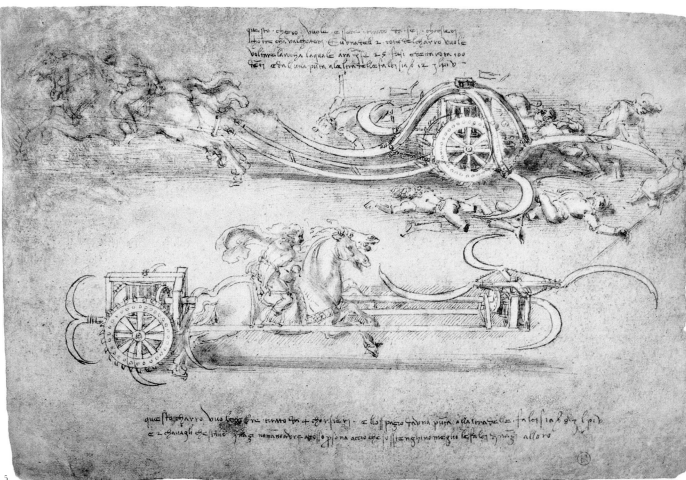

5

1483 to 1546
Martin Luther, German reformer.

1484 to 1531
Huldrich Zwingli Swiss reformer.

1506
Death of Christopher Columbus.

1520
Death of Raffael Santi the painter.

1543
Peru and Ecuador come under Spanish control.

1556
India is united into one realm under Akbar.

1569
Death of Pieter Breughel the Elder, Flemish painter.

1572
First mention of the Spanish Riding School in Vienna.

1577 to 1640
Peter Paul Rubens, the greatest of the Baroque Dutch painters.

The renaissance of the riding style is probably most obvious in Gozzoli's 'Journey of the Magi' in the chapel of the Palazzo Richardi in Florence, but most contemporary paintings depicted peaceful, often cheerful scenes like the hunting in this fresco. One exception was Uccello, who became famous for stirring paintings of battle scenes. His compositions are full of figures and clearly show the knowledge of perspective possessed by the artists of his time.

One feature of many Renaissance statues is rather curious. All the horses are pacing (see Gaits on page 60) — the

monument to Paolo Savelli in the Frari church in Venice, for example; the statue of David by Verrocchio de Calleoni; and even the famous horse of Gattamelata (Francesco de Narni) in Padua, created by Donatello, one of the most productive and successful sculptors, who emulated the works of antiquity. Many experts believe that the artists took such liberties with their subjects in order to cope with technical difficulties, but a more correct explanation would be that the models were, in fact, pacers. At that time horses which were able to pace were much sought after, and, at least in upper circles of society, quite common.

Later this gait was almost completely forgotten, although retained by Icelandic ponies and the Paso horses of South America, to be rediscovered only recently by enthusiasts for the subject.

125

THE CONQUISTADORS
IN THE NEW WORLD

1498
Louis XII becomes
King of France.

1509
Henry VIII becomes
King of England.

1515
Francis I becomes
King of France.

The castle of
Chambord, completed
in 1509, is one of the
magnificent French
Renaissance castles
on the Loire.

1522
Knights (Franz von
Sickingen, Ulrich von
Hutten) challenge the
spiritual power of
Princes.

1528
Death of Albrecht
Dürer, German
painter and graphic
artist.

1529
End of the siege of
Vienna by the Turks.

1530
Emperor Charles V is
crowned in Bologna.

1547
Henry II becomes
King of France.

The horse's primeval home was the American continent, but for some unexplained reason all the single-toed animals became extinct there about 10,000 years ago. They may well have been victims of an epidemic. Originally Alaska and Siberia were joined together by the Bering Way and horses and other animals, as well as Asiatic hunters, the ancestors of the American Indians, used this path to migrate from the Old World to the New, a route which was permanently closed when the narrow land bridge was covered by the sea.

Recent finds in the US indicate that the Vikings probably brought ponies to North America about a thousand years ago. Nothing is known of the descendants of these horses, however, and they seem to have played no part in the historical development of the horse in America. The Mustang, the horse which 'made' America and had such a profound effect on the course of its history, is said to be of Spanish origin.

Columbus brought horses to the New World. When in 1492 the Spaniards conquered Granada, the last bastion of the Moors, and put an end to 800 years of continuous suzerainty, they were ready for new adventures. Isabella of Castile, anxious to extend Spanish power to include India, commanded Christopher Columbus, the

1 Model of a Catalan ship from the sixteenth century. Ships like these were used to transport thousands of horses from Spain to the New World.

2 When Christopher Columbus discovered America in 1492 he brought about thirty horses with him.

3 Hernando Cortez conquered Mexico from 1519 to 1521.

Genoese mariner and geographer, to find the sea-route to this fabulous land. Columbus was convinced that the earth was round, and therefore sailed westwards until, seventy days after his departure, he reached the Caribbean Islands. He called them the West Indies, and their inhabitants Indians; till the time of his death in 1505 he was convinced that he had found India. On 6 December 1492 Columbus landed in Haiti and there took the first thirty Spanish horses ashore.

In the following years the Spaniards occupied a number of the Caribbean Islands, as well as some coastal areas of the mainland, and very probably took horses with them each time they landed. The serious campaign to conquer the American continent did not begin until 1519 when Hernando Cortez set off into the Mexican interior. Within three

years, after a series of bloody battles, Cortez, who in 1511 had been present at the occupation of Cuba, destroyed the ancient realms of the Mayas and the Aztecs, eventually becoming governor of Mexico, which was then renamed New Spain and considered to be a Spanish province. Cortez' army was amazingly small, and except for the conquistadors and some of the officers, contained only foot soldiers. At the start of his campaign Cortez had eleven stallions, five mares and a foal.

It is sometimes maintained that the Mustangs which now number in the millions are descended from Cortez' horses, but as this breed has existed in the American west for less than a century this is obviously nonsense. Every Spanish ship which landed in America in the following hundred years probably carried horses to be used as riding and pack animals in the New World, and as the ships had no cargo these animals were made to function as deck ballast during the journey. For an average of sixty to eighty days they were tied up on deck or suspended by wide straps, and given little protection against storms and inclement weather. On arrival those which survived the crossing were simply pushed overboard and had to swim to reach land about a hundred metres away. Despite heavy losses, thousands of Spanish horses reached America in this way.

Francisco Pizarro was another successful conquistador. In 1527 he discovered the Peruvian coast and between 1531 and 1535 he destroyed the immense flourishing realm of the Incas. He was even more cruel than Cortez and frankly admitted that his only interest was the enormous treasure

*4 Around 1540
Hernando de Soto
marched from Florida to
the Mississippi. About
ten years previously he
had supported Pizarro's
campaign to conquer the
Inca realm.*

*5 Statue of Francisco
Pizarro (1478 to 1541)
in Lima. The cruel
conqueror became Peru's
national hero.*

*6 Mexican Indians, bent
on revenge, cut off the
heads of their Spanish
prisoners and throw
them at Cortez' feet.*

5

6

of gold and silver belonging to the Incas. This wealth, however, became the cause of bloody feuds among the Spaniards themselves, one of whom claimed Pizarro himself as a victim. He was killed in 1541 in Lima, the city he had founded six years before. Since that time the Peruvian Indians have never regained their independence. For thousands of years the Indians' only domestic animals had been llamas and alpacas, but the Spaniards' introduction of sheep, cattle and horses was little compensation for their cruelty.

Two other conquerors made inroads into the North American continent. Around 1540 Francisco Vasquez Coronado left Mexico, taking with him about three hundred cattle to provide a continuous supply of fresh meat.

Cattle breeding had already developed into a flourishing industry there, and among his followers were a number of mounted Indian vaqueros whose job it was to drive the cattle. They were forerunners of the American cowboy, and the Western style of riding, which evolved in the American west, was derived from the Spanish.

Coronado's contemporary, Hernando de Soto began to search for the legendary 'Golden Cities' of Florida, and took about two hundred riding and pack horses with him. Some years after starting out, de Soto, then mortally ill, arrived at the Mississippi, and because the journey had to be continued by boat he instructed that the remaining forty of his horses should be slaughtered to provide provisions for the journey. Five horses are said to have escaped, a story which gave rise to the legend that the giant herds of Mustangs, in later centuries found grazing all across the prairies, were the descendants of these five horses.

In both North and South American large numbers of Spanish horses escaped and became wild, by far the majority of them probably Andalusians with a great deal of Berber and some Arab blood. They formed the basis of a large number of new breeds and types. As well as the Mustangs there were the various breeds of Western Horse (except for the more recent Quarter Horse breed); the Galiceños in Mexico; the Criollos and their various relatives in South America; the Paso Finos in Colombia; the Costeños and Peruvian Pasos in Peru and many others.

1556
Charles V abdicates.
His brother
Ferdinand I becomes
German Emperor.

1558
Ivan IV (the Terrible)
conquers Latvia.
Elizabeth I becomes
Queen of England.

1562 to 1598
Huguenot wars in
France.
Beginning of the
slave transports from
Africa to America.

1564
Maximilian II
becomes German
Emperor.
Death of the reformer
John Calvin.

1566
Death of
Nostradamus, French
astrologer and
physician.

1576
Death of Titian, the
greatest painter of the
Venetian High
Renaissance.

1581
Francis Drake returns
to England where he
shares the booty from
his adventurous
voyages with Queen
Elizabeth.

127

THE HORSE IN THE BAROQUE PERIOD

CONTEMPORARY
EVENTS

1585 to 1589
Civil war in France.

1606 to 1626
Building of St Peter's
in Rome.

1611
Gustavus II, Adolphus
becomes King of
Sweden. He is killed
in 1632 at the battle of
Lützen but his troops
are victorious against
Wallenstein's army.

1614
Death of El Greco, the
Spanish-Greek
painter.

1615
Cervantes writes *Don
Quixote.*

1632
Rembrandt paints
'The Anatomy
Lesson'.

1643
At the age of five
Louis XIV becomes
King of France.

The Baroque period, with its
extravagant displays of splendour,
produced a very distinctive type of
horse which corresponded exactly
to the style and taste of the upper
levels of society of that time.
Although compact and strong it
still managed to look very elegant.
Its body was rounded, its head
long and striking, and the profile
of its nose slightly convex. It
carried its strong neck high, had a
broad chest and a rounded
powerful croup, rather short but
strong, well-defined legs and small
hooves. In short its Berber
ancestry was unmistakable. This
type of horse was being bred in
Andalusia at the time of the
Moors, who, using Berber horses
as a basis, then cross-bred with
ancient Spanish and Arab breeds.
Very soon the breed was taken to
Naples, and to Portugal where it
was evolved into the Altèr Real
breed. During the Baroque period
the nobility of Europe tried to

outdo each other in splendid
parades and magnificent circus
spectacles, with the result that the
horses were introduced into
almost all Royal Stables. Most of
these noble stud farms then
developed their own breeds, using
the Andalusian and Neapolitans as
a basis. Some breeds which were
evolved in this way are the
Frederiksborger from Denmark,
which used to be bred for colour;
the Kladruber, a particularly hardy

horse which was bred in grey and
black colouring in what is now
modern Czechoslovakia; and the
famous Lipizzaners from the Karst
region in modern Yugoslavia.

Not many traces remain of these
Baroque horses which were once
so sought after: the modern
Andalusian has marked Arab
qualities; most of the
Frederiksborgers are of the
modern sporting type; few
Kladrubers and Altèr Reals are

*1 Louis XIV, after a
painting by the Court
painter Pierre Mignard
(le Romain, 1612 to
1695). It is hardly
credible however that the
French King would use
a leopard skin instead of
a saddle for dressage
exercises.*

*2 Diego de Silva y
Velazquez (c. 1599 to
1660) was Spain's
greatest Baroque painter.
This painting depicts
Philip IV on a
magnificent Andalusian
parade stallion of the
type which was much
sought after throughout
Europe.*

*3 Catherine II (the
Great) on a grey of
Spanish descent, depicted
by her Danish Court
painter, Vigilius
Erichsen.*

*4 This is how William
Cavendish, the Duke of
Newcastle, who was
driven out of England,
had himself portrayed on
the title page of his book
the* Art of Riding. *The
engraving is the work of
a pupil of Rubens
named Diepenbecke.*

*5 Queen Isabella, the
wife of Philip IV of
Spain, by Velazquez.*

1650
The Taj Majal in Agra is completed after taking twenty years to build.

1658
Death of Oliver Cromwell.

1675
Work begins on the Invalides in Paris and on St Paul's Cathedral in London.

1710
The porcelain factory in Meissen is founded.

1715
G. D. Fahrenheit invents the mercury thermometer.

Sala Terrana in Belvedere Palace in Vienna built by Lucas von Hildebrandt between 1721 and 1723.

1731
Death of Daniel Defoe (Robinson Crusoe).

1749
Birth of Johann Wolfgang Goethe.

bred now. Only the Lipizzaners are still bred in any numbers in Austria, Yugoslavia, Hungary and Rumania.

Although Baroque horses were to be found in the English Royal Stables at this time, and the classical school, which had spread there from Italy during the Renaissance, had its adherents, the English, always enthusiasts for sport and gambling, were more interested in hunting and racing.

While the breeders on the continent were concerned with breeding horses with well curved necks, well shaped rumps and a high knee action, and capable of doing the 'Spanish walk', the British selected the fastest horses for breeding and created the unique breed of the English Thoroughbred. Although a product of the Baroque, it is a departure from everything associated with that period.

The revival of the classical art of riding by the Neapolitan Grisone during the Renaissance could not have happened at a more favourable time. The cadenced and affected behaviour, with 'airs on and above the ground', was ideally suited to the pompous style of the Baroque which immediately followed the Renaissance. Throughout Europe schools sprang up based on the ideas fostered by Grisone and his successor Giovanni Pignatelli, and at these select academies for the offspring of the nobility, the art of classical riding played a central role. Among a multitude of teachers, three were outstanding: Antoine de Pluvinel, William Cavendish (Duke of Newcastle) and Georg Engelhard von Löhneysen. These three educators and riding instructors published voluminous works which contributed to their lasting fame. Undoubtedly the most famous of them all was Pluvinel, one of whose pupils was King Louis XIII of France. The following pages are devoted to his work, for which Crispin de Passe produced some marvellous illustrations.

Cavendish was apparently the only Englishman to write about the art of classical riding before the twentieth century, but his riding school was in Antwerp, not in England. He used bridle reins and a cavesson to help him bend the horse's neck into the desired position, and was such a fanatical advocate of collected gaits that he not only galloped on the spot but even did so backwards! Cavendish was able to achieve amazing results with his horses, but unfortunately these bore no relationship to the teachings of Xenophon.

The German Löhneysen adhered much more closely to the school of the Italian Grisone, but like Pluvinel he used much more humane methods. An equerry of the princely stables at Wolfenbüttel, he built his own printing works in order to publish his comprehensive book.

THE TURKS

1543
Death of Copernicus,
physician, lawyer,
astronomer and
presenter of the
heliocentric view of
the world.

1564 to 1642
The Italian scientist
Galileo Galilei.

1602
The Dutch found
colonies in South
Africa.

1603
The French settle in
Canada.

1612
The Dutch found New
Amsterdam (New
York).

1616
Death of William
Shakespeare.

In the course of its history Europe was continually plagued by hordes of horsemen from the East who came to pillage and murder. The most notorious of these were the soldiers of Attila, the leader of the Huns, and those of Genghis Khan, the Mongol, who were described as having greasy hair, walrus moustaches, and an odour of sour mare's milk. The Turks were the last of these 'scourges of God'. For over 150 years they were invincible, having not only better artillery but, most important of all, far superior horses.

By 1300 the Ottoman Turks — as they were called until 1920 — had separated themselves from the Seljuk sultanate and begun to spread out. In 1356 they first trod on European soil in the Balkans. A hundred years later, thanks to their 'modern' cannon, they conquered Constantinople and brought an end to the Byzantine Empire. Around 1512 they began their war against the Mamelukes, and were victorious. By conquering Syria and Egypt they gained control over the homeland of the finest horses of all. The Turks already possessed excellent riding horses — comparatively large, noble-blooded, tough, fast animals which apparently originated in Turkestan and were doubtless closely related to the Arab breed. In Syria and Egypt,

however, they now had access to the classical Arabs, the noblest breed of all.

Excellent riders endowed with acrobatic agility, the Turks waged war from the backs of their horses, shooting a hail of arrows at their enemies. They also had an extraordinarily intimate relationship with their animals. In the seventeenth century the hippologist Buskepius wrote that 'the gentleness of the Turkish horses is unsurpassed and their obedience to their masters and grooms is admirable. This is because the animals are always treated with great kindness. . . . Young foals are taken into the houses and cleaned, combed and petted as if they were children. . . . They are never beaten and the stable boys who look after them are as gentle as the masters. This treatment naturally produces animals which are very devoted,

obedient and easy to teach . . .'

The Ottoman Empire, then at its height, was protected by an army which had the fastest and hardiest horses. It controlled Mesopotamia in the east, Arabia and parts of North Africa in the south and extended to Hungary in the north. The tide did not turn until 1683 when the Turks tried to take Vienna. They were beaten by the western artillery, which in the interim period had become technically far superior, and from this moment the Ottoman Empire started to decline.

Horses from the Turkish army were much sought after as booty. During the seemingly endless years of Turkish dominance Europeans were seldom able to acquire Arab, Syrian or Turkestan stallions. Although anyone in the West with any sort of social pretensions would insist on riding a stallion, the Turks almost always

CONTERFACTVR WIE DIE HAVPTSTAD WIEN IN ÖSTERREICH VOM TVRCKEN IST BELEGERT GEWEST. ANNO. 1529.

1 The Turkish Grand Vizier, Ahmed Pasha, after a copper engraving by Paulus Fürst, c. 1665.

2 Jan III Sobieski became King of Poland after his victory over the Turks at Chotin in 1673. Ten years later he helped to raise the siege in Vienna.

3 In 1529 Vienna was unsuccessfully besieged by Suleiman the Magnificent. (Wood-cut from the Historical Museum in Vienna.) In 1683 the Turks made another unsuccessful attempt. Following this the Ottoman Empire began to decline.

4 Turks fighting in the Balkans in 1577.

5 The Turks loved to deck their horses out in magnificent trappings.

6 A Turkish rider with a spear. After a wood-cut by Niklas Stever, 1529.

4

1619
Dutch found Batavia on Java.

1625
French settle the Antilles.

1630 to 1650
Building of the Taj Majal in Agra.

1638
Death of the Flemish painter Pieter Breughel the Younger.

1643
Tasman discovers southern New Zealand and the Fiji Islands.

1660
Death of the Spanish painter Diego Rodriguez Velazquez.

1661
Work begins on the park of the palace at Versailles.

1664
The English conquer New Amsterdam (New York).

1669
Death of the Dutch painter Rembrandt (Harmensz van Rijn).

1685
Venetian bomb destroys the Parthenon which is being used by the Turks as a magazine.

1686
War breaks out between the English and French in Canada.

5

rode mares, often with a foal at foot. And they cherished their animals like life itself. Only rarely would a Turkish dealer sell a stallion and even then he would be unlikely to part with a first class animal. As the Ottoman Empire began to decline, however, more and more horses fell into the hands of the Imperial troops. Aleppo became an open trading city where there were plenty of Oriental horses for sale, among them first class Arabs from the Arabian plateau.

Almost a thousand years earlier the Islamic horsemen had taken Arab and Berber horses across the narrow strait of Gibraltar to Europe, where these animals had contributed a great deal to the breeding of horses. The Oriental horses which reached the western world through the Turks were to have an even greater influence.

Constantly evolving military tactics no longer required the heavy war horses of the Middle Ages. Instead, fast mobile animals were needed. As Arab and Turkmene breeds were the best recipe for providing them, Oriental horses were introduced into all the European breeds. Oriental blood was particularly highly concentrated in the racehorses bred in England.

Generally the mares on which the breeding of English Thoroughbreds was based are described as native ponies, but their origins are confused and they appear to have a larger dose of Oriental blood than British pony blood. Berber, Arab and Turkish stallions and mares had already been introduced into the British breeding scene by the end of the seventeenth and beginning of the eighteenth centuries, i.e., the time of the three great founding stallions — Godolphin Barb, Byerley Turk and Darley Arabian.

6

131

CONTEMPORARY EVENTS

1715
Louis XV becomes King of France.

1724
Birth of the German philosopher Immanuel Kant.

1725
Catherine I becomes Empress of Russia (until 1727).

1727
George II becomes King of Great Britain. In America the Quakers demand the abolition of the slave trade.

1730
Anna Ivanovna becomes Empress of Russia.

1732
Birth of Joseph Haydn.

1740
Maria Theresa becomes Queen of Bohemia and Hungary and Archduchess of Austria.

1741
Elizabeth becomes Russian Empress.

1744
Death of the Swedish scientist Anders Celsius who invented the centigrade thermometer.

1745
Franz I becomes Holy Roman Emperor.

FREDERICK THE GREAT

'. . . His Majesty orders all commanders of the cavalry regiments to direct their energy, hopes and endeavours towards making the common man into a capable, efficient rider.'

Frederick the Great had good reason for giving instructions like this, for when he ascended the Prussian throne in 1740 he inherited a useless cavalry force, criticized as unable to ride at an even tempo across smooth ground let alone on rough. Frederick's reform of the cavalry has earned him the right to be called the first modern cavalry leader.

Frederick the Great was born in Berlin in 1712. His despotic father Frederick William I made his life a misery and in 1730 he tried to flee to England, but was caught and imprisoned in the fortress of Küstrin where he was made to witness the execution of his closest friend Lieutenant von Katte. He was reconciled with his father a year later, however, and on Frederick William's death on 31 May 1740 became king as Frederick II.

During his forty years' reign he

1 Equestrian statue of Frederick the Great in the park of Sanssouci Palace, the summer residence of the Prussian Kings. This is where he died on 17 August 1786 at the age of 74.

made Prussia into a great European power, at the same time giving his people more rights, more educational possibilities and a higher living standard. As the king he appeared not so much in the customary role of demi-god, but rather as the good servant of his people.

2 Frederick the Great enters Berlin after the conclusion of the peace between Austria and Prussia at Hubertusburg. After a contemporary etching by J. L. Rugendas.

By December of the year he ascended the throne Frederick had initiated the War of the Austrian Succession. During this campaign it became abundantly clear to the Prussian King that the Prussian cavalry was far inferior to the Austrian, but among his own men he discovered one with whom he would create the most powerful cavalry of his time.

Friedrich Wilhelm von Seydlitz was a cavalry officer under Colonel von Rochow. He had made himself conspicuous by his wild, foolhardy riding escapades and was a real thorn in the flesh of Rochow, who was a devotee of classical dressage. One day, therefore, Seydlitz received an order to defend a village, although obviously hopelessly outnumbered. He put up an extremely skilful defence and only as a last resort did he try to break out on

3 Troops parading in front of Frederick the Great. After a contemporary copper engraving by D. Chodowiecki.

4 Frederick at the Battle of Leuthen where on 5 December 1757 he gained a conclusive victory over the Austrians. Exactly a month before, thanks to Seydlitz his cavalry commander, Frederick was able to pit twice as many cavalry against the French at Rossbach, the most famous battle of the Seven Years' War.

5 Ziethen Hussars from the time of Frederick the Great. After a watercolour from the eighteenth century.

1750
Death of Johann Sebastian Bach.

1752
Benjamin Franklin, American statesman, and both physicist and printer, invents the lightning rod.

1759
Death of George Frederick Händel. Birth of Friedrich Schiller.

1760
George III becomes King of Great Britain.

1762
Peter III becomes Russian Czar. After his assassination Catherine II (the Great) becomes Empress.

1765
Joseph II becomes Holy Roman Emperor.

1770
James Cook discovers Australia.

1771
Gustavus III becomes King of Sweden.

1774
Louis XVI becomes King of France.

1778
Death of Francois de Voltaire (picture), and of Jean Jacques Rousseau.

horseback with the few survivors. His horse was shot, he was taken prisoner and imprisoned in the Hungarian fortress of Raab.

But Rochow's triumph was shortlived, for Frederick heard of the incident and had Seydlitz exchanged for a much higher ranking Austrian officer. Soon Frederick promoted him to cavalry captain and appointed him a squadron commander of the Trebnitz Hussars.

The poor performance of the Prussian cavalry around 1740 was not the result of a lack of interest on the part of Frederick William, but was apparently due to the one-sided training which was given to the cuirassiers, dragoons and horses.

Frederick the Great's father, in fact, doubled the number of cavalry and also created Trakehnen, a military stud which became world famous. Six hundred people were employed to build the stud, and for six years they worked on clearing and draining the grounds which

stretched over an area of about 24,000 acres. The first buildings were not erected until 1732 when the first 1100 (!) horses arrived at the Royal Trakehnen Stud.

By Frederick the Great's time horses from this stud were already setting new distance records. Under Frederick William I the

Prussian cavalry did improve but the cuirassiers were still manège riders. Their horses with their arched necks were magnificent, and they could step out elegantly, but they had no conception of how to attack.

Frederick the Great soon changed all this. While retaining the basic manège exercises, in addition he instituted a tough and comprehensive course in attacking techniques. In Seydlitz he had an ideal cavalry officer for, although under his command the field exercises often resulted in frequent falls and even serious accidents, his squadron soon became famous and prospective

cavalry officers clamoured to be accepted into it.

By the time of the second Silesian War the Austrians were confronted by a vastly improved Prussian cavalry force. Shortly after the outbreak of the Seven Years' War in 1756 Seydlitz was made Commander of the entire Prussian cavalry, which even the British and French were forced to concede was far superior to any other.

133

NAPOLEON

1776
Benjamin Franklin
with Thomas
Jefferson and John
Adams draw up the
American
Constitution.
Building of La Scala
opera house begins in
Milan.

1789
George Washington
becomes the first US
President.
Start of the French
Revolution; on 14 July
the Bastille stormed.

1790
Goethe returns from
Italy and writes
Torquato Tasso.
Death of Benjamin
Franklin.

The constant threat of war at the end of the eighteenth century and beginning of the nineteenth gave a great boost to the horse-breeding industry. The armies of Austria and Prussia, and those of the British and Russians, had their own well-stocked studs, which were able to keep up with the huge demands for good cavalry horses. Napoleon, however, found at the beginning of his career as a dictator that in France the breeding of horses was in a disastrous condition, and during his first campaigns he had to give priority to the taking of horses as booty. In Switzerland alone Napoleon's soldiers captured some ten thousand horses *en passant*. They cleared out, 'to the last foal's tail', the stables of the farmers and small breeders as well as the stud belonging to the monastery at Einsiedeln.

Despite his victories, Napoleon's campaigns to Egypt and Syria (from 1798 to 1799) brought him no strategic gains, but the French cavalry were able to obtain many of the first class Oriental horses for which their commander had a special preference.

The revolution put an end to stud farms in France. The numerous Royal Studs were abolished, as was everything — good or bad — which had been part of the *ancien régime*.

When in November 1799 Napoleon became First Consul he ordered seven studs to be reopened and organized an intensive breeding programme to produce horses suitable for the cavalry.

Over the next few years he founded six more national studs,

1 On the way to Italy to fight the Austrians, Napoleon, in an unexpected move, took his troops across the Alps over the Great St Bernard Pass. Painting by Jacques Louis David, 1810.

2 After the defeat of the Prussians at Jena and Auerstädt, Napoleon entered Berlin through the Brandenburg Gate on 27 October 1806.

thirty depots for stallions, and three riding schools. The famous cavalry school in Saumur, which was founded in 1771 and closed down during the Revolution was not, however, reopened until 1815.

In 1806, two years after Napoleon had had himself crowned Emperor, there were about 1500 stud stallions in the Haras Impériaux. Some of these were former State stallions which had been bought back from the farmers; the rest were Arabs from Egypt and Syria.

Napoleon never had a close affinity with his horses. He always rode beautiful animals, but the fact that he had a particular preference for grey Arab stallions probably

3 On 9 March 1796 Napoleon married Marie Rose Joséphine Tascher de la Pagerie, the 'beautiful Joséphine', widow of General Beauharnais who had been executed

7 Battle of Eylau against the Russians and Prussians on 8 February 1807. Painting by J. Gross.

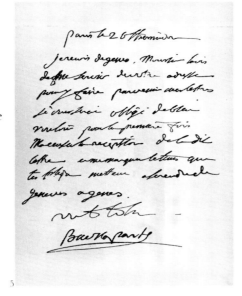

reflected his need to be admired rather than any deep love of horses.

The Emperor's most famous horse, Marengo, was part of the booty taken from Abukir in Egypt. Like many desert Arabs it had a height at the withers of only a little over 140 cm. Napoleon is said to have taken this horse on all his campaigns that followed the battle against the Austrians at Marengo. The stallion is sometimes spoken of with the same admiration as Bucephalus, the famous horse ridden by Alexander the Great in so many of his campaigns, and in fact Napoleon was still riding Marengo in 1815 at Waterloo, his last battle.

Afterwards the stallion fell into the hands of the British, along with Napoleon's travelling carriage and its six coach horses, and were put on display in London. The coach horses were then sold by public auction, and the coach was put in Madame Tussaud's Wax Museum where unfortunately it was lost in the fire which destroyed a large part of the gallery in 1925.

Marengo was bought by Lieutenant General J. J. W. Angerstein and put into his Thoroughbred stud at New

Barnes, but Marengo's descendants apparently had little success on the turf. The racing calendar of 1831 mentions one of his sons, who took part in the Spring meeting held at Newmarket but was not placed. Marengo died in 1832 at the amazing age of thirty-five years. His skeleton can be viewed in the National Army Museum in London.

As well as this legendary stallion Napoleon owned over two hundred saddle horses, along with a large number of coach horses, several of them grey Arab stallions

from Egypt and Syria. Like Marengo many were named after famous battles: Pyramid, Jaffa, Wagram, Austerlitz, etc. His stallion Fayoum had considerable influence on the horses bred at the Zweibrücken stud which Napoleon reopened in 1806, and in 1811 this horse was allowed to exchange the battle field for the stud farm.

Napoleon's stallion Vizir is said to have carried his master from Paris to Moscow and back. Perhaps the Emperor did ride Vizir during the most important battles of the Russian campaign, but on the immense stretches in between he preferred the comfort of the travelling carriage or, in winter, the sledge.

At least nineteen grey stallions are said to have been killed while Napoleon was riding them, and this could well be true as over a period of twenty years he took part in about sixty battles. It would be impossible to relate the history of all these horses, but the grey Arab stallion has become a permanent part of the Napoleonic legend.

From 1796 on Napoleon achieved a succession of victories which helped him to attain an apparently unassailable supremacy in Europe, a spread of power which was not halted until 1808. Napoleon wanted to 'liberate' Spain but could find no effective means to combat the religious fanaticism with which the Spaniards, particularly the partisans, defended themselves. That cost the Grande Armée about 300,000 men.

135

1 Again and again throughout the Russian winter the Don Cossacks on their seemingly indestructible horses, made surprise attacks on Napoleon's army as it retreated.

2 On the retreat from Russia at the end of November 1812 the Grande Armée was completely routed at the river Beresina.

3 The combined forces defeated Napoleon at the Battle of Leipzig 16 to 19 October 1813.

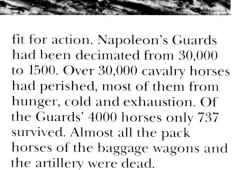

Over the following four years, by a series of strategic and diplomatic chess-like moves, Napoleon was again able to consolidate his position of supremacy, until there remained only one obstacle to the implementation of his idea for a new order in Europe — Czar Alexander of Russia. In order to make him more amenable Napoleon chose those tactics which had brought him success in almost all similar cases, believing that two or three defeats in battle would instil the necessary respect into his opponent.

When he embarked on his Russian campaign, and crossed the River Nieman on 24 June 1812, Napoleon had over 500,000 men, 20,000 horsedrawn baggage carts and 1000 cannon. His cavalry had a supply of 43,000 horses. At the end of November, after the retreat from Moscow back across the Beresina, the Grande Armée consisted of only 9000 soldiers still fit for action. Napoleon's Guards had been decimated from 30,000 to 1500. Over 30,000 cavalry horses had perished, most of them from hunger, cold and exhaustion. Of the Guards' 4000 horses only 737 survived. Almost all the pack horses of the baggage wagons and the artillery were dead.

Yet the catastrophic losses of the Russian campaign had no effect on Napoleon's delusions of grandeur. He hurried back to Paris, where he arrived on 5 December 1812, and in May 1813 successfully waged two further battles against the combined forces of the Russians and the Prussians. By this time East Prussia alone, once a flourishing horse breeding area, had lost 175,000 horses in the Napoleonic wars.

The end came that same year with the Battle of Leipzig and the invasion of France by the allied Russian, Austrian and Prussian

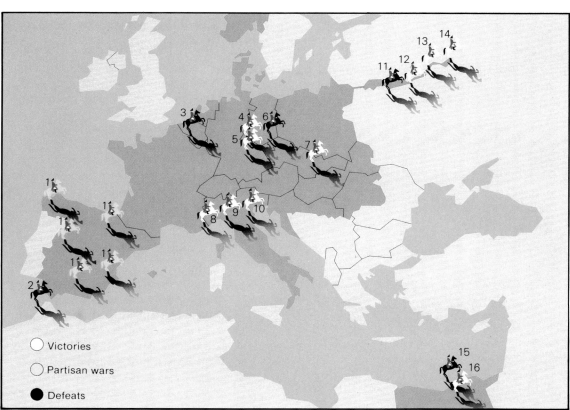

○ Victories
○ Partisan wars
● Defeats

1 Spain, March to July 1808.

2 Naval battle at Trafalgar, 21.10.1805.

3 Waterloo, 18.6.1815.

4 Auerstadt, 8.10.1806.

5 Jena, 14.10.1806.

6 Leipzig, 16 to 19.10.1813.

7 Austerlitz, 2.12.1805.

8 Arcola, 17.11.1796.

9 Milan, 14.4.1796.

10 Marengo, 14.6.1800.

11 Studzianska on the Beresina, 28.11.1812.

12 Smolenzk, 17.8.1812.

13 Borodino, 7.9.1812.

14 Moscow, 15.9.1812.

15 Naval battle at Aboukir, 1.8.1798.

16 Cairo, 30.6.1798.

4 Napoleon surrounded by his generals.

4

Towards evening Napoleon launched another attack. At first he achieved some successes against the Prussians, but then lost two-thirds of his men against the British.

In the middle of this disaster Blücher arrived with reinforcements and sealed the fate of the French. Around 45,000 soldiers and seventy-five per cent of the horses lay dead or wounded on the battlefield.

Barely a month later Napoleon was banished to the island of St Helena where he died on 5 May

1803
Friedrich Hölderlin becomes insane.

1805
Death of Schiller.

1806
Arc de Triomphe built in Paris.

1809
Death of Haydn. James Madison becomes third President of the US.

1809
The *Tales of the Brothers Grimm* appear. Kleist commits suicide.

1810-1813
Goya creates his 'Disasters of War', 85 pictures on the cruelty of the Spanish War of Independence against Napoleon.

1813
Births of Richard Wagner and Giuseppe Verdi.

1814
George Stephenson builds the first steam locomotive.

5

6

5 Waterloo, the final battle, fought on 18 June 1815, from which after sixteen hours the British, with the support of the Prussians, emerged the victors.

6 On 15 July 1815 Napoleon was banished to the island of St Helena. Here he dictated his memoirs to his faithful General Gourgaud.

forces. In 1814 Napoleon abdicated and retired to the island of Elba, but in March 1815 returned to Paris and once again attempted to take the reins of power.

At Waterloo on 18 June 1815 Napoleon fought his last battle. At this encounter, described as the last great cavalry battle, the Duke of Wellington had some 13,000 horses under his command; the Napoleonic cavalry consisted of over 16,000 horsemen. Although the British made use of rockets, their latest acquisition, the course of the battle was wholly determined by the cavalry.

About midday on this fateful day, Napoleon began his attack with the storming of Mont St Jean. The British put up such a fierce defence that after three hours his cavalry were forced to retreat.

1821 at the age of fifty-two. The cause of death was probably stomach ulcers, but he may have been poisoned.

137

AMERICAN INDIANS AND THEIR HORSES

CONTEMPORARY EVENTS

1499
The Florentine traveller Amerigo Vespucci names the continent of America and produces its first maps.

1518
Hernando Cortez lands in Mexico.

1585
Founding of the English colony of Virginia in North America.

1612
Founding of New Amsterdam (New York).

1643
Connecticut, New Haven, Plymouth and Massachusetts Bay form the New England Federation.

1664
The English take New Amsterdam (New York) from the Dutch.

1672
Isaac Newton uses the prism to show that white light can be separated into the colours of the spectrum and invents the reflector telescope.

1755 to 1763
Franco-British Colonial war in America.

1776
The Congress in Philadelphia publishes the Colonies' Declaration of Independence.

The charred bones of horses found in geological deposits 7000 to 10,000 years old indicate that the early American Indians in North America were acquainted with the prehistoric horses of the New World. It is unlikely that they rode them, but like the Europeans of the Ice Age they would probably have hunted and eaten them. When these animals became extinct, the Indians had no further contact with horses until the Spaniards and then other Europeans settled in America thousands of years later.

The peaceful tribes of the north and east lived mainly from agriculture and fishing, and as they had practically no contact with them, these new animals had little effect on their lives. The opposite was true, however, of the warlike Plains Indians of the West who were nomadic hunters, and the Apaches in particular are said to have taken to riding like ducks to water. Soon the Navahos, the Pawnees and the Comanches also learnt to ride and, in time, some of the pastoral tribes discovered the taste of freedom which horses brought into their lives. The Blackfeet Indians were originally farmers, but the horse turned them into hunters. Soon they no longer built villages of wooden huts but set up their camps wherever they happened to be.

Their whole culture was altered by the horse which, as well as a means of transport and a status symbol, became an article of value and cultural significance. The chiefs took their favourite horses with them to the grave in the manner of the various ancient horse people.

The Plains Indians desired horses greatly, for they very quickly discovered that animal's value in their struggle against the white intruders and in the hunt for bison. From the seventeenth century on there were, among the buffalo herds many wild Mustangs which, using leather lassos and a great deal of skill, the Indians were able to catch, very often choosing the pregnant mares which were slower and had less stamina, and also offered the possible bonus of a foal. We are told that the Mustangs were broken in immediately after capture, while still suffering from shock, a procedure for which the Indians showed extraordinary talent, and often within an hour of capture they were able to lead the animals quietly away, submissive and obedient. Nevertheless,

1 Navaho Indians by H. B. Möllhausen, 1853. The Navahos and the Apaches were the first Indians to obtain Spanish horses. Most Indians were excellent bareback riders but when they could get hold of a saddle they valued the advantages it gave them.

2 Blackfeet Indians, after a picture by the Swiss Karl Bodmer (1809 to 1893), considered by experts to be one of the most eminent painters of Indian life.

1789
George Washington becomes first President of the US. Proclamation of the Constitution.

1793
Founding of Washington, capital city of the US.

1797
John Adams becomes President of the US.

1801
Thomas Jefferson becomes President of US.

1809
James Madison becomes President of the US.

1810 to 1849
Frédéric Chopin.

1813 to 1901
Giuseppe Verdi.

1817
James Monroe becomes President of the US.

1837 to 1901
Queen Victoria of Britain.

1845 to 1848
Texas, Oregon, and California become States of the US.

1860
Abraham Lincoln becomes President of the US.

1866
Andrew Johnson, President of the US, abolishes slavery.

1897
William MacKinley becomes President of the US.

despite their skill, this method of obtaining riding animals was an exhausting process, to be avoided if there were alternatives. Raids on the Spanish haciendas in the frontier area were particularly popular, for the owners were not in a position to put up much resistance and the Indians were able to take a great many animals. The main advantage was that

these horses were tame and often already broken in. Moreover, there were always fresh supplies, as the colonial government imported thousands of horses from Spain and sent them to the settlers. Only under these conditions were the latter prepared to remain in the dangerous frontier area.

The Indians were extremely talented natural horsemen and able to keep control of their mounts even under the most difficult conditions. They rode either bareback or on a blanket which was firmly tied on. The

breeding of horses, however, had apparently no place in their restless mentality and the Nez Percé who settled in the Palouse Valley in Idaho were the only Indian tribe to breed horses both systematically and successfully. Like most Indians they preferred coloured horses and chose to breed animals with definite spotted patterns. These were formerly very common among the Spanish horses (see chapter on Breeds under Appaloosa, page 31). When the Nez Percé selected horses for breeding they naturally chose the most beautiful animals, but it would seem they also took account of the animals' hardiness, speed, stamina and character, for these are the modern characteristics of the Appaloosa breed. In 1877 the Nez Percé were overwhelmed by the US Cavalry, despite a desperate attempt to flee on horseback during which they, together with their women and children, had covered 2500 kilometres within eleven weeks. Some two hundred Appaloosa horses fell into the hands of the white men then. These beautiful animals proved first class horses. Their breed has found many devotees and now totals around 150,000 animals.

3 Sioux painting of the Battle of Little Big Horn, June 1876. The Sioux chief, Crazy Horse, is in the middle of the picture. This was the only successful battle that the Indians — Sioux and Cheyenne — fought against the US cavalry.

4 Kills Two, an Oglala Sioux who painted this picture, was a famous Indian artist.

5 This picture by Karl Bodmer shows that painter himself (far right) and his companion Maximilian Prince of Wied (second from right) with a group of Minitari Indians at Fort Clark. The symbols painted on the grey horse's coat indicate that the animal played a role in the cult customs.

139

1791
Death of Wolfgang
Amadeus Mozart.

1804
Death of German
philosopher
Immanuel Kant.

1809
Death of composer
Joseph Haydn.

1812
Birth of Charles
Dickens.

1813
Birth of Richard
Wagner.

1827
Heinrich Heine writes
the *Book of Songs*.

1830
Honoré de Balzac
writes *The Human
Comedy*.

1832
Death of Johann
Wolfgang von Goethe.

1849
Death of Edgar Allan
Poe.

THE UNITED STATES CAVALRY

The legendary US Cavalry, which more than any other military unit has been glorified by the cinema, was never a cavalry in the European sense of the word, i.e., one which attacked with drawn sword. Swords were useful for cutting grass and chopping wood; commanders used them to signal their men, but in battle they were only drawn as a last resort in a seemingly hopeless situation. Tactically it was more reliable to dismount at some distance from the enemy line and to shoot at him rather than to try to run him through from horseback, a traditional manoeuvre which survived in Europe even after the invention of the hand gun.

In the War of Independence (1775 to 1783) which marked the founding of the United States, the cavalry was given only a secondary role to play, even though mounted soldiers were far more suitable for covering the vast distances of North America. George Washington was an infantry man through and through. He deployed very few mounted soldiers, using them mainly for service as couriers and for reconnaissance. Many commanders never used the horses placed at their disposal in fighting, but only when large numbers of troops had to change their positions. Also the cavalry had had almost no training, although there was the Connecticut Light Horse, a cavalry troop which had been modelled on the European pattern. Its

1 *The last phase of the battle at Little Big Horn in which the Indians inflicted a bloody defeat on the US Cavalry and General Custer was killed (25 June 1876). Painting by the Oglala Sioux, Amos Bad Heart Bull.*

2 *In the first year of the Civil War (1861) Union troops were defeated at Bull Run, to the south-west of Washington, by the Southern States' cavalry, most of whom were mounted on first class Kentucky saddle horses.*

members were mainly recruited from the well-to-do levels of society and considered themselves much superior to the infantry. After their dashing training exercises they left the stable work and guard duty to the infantry, and went off to look for adventure in feminine company. They gave, however, only a brief performance at Washington's headquarters and were then sent back to Connecticut without having done much at all for the independence of the US.

The cavalry played a much more important role in the Mexican War (1846 to 1848), when the Mexicans were defeated and forced to cede an enormous tract of land in New

1854
Florence Nightingale
organizes a nursing
service to help the
soldiers.
Gottfried Keller writes
Green Henry.

1855
D. E. Hughes detects
electromagnetic waves
and contributes to the
development of the
teletypewriter.
Great Exhibition in
Paris.

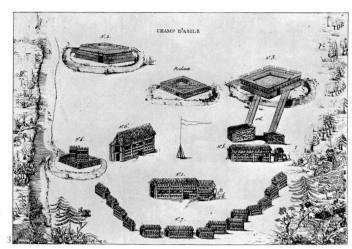

3 In 1818 French Bonapartists built the colony of Champs d'Asile on the Trinity River in what was then Mexican Texas, but in spite of the defences were forced to abandon it after a year.

4 Painting by Betsy Ross dated 1776, the year of the birth of both the US and the US Cavalry.

Mexico and Texas to the US. Since the War of Independence the Americans had not had to wage any major wars, but the number of mounted troops had been enlarged and improved, mainly to keep the Indians in check. By 1837 there were still about 50,000 Indians living in the east of the Mississippi, although both their living space and their rights were being continually reduced. About the same number had earlier moved across the Mississippi on to the giant plains of the West where there were already about 230,000 Plains Indians. Troops of dragoons formally controlled the Indians from about a dozen advanced bases, and for an amazingly long time there were no serious incidents simply because the Indians always believed the promises made by the white man's mediators.

When the Civil War (1861 to 1865) broke out, the heyday of the cavalry was already past in Europe. Even in the US many highly placed military men and politicians wanted to make drastic reductions in the cavalry and use it only for courier and reconnaissance duties.

Yet during the Civil War 272 cavalry regiments were deployed by the North along with 2144 infantry regiments, while the South had over 642 infantry and 137 cavalry regiments. There were over ten thousand skirmishes in this war and the cavalry played a major part in many of them.

The US Cavalry rode horses of the most varied origins, among them many tamed Mustangs, but one breed very soon proved superior to all others. This was the American Saddle Horse which had been developed in Kentucky and Virginia during the Colonial Period. By the outbreak of the Civil War there were already enough of the breed available to supply a large part of the Southern States' Cavalry, which in consequence was superbly mounted. The North on the other hand had the Morgan breed, a small but very fast and tough horse with plenty of stamina. Many historians maintain that the Morgan horse was a decisive factor in the eventual victory of the Union troops.

At the end of the Civil War the West was finally settled, a situation which resulted in the Indian Wars, the blackest chapter in the history of the US. The Indians, mounted on their tough hardy ponies, were incomparable riders and brave fighters but, despite their great numbers, in the long term they had no chance of successfully defending their land against the Europeans, mainly because there was almost no liaison between the individual tribes. Less than fifty years after the Civil War there was not one Indian left who could describe himself as genuinely free. In the final conquering of the West the US Cavalry was the decisive instrument of a completely unscrupulous 'civilizing' policy. Very few of the officers and soldiers were capable of assessing the situation properly and simply carried out the orders from Washington.

1859
Charles Darwin publishes his revolutionary theory of evolution. Death of the German naturalist Alexander von Humboldt.

1860
Death of the German philosopher Arthur Schopenhauer.

1862
Abraham Lincoln, President of the US, tries to persuade Congress to free the negroes.

1867
F. M. Dostoyevsky writes Crime and Punishment. Karl Marx writes Das Kapital.

1875
Death of Danish author Hans Christian Andersen.

1876
Mark Twain writes Tom Sawyer.

1879
The Russian Nikolai Prjevalsky discovers Prjevalsky's Horse.

1893 to 1896
North Pole Expedition led by Fridtjof Nansen.

1901
W. C. Röntgen receives the Nobel prize for the discovery of X-rays.

141

THE GREAT CATTLE DRIVES

1867
Feodor M.
Dostoyevsky writes
Crime and Punishment.

1869
Suez Canal is opened.

1879
Nikolai Prjevalsky
discovers Prjevalsky's
Horse.
Death of Charles
Dickens.
Death of Alexandre
Dumas.

1870-1871
Franco-Prussian War.
Proclamation of the
Second Reich.

1875
Death of Georges
Bizet after the
production of *Carmen.*
Death of Hans
Christian Andersen.

1877
T. A. Edison invents
the phonograph.

1879
Peter Tchaikovsky
writes *Eugene Onegin.*

1883
Death of Karl Marx.

In 1523 the Spaniard Villalobes brought the first eight cattle to the New World with the intention of using them to start a farm in Mexico. He was extremely successful. Seventeen years later Coronado took 300 head of cattle with him on his ill-fated expedition in search of the legendary 'Seven Golden Cities'. These beasts were intended to furnish him with a continuous supply of fresh meat, but in the high country of the north of Mexico the company was caught in a fierce thunderstorm which caused the cattle to stampede in panic. Afterwards Coronado's men were able to find only a few animals — the rest had run off.

Three hundred years later the number of wild cattle in Texas was estimated to be about five million. By 1850 there were about six cattle for every Texan. These could simply be caught as required, and there was no need for anyone to go hungry, but the abundance of meat was difficult to convert into cash. Although the value of a steer ready for slaughter was only about three dollars, cities on the east coast and hungry gold diggers in California would pay sixty to eighty dollars a head.

The logical conclusion was that if any money was to be made then the cattle had to be taken to where the demand was greatest. Between 1850 and 1860 mounted herdsmen, the first 'cowboys', had driven small herds to the Mississippi and embarked them there; some had even been taken to California, but the losses en route were high and the profit not worth mentioning.

The true era of the cowboys, and with it one of the most fascinating chapters in the history of the US, began in 1866 with the first great cattle drives. Over 250,000 longhorn cattle were driven from Texas in the south across the Red River northwards, sometimes for stretches of 2000 kilometres at a time. By 1877 Joe McCoy had already founded Abilene (the first and most famous of all the cattle towns), in an

1 The cowboy feared nothing so much as a stampede. A roll of thunder, the howl of a coyote, or even the neigh of a horse could cause panic among the half-wild longhorn cattle. It could take a horse and rider days to calm the herds down again, a highly dangerous task.

2 The separating off and catching of individual cattle demanded skill from the cowboy and active co-operation from the horse.

3 The most important trails which led from Texas to the cattle towns on the railway lines in the north.

Federal States
1 *California*
2 *Nevada*
3 *Oregon*
4 *Idaho*
5 *Washington*
6 *Montana*
7 *Wyoming*
8 *North Dakota*
9 *South Dakota*
10 *Nebraska*
11 *Kansas*
12 *Arizona*
13 *New Mexico*
14 *Utah*
15 *Colorado*
16 *Oklahoma*
17 *Texas*

18 *Arkansas*
19 *Louisiana*
20 *Missouri*
21 *Minnesota*
22 *Iowa*
23 *Illinois*
24 *Wisconsin*

Trails
25 *Nelson Story Trail*
26 *Goodnight-Loving Trail*
27 *Western Trail*
28 *Chisholm Trail*
29 *Shawnee Trail*

Places
30 *Stanford*
31 *Virginia City*
32 *Fort Kearney*
33 *Buffalo*
34 *Casper*
35 *Fort Laramie*
36 *Cheyenne*
37 *Fort Leavenworth*
38 *Chicago*
39 *Kansas City*
40 *Sedalia*
41 *St Louis*
42 *Denver*
43 *Hayes*
44 *Ellsworth*
45 *Abilene*
46 *Dodge City*
47 *Newton*
48 *San Francisco*
49 *Santa Fe*
50 *Fort Sumner*
51 *Lincoln*
52 *Fort Becknap*
53 *Fort Worth*
54 *Dallas*
55 *San Antonio*
56 *Houston*

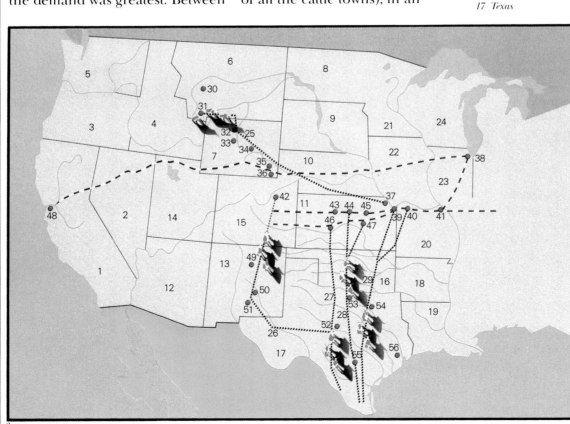

4 Cattle brands from Texas. A cattle owner's burnt-on symbol was a simple but effective means of identifying the animals, as herds so often got mixed up on the unfenced 'open range'.

5 Bloody disputes broke out between the cattle breeders when pastures were fenced in after the introduction of barbed wire.

unsettled region of Kansas which had a plentiful supply of grass and water. To transport the cattle further, McCoy had secured contracts with the Hannibal and St Jo Railway Companies, and in the same year, 35,000 cattle were driven from Texas along the Abilene Trail.

As the railroad spread westwards, new routes like the Chisholm and Panhandle Trails were opened up, along which the animals of the Texan 'cattle kings' were driven north and north-west.

The cowboy was soon glorified into a romantic hero figure, the symbol of the American West; in reality his job was extremely hard and often very dangerous. The herds sometimes consisted of over two thousand animals, travelling for months at a time across what was mostly a very raw landscape. The men were in the saddle for up to twenty hours a day. For weeks

they wore the same clothes and were out in the open in all weather, day and night, frequently under attack by Indians and professional cattle thieves. Often the difference between life and death depended not only on who could draw a gun the fastest but also on who had the fastest horse. Little wonder that the breeds of horses which developed under these conditions are some of the most robust. The period of the great cattle drives came to an end about 1890, but the horses have remained indispensable.

1883
Death of Richard Wagner.

c. 1885
Flowering of French Impressionism: Dégas, Manet, Monet, Renoir.

1886
Gottlieb Daimler inventor of the gas engine, builds the first car.

1887-1889
Building of the Eiffel Tower.

1887
First performance of Othello by Verdi.

1887
Wilhelm Busch publishes humorous tales including Max und Moritz

1888
Friedrich Nietzsche writes Ecce homo.

1890
Emil von Behring discovers a serum against diphtheria.

1914
Franz Marc completes
the picture 'Tower of
the Blue Horses'.
Marc is killed in 1916.

1914
Mahatma Gandhi
advocates policy of
non-violent resistance
to free India from the
British.

F. Sauerbruch invents
artificial limbs.

1917
Death of Count
Zeppelin.

1918
C. G. Jung publishes
his main work on
psychoanalysis.
Death of composer
Claude Debussy.
Igor Stravinsky writes
The Soldier's Tale.
Max Planck receives
the Nobel prize for
Physics.

1939
Death of Sigmund
Freud, the
psychoanalyst.

1939
John Steinbeck writes
The Grapes of Wrath.

1914 to 1918, 1939 to 1945

HORSES IN THE TWO WORLD WARS

The invention of gunpowder heralded the end of the cavalry horse. Until guns were used the cavalry had been far superior to the infantry, but soon expert marksmen were able to drive off a cavalry attack, for horses were large vulnerable targets. Yet even in the wars of this century the horse played a much greater role than might have been expected. In the South African Boer War of 1899 to 1902, for example, over 500,000 horses were used. Of these 150,000 did not survive.

Soon after the turn of the century the military made great technological advances. The means of transport were mechanized and the automatic machine gun became the devastating weapon of the infantry. At the beginning of World War One few officers authorized traditional cavalry attacks with drawn sword. In most cases the cavalry man was turned into a dragoon, i.e., a mounted infantryman who used his horse, not for attacking, but merely to help him change position quickly.

Yet in 1916, when tanks made their first terrifying appearance, there were about a million saddle horses deployed on all fronts, more than in any previous war.

Draught horses, too, were still being used in large numbers. All the cannon, for example, were drawn by horses; the lighter weight ones by six, the heavier by eight to twelve animals.

In World War One the German army had a total of fourteen million horses and the British alone lost 256,000 animals. This number would have been much higher without the British veterinary organization, which was

1 August 1914:
Dragoons moving out of
Berlin.

2 British troops
transporting artillery
munition on the road
from Ypres to Menin in
Belgium during the
battle fought near Ypres
in September 1917.

3 Mules were invaluable
for transporting the
wounded over rough
terrain.

4 Horses, too, could use gas masks to give them some protection from gas, the terrifying new weapon.

5 The great majority of the horses did not die from their wounds but from exhaustion, hunger, cold, infections or parasites. Only rarely was a horse as fortunate as the one pictured here which is being given a special bath to clear its skin of parasites.

6 Camouflage paint was used on horses too.

7 On the Eastern front: the German Wehrmacht was not, as it claimed fully mechanized. Hitler sent more than 2.75 million horses into the war.

8 Draught horses in particular were completely helpless against modern war technology. The picture shows French artillery horses after a German attack.

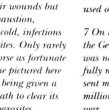

at the time a revolutionary idea. The British even had ambulance wagons for horses — large two-wheeled vehicles drawn by two horses in tandem. In France during the four years of the war over 2.5 million horses and mules were treated in the British field hospitals and seventy-eight per cent recovered.

Even in World War Two horses played an important role. The East Europeans deployed large numbers of them, and a so-called 'Don Quixote' attack made by the Polish dragoons against the German tanks became a legend. Russian tanks were always accompanied by mounted units and the Red Army deployed a total of over 3.5 million horses. Hitler was inaccurate when he led his people to believe that the Wehrmacht was full mechanized.

No fewer than 2.75 million horses took part in the war for Führer and Fatherland.

World War Two was not only tragic for people, but for horses too, who were completely helpless and at the mercy of modern technology. The war lasted more than two thousand days and on average 865 horses were killed daily in the German Wehrmacht. Around 52,000 of their horses were lost in the Battle of Stalingrad alone. In 1944 about the same number were shot by German soldiers on the orders of headquarters before they were finally able to withdraw, defeated, from the Crimean peninsula.

1940
Death of Paul Klee.

1940
Ernest Hemingway writes *For Whom The Bell Tolls*.

1940
Death of Swedish author, Selma Lagerlof (Nobel prize 1909).

1941
Bert Brecht writes *Mother Courage*.

1942
Stefan Zweig commits suicide.

1943
Jean Paul Sartre writes *The Flies*.
Hermann Hesse writes *The Glass Bead Game*.
Death of the Russian composer Sergei Rachmaninov.

1944
The painter Hans Bendel works on his studies of the anatomy of the horse.

Antoine de St Exupéry, author of *The Little Prince*, and French military pilot, shot down.

145

1 *Toy horse, England, carved in wood, painted, on iron wheels, second half of the nineteenth century.*

2 *Baroque rocking-horse, Switzerland, carved in wood, painted, c. 1800.*

3 *Horse from a merry-go-round, Vienna, carved in wood, painted, c. 1900.*

4 *Rocking-horse, England, mounted on a stand, carved in wood, painted, saddle and bridle made of leather, first half of the nineteenth century.*

5 *Rocking-horse, Switzerland, carved in wood, painted, second half of the nineteenth century.*

6 *Toy horse, southern Germany, carved in wood, painted, second half of the nineteenth century.*

7 *Rocking-horse, Switzerland, carved in wood, painted, second half of the nineteenth century.*

8 *Baroque rocking-horse, Switzerland, carved in wood, painted, c. 1800.*

9 *Baroque rocking-horse, Switzerland, carved in wood, painted, c. 1800.*

10 *Toy horse, Switzerland, carved in wood, painted, c. 1920.*

11 *Tiny toy horse, Switzerland, wooden, painted, on iron wheels, c. 1940.*

12 *Baroque toy horse, Austria, carved in wood, painted, c. 1800.*

13 *Baroque toy horse, Austria, carved in wood, painted, c. 1800.*

14 *Toy horse, Switzerland, carved in wood, c. 1900.*

TOY HORSES

For centuries they have made children's hearts beat faster with excitement. Designed with loving care, they bear witness to the artistic talents of their creators, the fathers and grandfathers, who were often extremely talented wood carvers and craftsmen. Nowadays they are much sought after as collectors' items.

SADDLES THROUGH THE CENTURIES

An eighteen-metre high grave mound, found near Certomlyk on the river Dnieper, contained a decorated vase which included a picture of a saddled horse among its designs. The saddle is fastened with a girth, and a rein which seems to end in a leather loop hangs loosely from the side of the saddle. The grave mound dates from around 300 BC, so this could well be the earliest drawing of a saddle with stirrups, indicating that a good two and a half millennia had elapsed before man took this vital step forward.

Long before this, members of the ruling classes had put covers on their horses' backs. Often very valuable, these were intended to give the rider a softer seat as well as protect him from the horse's sweat. But this underlay slipped around and made his seat even less secure until someone, probably an Assyrian, thought of fastening the covers in place with girth and chest straps. The soldiers of the Persian King Darius sat on covers like these, causing their Greek opponents to refer to them mockingly as 'soft-bummed'! Even during the Roman Empire, however, by which time the art of saddlery had made great progress, many soldiers still fought riding bareback.

Although Scythian saddles were fitted with stirrups some centuries before the birth of Christ, they were very simple, being made only of pieces of leather sewn together one on top of the other. Yet it seems the Scythians were the inventors of that very important innovation, the saddle tree. At first this consisted of two small boards covered in leather, moulded to the shape of the horse's back and placed on each side of its backbone. A girth strap, used to keep this construction firmly in place, and preventing it from moving sideways, was a definite step forward. Then for a long time the wood seems to have been dispensed with altogether. Instead two longish, flat, leather cushions stuffed with horsehair were sewn on to the actual saddle leather. This made an excellent base and was used for centuries, particularly in southern Russia.

Sooner or later all the equestrian peoples were using wooden saddle trees. It then became popular practice to raise both the front end of the saddle and the rim at the back. This gave the rider even more support and was the pattern for the knights' saddles in the Middle Ages.

The art of saddlery flourished during the Baroque period, and extravagantly sumptuous pieces were designed to keep up with fashions of the day. While the rider may have found them to his liking, it is doubtful whether they gave the horse much enjoyment.

The 'English' saddle now used throughout Europe was designed in England around 1600. Originally intended to be a hunting saddle, it was later modified to suit the various needs of different sports. On the other hand the western saddle, which was designed about two hundred years ago in California, was basically a knights' saddle adapted for working with cattle.

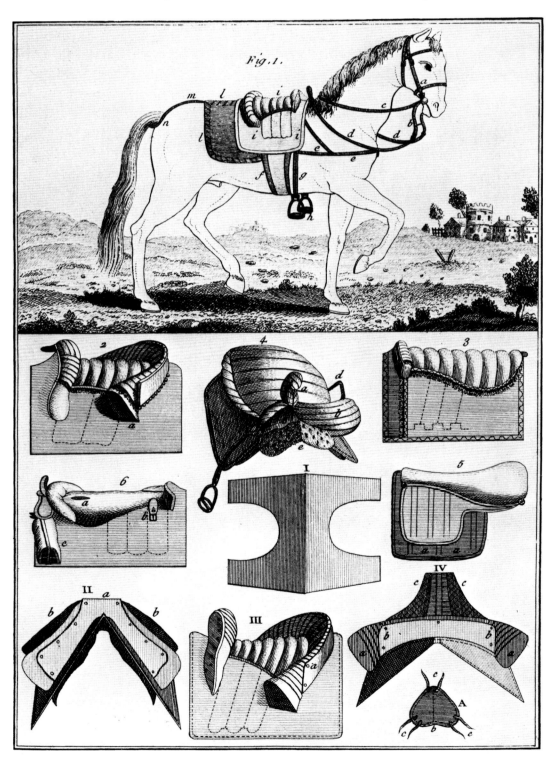

Left: Table XI from L'Art du Bourrelier et du Sellier. A horse saddled and bridled, with, below, a collection of saddles dating from around 1750: 2 Knights' saddle; 3 Flat saddle; 4 Ladies' saddle; 5 English saddle; 6 Mail saddle. I, II, III and IV are older types of tournament saddles.

Right: A saddle, said to be Persian, which possibly originated in the Caucasians or southern Turkestan.

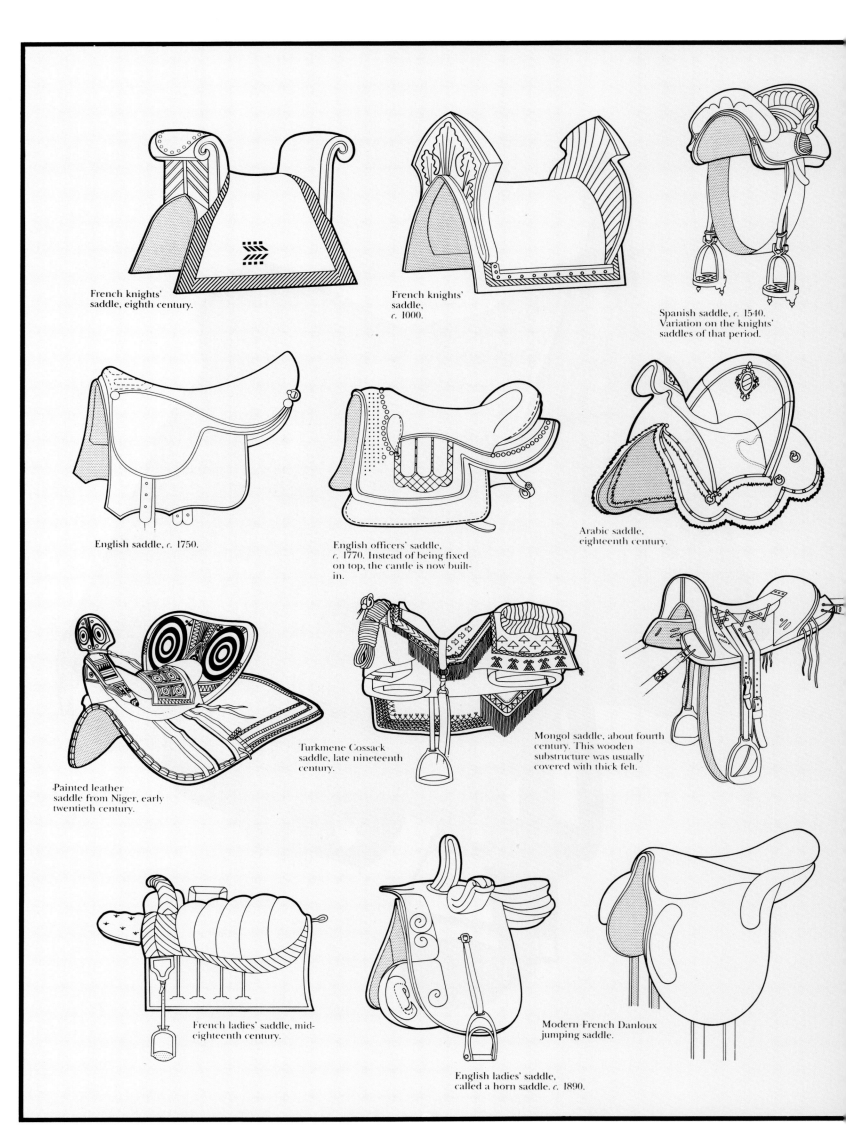

French knights'
saddle, eighth century.

French knights'
saddle,
c. 1000.

Spanish saddle, c. 1540.
Variation on the knights'
saddles of that period.

English saddle, c. 1750.

English officers' saddle,
c. 1770. Instead of being fixed
on top, the cantle is now built-
in.

Arabic saddle,
eighteenth century.

Painted leather
saddle from Niger, early
twentieth century.

Turkmene Cossack
saddle, late nineteenth
century.

Mongol saddle, about fourth
century. This wooden
substructure was usually
covered with thick felt.

French ladies' saddle, mid-
eighteenth century.

English ladies' saddle,
called a horn saddle. c. 1890.

Modern French Danloux
jumping saddle.

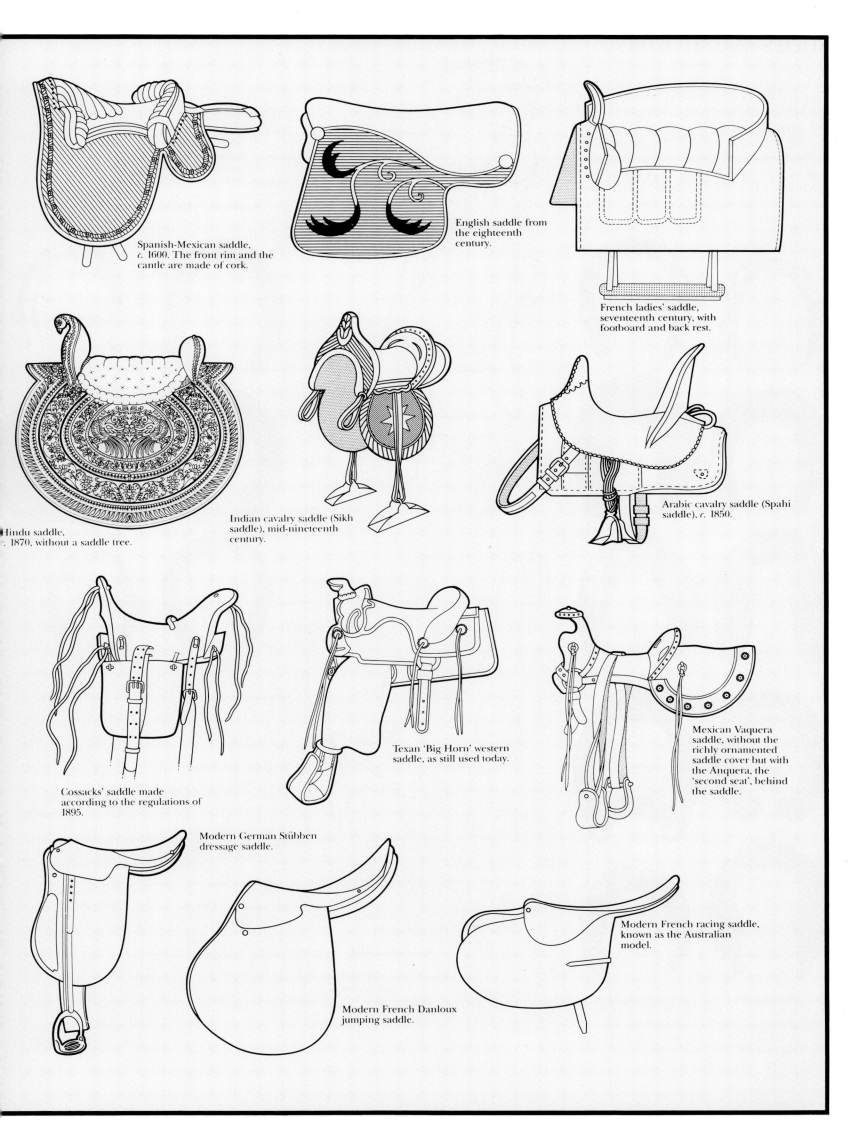

Spanish-Mexican saddle,
c. 1600. The front rim and the
cantle are made of cork.

English saddle from
the eighteenth
century.

French ladies' saddle,
seventeenth century, with
footboard and back rest.

Hindu saddle,
c. 1870, without a saddle tree.

Indian cavalry saddle (Sikh
saddle), mid-nineteenth
century.

Arabic cavalry saddle (Spahi
saddle), *c.* 1850.

Cossacks' saddle made
according to the regulations of
1895.

Texan 'Big Horn' western
saddle, as still used today.

Mexican Vaquera
saddle, without the
richly ornamented
saddle cover but with
the Anquera, the
'second seat', behind
the saddle.

Modern German Stübben
dressage saddle.

Modern French Danloux
jumping saddle.

Modern French racing saddle,
known as the Australian
model.

SHOES AND SHOEING

The discovery of a nailed horseshoe in the burial chamber of Chilperic I, the Merovingian king of the Franks from 561 to 584, seems to support the theory that horseshoes were in use at that time and that nails were used to fasten them to the horse's hooves. However, as no other nailed horseshoes have been found which date from earlier than the year

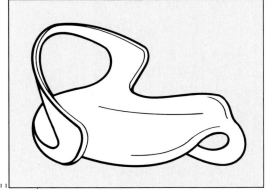

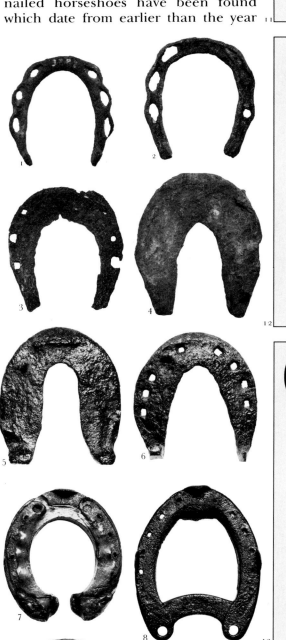

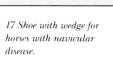

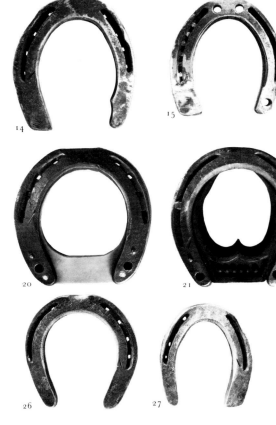

11 to 13 If the Celts had known about horseshoes, as is so often alleged, then the Romans would certainly have appropriated their invention. Instead the Romans made 'Roman hipposandals', which were fastened on to the hooves.

28 Anvils.

29 The blacksmith's tools.

30 The blacksmith at work.

1 and 2 These horseshoes with wavy rims are the oldest known form of nailed horseshoe. Although often called 'Celtic horseshoes', it is unlikely that the Celts invented them as they apparently date from only a thousand years ago.

3 to 10 Different kinds of horseshoes which were in common use from about the twelfth into the nineteenth century.

14 Shoe for a horse which tends to wear down the outer rim of the hoof more than the inner.

15 The outer rim of this shoe is raised to relieve pressure on a hoof infected with spavin.

16 This feather-edged shoe prevents the hoof from brushing against the pastern joint on the opposite foot.

17 Shoe with wedge for horses with navicular disease.

18 Handmade, lightweight sporting shoe.

19 Shoe for a mule.

20 Handmade sporting shoe with a plate to temporarily relieve pressure.

21 Shoe with tolouette for hooves incapable of bearing a heavy load.

22 An inset made of synthetic material is inserted between shoe and hoof for better grip.

23 Racing shoe made of lightweight metal.

24 A shoe with a leather sole, used if the sole of the hoof is too thin, to prevent it being injured.

25 Regulation shoe with four calkins: winter shoeing for working horses; mountain shoes for training horses (Swiss army).

26 Normal right front shoe (round shape).

27 Normal shoe for back right foot (oval shape).

31 and 32 Where show gaits with high action are demanded, as, for example, in the Hackney, American Saddle Horse, or Tennessee Walking Horse, shoeing often becomes a torment for the animal. The pictures show the kind of shoes which are commonly put on a Tennessee Walking Horse. Its front hooves are weighted down with heavy rubber blocks. The chains around the fetlocks, which are intended to make the horse lift its legs even higher, hit painfully against the sensitive coronary band, often making it very sore.

1000 we cannot accept this as conclusive proof.

Eligius, the patron saint of farriers, lived around the year 600, but it is not known if he forged horseshoes. There is also a legend that a horse belonging to an uncle of Mohammed wore shoes which would support the assumption that the art of shoeing was invented in the Orient. The term 'Celtic shoes', used to describe the ancient horseshoes with the wavy rim, is misleading as they do not

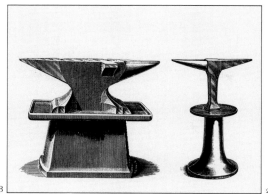
28

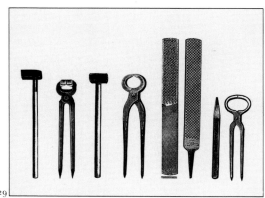
29

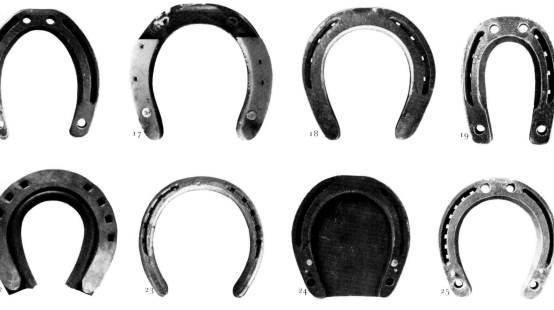

17   18   19

23   24   25

30

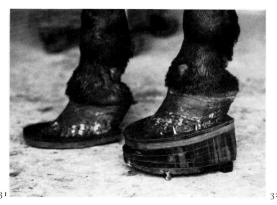
31

32

date from the pre-Christian times, being only about a thousand years old, and the Celts are unlikely to have invented them.

So long as horses lived in their natural environment they had no problems with their hooves, wear and tear being kept under control by natural means. Alexander the Great and his contemporaries apparently had no foot difficulties with their animals during their extensive campaigns on horseback, and it was only after the development of permanent hard-surfaced streets that troubles arose. The Romans countered these by producing a kind of horseshoe. First made from leather, which wore out very quickly, an iron sole was added, then a kind of sandal was moulded out of iron, and this was fastened to the hooves with leather straps. The Romans continued to use these 'hipposandals' for years.

Horseshoes became more widely used out of necessity as the network of roads spread out and an increasingly greater proportion of travelling and transporting had to be done on hard surfaces. In the meantime the work of the blacksmith had become almost a science, for besides a pair of strong fists it required a great deal of sensitivity in the fingertips, plus a precise knowledge of the anatomy and mechanics of the horse's foot.

The farrier has to have a high level of technical expertise. Even the shoeing of a normally developed hoof for ordinary use requires skill to ensure uneven wear is prevented, and in addition he has to make corrective or orthopaedic shoes. Shoes which are used either to encourage or radically change certain gaits require particularly skilled work, though the greatest skill is not enough to prevent the suffering such shoes cause to the animal.

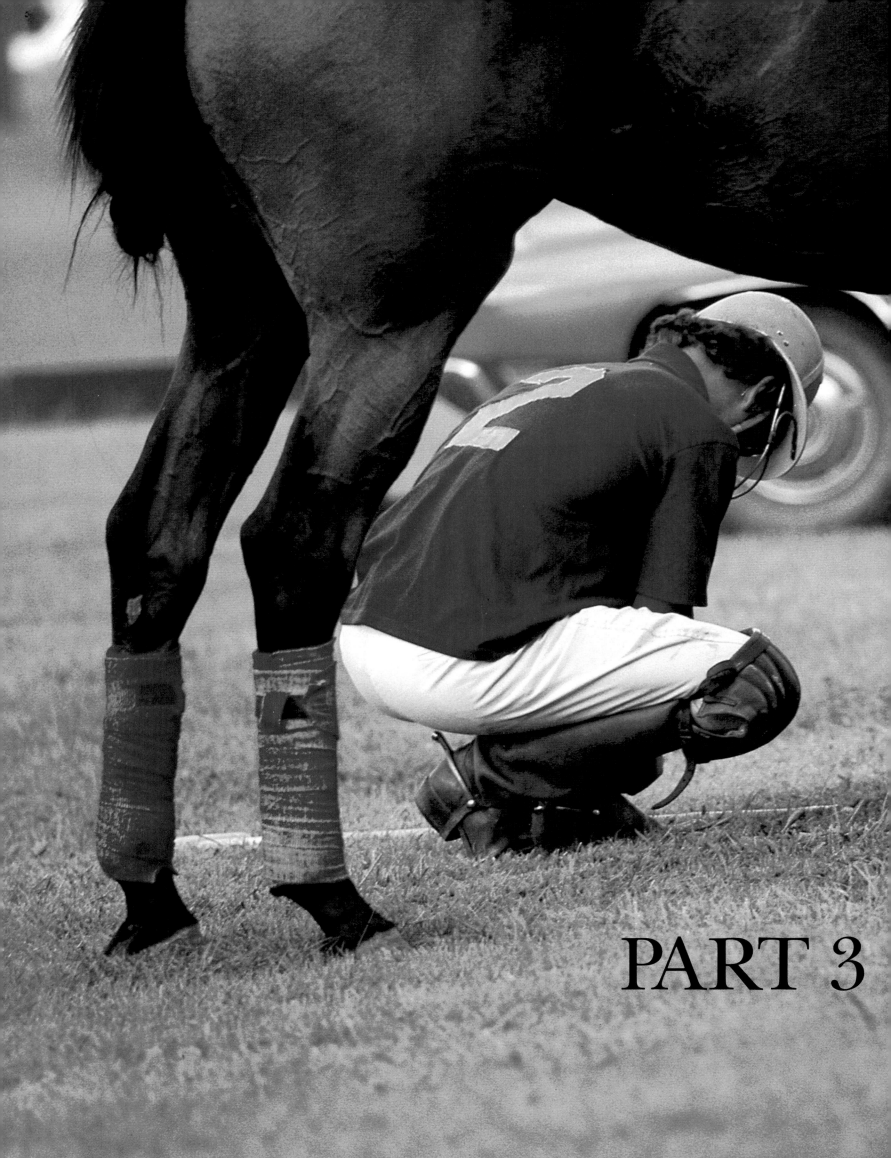

PART 3

HORSE AND MAN
TODAY

HORSES AT WORK IN THE MODERN WORLD

In Sweden in 1940 over 60,000 Swedish Ardennes mares were covered, but in 1976 this cold-blood breed numbered only 1700 broodmares — a reduction of over ninety-seven per cent. In the Saint Lô stud in northern France, out of some two hundred stud stallions, only about twenty are Percherons. Yet this region was formerly the heart of European Thoroughbred breeding. Forty years ago the cold-blood breeds comprised between eighty and ninety per cent of the total complement of horses in western Europe; today they make up less than ten per cent. Those that remain are kept more as a hobby than to satisfy a serious demand, although as working animals the cold-bloods have an important role to play in more remote mountain or forest areas.

The sight of a draught horse at work has become a rare occurrence which awakens feelings of nostalgia, and makes it a pleasant experience to travel in countries where teams of working horses are still part of the normal scene. In the countries of the Eastern bloc, for example, farmers with small holdings, who cannot afford a tractor, harness their horses to plough and wagon as a matter of course, but draught horses are also a frequent sight on the large collective farms. It is therefore appropriate that the breeding of working horses is considered to be far more important

than the breeding of horses merely for sport and leisure time activities.

Poland, for example, has about three million horses, the highest number of any European country, and is particularly renowned for the outstanding Arabs produced by the Janow Podlaski stud, for the noble Polish Trakehner or Wielko-polski breed and for its Anglo-Arabs or Malapolski, all of which are valuable exports to the West.

At home, however, two other breeds are much more in demand: the Huzule pony from the Carpathians, which is particularly efficient in the mountains, and the industrious Konic. The number of Konics in Poland is greater than that of all the other breeds combined.

In Yugoslavia there are about a million horses, over eighty per cent of them used in agricultural work. The Bosnian pony, of which there are said to be over 400,000 animals, is the most important breed. It is similar to the Huzule, and although only about 130 to 140 cm tall, is hardy, undemanding and amazingly strong. As a pack and draught animal it will remain a part of the Yugoslavian mountain scene for a long time to come. The famous Lipizzaner breed, which originated in the former Imperial stud at Lipica in the Karst, is also bred here for agricultural

1 A draught horse harnessed in front of the farmer's wagon with its iron clad wheels has remained a very familiar scene in Ireland. One reason is, of course, the proverbial affinity the Irish have with their horses, but another is that many Irish farmers cannot afford a tractor.

2 Over the last decades the complement of cold-blood horses in France has decreased by about eighty per cent, but in the north of the country many an Ardennais, Breton, Percheron, or Trait du Nord can be seen grazing or working.

3 In central Europe mules or horses are no longer used to thresh grain, but they are still a common sight elsewhere as, for example, here in Turkish East Anatolia.

4 An old-time village scene? No, a modern sight in a Hungarian village. The horse is still indispensable for agricultural work in the states of the Eastern bloc.

5 Mules ploughing the fields. This still happens even in the US. For religious reasons, members of certain sects use no motorised vehicles.

work rather than for the performance of classical dressage movements. The Hungarian Nonius breed, too, is often used as a draught horse.

Around the turn of the century the world's equine population was estimated to be about a hundred million, and of these, 34 million, i.e., about one-third, lived in Russia alone. Today Russia has about eight million horses. There, too, draught horses are the predominant breeds. After World War Two, when the numbers of cold-bloods in western countries dropped rapidly, the Soviet Union was actually developing new breeds of this type. Cold-bloods now account for about eighty per cent of their horses, and no less than six different native breeds are still being bred in quantity.

The most ancient must be the Bitjug breed which was already in existence by the year 1700. At the instigation of Peter the Great, the breed was developed by crossing mares native to the region of the river Bitjug with cold-blood stallions from the Netherlands. The result was a lighter weight, lively animal. By the turn of the century this breed had lost a great deal of its original quality (the result of various breeding errors), but between the two world wars, by a process of careful selective breeding, and particularly under the influence of hardy Orlov Trotter stallions, a new lightweight cold-blood breed was developed. It is known now as the Woronesh breed.

In the region to the east of Moscow, the Vladimir Heavy Draught horse was developed about a hundred years ago, although as a breed it has only been known by this name since 1946. With tremendous stamina, and capable of

pulling very heavy loads, its development owes something to a number of western cold-blood breeds, including the Ardennais, Percheron, Suffolk Punch, Clydesdale and the Shire Horse.

The make-up of the Russian Heavy Draught breed was much simpler, merely a cross between mares of the native Ukrainian breed and Belgian Heavy Draught stallions. The larger Soviet Heavy Draught breed, which weighs around 800 kg, was first developed about forty years ago, as was the Belorussian or White Russian Heavy Draught. The latter weighs about 500 kg and is about 150 cm tall.

A few of the West European countries still have large numbers of draught horses. Out of Norway's total complement of around 45,000 horses, about 30,000 Döle horses are kept for agricultural work. In that country, too, there are also a large number of hard-working Fjord ponies. There are about 35,000 horses in Austria, about 15,000 of them Norikers. The number of Haflingers continues to increase, and there may well

be more than 15,000 of these small, agile, chestnut-coloured horses from the Tyrol. In their native land the Haflingers, too, are used mostly for agricultural work, but they owe the upsurge in their numbers to the fact that they make excellent horses for leisure time pursuits.

Switzerland is a highly mechanized country, but even there the number of cold-blood horses is about sixty-five per cent of the total. The Freiberger breed, of which there are about 150 stud stallions, is the most numerous. Much sought after by the farmers in the Juras, the army also uses a great many of them as pack animals in the mountains.

EQUESTRIAN SPORTS

'Lots are drawn for position and then the stable boys, wearing their best outfits, lead the horses into the marked-off areas behind the rope. The horses have no bridles or any other covering. String has been used to fix spiked balls on to their bodies. The spikes will act as spurs but the sensitive parts they are aimed at are covered with pieces of leather until they are ready to start. The horses also have large pieces of gold foil stuck on to their bodies. . . . Finally the rope is dropped and they are off.

'While they are in the wide, open square they try to get ahead of each other, but when they reach the narrow space between the two rows of coaches all competition is in vain. By this time a few are usually in front and are making a tremendous effort. Their hooves strike sparks from the cobblestones in spite of the ashes which have been strewn over them, their manes stream back, the gold foil on their bodies sparkles and in a flash they are gone.'

In his *Roman Carnival* Goethe gives this description of the equestrian sport known as the Corso die Barberi. It has since lapsed into oblivion and only the name of a street in Rome, the Via del Corso, is a reminder. The Palio di Siena is the sole survivor of the various races which were once held in many Italian towns and villages, the prize for which was always a *palio*, a piece of expensive brocade. Nearly all the other European equestrian sports, once so widely spread, have also disappeared, the remainder confined to a few local events such as races held by Swiss farmers, tilting at the ring staged in northern Germany, tub-sticking in Austria, and gymkhanas in Britain and Ireland.

Equestrian sports on a grand scale are as old as riding itself, many of them retaining their original qualities, and often wild and exuberant. They are still played in areas inhabited by groups of equestrian peoples, such as North and South America, Australia, Mongolia, Turkmenistan, and Afghanistan where this photograph was taken.

CLASSICAL DRESSAGE

The earliest mention of classical dressage is probably the description in the Greek *Iliad* of horsemen circling the funeral pyre of Patroclus, for riding in circles is one of the three main elements. The other two are evolutions, performed as a group, and intricate routines in which each rider rides towards or away from the other.

Classical dressage movements, like many other equestrian sports, had their origins in military exercises. Every rider knows the importance of the volte in the horse's training. Simply riding in circles requires that the rider has a secure seat, and that the horse is thoroughly amenable to his wishes.

Evolution and figure riding is also known as the Trojan Game, for it is believed to have originated in Troy. The son of Aeneas, Ascanius, who escaped from the city when it was sacked, is said to have introduced this sport to the Latins. With one person in overall command, a group of thirty-six boys was divided into three sections, each with a captain and a leader. On command, the boys rode away from each other, formed into groups, wheeled and turned in intricate routines of circles and about-turns. This spectacle, exactly like modern classical dressage or figure riding, was originally an equestrian sport for boys involving manoeuvres on horseback

without weapons, and seems also to have been important during the period of the Roman Emperors.

In most cases figure riding was a part of military training which taught riders how to manoeuvre and how to move as a group in an orderly fashion. The routine contained a brief outline of all the formations and movements which the cavalry would have to use in the field and in battle, so that cavalrymen gained confidence and obtained a feeling for tempo, intervals and distances, learnt how to wheel about and to stay together

and how to maintain spacing and distance between each rider. All these advantages have been retained in figure riding to the present day. The rider dare not let his attention wander for an instant from the commands, which sharpens both his concentration and his hearing. With little room to spare in the arena, he must be able to estimate distance and tempo correctly — training for both instinct and eyesight.

In figure riding horses learn to perform the sharpest turns quickly, to move smoothly from one gait to another,

1 When performed in front of a circus audience, figure riding was, and still is, a feast for the eyes. This drawing of the Cirque des Champs-Elysées dates from 1843.

2 The main purpose of classical dressage was to help the cavalry gain experience in certain battle formations in which, as a closed phalanx, it had to approach the enemy. This painting by T. Schneider depicts the 'Battle on the White Hill which was fought near Prague on 8 November 1620'.

3 Portugal's Guarda Nacional Republicana give a display of riding.

4 The epitome of classical dressage. Members of the Spanish Riding School performing at Schönbrunn.

5 Dragoons of the Swiss army taking part in an impressive display of classical dressage, though the usual standard of Swiss precision seems to be momentarily lacking.

to maintain an even tempo and to move freely towards, away from and across in front of each other. This is learnt gradually, but soon becomes instinctive: 'Character-ruining, bone-ruining scraps and tussles which are so common in the individual rider simply disappear' (O. Fritz).

Historically, figure riding is based on the duodecimal or twelve-fold system. The division by six, four, three or two allows the riders to wheel in columns (one behind the other) or in lines (next to each other), in circles, semi-circles, quarters and eighths. Thus two groups can face each other, from the sides or ends of the arena, sometimes moving in the same, sometimes going in opposite directions. In all three gaits the riders then have to ride to the right or left, keeping varying distances between them, or perform circling and wheel-abouts in various combinations. A few simple commands can thus produce thousands of variations.

Figure riding is also an excellent means of judging the level of training of a team and its horses.

Classical dressage flourished amid the splendour and pomp of the Baroque age. Performers arrayed in marvellous costumes, mounted on noble, superbly collected horses of Spanish and Neapolitan blood, demonstrated their routines with great skill and assurance. Display often became more important than any other aspect, although the military origins were retained. The tournaments so popular at that time were simply mock skirmishes, consisting of elegantly arranged displays of single combats, mock battles between large groups, and equestrian evolutions. These splendid processions on horseback became very fashionable and the nobility relished every opportunity to show off their magnificent steeds and their own skilled horsemanship.

One of the most famous of all riding displays was a carousel organised by Louis XIV in Paris in 1662, in memory of which the square between the Louvre and the Tuileries in Paris was named the Place du Carrousel. The 'Equestrian Ballet' performed in January 1667 in the Imperial Palace in Vienna, was given a similar accolade. The title reveals how much of the original military character had been lost in favour of the gala atmosphere of the circus.

In the following centuries classical dressage regained its importance as a means of training a quick-thinking cavalry until it finally lost all its military relevance when the invention of reliable hand-weapons signalled the end of the classic cavalry attack. Yet this is indisputably a valuable form of equestrian training. Whoever has once taken part in a quadrille will have discovered that afterwards his horse obeys the aids more willingly and more dependably.

CIRCUS ACROBATICS

Circus acrobatics are gymnastics performed on a galloping horse. Although acrobatics like these have been performed for many centuries, again and again this form of riding has almost lapsed into oblivion. During the past fifteen years or more, however, it seems to have become more popular once again, and both in Europe and the US the number of enthusiasts continues to increase.

From the writings of Vegetius, a Roman military theorist who also bred horses, we know that acrobatics on horseback were part of the cavalry training on the Field of Mars in Rome. Certainly these exercises would improve the balance of prospective riders, and give them a thorough understanding of the movement of a horse. Acrobatics were also performed in many other cavalry schools, and from the sixteenth to eighteenth centuries young men who aspired to enter the French army frequently performed gymnastics on the backs of galloping horses. At the same time acrobatics riding became a permanent part of equestrian circus events. It is still extremely popular. The oldest textbook on acrobatics in the German language, written by J. G. Pascha, appeared on the market in 1657, and acrobatics reached one of their high points in popularity in 1928 when they were part of the Olympics.

The most recent upsurge began in the sixties when championships were re-introduced. Today national and international competitions are held regularly, and in Germany alone there are around 35,000 acrobatics riders. Competitions for acrobatics on horseback are also held in Switzerland, France, England, Denmark, Holland, Belgium and the US.

Between the ages of six and sixteen, riders compete in groups; over the age of sixteen they are allowed to compete as individual riders.

A competition team comprises eight acrobats, one substitute and a trainer. The competition programme consists of a compulsory routine and one which the teams can choose for themselves. There are six exercises which must be performed by all eight members of the team: the basic seat, flag, mill, flank-vault, stand and scissors. The team may then display

1 Acrobatics on horseback form part of the repertoire of every circus. 'Picture of equestrian acrobatics' from the early nineteenth century.

2 Acrobatics are a sport for young people which is growing in popularity.

3 The ideal horse for acrobatics is compact, agile, strong, rather short-legged, perfectly even-tempered and with no trace of nervousness.

4 Learning how to look after a horse is part of the basic training of every acrobatics rider.

5 to 10 Some acrobatics figures. Basic seat, flag, scissors, flank-vault, scissors, stand. Naturally all are performed on a galloping horse!

5

6

7

8

9

10

exercises of its own choice, the only restriction being that no more than three riders are allowed to be on the horse at the same time. Both the compulsory and the free choice routines have to be completed within a total of fifteen minutes.

The individual acrobatics rider also has to perform the compulsory routine first, and is then allowed one minute for individual exercises of his or her own choice.

Acrobatics are very closely related to gymnastics performed on apparatus, except that the 'apparatus' is not a motionless object, but a horse that is galloping round in a circle thirteen metres in diameter at the end of the longe line held by the trainer.

There are many different ways in which the riders can jump on and off the horse, and they need to be well trained in gymnastics to perform even comparatively simple mounted exercises. They also need a thorough grounding in acrobatic skills to perform some of the figures in the free exercises, partic-

ularly those which require two or three people to be lifted and then supported. Gymnastics on horseback are an excellent preparation for riding itself. The acrobatics rider becomes familiar with the horse's character and with its physical attributes, and acquires an excellent sense of balance.

Although a horse used for acrobatics has simply to learn to gallop evenly in a circle while on the longe rein, it also has to comply with certain basic requirements. It must be strongly built yet not too heavy, for although it has to be able to carry 150 kilograms it should also have enough stamina to gallop steadily for a quarter of an hour. As well as being correctly aligned, its legs must be strong and robust if it is to keep galloping in the narrow circle and also cope with the added strain of a rider jumping on and off its back. The saddle area must be beautifully rounded and the croup broad with smoothly sloping sides. Its back must not be too long, and therefore unsuitable for carrying a heavy burden, but must be long enough to accommodate up to

three acrobats. Rather short legs are actually preferable as they are normally very robust, and the correspondingly lower withers height makes it easier for riders to jump on and off. The horse needs to be fairly spirited so that it will continue to gallop happily without having to be continually urged on, but it must not be nervous or fearful, and, of course, it must not be ticklish. The most important prerequisite of all is a placid, friendly, honest nature, for only a horse with these characteristics should be allowed near children.

The American Quarter Horse, or a horse of a similar type, would actually make an ideal horse for equestrian gymnastics — it would also be an ideal cross-country horse — but so far as Europe is concerned, the breeding of riding horses is directed almost exclusively at jumping ability.

POLO

Polo is one of the oldest team sports in the world. It originated in Persia probably long before the birth of Christ and was soon popular in India and China as well. Indisputably one of the most thrilling of all team games, it used to be one of the highpoints of the modern Olympic Games until 1936, when it was dropped from the programme because so few nations could provide teams of a sufficiently high quality. Polo could only prosper in countries with a plentiful supply of horses, and where the upper levels of society were financially secure.

Returning crusaders introduced the game into France as early as 1200, but it did not become established in Europe until 1872, when British cavalry officers, who had played this sport in India,

founded the Monmouthshire Polo Club.

Apart from England, this sport is widely played only in the US and Argentina. The reasons are simply that, in addition to natural aptitude, each polo pony needs to undergo a lengthy training period and each player needs at least two, preferably three or four, ponies as the animals are so exhausted after each playing period that they need to be rested.

Polo is usually played on a field measuring 250 by 150 metres. There are

four players in a team, and the aim is to use the mallets to hit the white wooden ball, weighing 125 grams, into the opponent's goal which is 7.5 metres wide. In Europe each game usually consists of four chukkas or playing periods, though six are played in South America where more horses are available. If the game is a draw, i.e., the same number of goals have been scored, then an additional chukka is played.

Polo is a tough sport which can be quite dangerous. The rider must be thoroughly trained, for he needs a great deal of skill, an instinct for balance and handling a ball, plus lightning fast reactions and nerves of steel. In addition there must be complete trust between rider and horse. The four basic hits — a forwards and a backwards hit on each side of the body — are difficult enough in themselves, but become doubly so when they have to be executed from a galloping horse on to a moving ball. Only very good players master the hits under the horse's neck or tail and the real experts include the hit under the animal's belly in their repertoires.

Nowadays polo ponies are rarely ponies, but it is traditional to refer to them as such. The necessary attributes are speed, agility, stamina and toughness, intelligence, eagerness to learn, and excellent nerves. The ponies need to be fairly spirited animals, for only horses with a high proportion of noble blood in them can last through a chukka without a noticeable decrease in performance, and then recover sufficiently to be able to gallop at top speed in a later playing period.

EL PATO

In its original form this Argentinian game was played with a duck, *el pato*. The earliest mention is found in an ecclesiastical publication of 1610, which tells of a game during which many of the young riders are said to have been crushed to death or trampled by the horses.

The church eventually banned the sport as being too dangerous, but in outlying regions the gauchos continued to play it with passionate enthusiasm.

Just before the start of a game a duck was sewn into a piece of leather. Then, in front of the church, it was thrown in to the air above the assembled riders, each of whom would try to catch it and then ride to the house of his beloved and throw it down in front of the door. At least several dozen riders, frequently several hundred, would take part in each game. When there were two teams, the competition was fierce and ruthless for the winners were fêted like heroes. The game usually lasted for hours and required daring riders with a good seat as well as tough, fast, agile horses with a great deal of stamina.

In 1822 el pato was officially banned by the State, and it was not until 1937 that a more humane version of the sport

was permitted, with fixed rules. Each game now permits only eight riders, i.e., two four-man teams. The venue is usually a playing field measuring 90 by 200 metres. 'El pato' is no longer an unfortunate bird but a heavy ball weighing 1250 grams, with four leather hand grips, which, as in basketball, has to be thrown into the opponents' basket. Play normally consists of six playing periods, each of seven minutes, with a five minute break between each one. Usually each rider has two horses which he rides alternately.

Although no longer such a dangerous game el pato still demands a high degree of acrobatic skill. At full gallop the riders have to be able to pick the ball up from the ground, throw it with precision to their partner or into the net and yet remain completely in control of their horses throughout. The game requires animals which are robust, extremely agile, eager for action and with tremendous stamina. They also have to be intelligent for, as in polo, the horse plays the game too.

GYMKHANA

When boys rode in columns and then dispersed in circles in ancient Greece; when Roman cavalrymen practised sword thrusts on the *palus* (the wooden post set up in the training area); when riders of the Middle Ages used their lances to try to lift each other out of the saddle; or when Austrian Hussars, riding at a fast gallop, tried to spear artificial turban-wrapped heads with their lances — they were all first and foremost concerned with developing their fighting skills. In all these forms of military training the art of riding took second place.

The riding exercises of the Indian soldiers during the British Colonial period were much more refined and versatile. They were called *gymkhana* which, when translated, means almost the same as riding school. These games made the riders more agile, sharpened their reactions, made them physically fit, and encouraged a feeling of mutual trust. Soldiers became very relaxed riders with an exceptionally good sense of balance, and their tough ponies were turned into amenable riding animals which responded to the lightest touch of the aids, quite prepared to tackle the most unusual tasks.

The British soon realized the great value of these exercises, which also appealed to their innate passion for games. Very soon gymkhana exercises were an integral part of the training and

sporting activities of the English riders in India, who took them home with them to Britain. There they have retained their popularity as riding games, particularly for youngsters.

Gymkhana has also become very popular in the US, especially in the West, and it is interesting that these games have gained such a firm hold where riding is taken for granted as a natural way of life and does not have the notoriety of being a sport for the upper classes. There, too, the most important aspect of riding is that a horse 'functions' well. Above all else it must be willing and dependable, without the slightest tendency to nervousness, agile, skilled, obedient, and yet self-confident as well. Gymkhana fosters all these traits. A good gymkhana pony is usually, therefore, an excellent animal for cross-country riding and for trekking.

On the continent of Europe, however, gymkhana has not been accepted nearly as readily, and there are still only a few experts there able to train ponies or horses and their riders in gymkhana

games. To make the public more aware, riding games for children are now being included in European riding tournaments, but most of the young riders and their ponies are ill-prepared for such tasks. Spectators tend to laugh, and the children who have taken part in them do not want to do so again. Jumping and racing events for ponies are, on the other hand, much in demand, though these two sports in particular can be very harmful to ponies.

There are many different gymkhana games. Some do require that the ponies gallop for short stretches and jump small obstacles as well, but all these games are aimed at developing skills, at encouraging rider and pony to trust each other, not at achieving fast speeds or increasing the ability to jump. The advantages which result from such exercises are clear-cut. On the one hand the ponies become skilled and amenable and on the other their worth is based, not on their cash value in the sale ring, but on their training and on a relationship of unshakable trust which has been built up between animal and child.

There are a great many gymkhana games. Here are just a few examples. The keyhole race is included in almost every gymkhana in the US. It is a simple game and not very exciting for the spectators but an excellent test of skill. A keyhole-shaped figure is drawn on the ground with sawdust at a distance of 5 to 25 metres from the starting line. Each rider has to gallop to the figure, walk or trot through the small neck opening, and

3

3 Missed by centimetres. Here the aim is to pick up a tennis ball from the ground from the back of a galloping pony. Beginners practise this game with a jute sack. Experts use a coin and often ride bareback as well.

4 A combination game for beginners. Among other things the rider has to put on a jacket while on horseback and throw some potatoes into a bucket. That sounds very easy, but a pony which is unprepared will shy at the fluttering jacket and certainly make life difficult when the potatoes clatter into the container.

4

5

5 Gymkhana games consist of slalom courses of all kinds. The horse has to be agile, able to change direction quickly and accurately at the gallop, and must also allow itself to be guided. In this photo Jack Huyler on El Paso Gap makes a turn which is a little too wide around the last post of a slalom course. He has been the Californian gymkhana champion several times.

make a turn in the circle, which has a diameter of two metres for smaller ponies and 2.5 metres for larger ponies and horses. The rider then leaves the keyhole again through the neck and gallops back to the starting line. If the pony steps on or crosses over the sawdust line it is disqualified. Speed is not a factor: what is much more important is that a pony remains under control and performs its turns quickly and neatly.

Many gymkhana games are variations of a slalom, usually with six sticks set in a straight line, each five metres apart, which riders have to negotiate in zigzag fashion. This requires skill from the rider in quickly changing his weight from one side to the other, and only a pony which has learnt to keep its balance throughout such changes will be able to gallop smoothly through a slalom course. Such a pony is also unlikely to lose its balance when being ridden across country. Often two or even more slalom courses are set up side by side, and several individual riders or whole relay teams then race simultaneously, which makes the game much more exciting.

In the US the most popular gymkhana game is barrel racing. Three empty barrels, set up in a triangle at distances of 30 to 35 metres from each other, have to be ridden round in a clover-leafed pattern. That, too, looks very simple but only riders and ponies with a great deal of training are capable of completing a good barrel ride.

There are many similar races of this kind. Other exercises, like the potato race, are included just for fun, and intended particularly for the youngest participants. As each rider passes a pail set on the ground he has to throw some potatoes into it: the pony should not take fright at the noise.

Another game involves the rider changing his clothing while riding, during which the pony should not be upset by the flapping garments.

RODEO

The word Rodeo usually conjures up a picture of wild horses racing around a corral while despairing cowboys try to stay on their backs. Riding a bucking horse is certainly part of the proceedings, but only one out of the six competitions which constitute a rodeo.

Rodeos, which have an enthusiastic following in Australia and New Zealand as well as in the US and Canada, evolved from the cowboys' daily chores which, as well as breaking in horses captured in the wild, included capturing and overpowering calves and cattle which had grown up semi-wild. Although bareback and bronc riding — the wild rides on bucking horses — are spectacular events and consequently have a great deal of public appeal, in reality they require nothing much more than that the rider has a very secure seat, the necessary amount of courage, and of course a bucking horse. The 'ropers' on the other hand, who use lassos to catch the cattle, have to be outstanding riders although, apart from requiring many years of training, their style has little in common with classical dressage.

In calf roping a calf has to be first lassoed and then secured by three of its legs. The calf is kept ready in a chute behind a gate, the one thought in its mind being the urgent desire to rejoin its companions in the pens at the other end of the stadium. The cowboy waits behind a barrier next to the chute. He has tied one end of his lasso firmly to the saddle pommel while he holds the other at the ready. Between his teeth he

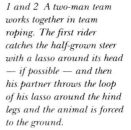

1 and 2 A two-man team works together in team roping. The first rider catches the half-grown steer with a lasso around its head — if possible — and then his partner throws the loop of his lasso around the hind legs and the animal is forced to the ground.

3 In steer wrestling the rider tries to get as close as possible to the half-grown steer. He then throws himself on to the animal's neck and tries to push it down to the ground.

4 to 11 In calf roping the rider demands a great deal of active participation from his horse. It follows the calf of its own accord and comes to an immediate stop when the loop of the lasso lies around the calf's head; then it tries, by walking backwards, to keep the rope taut. In this sequence of pictures the course of events did not run as planned. Instead of having a calf tied up at his feet the rider lands in the dust.

has a small piece of rope which he will use to tie up the calf's legs.

At a signal the gate is opened, and in an amazing burst of speed the calf erupts into the stadium. The cowboy dashes after it, helped not a little by the legendary accelerating power of the Quarter Horse or Appaloosa he is riding. At the moment he throws the lasso over the calf's head he leaps from his horse, which immediately stands quite still. The rope suddenly becomes taut and the calf is thrown to the ground. Before it can scramble to its feet again the cowboy kneels on it, grabs three of its legs, ties them up with lightning speed and stands up. The calf struggles but must remain tied up for at least ten seconds.

An experienced rider can complete the entire process from starting signal to when he stands beside the calf in about eight seconds!

For about half the participants, calf roping does not run nearly so smoothly. The cowboy's first throw may miss and, as a second throw is not allowed, he is out of the game. The calf may get to its feet before the rider reaches it and have to be thrown to the ground again before it can be tied up. That is not always easy, and the rider is allowed only a total of twenty seconds. The amazing part is that the horse practically never refuses, but follows the calf of its own accord without needing to be spurred on or guided in the right direction. Within seconds after the lasso's loop lies around the calf's neck, the horse can come to a 'sliding stop'. This is a typical movement in western riding in which the horse comes to a dead halt with its hind legs well under the rest of its body. And finally the horse ensures that the lasso remains taut. If the calf is trying to scramble up, a well-trained roping horse will immediately step backwards to prevent it from standing.

The prerequisites for obtaining such a standard of performance are a clever horse that enjoys learning, a trainer who is blessed with an 'understanding for horses', and a great deal of patience. In America young, untrained western horses with potential can be bought for what seem to Europeans as unbelievably low prices, but it is less surprising that a fully trained cowboy's horse on the other hand can be worth a small fortune. At least five or six years of training are required before a horse can be depended on to cope with all aspects of cattle work.

Team roping is another competition involving lasso work; in this case to catch a half-grown steer. The behaviour of these animals, too, like that of the small, very lively calves, bears no resemblance

4

8

5

9

6

10

7

11

to that of dairy cattle. These steers are bred for meat. They grow up on the huge ranches in an almost wild state and are strong, agile and very wary of humans. When big enough they are also well able to defend themselves.

Two cowboys have to work together to catch the half-grown animals and this competition is a test of teamwork. The two riders wait beside the chute opening, and at the signal race one behind the other after the steer. As fast as he can the front rider throws the loop of his lasso over the head of the steer or over its horns, and, without stopping, imme-diately rides off to the side. The second rider throws his lasso around the hind legs of the galloping steer and rides off to the opposite side. In a few moments the two lasso ropes become taut and the steer falls helpless to the ground.

The important factor here is that both riders and horses have the ability to react with lightning speed, for although the steer's main preoccupation is to reach its fellows at the other side of the stadium as quickly as possible, its movements are extremely unpredictable. Throwing the lasso around one or both hind legs is the most difficult part.

Steer wrestling is cattle work as seldom practised in reality. A half-grown steer is put in the chute, flanked by a cowboy on either side. When it is released, one rider has to prevent the animal from breaking out to the right. His partner, who is usually very solidly built, has almost immediately to lower himself down to the steer's level, hurl himself sideways on to the animal's neck and, using the force of his impact, pull the animal to the ground. Then he must turn the steer's neck and head so that the tips of both horns touch the ground, render-ing it defenceless for at least a few

2 When the rodeo rider has lasted the required length of time, he is allowed to clamber on to the back of another horse which is brought out to rescue him.

3 The rider is permitted to sit in a saddle in bronc riding but he is allowed to use only his left hand to hold on to a piece of rope which is fixed to the halter.

1 Bareback riding. This rider's hands have already lost their grip on the chest strap and he has no hope of keeping his seat on the back of the wildly bucking horse for the required fifteen seconds.

4 Bull riding. Fifteen seconds without a saddle on a half-wild steer. This is often very dangerous as the animal can be incredibly lively.

5 and 6 Preparations for bareback riding. While the horse is standing ready in the narrow chute the rider very carefully puts the chest strap in place.

7 Painful falls are commonplace at every rodeo but, surprisingly, serious injuries are rare.

seconds. Frequently the rider ends up under the steer, and he nearly always receives a few bruises for his efforts. Sometimes the steer manages to get out of the way at the last moment, and the rider lands in a heap on the ground where the animal is quite likely to run over him.

Bull riding is also a game with steers — and the craziest and most dangerous of all the rodeo competitions. The steers used in this event are fully grown and muscular, mostly zebus of Asiatic origin or the products of crosses between zebus and other breeds.

Before the start the bull is driven into a narrow chute, where a rope is bound around the front of its body and the rider seats himself carefully on the massive back. Most of us can visualize a horse bucking wildly and throwing itself

around like a tornado, but those who have not seen it for themselves would not believe that a fully grown steer is capable of such leaps in the air or such lightning fast pirouettes. The riders are allowed to hold on to the rope with the left hand only, and most of them are lying in the sand long before the prescribed twenty seconds have elapsed.

If a rodeo rider falls off a bucking horse he has to watch out for his horse's kicking hooves. The steer kicks out just as energetically, and it may also deliberately attack the fallen cowboy. Bull riding can cause serious injuries.

Bareback riding and saddle bronc riding have basically the same format. In bareback riding the horse is ridden without a saddle. A strap is buckled around the front of the animal's body and a solid leather grip attached to it, but the rider is allowed to hold on only with his left hand.

In bronc riding, although the rider is allowed a saddle and therefore has a much more secure seat, he has only a rope to hold on to, also with his left hand. This rope is about a metre long and is tied to the halter. If he remains on the horse for the stipulated twenty seconds, then his style and the degree of difficulty are also taken into account, for not all horses are equally unmanageable. Mustangs are most frequently used. A leather strap buckled around the horse's belly just in front of its hind legs ensures that

it will continue to buck. When it is removed the horse immediately stops kicking, and calmly trots back into the pen with its companions.

THE GAMES OF THE GAUCHOS

The mounted cattle herders of Central and South America, just like the cowboys of the American West, have evolved games which test both their occupational skills and their courage. A *Jineteada*, a South American rodeo, may be simply a rural Sunday pastime, and usually gives the impression of being improvised. No one seems to know for certain whether it will take place at all, when it is meant to start, or when it has finished; but it is very exciting and well reflects the South American temperament.

Organised Jineteadas usually include two competitions. The first one is for amateurs, whose prize is simply the crowd's applause and the food and drink which is provided after the events. The second is for the professional riders who move from fiesta to fiesta and live off their winnings.

The most popular event is riding unbroken horses, where there are a wide range of regional variations. In the north-west of Argentina the horse is ridden bareback, the rider holding on to a leather strap placed loosely around the horse's neck. A ride which lasts for ten seconds is considered to be an amazing feat. On the Argentinian pampas and in Uruguay the rider sits on a kind of cushion or sheepskin held firmly on the horse's back by a chest strap. Or the gaucho may put on his own

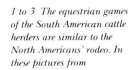

1 to 3 The equestrian games of the South American cattle herders are similar to the North Americans' rodeo. In these pictures from Argentina the unbroken horse is tied to a post and has his eyes blindfolded so that he can be saddled and mounted.

saddle and use a simple bridle with a wide rein.

At all North American rodeos narrow, partitioned areas are set up for bridling and mounting the animals, but in South America the horse is usually bound to a post instead, its eyes blindfolded so that it remains fairly quiet. When the rider is seated, the horse is untied and the bandage around its eyes removed. Then begins the maniacal dance, to the accompaniment of lively calls of encouragement, applause, abuse, or even gloating laughter from the spectators. The commentator is often extremely

eloquent and enlivens the proceedings by making his comments in rhyme. Sometimes the post is dispensed with and half a dozen gauchos hold on to the horse until the bandage around its eyes is removed — when each one tries to get out of reach of the flailing hooves as fast as possible.

The rodeo rider is most vulnerable when he falls off, as the horse kicks out wildly and can easily cripple him. This is an ever-present risk. The rider who lasts the prescribed time on the bucking horse, on the other hand, receives help from other riders who try to reach his

5

6

are often hurt, though seldom seriously injured. Points are awarded according to which part of the horse's body is used to block the steer.

At first glance many gaucho games seem to be very simple but in reality all demand a great deal of skill. One, for example, requires the players to ride at full gallop towards a rope stretched across the course at the height of a man's knee and to stop as close to it as possible. The best riders just touch the rope; the courageous but less skilful ones can come an awful cropper.

The *Carrera de sortijas* is very popular. It is a form of tilting at the ring, a game which occurs in many different guises throughout the world. The gauchos use a ring no larger than a finger ring, and hang it up so high that the rider, as he gallops past, has to stand up in his stirrups and stretch out his arm in order to reach it. A piece of wood about the size of a pencil takes the place of the 'lance' and is used to pick up the ring. Usually two riders start off at the same time, and two rings are hung side by side, with sometimes a second pair of rings a few metres further on. Both have then to be collected in the same round. Many players are so skilled that often a whole series of rounds has to be played to determine the winner.

7

side as quickly as possible so that he can save himself by getting on to the back of a tame horse. It obviously requires a great deal of skill to clamber from one horse on to another, but it is one foolhardy act well worth practising.

In the US bull riding is usually an organized competition, and as such does not exist in South America. At a village fiesta, however, a tipsy gaucho will often take great delight in proving his prowess by riding a steer or a pig, which is naturally a source of great amusement to the onlookers.

Cattle blocking is another very popular rodeo game. The event is held in a round

arena which is surrounded by a wooden partition and often a primitive grandstand or two as well. Many estancias can provide such a venue, which are normally used to sort out the young cattle when they are first brought in from the wild to be branded or sold. The competition is simply a game with fixed rules based on the skills required for this sort of work. The gaucho has to wear his usual working clothes and, of course, uses a horse which is trained to manoeuvre a steer into position up against the wooden partition, and then block it there with its chest and forelegs. This is a really difficult undertaking and the participants

FANTASIA

The Moroccans' holy festivals are the most colourful of any religious occasions. They are markets which sell almost anything, from the most secret medicines to camels for riding. Camel races are held. Entertainment is provided by Shluh musicians and dancers from Chaouen. There are fortune-tellers, snake charmers, and story tellers as well.

The Fantasias are the high point of each great festival, equestrian performances which are reminiscent of the warlike quarrels of the past. Suddenly, as from nowhere, a band of horsemen appears on the horizon followed by an immense cloud of dust, and, at a given signal, fire a volley from their long, richly ornamented weapons. Now at close range the horses' magnificent trappings are clearly visible. The animals are mostly greys and blacks and often of the noblest Berber descent.

These Fantasias are, in fact, not games at all for no opposing parties compete with each other. They are simply mock attacks enacted in a thrilling manner.

The greatest of all the religious festivals is held annually in August in Moulay Idris, in honour of Moulay Idris al-Akbar, the 'father of the nation', who in 788 founded the first Arabic dynasty in Morocco.

1 At the great festivals whole towns are created under canvas. There are bazaars which sell almost anything and where arts and crafts of all kinds are on display.

2 Moroccan saddles have remained unchanged for centuries. As Moroccan boots often have thin soles, stirrups are made with a flat surface large enough to accommodate the whole foot.

3 The religious festival held at Moulay Abdallah is one of the most important in Morocco.

Right: When Mohammed's hordes arrived they brought their Arab horses with them and consequently there are hardly any pure-bred Berbers left.

Overleaf: Fantasia riders staging a mock attack.

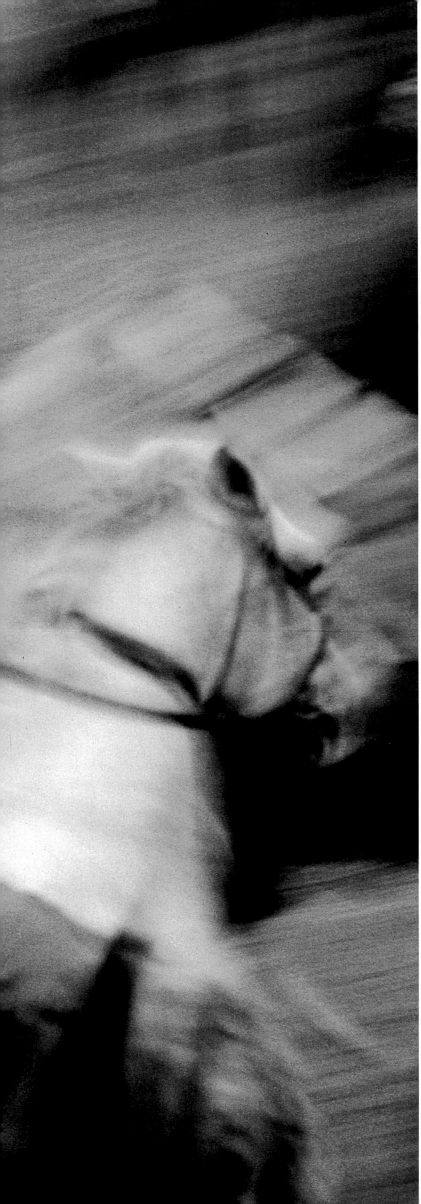

Buzkashi is not simply a sport. Like many of the ancient equestrian games, it is also a cult custom, played on special holidays during the winter, usually in conjunction with other festivities. All the young men dream of becoming a Buzkashi rider, a desire probably aroused in them the first time they sat on a small wooden horse on a merry-go-round, but for most of them it will remain a dream. Buzkashi horses are so valuable that they are owned almost exclusively by the rich Beys, who choose only the best and most fearless riders.

Just as much care is devoted to the breeding of the horses, and selection is based on toughness, speed, stamina and agility. Pregnant mares have a dozen eggs poured down their throats each day, and it is said that when a foal with the potential of becoming a Buzkashi horse is being born, it must never be allowed to fall to the ground for fear that 'its wings' might be broken.

BUZKASHI

Buzkashi is the wildest of all equestrian sports. It has a long tradition and is still very much alive among the Turkish people, and particularly in Afghanistan. When, on winter Sundays and holidays, the Chapandaz (master horsemen) gather to play the game they receive as much attention and admiration as football stars.

Buzkashi means 'to steal a goat'. On the day before the game, a goat or calf is killed and skinned, the skin filled with sand, sewn up and left to soak in water overnight. On the day of the game the pelt, which now weighs thirty or forty kilograms, is put on the playing field in the Hallal, or 'circle of justice'. The object of the game is to grab hold of the skin from horseback, ride at the gallop around a post set up out on the steppe, and throw the skin back into the circle again. This sounds simple, but with at least ten, and usually more, riders all competing fiercely with each other, and using whips to fend off their opponents, the ensuing wild turmoil inevitably causes injuries, some serious. The riders usually suffer more than the horse.

EQUESTRIAN SPORTS IN RUSSIA

Racing is probably the most ancient equestrian sport, and it seems certain that races were first held about five thousand years ago in the southern part of what is now the Soviet Union. Long-distance races were especially popular as an exciting test of a horse's hardiness, speed and stamina. Even in antiquity Turkmene horses were widely renowned, and the Persian king Darius is said to have had in his army an elite troop of 30,000 riders mounted on these animals. Alexander the Great's famous stallion, Bucephalus, is reported to have been one of this noble breed.

Akhal-Teké horses, which are similar to Arabs and English Thoroughbreds and closely related to both, are direct descendants of the Turkmenes and also capable of tremendous speeds. In one long-distance race, Akhal-Tekés covered the stretch from their Turkmene homeland across the Kara-kum desert, a distance of around 4300 kilometres, in eighty-four days.

The distance races organized with Kabardin horses are even more amazing. These animals are native to the northern Caucasus and renowned as extraordinarily sure-footed mountain horses. They,

too, are closely related to the Arab breed and have exceptional speed and stamina. With Cherkassian riders these animals took part in races held in the mountains, in winter, over distances of around three thousand kilometres. The fastest are said to have finished the course in forty-seven days!

History was made in a race over seventy-five kilometres which took place on 4 August 1825 in the public streets of St Petersburg. Two Don horses, the steppe breed made famous by the Don Cossacks, competed against two English Thoroughbreds. Halfway through, one of the Thoroughbreds began to go lame and had to be withdrawn, and one of the Don horses was also obliged to give up, totally exhausted. Although considerably heavier, the second Thoroughbred won the race by eight minutes. The Russians, impressed, imported many Thoroughbreds from England and in 1836 published their first Thoroughbred Studbook. Racing in the English style arrived at the same time and the first racetracks were built in Moscow and St Petersburg.

Professional racing has an enthusiastic following in Russia, but the traditional long-distance races are still very popular. In the Caucasus mountains, for example, such competitions are known as *Mtidaudaschweba*. The course covers five to

seven kilometres and the competitors, who ride bareback, are mostly herdsmen and workers on stud farms.

The *Baigas*, usually fifteen to thirty kilometres long, are also held out in the countryside. These are extremely popular in Kazakhstan, where children, also riding bareback, participate in these races which are held on various holidays and often attract over two hundred riders. Other *Baigas* are ridden on the racetrack. Each race is fifteen to twenty kilometres long and there is a maximum limit of twenty riders.

In addition to racing, more than forty other equestrian sports are played in the Soviet Union, many of them favourite Sunday pastimes on the collective farms. Some are decidedly amusing; the *Khis-Kouhou*, the 'bride hunt' of the Mongols, for example, in which the young men ride after the girls and try to kiss them. The girls retaliate fiercely with their whips. Another game, the *Papach-oinu*, which takes place in a marked-off playing field, lasts for ten minutes, during which time each rider tries to snatch as many caps as possible off the other riders' heads without losing his own.

Sais, an ancient but still very popular game among the mounted herdsmen, is a duel in which each rider tries to grab his opponent by the hands or arms and pull him off his horse. Participants are divided into various classes according to weight.

Abats-le-Sultan is an aggressive eques-

1 Sjurpapach is similar to the Argentinian game of pato. A stuffed, long-haired sheepskin hat has to be thrown through the opponents' ring fixed on top of a high post.

2 In Kabachi the rider, while galloping past, has to throw a spear through a small hoop.

3 Sais is an ancient game from Kirghiz in which each rider, by grabbing his opponent's hands and arms, tries to pull him off his horse. For Sais competitions the participants are divided into classes according to weight.

trian sport. Because it is more expensive — each rider must wear a fencing mask and padded shirt — it is played less often. On top of each rider's mask a feather is fixed upright, which his opponent must try to slice off with a razor-sharp dagger.

Nisakinetum is similar to the Middle European game of head-sticking which dates from the Baroque period. Balls, about the size of a man's head, are arranged on top of several wooden posts, set up in a line. The riders have to gallop past as fast as they can and knock the balls down with a spear.

Kabachi is a version of tilting at the ring. As each rider gallops past he has to throw a spear through a ring set on a post at a height of three metres.

Tschenburti is similar to polo, played by two teams each of six riders. The aim is to hit the ball into the opponents' goal using sticks like long tennis racquets.

Equestrian football is another team game in which the horses have to push a ball of 1.5 m diameter into the goal.

HUNTING ON HORSEBACK

Hunting on horseback is almost as old as hunting itself. For thousands of years man's existence, until he learned how to breed cattle and cultivate fields, depended on his skill at hunting, and to make use of the horse's speed and stamina was only logical.

The hunting instinct is as elementary and basic as the reproductive urge. Civilization has not driven it out of the repertoire of instincts, merely suppressed it, as each of us discovers when for the first time we share with other riders the incomparable excitement of dashing behind the hounds up hill and down dale, over ditches, hedges and walls, putting our trust blindly in our horses, and surrounded by the baying of the hounds, the high-pitched calls of the huntsmen, the snorting of the horses and the clattering of their hooves. Even when the course is over an artificially scented trail which has been carefully prepared, the hunt is exciting: much more so when the trail is laid by a live fox, for he is a shrewd customer whose escape path cannot be plotted in advance. During the pursuit a rider will often sail over obstacles which, when viewed later, make even an experienced huntsman blench.

HUNTING IN EARLIER TIMES

From the discovery of the bones of over ten thousand wild horses at the foot of a cliff in Solutré near Lyon in France, it seems likely that hunters of the Ice Age, in order to obtain large quantities of meat, repeatedly drove herds of wild horses over the top of this cliff to their deaths. Whistles made of stag antlers, dating from the same period, were probably used by the hunters to communicate with each other and to drive the game. They would also have created as much noise as possible by shouting, and used torches and possibly tame wolves (the first 'domestic' animals) to make the horses panic.

This is one of many indications that horses were prized as game animals, and no Ice Age hunter could have imagined that, along with dogs, they would eventually become man's most important assistants on the hunt itself.

The earliest horse breeders probably lived in the vast steppes to the north of the Caucasus mountains, but we cannot be sure whether they first used horses as riding animals or harnessed them in front of their wagons, though many historians firmly believe the latter. These nomads were cattle breeders and it can probably be assumed that they used horses to hunt game.

Drawings and inscriptions found on broken pieces of pottery and writing tablets indicate that the Sumerians hunted on horseback over four thousand

1 A pause in the hunt. Persian miniature from the fifteenth or sixteenth century.

2 Picture of a hunt on a fresco in the Hair al Gharbi palace. Syrian museum, Damascus.

3 Fresco on the Piazza Armerina in Florence.

4 Miniature from an Italian book: 'Riding out to hunt with falcons' from Treviarium Grimani, c. 1500.

5 Coloured copper engraving by Johann Elias Ridinger, 1698 to 1767: 'The procession at a bend in the track on the deer-hunt'.

years ago, but what seem to be the earliest detailed depictions of hunting with horses originate from the age of the Egyptian Pharaohs. A wall picture from the grave of Userbet, the secretary of the Pharaoh Amenophis II, dating from around 1450 BC, is one of the most beautiful of all Egyptian hunting scenes. The hunter stands on a two-wheeled war chariot drawn by two galloping horses. His bow is drawn and his arrow is aimed at some gazelles, hares and hyenas fleeing in front of him.

A similar though much smaller picture of a hunt was found on the quiver belonging to Tutankhamen, dated about 1340 BC.

The Egyptians also used their dogs to drive the game from cover. These were slender, long-legged greyhounds which seem as nobly bred as the small finely-limbed horses.

The hunting scenes depicted on the monumental reliefs in the palace of the Assyrian king Assurbanipal II in Nineveh are particularly impressive. From the seventh century BC, they show the bearded king, on horseback and in his war chariot, hunting lions with spear, and bow and arrow. The Assyrians' horses were bigger and more heavily built than those of the Egyptians, and their dogs were not greyhounds, but massive animals trained to fight. The Assyrians were as bloodthirsty when hunting as they were in battle, and it is said of Assurbanipal II that on one single hunt he killed 450 lions, 390 wild cattle, 200 ostriches and 30 elephants.

It is known that the Assyrians, like the Persians, caught large numbers of all kinds of wild animals and then kept them in enclosures ready for royal 'hunts', but the slaughtering of these animals, though containing an element of danger, can hardly be described as the noble art of hunting.

The ancient Greeks seem to have frowned upon such methods. They organized hunts on horseback in large hunting preserves, and skilled hunters were treated with as much honour as champions in the Olympic stadia.

The Romans also had high standards for hunting. A famous huntsman named Arrian had greyhounds brought from England because he considered them the finest dogs, and wrote the first book of instructions for hunting. But the ancient Romans are more likely to be remembered for the mass slaughterings of wild animals in the arenas, delighting nobility and mob alike; those who hunted for sport are not renowned. Yet at that time other peoples, such as the Germanic tribes, the Celts and the Manchurians, also hunted on horseback.

When the Roman Empire collapsed and the Romans withdrew from England they left the pheasant, a much prized game bird, which they had introduced from southern Europe. But they also left the English defenceless, and over the following centuries, constantly harassed by the Vikings and Danes, they had little time to develop the art of hunting. The English did not finally learn to defend themselves until the time of the Anglo-Saxon king, Alfred the Great (871 to 899). This same Alfred was primarily responsible for making hunting a favourite sport

of the nobility, when he exhorted the young noblemen 'to train themselves in all the arts, but particularly in hunting and riding'.

Hunting was not legally controlled in England until in 1016 the Danish king Canute introduced the death penalty for any unauthorized hunting in his preserves. On the continent the Frankish king Dagobert had already passed laws to make hunting the exclusive prerogative of the nobility. The sport of hunting, particularly on horseback, was no longer simply a chase after booty and began to assume the trappings of a ceremony. Strict rules and laws evolved, and hunting became a science with an extensive vocabulary incomprehensible to outsiders. Today hunting is inseparable from its traditions and ceremonies.

PRESENT-DAY HUNTING

The traditional sport of hunting on horseback remains popular in England and Ireland, and, despite its heavy demands on both rider and horse, people from many walks of life are enthusiastic participants.

With the clearing of the forests the numbers of hoofed wild animals decreased markedly and for the past two centuries the fox has been the most usual quarry. There are some 300 packs of hounds in England, of which about 240 are foxhounds, a good 50 are harriers, that is, packs specifically for hunting hares, and a mere six are staghounds, used for hunting red deer.

The necessary choice of the fox as a game animal was crucial in the development of hunting as a sport. Hunted foxes are extremely cunning, and will jump over ditches and walls, and squeeze their way through undergrowth and

barriers of all sorts. Riders and horses have to find negotiable places in all the hedges and walls, jump hair-raising obstacles and always be ready to react with lightning speed, if they are to keep up. They also have to be able to keep going for hours at a time and often in all weathers, so it is not surprising that riders from the British Isles consistently attain the highest levels of horsemanship, for from childhood most of them have ridden their ponies behind the

1 The 'Scarteen Black and Tans', an outstanding pack of black and brown foxhounds, from the county of Limerick in Ireland.

2 In Germany the huntsmen also ride behind a pack, but instead of pursuing live game they follow a carefully prepared artificial trail. Nevertheless the hunt is still exciting and demanding.

baying pack. For this same reason horses from England and Ireland are noted for their speed, stamina and tremendous jumping ability.

The sport is also popular in the eastern US, where there are about 130 foxhound packs. By comparison, New Zealand has 17 packs, Canada 11, and Australia 7.

The traditional pattern of the English fox hunt has comparatively simple rules. So long as the master is never overtaken, each rider is free to select his own way

3 Hunting the hare in Ireland. In addition to thirty-three packs of fox-hounds there are at least thirty harrier packs, which specialize in coursing, and two packs of staghounds.

4 The fox has gone into the pipe. The large hounds are helpless, but smaller fox terriers are often brought along on the horses, expressly to try to force the wily animal out.

5 The hunting horn is an indispensable means of communication when hunts are held in large forests. It is also the traditional accompaniment to the drag hunt, and horn players have to master a wide repertoire of different signals.

3

4

5

of keeping in contact with the pack. Each pack is controlled by a Master of Foxhounds, a title which is usually inherited and which carries at least as much weight as a doctorate. The foxhounds are never called dogs like ordinary canines, but always referred to formally as hounds, a privilege shared by greyhounds, which originally were also hunting dogs.

Vénerie, or hunting French-style, is much more complicated than English hunting, and has its origins in the courtly hunts staged by the Frankish kings. The basic difference is that the French hunt takes place in a forest, where the mounted huntsmen follow a very carefully planned strategy as they move through the network of the ancient pathways. They keep in close touch with each other among the trees by a wide repertoire of horn signals. The huge packs of hounds are divided into groups or shifts. Much larger than English foxhounds, particularly those known as the *Blanc et Noir* and *Francais Tricolore*, which have tri-coloured coats and are over 70 cm tall, they need both strength and size for their prey are deer and wild pig.

The complicated ceremonial of the *vénerie*, which includes seventy-two

different horn signals for the deer's movements alone, has remained basically unchanged for centuries.

Hunters in France still have about a million hectares of forest at their disposal, and there are almost a hundred hunting associations, each with their own packs known as *équipages*. Outside that country, *vénerie* is almost unknown, with only five *équipages* in Belgium and one in French-speaking Canada. The latter pack is remarkable, for it specializes in hunting wolves and coyotes.

Although hunting live game with dogs is forbidden in Germany, in the autumn thirteen packs of English foxhounds and beagles still dash through the fields and forests. They are accompanied by the Master of the Hounds and his assistants, the *piqueurs* or whippers-in with their long whips for keeping the hounds in order, and followed by large groups of riders who wear either red or black coats or tweed jackets, which indicate their status based on previous performance in the hunt. Baying enthusiastically, the hounds follow the invisible trail. Although it has every appearance of a genuine hunt, it is in fact a drag hunt. The trail of scent which the hounds are following has been laid artificially using, for example, fox droppings, and the hunt

follows a course laid out in advance, which includes obstacles made to look as natural a part of the countryside as possible. These courses have varying degrees of difficulty so that each rider can select a hunt which suits him personally.

In some countries 'foxhunts' are merely equestrian games which give the 'hunt' and their friends the opportunity for a ride across country. The course varies from easy to demanding, and at the end, the riders take part in a competition for the fox's brush. In this a rider taking the part of the fox fixes a fox's brush to one shoulder — let us assume it is the right one — to be pursued by the other riders who try to seize the trophy, which they are only allowed to grab from the opposite side, in this case the left.

Alternatively the fox's brush is hung up on a taut line but within reach. At a given signal all the riders dash off to try to pull it down.

HORSE RACING

Horse racing epitomises equestrian sport. From the moment the horse first emerged from the primeval swamps on to the open grassland, his most important weapon in the fight for survival has been speed. And probably ever since men learnt to ride horses they have tested them in races — just for the fun of it; or to separate the wheat from the chaff for breeding purposes; or quite simply to earn money.

In the time of the early Greeks, horse racing had already become a disciplined sport with strict rules, and from 680 BC chariot races were one of the highlights of the Olympic Games. About forty years later races under saddle were introduced, which included races for horses of all ages over various distances as well as races specially for mares. The best drivers and riders were fêted; the most successful horses were taken to exclusive studs to breed animals of the highest nobility and performance.

Identical objectives were behind the development of the Thoroughbred breed in England about two hundred and fifty years ago. Not only does this breed of horse now dominate most racetracks of the world; without it the modern horse breeding industry would not exist.

ORIGINS OF RACING IN ENGLAND

In AD 208 the Roman Emperor Lucius Septimius Severus (193 to 211) led a campaign to Britain. There he settled and lived out the rest of his life in Yorkshire, where he is reported to have laid out the first racetrack on English soil, and organized horse races. This imperial amusement may well have had some influence on the development of racing in England, for the Romans are said to have brought in Oriental horses for their races, which would suggest that the indigenous ponies which later contributed to the development of the English Thoroughbred had some noble desert blood in them.

Ecclesiastical records confirm that during the centuries after the Roman occupation, horse racing, though probably not widely spread, was certainly a popular amusement, and Church dignitaries who recorded such things were outraged at its continuing existence. In 1074 William Fitzstephen published his *Description of the city of London*, in which he gave the first detailed account of these events. According to this, horses were brought to Smithfield every Friday to be sold. To show off the animals' potential, professional jockeys took them at a gallop up and down a marked course in front of a grandstand which was always well filled with spectators and prospective buyers. And no doubt many of the onlookers made bets with each other.

Similar races were also held a little later on at the market in Newmarket. No one would have dreamt then that this small town set in the open rolling landscape of Suffolk would one day become the mecca of the Thoroughbred breeding industry.

Although racehorses were not being bred specifically, expert breeders would have followed a selective process and chosen only the fastest horses for their studs, a selective process in which Oriental horses soon began to play an important role. The superior speed and stamina of the desert horses were obvious, and from the fourteenth century an increasing number of Arab, Barb, Turkish and Persian horses were imported into the British Isles.

Thomas Blundeville, a highly respected expert on horses with an instinctive talent for breeding, was one of the founders of the Thoroughbred breeding industry. In a publication which appeared in 1565 and attracted a great deal of attention, he put forward a persuasive argument for the consistent breeding of noble blood-lines — following the procedures recommended by Mohammed about a thousand years earlier.

In the following century the industry received considerable encouragement from the Stuart kings, and both James I (1603 to 1625) and Charles I (1625 to 1649) fostered the development of racing as a sport. Under Charles in particular Newmarket became the centre of the horse racing scene. There in 1627 the famous Spring and Autumn races were inaugurated, which always attracted the fastest horses in the country. In 1634 the king donated the first of the Gold Cups which have remained sought-after trophies up to the present day.

In 1654 Oliver Cromwell (1649 to 1658) banned public horse races although, with his 'Ironsides', he had built up an

1 Byerley Turk, an Oriental stallion from Turkey, was brought to Yorkshire in 1691. He became the first of the three founding sires of the English Thoroughbred breed.

2 Of the three founding sires Darley Arabian was probably the only pure-bred Arab, and the greatest as a lineage founder. He first stood at stud in England in 1704, and now about ninety-five per cent of all English Thoroughbreds trace their descent from him.

3 Godolphin Barb is also known as Godolphin Arabian, although he came from Tunis and was obviously a Berber. In 1731 he founded the third of the three famous lineages.

4 The most important of the later sires from the line founded by Byerley Turk was his great-great-grandson King Herod — often referred to simply as Herod.

5 The most famous sire of all was a great-great-grandson of Darley Arabian, called Eclipse because he was said to have been born during an eclipse of the sun.

6 The most successful of Godolphin Barb's descendants was his grandson Matchem, foaled in 1748.

Opposite: Flying Childers, a son of Darley Arabian, is described as the first great racehorse and often as the first English Thoroughbred as well. In his time the stallion was unbeatable and was dubbed the swiftest horse that had ever been bred.

outstanding cavalry force, and was personally anxious to improve the breeding industry.

The evolution of the Thoroughbred could not be halted, however, and under Charles II (1660 to 1685) the sport of racing was soon flourishing again. Races were held regularly on twelve courses, including Epsom where the English Derby is still run, and the King provided the prizes in the form of valuable silver 'King's Plates'. These races were the precursors of what are now the classic races.

More and more Oriental stallions were brought in and their influence on the breeding of racehorses increased; but few of these lineages had any staying power. Although 103 Oriental stallions were registered in the *General Stud Book* as the founders of the Thoroughbred breed, only three blood-lines have been able to maintain themselves to the present day. By 1850 traces of all others were obliterated, and only these three can be considered to be genuine found-

ing sires: Byerley Turk, Darley Arabian and Godolphin Barb.

Like most of the Oriental stallions of that time they bore the names of their owners. Byerley Turk fell into the hands of a Captain Byerley in 1683 at the siege of Vienna. Like so many of the Turks' horses, the light bay stallion was very nobly bred, perhaps even a pure-bred Arab, and because he had an iron constitution the English officer kept him as a cavalry horse. He rode him in the Irish campaign undertaken at the instigation of King William III in 1690, and then the horse was sent to stud in England where he covered a very few mares. Unfortunately little is known about them, though some doubtless had excellent qualities, and Byerley Turk sired outstanding progeny, the most noteworthy of his direct descendants being Jig, whose great-grandson King Herod, foaled in 1758 on the Duke of Cumberland's Stud, became one of the most prepotent of all sires.

Darley Arabian was bought by Thomas

Darley, the British Consul in Aleppo, Syria, for his brother Richard (according to one story he was exchanged for a gun). The stallion reached England at the beginning of 1704, in good health despite the conditions of war that prevailed at the time, and the beautiful, dark bay, pure-bred Muniqi Arab became the stud stallion on the Darley estate in Aldby, Yorkshire, where he lived to the ripe old age of thirty years. It is hard to imagine how the Thoroughbred breeding industry would have developed without this stallion. Of the something like 800,000 Thoroughbred horses in the world today, ninety per cent of them are his descendants through his great-great-grandson Eclipse.

Godolphin Barb, the third of the founding sires, had the most remarkable history. Despite the name of Godolphin Arabian, he was probably a Berber; although like many members of his race he would have had some Arab blood. Unlike the other two founding sires, his appearance, with tiny ears and a pow-

1 *The Duke of Cumberland who, on his Stud at Windsor Great Park, bred Eclipse — one of the most remarkable horses of all time.*

2 *Although Marske was never an outstanding racehorse, he was an excellent stud stallion. He sired Eclipse — or so the equerry claimed.*

3 *Eclipse at Beacon racetrack.*

4 *Dungannon, along with Pot-8-Os, Empress, Young Eclipse, Gunpowder and Meteor, was one of the most impressive of Eclipse's sons. He was also famous for his friendship with a sheep.*

5 *Hambletonian, the winner of the St Leger in 1795, was a grandson of Eclipse through King Fergus. He proved himself to be one of the most prepotent sires in the history of Thoroughbred breeding.*

Cambridgeshire, where he is reputed to have served as a teaser, until a mare named Roxana obstinately refused to receive the stud stallion Hobgoblin, and for want of a better alternative Sham was allowed to cover her. The facts, however, are that by 1731 Sham had already covered Roxana at Coke's stud, and it is unlikely that the stallion ever had to endure the humiliating role of a teaser. The result of the mating was Lath, one of the greatest racehorses of his time. Sham remained on Lord Godolphin's stud and continued to cover numerous mares until his death on Christmas Day 1753, aged twenty-nine.

His most noteworthy descendant was Cade who sired Matchem. Like King Herod and Eclipse, the descendants of Byerley Turk and Darley Arabian respectively, Matchem was the only descendant of Godolphin Barb able to perpetuate his great qualities through a lineage which has been maintained to the present day.

William Augustus, Duke of Cumberland and son of George II, might have been an unlucky commander, but he was an outstanding horse-breeder. King Herod was among many fine horses bred in his stables, and a horse which was born on 1 April 1764 on his stud at Windsor Great Park deserves at least as much recognition as the three founding sires. He was called Eclipse because he was said to have been born during an eclipse of the sun. There was a problem, however, in that the colt's mother, Spiletta, had been covered by two stallions, Shakespeare and Marske. Although the Duke's equerry declared publicly that Marske had been the sire of Eclipse, and this was recorded in the *General Stud Book*, lingering doubt remains.

In 1765 the Duke died of a stroke at the early age of forty-four, and did not live to enjoy the unprecedented success of this most outstanding of all his horses — Eclipse, later sold at an auction. A livestock dealer named William Wildman, who bought the horse, almost decided to have the young stallion gelded. Fortunately — an event which merits the eternal gratitude of the whole Thoroughbred breeding industry — a man was found who was able to cope with the animal's unruly temperament.

erful fat neck, would not have created a very good first impression, although if contemporary drawings can be believed he was otherwise splendidly built. Originally taken to France as a present for Louis XV from the Bey of Tunis, because Baroque parade horses of Andalusian and Neapolitan descent were currently in fashion there, the stallion was not considered suitable for the Royal Stables. One story is that he then pulled a water-cart through the streets of Paris, but that is probably only an embellishment to his Cinderella-like tale. What is certain is that in 1729 he was discovered by an Englishman named Coke, who took him to England.

When Edward Coke died in 1733 the stallion, which was originally called Sham, is said to have been bequeathed to one Roger Williams, a coffee-house owner who, as a sideline, also dealt in racehorses. He in turn sold the horse to Lord Godolphin who took him to

Wildman did not allow Eclipse on the racetrack until he was five years old, but even before the stallion had run a race the spies at training had noticed that they were dealing with an unusually fast horse. In his first race, at Epsom on 3 May 1769, the odds were already four to one in his favour. One of the spectators, an Irishman named Colonel O'Kelly who owned a stud and racing stable close by, was so impressed by this first run that he made the now famous comment, 'Eclipse first — and the rest nowhere.' Thereupon he placed very high bets on the horse's next race — and won. The following year he bought the stallion for 1750 guineas. (The previous owners had auctioned the horse for seventy-five guineas.) With this the Irishman made the most successful business deal of his life; as a racehorse and as a stud stallion Eclipse brought him the unprecedented sum of thirty thousand pounds.

Although many writers describe Flying Childers, the son of Darley Arabian, as the first English Thoroughbred, Eclipse was certainly the greatest representative of this breed, and therefore possibly the most outstanding horse of all. During his short racing career of only one and half years, he ran in eighteen of the most important races of that time, always winning by a considerable margin. His jockey John Oakley never needed to urge him on. Understandably enough, no one liked to enter his horse against such a vastly superior rival, and in seven of his races he had no competition and had to race alone! On the racetrack only one horse managed to get its nose near Eclipse's shoulder. This was Bucephalus, which had up till then won many races and acquired a reputation worthy of his name, but after a bitterly fought duel Eclipse clearly outdistanced him from the halfway point on, and finally Bucephalus's will to win was broken.

Eclipse's unique prepotency was even more important, and 344 of his foals won a total of 862 races. His most notable descendants were King Fergus and Pot-8-Os, horses whose blood-lines have been maintained to the present day.

When Eclipse died on 27 February 1789 he was dissected and measured by the French anatomist Charles Vial de St Bel. The skeleton of this wonder horse was much sought-after by collectors. In fact, no one knows for certain where the genuine one is, for there are at least six, all said to be Eclipse. Great honours can be bestowed on a horse!

A great deal more is known about these great sires than about the mares which were the founding dams of the Tho-

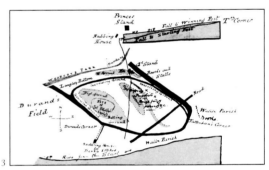

1 Orville, foaled in 1799, was the St Leger winner in 1803. He was a difficult horse but his jockey, Will Edward, described him as the best he had ever ridden.

2 Touchstone won the St Leger in 1834. He became one of the leading sires of his time.

3 A drawing of the track at Epsom, dated 1823. Since 1780 the English Derby, the most famous race in the world, has been run here annually.

4 The Derby at Epsom, after a painting by James Pollard, 1834.

roughbred breed. The story that these mares were ponies is probably just as incorrect as the report that they were fifty Oriental mares imported specially by King Charles II. If they were ponies, they were probably animals which had a high proportion of Oriental blood, and which for generations had been bred for speed. There may well have been some pure-bred Oriental mares as well. Research done about 1890 by an Australian named Lowe, and in 1953 by a Pole called Bobinski, indicates that of some hundred mares who founded the breed, forty-three formed maternal lines which still exist today.

Racing was very well organized even before Eclipse was born. The English Jockey Club had been founded in 1752 with the object of laying down strict rules to regulate horse racing and breeding, and a century later the Jockey Club, under its then president, Admiral Henry John Rous (often called the Dictator of the Turf), had become very influential.

At that time most races were run over two miles or even greater distances, and the horses were normally at least five years old before they were raced. The first races for three-year-olds were held in 1756 and only from 1776 onwards were there races for two-year-olds. So that these young horses should not be overtaxed, distances were reduced, and it was in these races that the so-called 'Classics' had their origins. They have remained the supreme tests. The St Leger, inaugurated in 1776, and named after its founder, is one and three-quarter miles long.

Three years later the Oaks was run for the first time. This one-mile race is

5 The Derby at Epsom in 1847. In this coloured etching by Charles Hunt, Cossack, the winner, is in the middle; War Eagle, placed second, is on the left; and on the right is Van Tromp who came third, but in the same year won both the St Leger and the Ascot Gold Cup.

6 Persimmon won the Derby in 1896 and as a sire produced outstanding mares.

7 In 1902 Sceptre won all the classic races except the Derby. She is considered one of the greatest racing mares of all time.

8 In 1900 Diamond Jubilee, the son of the unbeaten St Simon, won the Triple Crown, i.e., the three classic races — the Two Thousand Guineas, the Derby and the St Leger.

named after the country house of the twelfth Earl of Derby near Epsom. Lastly, in 1780 came the Derby, which has remained the most prestigious of all horse races. Lord Bunbury, the first president of the Jockey Club, and Derby tossed a coin to see who should name the race. Derby won, but it was some consolation to Bunbury that his horse Diomed was the winner of the first Derby at Epsom on 4 May 1780. At that time the race was still being run over a distance of a mile. Later it was increased to one and a half miles.

The Two Thousand and the Thousand Guineas, the other two classic races, were founded in 1809 and 1814 respectively. All these classic races are tests for three-year-olds; but only mares are allowed to race in the Thousand Guineas and the Oaks. All stallions carry the same weight; mares carry four pounds less. A horse that wins over all three distances is called the Triple Crown Winner, and when this happens in the classic races of England, France or the US, then that horse earns a permanent place in the history of the Turf.

In 1791 the handicap was added to the rules of the Jockey Club, when, in the Oatland Stakes at Ascot, a race was run in which for the first time horses carried different weights, which were based on their previous performances. The handicap system gave every horse an equal chance of winning, and considerably increased the excitement for the owners and the betting public. Admittedly the task of the handicapper has remained a very difficult and thankless one.

THE TWENTIETH CENTURY IN ENGLAND

Ascot and Epsom may have the more evocative and prestigious names, but Newmarket is the real centre of the Thoroughbred empire. Although originally little more than a small market town some seventy miles (112 km) to the north of London, it is certainly not lacking in tradition. In the early seventeenth century James I used to hunt there, while his followers amused themselves by organizing 'matches', that is, races run between two horses to settle a wager or argument between the owners.

Newmarket is the headquarters of the all-powerful Jockey Club, whose Georgian exterior dominates the main street, and Tattersalls, the famous auction house, is also there. It has been auctioning Thoroughbreds since 1750. Breeders from all over the world gather at Newmarket and the annual turnover is about eight million pounds.

There are thirty-five stables in the district, and about two thousand horses are in training. Early each morning they are exercised by their jockeys over the two main working grounds, which are extensive and scenically very beautiful. Newmarket has two first class racetracks which cater for many other races as well as the celebrated One Thousand and Two Thousand Guineas. These two are run on what is called the Rowley Mile, the name a reminder of Charles II, who, from about 1660, was a great promoter of horse racing. He also enjoyed taking part in the sport himself (he won the Newmarket Town Plate twice), and owned a horse called Old Rowley, after

Above:
At the entrance to Woodland Stud, Newmarket, there is a statue of Hyperion, probably the greatest Thoroughbred this century has produced.

Right:
In keeping with tradition, English racecourses have changed little in two hundred years — except for the people with cameras. This is a picture of the winners' enclosure at Ascot.

FIRST

which he was later nicknamed. The Newmarket Town Plate is still run today.

The flat open countryside is ideal for breeding horses, and there are at least forty stud farms in the neighbourhood.

There are a total of sixty-three race-courses in England, Scotland and Wales, and horse racing in Britain is particularly interesting because there is so much variety in the courses. Some, like Ascot, are very formal. There, before the main race, the Queen, amid cheers, is driven along a part of the track in an open landau drawn by the famous Windsor Greys. (Coach horses used on ceremonial occasions are traditionally grey, even though the Queen has her own stud of coach horses consisting of brown Cleveland Bays.)

The racetrack at Windsor, tucked into a bend in the River Thames, is also very formal, as befits its surroundings, whereas Pontefract in Yorkshire, for example, is in a coal-mining area where most of the local people are miners, who go just to enjoy themselves.

The racecourse at Chester is built on historic ground; the Romans are said to have held horse races there, as they did in Wetherby in Yorkshire. At Chester a large crowd of people can follow the course of the race from the vantage point provided by the ancient city walls.

The tracks themselves are laid out in a variety of ways. Twenty-three, including Ascot, are right-handed courses, that is, the horses gallop in a clockwise direction. Thirty-eight, including Epsom, are left-handed courses, which the horses prefer, according to the experts. The other two, Windsor and Fontwell, are laid out as figures of eight. Many tracks are uneven, with rises and dips in them; curves can be wide or sharp; ground conditions may vary, and are also affected by the weather.

In addition almost all racehorses have their own specific strengths and preferences. Some do particularly well on a springy turf; others show their mettle when the gradient of the course rises towards the finishing line. Races on such a variety of courses are always exciting because not even the experts can predict the outcome with any degree of certainty.

About eight thousand racehorses are in training throughout the whole of England. They are in the care of about four hundred licensed trainers, and possibly a hundred private trainers — who are allowed to work only with privately owned horses. The annual number of race days is about eight hundred and fifty.

One of the many breeding establishments concentrated around Newmarket is the National Stud. It is a national stud

in name only, as it has received no government subsidy since 1963 and is now an independent enterprise.

The history of the English National Stud actually begins in Tully, Ireland, which is presently the home of the Irish National Stud, near the famous Curragh racecourse. Originally it belonged to William Hall Walker, who was one of the most colourful racing personalities of his time. In 1915 he donated his string of six stud stallions, forty-three broodmares and twenty-nine young horses to the British government on the condition that it used them to found a National Stud. He also offered to sell them the premises.

During its first decades the National Stud produced no less than four Derby winners (Trigo, Blenheim, Windsor Lad and Bahram), as well as Royal Lancer and Chamossaire, winners of the St Leger, Big Game, a winner of the Two Thousand Guineas, and Sun Chariot, the 1942 winner of the One Thousand Guineas, the Oaks and the St Leger.

During World War Two the British government sold the premises to the Irish government, which used them to set up its own National Stud, and the

1 Hyperion was often spoken of disparagingly and called small, lazy and difficult; but as a racehorse and as a sire he was outstanding. This stallion was foaled in 1930 and his sons were subsequently sold to America, France, Argentina, Australia, New Zealand and South Africa.

2 Blakeney, the winner of the Derby in 1966, now a stud stallion at the English National Stud. He is a first class horse and one of a now small number which trace their descent from Byerley Turk.

3 Grundy, foaled in 1972. As a two-year-old he won four races, and as a three-year-old he won five. Like Blakeney he, too, now stands at stud in the National Stud at Newmarket.

4 Internationally Lester Piggott is probably the best known of all contemporary jockeys. He has ridden winners on all the larger racecourses in the world.

5 The jockey Gordon Richards was born in 1904. Between 1925 and 1953 he rode in 23,834 races and won 4,870 times.

6 Steve Donoghue, born 1884. Up to 1937 he won no fewer than fourteen classic races.

7 Wolverton, one of the Royal Studs. Here, as at Sandringham, there is one stud stallion and about twenty broodmares, all belonging to HM the Queen.

8 In Newmarket at the turn of the century the 16th Earl of Derby built Woodland Stud. This is where Hyperion was foaled.

9 The stallions' quarters at the English National Stud at Newmarket which was built between 1965 and 1969.

horses were removed to Gillingham in Dorset.

Once the new administration was autonomous, it proceeded, between 1965 and 1969, to build the ultra-modern stud near Newmarket. This houses only top quality stud stallions, and broodmares are brought in to be covered and to foal.

Dalham Hall is one of the most remarkable studs in the Newmarket area. While the complement is small — about seventeen broodmares and only one stallion — it is of excellent quality. In 1975 the stud stallion Great Nephew was the leading sire, and in the same year the seven yearlings were sold for an average price of 52,714 guineas — an unprecedented sum for that side of the Atlantic.

Someries Stud, with its seventy-five horse boxes, is situated nearby. It is a medium-sized stud which has produced two outstanding horses. Precipitation, the winner of the Ascot Gold Cup and six other races, sired progeny which won over five hundred races and together accumulated over £333,000. Meld was one of the best Thoroughbred mares of the century (and one of the most popular with the racing public). She won the One Thousand Guineas, the Oaks, and the St Leger, and produced among others the Derby winner Charlottown.

Stanley and Woodlands, the stud founded shortly before the turn of the century by the 16th Earl of Derby, is also near Newmarket. On Good Friday 1930 a small weak foal was born here. It was called Hyperion and although always small, in every other respect he was anything but weak. In fact, he became one of the most influential stallions in the history of Thoroughbred breeding. This apparently lazy and difficult horse easily won the Derby and the St Leger. After retiring from his racing career he was six times leading sire of the year. In the years after World War Two his sons were the most valuable of all the Thoroughbreds then available and a large number of them were taken to the US, Argentina, France, Australia, New Zealand and South Africa. His most famous descendant from that period is probably his great-great-grandson Vaguely Noble.

Out of all the many other studs dotted throughout the country the Royal Studs deserve special mention. Their history can be traced back to the sixteenth century when Henry VIII started the Royal Stud at Hampton Court — an eventful history which fluctuated according to the moods and hobbies of the sovereign. Hampton Court was neglected more than once, and that venerable institution was finally closed in 1894, when the horses were moved into today's Royal Studs — Sandringham and Wolverton.

Sandringham became famous very early on through the mare Perdita II which, covered by St Simon, produced such successful horses as Florizel II, Persimmon and Diamond Jubilee. More recently the most outstanding royal horse was Aureole. He came second in the Derby five days after the coronation of his owner, HM Queen Elizabeth II, and in 1954 was chosen as the best European racehorse. He was also twice acknowledged as the leading sire of the year.

Childwick Bury near St Albans, northeast of London, is one of the most beautiful and well kept studs in the whole of England. There are three hundred horseboxes, each with direct access to the open air, and the spacious park-like grounds include a beautiful rose garden. It was in the early years of this century that this stud first achieved success. In 1903 Our Lassie, and in 1907 Glass Doll won the Oaks; in 1907 Sunstar won the Two Thousand Guineas and the Derby; in 1912 Jest and in 1913 Princess Dorrie won the One Thousand Guineas and the Oaks; and in 1921 Humorist won the Derby. The stud then went through a low period which lasted for over twenty years, but after World War Two it gradually regained its good name. Since then Childwick Bury has produced about seven hundred winners.

10 February 1916. Lord Derby's trainer, George Lambton, who also trained the Aga Khan's first racehorses (among them the marvellous mare Mumtaz Mahal) is standing on the right of Bellhouse, the jockey. E. de St Cebry and Lord Derby, the breeders, are behind Lambton on the right.

11 Epsom Derby 1930. The Aga Khan leads his winning horse, Blenheim, and its jockey H. Wragg into the ring.

12 Oaks Day 1925. Lord and Lady Astor on the course at Epsom.

12

EPSOM

Any uninitiated spectator, who arrived at Epsom on Derby Day expecting to enjoy a formal traditional race meeting, would be surprised to find himself instead in the middle of a noisy fairground. Quite possibly Derby Day owes its immense popularity to the fact that it has very much the air of a village festival. Many different types of people can be found among the enormous crowd of spectators, some of whom take no interest in racing at all for most of the year, but feel it is almost a duty to attend the Derby and place a bet on the outcome of this famous race.

For over two hundred years the Derby has been run at Epsom, fifteen miles (24 km) south-west of London. The most important of the classic races, although not the longest, since 1872 it has been run over a very unusual course. Shortly after the start the track rises uphill in an easy right-hand curve, and, after a straight of about half a mile, or one kilometre, bears downhill into Tattenham Corner, which is a sharp left-hand curve, and ends with a half mile straight to the finish.

Although few jockeys would admit that the Epsom Derby is an extraordinary race, for each one it is just that, and even more so if they are led into the winners' enclosure afterwards. When a French horse won the race for the first time the event was described as revenge for Waterloo, and when for the first time an American horse won, the stock exchange on Wall Street is said to have been given a boost.

In this century some of the most outstanding winners of this classic race have been Diamond Jubilee (1900), Spearmint (1906), Orby (1907), Sunstar (1911), Sansovino (1924), Hyperion (1933), Bahram (1935), Pinza (1953), Sea Bird II (1965), Nijinsky II (1970), Mill Reef (1971) and Troy (1979).

Left: Royal Ascot offers, in addition to the marvellous race, a view of the latest fashions in women's hats and men's borrowed morning coats.

Right: Horses and jockeys leave the starting stalls to compete for the much sought-after Ascot Gold Cup.

Below: Arrival of HM the Queen and Prince Philip in their coach and four, which is driven from the saddle.

ASCOT

The atmosphere at Ascot, the Royal racecourse thirty miles (48 km) to the west of London, is completely different from Epsom. It is undeniably regal, particularly during the traditional four days of Royal Ascot. Not one of the five classic English races is run here (the One Thousand and Two Thousand Guineas are held in Newmarket, the Derby and the Oaks at Epsom and the St Leger in Doncaster), but the Ascot Gold Cup is one of the most sought-after trophies. It has been competed for here since 1807.

Annually, in the third week in June, a field of élite horses is assembled to race for the valuable cup and prize money of over ten thousand pounds.

A month later the King George VI and Queen Elizabeth Stakes, the second great event, calls the best of the three-year-olds out on to the track. This race has been run since 1946, and is a particularly valuable one for horses in this age group.

Royal Ascot meetings are not merely horse races; they are also some of the most important social events of the year. When the Queen is driven in a coach and four, behind the red-coated grooms, along the course in front of the grandstand she encounters a very formally dressed crowd of dignified spectators: thousands of women dressed in expensive and fashionable outfits topped off with the latest in millinery, thousands of men in morning coats and grey top hats, landed gentry in large numbers, hordes of *nouveaux riches*, and an even larger number of gentlemen wearing hired morning coats.

Queen Anne was too stout to be a good equestrienne, but she was an extremely enthusiastic supporter of the sport. The course at Ascot was laid out at her instigation, and in 1711 she presided at the opening ceremony. Until World War Two only four royal racedays were held annually. Nowadays there are about twenty-five, and recently a steeplechase course was added.

In 1955 Ribot, the greatest Italian racehorse of all time, was one of the entrants in the King George VI and Queen Elizabeth Stakes. Two days before the race, while training at Ascot, this 'wonder horse', bred by Federico Tesio, just missed breaking the track record by six-tenths of a second. Afterwards he was still as fresh as any horse after a normal training run.

On the following day, however, it rained, and it was common knowledge that Ribot never did very well on slow, muddy ground. At the start the outstanding Belgian horse, Todrai, was in the lead, closely followed by Ribot. But then, to tumultuous applause, the Queen's horse, High Veldt, overtook both of them. For the first time in his career Ribot looked as though he was going to be beaten — but in the finishing straight he exceeded all expectations and won by five lengths.

Goodwood, on the Sussex Downs, sixty miles (96 km) to the south-west of London, is the only other English racecourse where the atmosphere is as formal as it is at Ascot. The course is situated in the park belonging to the Duke of Richmond and Gordon. The meeting, which lasts for four days in July, is just as popular as Royal Ascot, and the Goodwood Cup, the Gordon Stakes and the News of the World Stakes are all high points of the British racing scene.

RACING
IN THE UNITED STATES

Every year about eighty million spectators gather on the hundred and forty American racecourses, where they place about $5 billion dollars' worth of bets on the horses they hope will win. Racing is an even more popular sport than football, which comes second with its 'mere' forty-five million supporters. And such astronomical figures are possible despite pressure from certain religious and other groups who have succeeded in having racing banned in twenty-two states of the US — even including Texas, whose history is perhaps much more closely tied up with horses than any other US state, and Virginia, the cradle of American Thoroughbred breeding. In these states, races are held at agricultural fairs and similar functions, but as betting is forbidden much of the point of racing is lost.

Nevertheless, the breeding of Thoroughbreds is a thriving industry in America, and only France is in a comparable position. Although to a large degree this is due to business acumen, the American people also have a very strong interest in and liking for horses.

In 1897 a jockey appeared on the English racing scene whose unconventional riding style caused considerable mirth. At that time all riders still adopted the Victorian riding style, which is, in fact, very similar to the Western riding style. They sat deep in the saddle, with straight backs and legs stretched out. This particular jockey, however, had adjusted his stirrups so that they were very short

and he apparently floated along, crouching low as he bent forward over the horse's withers. He was James Forman Sloan, an American, known as Tod Sloan or 'The Monkey up the Stick'.

But he was not laughed at for long, for very soon the public, the horses' owners and his competitors realized that this style was bringing Sloan considerable success, and that he was able to achieve faster speeds on his horses than any other jockey.

In a very short time he had won twenty

1 Willie Shoemaker, 'The Shoe', born 1931 in El Paso, Texas, rode his first winner on 20 April 1949, and in the same year came first a further 218 times. Up to 1976 he had ridden in over 29,000 races and won 700 times.

2 In October 1979, Laffit Pincay, Jr., from Panama, set a new world record. The horses he had ridden — Affirmed was one of them — had won over US$7 million in a single season.

3 The statue in the cemetery at Calumet Stud, Lexington, Kentucky, was erected in memory of Bull Lea, the sire of three Kentucky Derby winners. His sons and daughters won over US $13 million on the racetrack.

4 In 1919 Sir Barton, by Star Shoot out of Lady Sterling, was the first Triple Crown winner in American racing history.

5 Gallant Fox, by Sir Gallahad III out of Marguerite: Triple Crown winner, 1930.

6 Omaha, by Gallant Fox out of Flambino: Triple Crown winner, 1935.

races, and the following season he was signed on by Lord William Beresford, for whom he achieved fantastic results. Within a very few years Sloan had ridden in approximately two thousand races and won about seven hundred of them. He earned a great deal of money, but much of this went on illegal betting, and at the beginning of 1901 the Jockey Club revoked his licence. He died in 1933 from an excessive consumption of alcohol.

In the meantime his style had long since ceased to be a sensation, and had been adopted by jockeys all over the world. Tod Sloan did not invent the monkey seat, but he had watched blacks in the southern states riding bareback in their quarter-mile races out in the country and noticed that they crouched well forward and held on tightly with their knees to the horse's withers.

The most famous American jockey of modern times is Willie Shoemaker, also called 'The Shoe'. He was born on 19 August 1931 near El Paso, Texas, a town which is as unattractive as it is famous. At birth he is said to have weighed not

much more than a kilogram, and he owed his life to his grandmother who, as they had no incubator, put him in the oven. As an adult, at only 1.50 metres tall, he is still very small even for a jockey, but his career by contrast is all the more spectacular.

In 1949, as an eighteen-year-old apprentice, he won 219 races. This immediately made him American vice-champion behind Gordon Glisson. Since then 'The Shoe' has raced in approximately thirty-five thousand races, and won some eight thousand times. Such a success story requires both extraordinary talent and tremendous application and is also only conceivable in the land of unlimited possibilities. It is only in the US that races are held on afternoons and evenings throughout the year, and it is possible, for a period of over thirty years, to ride in an average of three races per day and to win almost five races a week!

Both Eddie Arcaro, with 4779 wins, and John Longden, with 6032 wins, also have extremely successful track records as jockeys. At present the most talented and successful jockeys are Laffit Pincay, Jr., Angel Cordero, Jr. and Chris McCarron.

Left: The start at Santa Fe Downs in New Mexico, US.

Above: Man O'War, foaled in 1917, by Fair Play out of Mahubah, a great-great-grandson of St Simon. Out of twenty-one races he came in second once and won the other twenty. He is one of the most outstanding Thoroughbreds to come from the US.

205

1 War Admiral, by Man O'War out of Brushup: Triple Crown winner, 1937.

2 Whirlaway, by Blenheim II out of Dustwhirl: Triple Crown winner, 1941.

3 Count Fleet, by Reigh Count out of Quickly: Triple Crown winner, 1943.

4 Assault, by Bold Venture out of Igual: Triple Crown winner, 1946.

5 Citation, by Bull Lea out of Hydroplane II: Triple Crown winner, 1948.

6 Secretariat, by Bold Ruler out of Something Royal: Triple Crown winner, 1973.

Of course they share their triumphs with the magnificent horses they ride, the champions who earn vast sums for their owners. John Henry is presently the leading money-earner, with over US$6 million in prize money.

Spectacular Bid has also earned a great deal of money. When he first raced as a three-year-old he had amassed for his owner the then unprecedented sum of US$2,781,607 after thirty races and twenty-six wins. A syndicate bought him for the unusually high price of US$22 million. Whether as a stud stallion he will justify their outlay depends on his potency as a sire.

In spite of the large sums he has won and his fantastic achievements on the racecourse, Spectacular Bid has not been accepted into the small guild of 'super champions', even though he is probably better than some who have. In the US this term is reserved only for Triple Crown winners, that is, for those horses which have won the classic races, the Kentucky Derby, Preakness Stakes and Belmont Stakes. Spectacular Bid won the

first two but came only third in Belmont Park in the state of New York.

To date eleven horses have won the American Triple Crown. Sir Barton was the first super champion. His sire was Star Shoot, an English horse, by Isinglass, and his owner was Canadian. He won the American Triple Crown in 1919 when officially it did not yet exist. Although Sir Barton was a beautiful stallion, temperamentally he was very difficult. Even when he was a foal his owner, John E. Madden, judged him to be a real crackerjack. As a two-year-old he was allowed to race only six times and was always ridden very gently. He was only placed once, when he came second. Many a racehorse is completely ruined as a two-year-old simply because its owner wants to recoup the high costs of training as quickly as possible. Sir Barton made all the patient waiting worthwhile. As a three-year-old he ran in thirteen of the most important races and came in first eight times, second three times and third twice. Even in his third season he started twelve times, and ten times was placed in the first three. In total he

7 Seattle Slew, by Bold Reasoning out of My Charmer: Triple Crown winner, 1977.

8 Affirmed won the Belmont Stakes in a dramatic neck and neck race against Alydar and became Triple Crown winner for 1978.

9 Willie Shoemaker riding Spectacular Bid in the San Fernando Stakes (worth US$108,300) at Santa Anita Park, California. At the beginning of the eighties Bid was the most outstanding horse in the US.

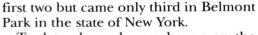

won the enormous sum of US$116,857.

Not until 1930 did a horse win the Triple Crown again. This was Gallant Fox, who came from Claiborne Farm, near Lexington in Kentucky, by that time already a world famous Thoroughbred stud. This horse was undoubtedly lazy and could not always be persuaded to perform at his best, but when it suited him he beat every opponent. Unfortunately he could easily be distracted from his task. In one race he was so fascinated by the sight of an aeroplane that he forgot about the race and for the only time in his career was not placed. As a three-year-old, Gallant Fox won nine out of ten races and came second once.

He was the only Triple Crown winner who sired a Triple Crown winner — Omaha, also bred at Claiborne Farm, who became super champion of 1935. When this horse was sent to James Fitzsimmons in Belmont for training, the trainer thought he was the most charming horse he knew. At the same time Smokey Saunders, the jockey, described him as the best racehorse he had ridden in his whole career. And he was right.

Man O'War, foaled in 1917, was an immensely popular horse. Since then only Secretariat, in the seventies, has enjoyed a comparable popularity. Man O'War won the Preakness and the Belmont Stakes, but did not start in the Derby. War Admiral, the Triple Crown winner of 1937, is one of his many successful descendants.

In the next ten years there were four Triple Crown winners — 1941, Whirla-way; 1943, Count Fleet; 1946, Assault; and 1948, Citation. Then something strange happened. Over the next twenty-five years fifteen horses won two of the three great classic races, but the Triple Crown seemed jinxed, and eluded them all. Then in 1973 Secretariat safely won both

the Derby and the Preakness and finally won the Belmont Stakes as well by a lead of thirty-one lengths.

Jamestown is the cradle of American racing in Virginia. By the year 1620 the English settlers were already organizing races there along the main street. Soon the town authorities banned these races, and moved them out into the countryside, where the course was usually a quarter of a mile long. Horses with the ability to make a very fast start and to maintain high speeds over a short distance were much in demand; that is, 'sprinters' as opposed to 'stayers'. These horses all came of the most diverse stock, but in time, through the introduction of English and Oriental bloodstock, a type was developed which was superbly equipped for the Sunday race over short stretches. They were described as 'Quarter Miler' or 'Quarter Horse' and were very versatile, being suitable for hard work on the farms and plantations as well as for service in the cavalry.

Surprisingly enough, it was only in recent years that a definite breed was developed from this horse, which was then named the Quarter Horse breed. It has had an amazingly successful breeding history. In 1940 the standard requirements for the breed were laid down and a stud register begun. There are now, only a few decades later, more than a million registered Quarter Horses, far more than there are of any other breed in the world. Today Quarter Horses are much sought after by those who want a horse for Western riding, or one suitable as a family horse. Many are still raced in quarter-mile races in the western states of the US, and some of these races offer a large amount of prize money.

The selling price for a top quality

decades as a stud stallion, and the inevitable question was why anyone bothered to take this twenty-two-year-old veteran from England to America at all. But the unbelievable happened. He founded one of the most important bloodlines in the US. His great-grandson Boston ran in forty-five races and won forty of them, and his great-great-grandson Lexington, foaled in 1850, became, as the result of his achievements on the racetrack and as a sire, the legendary American Thoroughbred of the nineteenth century. His racing career ended when, as a five-year-old, he went blind. Afterwards he stood at stud and sired 236 winners of 1776 races.

Today the breeding of American Thoroughbreds is centred on Lexington, Kentucky, in that part of the US which

1 The horses trained by Charles Whittingham won 362 victories and earned over US$1.5 million in 1977 alone.

2 In 1977 Grover G. Delp, a trainer in Keeneland, Kentucky, had 928 victories and received prize money totalling almost US$1.5 million.

3 Nelson Bunker Hunt and his wife, the owners of Bluegrass Farm in Kentucky. They arrange their own auctions, known as Hunt Sales.

4 Darby Dan stud in Lexington, Kentucky, produced six Kentucky Derby winners and one winner of the Epsom Derby. At present its most famous stud stallion is Ribot's son, Graustark, considered to be the fastest horse in America. He was the undisputed winner in seven races and in spite of breaking a bone in his foot came second in the eighth.

stallion can be over a million dollars, and in the US this side of racing has also developed into a thriving trade. Quarter Horses, Arabs and Thoroughbreds may all share the same racetracks, but the business side of all three breeds is kept quite separate.

In 1665 the first racecourse was laid out on the English model on Long Island, New York. Only a short while before, the English had driven the Dutch out of New Amsterdam and renamed the town New York, and it was the first British governor who ordered the racecourse to be built.

As far as is known the first Thoroughbred, whose name was Bull Rock, was brought to America in 1730, but he left behind no descendants worth mentioning. Diomed was, however, a noteworthy import. Although this stallion had won the English Derby, he had sired no great progeny during his following two

is called the Bluegrass Region because of its lush meadows. There are, of course, still excellent studs in Virginia, Florida, California and some other states, but nowhere else is there such a concentration of superb horses. Some of the most famous trotting breeders also live there.

Claiborne Farm, owned by the Hancock family, has been the leading Thoroughbred stud for some time. Usually the stud has about two hundred broodmares and fifteen stud stallions. Among them at present are two of American's leading sires, Secretariat and Spectacular Bid. Blenheim II, Gallant Fox, Sir Gallahad III and Johnstown are only some of the names which have made Claiborne world-famous.

Calumet Farm is also an extraordinarily successful stud. In 1931 the first three Thoroughbred yearlings were brought there. Since then horses from the Calumet stables have won over US$22 million. In 1947 Calumet horses achieved one hundred wins, forty-four seconds and twenty-six thirds, and won a total of US$1,402,436. The stud became especially famous for its Derby winners. Of eighteen Calumet horses which competed in the Kentucky Derby, eight won, and six were second or third. That makes four more than the number of winners produced by any other breeder.

Bull Lea was one of the greatest horses from Calumet. From 1947 to 1953 he was five times the leading sire in the US. He was still siring winners even at twenty-eight years old. Mon Zigue is one example. He died aged twenty-nine.

The stud's most successful racehorse was the Triple Crown winner, Citation. Today the stud has about six stud stallions and thirty-five broodmares.

Darby Dan Farm has produced four Derby winners. Ribot's son Graustark became, however, more famous than any of these four. He easily won his first seven races, and in 1967 he was the racehorse most frequently mentioned in the United States. Ten days before the Derby, he was racing in the Bluegrass Stakes when he broke a bone in his foot, but in spite of that he finished the race and came second. Afterwards he was bought by a syndicate for the then record sum of US$2,400,000.

When Leslie Combs II acquired Spendthrift Farm near Lexington in 1937, his first discovery was that it was almost impossible for a newcomer to get hold of a really first class stallion, and it was almost ten years before he was offered the outstanding Bean Pere for a hundred thousand dollars in California. Together with nineteen acquaintances, he founded the first stallion syndicate, in which, for five thousand dollars each, members acquired a part share. They bought Bean Pere and took him to Lexington — where the twenty-year-old stallion died without covering a mare

and before he was insured. Six months after this disaster, Combs acquired Hyperion's son, Alibhai, for five hundred thousand dollars, again with a syndicate. This horse started Spendthrift Farm off on a magnificent series of breeding successes, and at the famous summer auction staged at Keeneland, Combs held the sale record about twenty times. Today the stud has approximately two hundred broodmares and thirty stud stallions, that is, more Thoroughbred stud stallions than any other stud.

Ocala Stud Farm in Ocala, Florida, the giant King Ranch in Texas, Blair Farm (from which Nashua came) and Sagamore Farm (with Native Dancer) in Maryland, are some of the most famous studs outside Kentucky.

The American Jockey Club, which was founded in 1893, at first laid down its own rules and controlled all the important facets of racing and the breeding of Thoroughbreds, exactly as was done in England. Later, however, its power was drastically curtailed. Except in the states of New York and Delaware, the control of racing was taken over by State Racing Commissions, each one answerable to the current Governor, and also subordinate to the National Association of

5 Since 1875 the Kentucky Derby has been held at Churchill Downs in Louisville, Kentucky.

6 The racing season on the east coast of America ends in the fall, and horses, trainers, jockeys, etc., move to southern Florida. Hialeah Park is one of the most famous courses. It is laid out around a lake populated with flamingos and other aquatic birds.

7 At the giant Aqueduct racetrack in New York the grandstands alone cover twenty-eight thousand square metres. It could be described as a racing supermarket. Every year over two thousand races are run and every raceday up to US$6 million in bets are made.

8 The Preakness Stakes, the second of the classic races which make up the American Triple Crown, is run at Pimlico, Maryland. Pimlico was opened in 1871.

9 Keeneland racecourse was opened in 1935 in Lexington, Kentucky. It serves as a testing course for the many Thoroughbred studs in the neighbourhood.

10 An idyllic scene at the September yearling auction held at Keeneland.

1 The first American race to be worth a hundred thousand dollars was held in 1947 at Santa Anita near Los Angeles. The racing season always begins on 26 December and then runs continuously for seventy days.

2 For twenty-four days in midsummer, Saratoga, in the north of the state of New York, is the centre of New York racing.

3 The classic Belmont Stakes, the third race for the Triple Crown after the Preakness Stakes, and the Kentucky Derby, as well as a number of other races with high stakes, are all run at Belmont Park, the third great racecourse in the state of New York.

4 In summer some of the most important Thoroughbred auctions in the US are held at Saratoga.

State Racing Commissioners, which was established in 1934. In spite of this attempt to achieve a unified national policy, the rules are not the same in all states, although basically they agree. A few years after the Association was founded it banned bookmakers, just as was done in France and some other countries, so that all bets now go through the totalisators at the race track. This measure contributed considerably to the growth of racing and to the improvement of its financial position.

On the other hand, the Association has not sufficient influence to introduce racing into all states. In nineteen states opponents of racing (usually for religious reasons) have been able to have laws passed which forbid the combination of gambling with racing, despite the fact that this sport brings in considerable revenue from taxes. This makes it all the more astonishing that, not only does the American Thoroughbred industry have more power than any other in the world, but the racecourses attract about twice as many spectators as football matches.

It is probably impossible for any non-American to imagine the scene at the New York Aqueduct. Although none of the classic races are run here, over two thousand races are held annually, among them some of the most valuable races with prize money of over a hundred thousand dollars. Despite its rather sober and businesslike atmosphere, its position on Long Island, right next to the city, is so convenient that on good days it attracts as many as seventy-five thousand spectators.

Belmont Park, the site of the Belmont Stakes, which is one of the three great classic races, is also in New York, as is Saratoga where each summer after the races, the yearling auctions are held.

These have an international reputation. Each of these two racecourses also attracts enormous crowds of spectators, and the state of New York collects around eighty million dollars in taxes from all three courses.

The racetrack at Louisville in Kentucky, with its old wooden grandstand and two characteristic towers, has a charm unique to America. The American Derby has been run here since 1875, always on the first Sunday in May, and as a national event it occupies a similar position to that of the Epsom Derby in England.

The Preakness Stakes are run in Pimlico racecourse in Maryland two weeks later. Many experts judge this to be the most difficult race in the US. The Belmont Stakes, mentioned above, are held three weeks after that.

Since 1952, the Washington DC International, the most important international race in the United States (probably second only to the French Prix de l'Arc de Triomphe), has been run on the Laurel racecourse in Maryland. Horses from some seventeen nations come to the US to take part.

STEEPLECHASING

There are two kinds of steeplechase — the hurdle race and the steeplechase proper. In a hurdle race the obstacles to be jumped are lightly built and designed either to give way or fall over when knocked. The steeplechase proper, on the other hand, is the toughest racing sport of all. Older and more experienced horses compete, distances are usually comparatively long, and the obstacles are sometimes very difficult and often dangerous for both rider and horse. A steeplechase course may cover over seven thousand metres, and the length combined with the varying difficulty of the jumps gives it a unique excitement. A horse apparently hopelessly out of the running, and many lengths behind the rest of the field can sometimes still win; for horses in the lead may perhaps have been overextended and no longer have the strength to cope with the final jumps and finish the race, or a falling horse may become entangled with others and disrupt the proceedings. There was a classic example of this in the 1967 Grand National Steeplechase at Aintree, when a riderless horse caused practically the whole field to fall at the twenty-third jump and Foinavan, a hopeless outsider, came from behind, slipped through the frightful mêlée and won.

The term steeplechase has its origin in an entertaining but rather risky activity which apparently became popular in Ireland in the mid-eighteenth century. Two riders would race across the fields towards a chosen goal just visible far in the distance, usually a church tower or a steeple. The essence of the sport was to ride off in as direct a line as possible towards that goal and simply jump any

Left: Hurdle racing, the less arduous form of 'racing between the flags' (small flags are used to mark out the obstacles). On the European continent about a third of all races are steeplechases or hurdle races. There are far fewer in the US, and many more in Ireland, where the sport originated, and in Britain.

Above: In the early steeplechases in England and Ireland the competitors raced towards a particular goal visible in the far distance across the countryside. Engraving after a painting by Henry Alken.

1 Red Rum in his stall. The product of Irish breeding, he became England's 'National Hero'.

2 Red Rum at his morning workout on the beach near Southport.

3 The steeplechase at Aylesbury in 1836 which was won by Captain Becher. The most difficult jump in the Grand National was named after him.

obstacles in the way. Naturally bets were placed on the outcome! A Mr Edmund Blake and a Mr Sean O'Callaghan took part in the first recorded race of this kind. The course was from the church in St Leger in the County of Meath to the steeple at Buttevant. It was not until about forty years later that the first steeplechase was run in England.

In 1810 the first steeplechase racetrack, just under five miles or eight kilometres long and with eight obstacles, was laid out in Bedford. The steeplechase track at St Albans was developed in 1830; and

the Grand Liverpool Steeplechase was first held in 1837. According to some reports the latter is said to have been run for the first two years on the track at Maghull, and only afterwards at neighbouring Aintree near Liverpool, but whatever its beginnings the fame of the Grand National Steeplechase soon spread far and wide.

The popularity of these new races grew rapidly and by 1842 there were sixty-six steeplechase tracks in England.

Originally hunters, usually the product of a cross between a medium to heavy

warm-blood mare and a Thoroughbred stallion, were most often used.

As organized races began to replace private cross-country entertainments, horses were required with both the speed and stamina of the Thoroughbred and the strength and calmness to cope with the difficult jumps. Towards the end of the nineteenth century a type of horse with these particular qualities was being bred in Ireland and England. It was named the 'steeplechaser' or simply the 'chaser'. Some steeplechasers are halfbreds, the rest Thoroughbreds, but

4 Red Rum after his exciting win in the 1977 Grand National. In 1973 he was first past the finishing line in this the most difficult steeplechase in the world, was victorious again in 1974, and in 1975 and 1976 he came second. Then in 1977 when he was already twelve years old, he had his third victory and proved himself to be the greatest steeplechaser of all time.

5 and 6 Inevitably Red Rum's unusual popularity has been exploited. In Southport, for example, there is a Red Rum Hotel and a Rummie's Bar.

Overleaf: At Becher's Brook, the most notorious jump in the Grand National Steeplechase at Aintree.

normally they are such powerfully built animals that they could almost be described as a breed of their own. About twenty per cent of the Thoroughbred broodmares of England and Ireland are used to breed steeplechasers, more than half of them in Ireland, for the Irish are the undisputed masters of the breeding of these horses. This shows up very clearly in the fact that Irish horses comprise more than seventy-five per cent of the winners of the Grand National Steeplechase at Aintree, often described as the world's most difficult steeplechase. Red Rum came from Ireland. He won at Aintree three times and was twice placed second.

To cope with these difficult races the horses have to be at least five, or even six years old, and steeplechasers reach the peak of their performance at eight or twelve years. Almost all chasers are geldings; only a very few are mares.

The Grand National at Aintree is without doubt the most famous steeplechase in the world. Many people have never heard of any other, and it deserved a chapter of its own (see page 218). But many consider the Cheltenham Gold Cup to be at least as important, for the track at Cheltenham is just as demanding, and it is often described as the heart of the forty-six English steeplechase courses.

Ireland has twenty-seven courses. The Irish Grand National is run at Fairyhouse, and the Galway Plate, the Leopardstown Chase, and the Guinness Hurdle in Galway are equally famous races.

As a rule the French steeplechase courses are designed to test speed more than jumping ability, and the obstacles are less difficult, which places the comparatively heavy Irish and English chasers at a disadvantage compared with the French Thoroughbreds. The Grand Steeplechase of Paris, which originated in 1874, is the most prestigious French race of this kind. Oddly enough its first winner was an English mare named Miss Hungerford.

The Pardubice Steeplechase in Czechoslovakia is the most arduous of the steeplechases held on the European continent. As at Aintree, many horses are forced to withdraw from this race, in particular because of two obstacles — the Taxus Ditch and the Irish Bank — which are more formidable even than any at Aintree. At one stage, too, the course crosses fields, which is a drain on the horses' energy and puts their tendons and joints at risk.

There is one notorious difference between Pardubice and Aintree. Pardubice has many more serious accidents, mainly because of the quality of the horses. Before they are allowed to compete in the Grand National, horses must qualify and only those animals which put up an excellent performance are allowed to start. Horses sent to the Pardubice, however, are often not considered absolutely first class, although naturally they must have some sort of qualifications. The Grand National still qualifies as sport, though the term is sometimes stretched to its limits; Pardubice, on the other hand, is a spectacle very reminiscent of the Roman circus.

AINTREE

The owner of the Waterloo Hotel near Liverpool was an ambitious man by the name of Lynn. He was also a horse racing enthusiast who one day conceived the idea of building a racetrack next door, on the open country at Aintree.

The first race over this course was a flat-race run in 1829. Seven years later Lynn advertised the race as the Grand Liverpool Steeplechase, in which horses and riders had to overcome a total of forty-two obstacles. This is where the history of the most difficult steeplechase in the world begins. The winner of this first race was Captain Becher on his horse, The Duke. A year later the race was won by the same horse, but under a different rider, for Becher was ill.

In the meantime Mr Lynn had

famous. A good many great winners as well as some great losers shared its fame. Whole books could be filled with tales.

There was, for example, the mystery of Devon Loch, ridden in 1956 by Dick Francis for the owner, the Queen Mother. After a thrilling race Devon Loch had a tremendous lead as he came into the straight to the finish. But suddenly, on the rise at the water ditch just before the finish, he seemed to see an obstacle. When the horse landed after this jump into the air his forelegs buckled and Francis was flung out of the saddle on to the horse's neck. By the time Devon Loch got to his feet again he had been passed by the horse called E.S.B., ridden by D. Dick, and had lost the race. Notwithstanding, the magnanimous owner was the first to congratulate the winner. But what had caused this misfortune? Did the horse mistake the

without hesitating he remounted Highlandie again, and passed the finish line in fifteenth place. He donated the five hundred pounds to the fund for helping injured jockeys.

The winning horse in that race was called Red Alligator. He was a son of Miss Alligator, who was also the dam of Anglo who won the Grand National in 1966. The breeder of both these top class horses was a farmer from Northern Ireland by the name of William Kennedy, who had bought Miss Alligator for seventy pounds, received a hundred and forty pounds for Anglo as a foal, and four hundred pounds when he sold Red Alligator as a yearling. Kennedy undoubtedly did well out of the transactions, but his profit was small when compared with the weighty sums which both horses won for their new owners.

Betting on the Grand National begins

invested all his money in his Aintree course and lost the lot, and the story would almost certainly have come to an abrupt end if Lord Bentinck, and some of the other leading personalities of the English Turf at that time, had not decided to support the Grand Liverpool Steeplechase. As a result, in the spring of 1839, there were seventeen riders at the start, with Captain Becher, the winner of the first race, again one of the field. He fell in a ditch on the first circuit, but without a moment's hesitation swung himself back up on to his horse Conrad again. On the second circuit, however, he landed once again in the same ditch and this time had to put up with the whole field going past him. This obstacle is still called Becher's Brook and is the most notorious jump in the whole race.

The Grand National Steeplechase, or simply the Grand National, as the race has been called since 1847, became world

shadow of the water ditch's low barrier for an obstacle? This puzzle remains as fascinating as the stories which jockey Dick Francis then began to write and which made him into the Turf's best known crime writer.

In 1967 a horse named Foinavon was one of the starters, with chances of winning considered to be so slight that the bookmakers were offering odds of a hundred to one for a win. At the twenty-third jump a riderless horse ran across in front of the field and caused all the horses either to stop in front of the obstacle or to fall. But Foinavon, who was right at the back of the field, found a gap in the chaos, jumped the obstacle, gained an unassailable lead and won.

An American, Tim Durrant, wanted to ride with the Grand National field right to the finish in order to win a bet of five hundred pounds. During the second circuit he fell at Becher's Brook, but

1 View of the track at Aintree which was opened in 1829 and has since seen many changes.

2 Crack horses at the morning workout before the race.

3 Members of 'high society' are also represented at the Grand National.

4 The field as it passes in front of the grandstand for the first time.

5 The first of two runaways at Becher's Brook in 1982. Falls are almost unavoidable at this obstacle.

months beforehand, and long reports on the races and preparatory training of the entrants are published during the weeks leading up to the race. Theoretically every horse in the Grand National has an equal chance of winning, because weights are specified by a handicapper on the basis of the horse's previous racing performances. Each horse has to carry somewhere between sixty-four and eighty kilograms.

The basic prerequisite is, of course, that both horse and rider are in tiptop condition, but it is also important to get a good position in the field right from the start so that horse and rider can concentrate on negotiating the jumps without the added hazard of having to cope with the possibility of other horses and riders falling. The huge obstacles demand that a horse has a tremendous jumping ability, but it must also be in the peak of condition if it is to perform at its best on the straights. Riding ability, even acrobatic skills, can often determine whether the jockey remains in the saddle after the horse has made a mistake. And finally this race requires a great deal of courage from the participants. The dramatic pictures, especially those taken at Becher's Brook, make this more than clear. Riderless horses are greatly feared for, if they block the way in front of an obstacle, they can be the downfall of many a hopeful pair.

During the sixties a start was made on toning down the jumps of the Grand National. This was done probably not so much to appease the supporters of the animal protection societies, who regularly climb the barricades, but rather because for many years no amateur rider had won the race. Professional jockeys were clearly dominating the race, which had become much more commercially oriented than was thought desirable.

In 1965 a record number of spectators attended Aintree. The previous year, the owner of Aintree, Mrs Topham, had decided to sell the piece of land for building purposes, and it seemed as if the last Grand National was about to be held. But Lord Sefton was finally able to save this racecourse which is so rich in tradition.

In that same year the effects of the toning down process also became apparent. The race was won by an amateur American rider on Jay Drum, after an exciting duel at the finish with an outstanding horse named Freddie. In 1980 another amateur American rider, C. Fenwick, won on Ben Nevis.

In the seventies Aintree's existence was again threatened. It changed owners several times and there was renewed talk of selling the land for building purposes. But once again a solution was found. In 1980 Ladbrokes, the largest firm of English bookmakers, acquired the track.

They were also able to give it a new lease of life when they organized continuous steeplechase meetings which lasted for three days at a time. In 1980 the total prize money was £45,595 which, of course, speaks for itself.

In 1983 the track was sold to the Aintree Race Course Company Limited, a trust set up to administer the appeal to raise money to prevent Aintree from being bought for some other purpose. It was sold for £3.4 million.

There are naturally still problems to be solved. Most of the old grandstands at Aintree have now been demolished, but the County Stand still remains with temporary stands on one side and a tarmac mound on the other. The track is used only for three days in the year and the maintenance costs are enormous. However, the total prize money in 1984 was £199,000.

Nevertheless, in spite of all these problems, the world's greatest steeplechase will continue to attract the most brilliant jockeys and the finest horses, and to fascinate both them and millions of people for ten minutes each year.

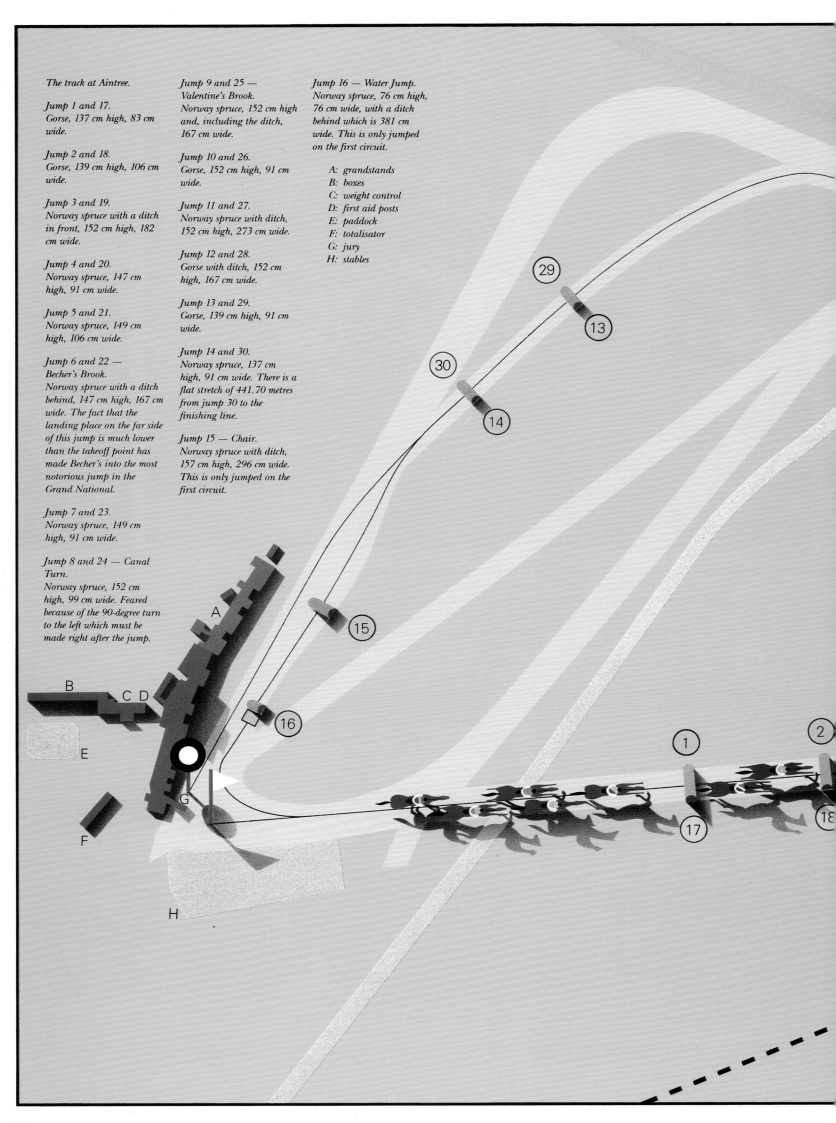

The track at Aintree.

Jump 1 and 17.
Gorse, 137 cm high, 83 cm wide.

Jump 2 and 18.
Gorse, 139 cm high, 106 cm wide.

Jump 3 and 19.
Norway spruce with a ditch in front, 152 cm high, 182 cm wide.

Jump 4 and 20.
Norway spruce, 147 cm high, 91 cm wide.

Jump 5 and 21.
Norway spruce, 149 cm high, 106 cm wide.

Jump 6 and 22 — Becher's Brook.
Norway spruce with a ditch behind, 147 cm high, 167 cm wide. The fact that the landing place on the far side of this jump is much lower than the takeoff point has made Becher's into the most notorious jump in the Grand National.

Jump 7 and 23.
Norway spruce, 149 cm high, 91 cm wide.

Jump 8 and 24 — Canal Turn.
Norway spruce, 152 cm high, 99 cm wide. Feared because of the 90-degree turn to the left which must be made right after the jump.

Jump 9 and 25 — Valentine's Brook.
Norway spruce, 152 cm high and, including the ditch, 167 cm wide.

Jump 10 and 26.
Gorse, 152 cm high, 91 cm wide.

Jump 11 and 27.
Norway spruce with ditch, 152 cm high, 273 cm wide.

Jump 12 and 28.
Gorse with ditch, 152 cm high, 167 cm wide.

Jump 13 and 29.
Gorse, 139 cm high, 91 cm wide.

Jump 14 and 30.
Norway spruce, 137 cm high, 91 cm wide. There is a flat stretch of 441.70 metres from jump 30 to the finishing line.

Jump 15 — Chair.
Norway spruce with ditch, 157 cm high, 296 cm wide. This is only jumped on the first circuit.

Jump 16 — Water Jump.
Norway spruce, 76 cm high, 76 cm wide, with a ditch behind which is 381 cm wide. This is only jumped on the first circuit.

A: grandstands
B: boxes
C: weight control
D: first aid posts
E: paddock
F: totalisator
G: jury
H: stables

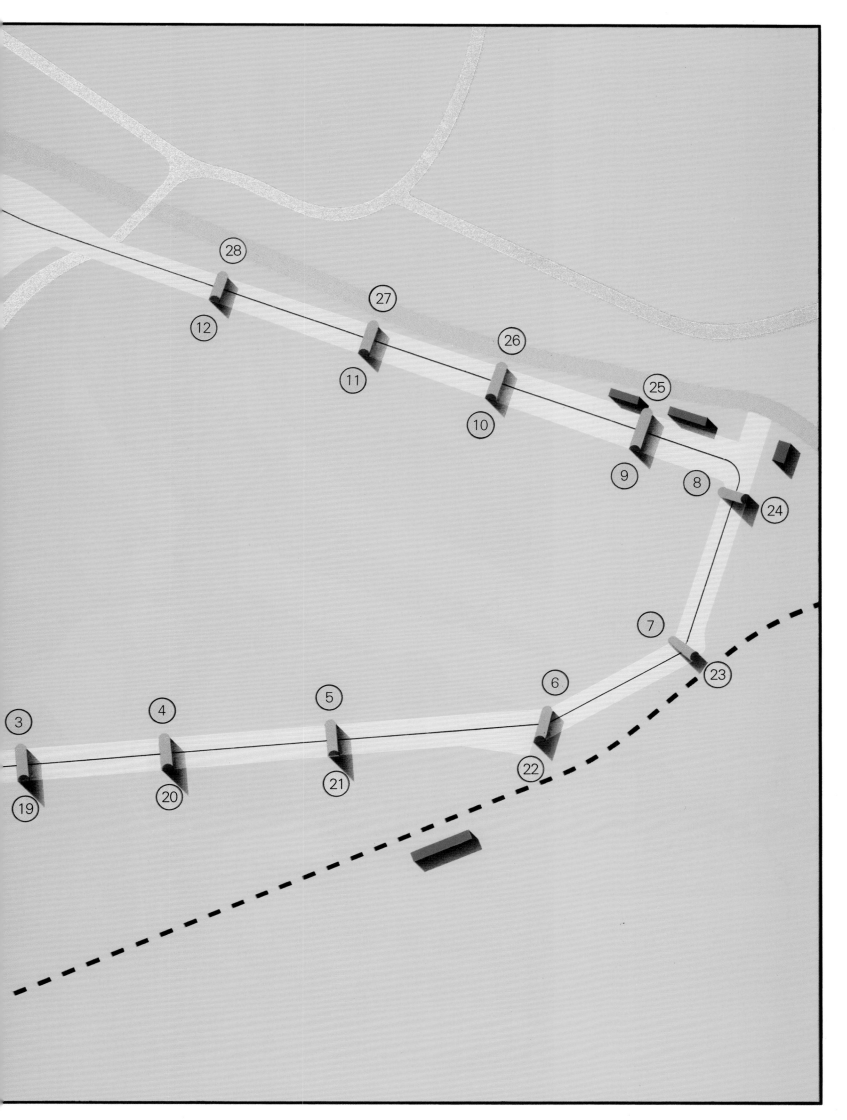

TROTTING

Although the modern sport of trotting had its origins as early as the end of the eighteenth century, for a long time it led a wallflower existence beside conventional racing. In most countries trotting did not become popular until only a few decades ago, but now, in France and the US in particular, the sport of trotting and the breeding of trotters has reached a highly specialized level. The Hanover Shoe Farm in Pennsylvania is the largest trotting stud in the world and has some 1700 breeding horses each spring. The American stallion Tar Heel has accumulated winnings of US$1,684,119 and the French mare Une de Mai has won 8,839,478 francs. The Prix d'Amérique, the most prestigious trotting race in France, provides a million francs in prize money, of which the winner receives 580,000 francs. Some 7500 trotting races are held annually in France alone.

As the word implies, the basic difference between trotting races and other races lies in the gait. In most contests, horses use the gait they would normally adopt to travel at speed; in trotting races they have to use a slower gait. Horses living in the wild would trot only when making the change from a walk to a gallop and vice versa, but by breeding, and using mechanical training aids, the trot has been increased to a racing tempo of about fifty kilometres an hour! The world speed record over a mile is 1:53.3 minutes, held since 1966 by Bret Hanover, an American stallion (a pacer). During a race, even when the will to win is greatest, a horse may not continually break into a gallop; nor may it continue to gallop for more than thirty metres, improve its placing or pass the finishing

Above: Smuggler, foaled in Massachusetts in 1874, created a sensation by trotting the mile in 2 minutes 15 seconds. The history of trotting races began a good hundred years earlier.

Right: Trotting race. The horses, harnessed to the sulkies, are at the first bend.

line at the gallop. Infringement means disqualification. In trotting races in Europe only the normal trot with diagonal footfalls is allowed, but in the US and Australia about seventy-five per cent of horses trot at the pace (see Gaits, page 76). Because, on average, pacers are somewhat faster than normal trotters, they have their own races. The pictures on the following pages show pacers in action. In France some trotting races are still ridden under the saddle, but usually they are raced in front of the sulky — a two-wheeled racing cart which weighs only about twenty kilograms.

Archaeological finds indicate that trotting races were organized in Asia Minor as early as 1300 BC, but the sport apparently fell into oblivion for a very long time, for it was unknown to the Greeks and Romans. A twelfth century report from Norfolk mentions a stallion which aroused a great deal of interest because of his distinctive, elegant and unbelievably fast trot. This is said to be the founding sire of the Norfolk Trotter breed which, around 1750, became famous for the elegance of its trotting action and consequently played an important role in many breeding programmes. About the same time the Netherlands, too, had developed a breed of horse which, besides having a special aptitude for the trot, was also fast, with

1 Count Alexei Orlov, c.1780, with Bars I (or Barss), harnessed in front of the sleigh.

2 A typical Orlov Trotter stallion on a Soviet State Stud. This breed was once world famous.

a great deal of stamina — the Harddraver. Many of the Danish Frederiksborg breed were excellent trotters. Sleigh races were popular in Sweden, Norway, Austria and Lower Bavaria, and because the horses had to cover longish distances they would usually trot. Surprisingly, however, the three great racing breeds of trotters did not develop in any of these places; instead they evolved, completely independently of each other, in Russia, America and France.

In seems that Count Alexei Gregorevitch Orlov Tchesmensky was not primarily concerned with producing a racehorse, but was more interested in developing a breed of horse that could pull a cart and sleigh as fast as possible.

Such a horse needed to be tough, to have plenty of stamina and to be able to trot so that it could keep up a regular even tempo for long stretches, and to achieve his aims Orlov was quite obviously prepared to experiment. In this he reflected an attitude wide-spread throughout all the studs of Europe at that time. Orlov crossed every imaginable breed, until in 1773 he led a grey-coloured Oriental stallion from Persia named Smetanka to a Frederiksborg mare, and from the mating obtained the stallion Polkan. This in turn he mated with a Dutch Harddraver mare, and the result was Bars I. This stallion inherited his grey colour, his fire, nobility and stamina from his grandsire, and the ability to trot

3 Bret Hanover, a pacer which in 1966 ran the mile in 1:53.3 minutes. He was immortalized during his lifetime by this statue on Castleton Farm in Lexington, Kentucky.

4 Albatross, the American pacer stallion which was foaled in 1968, set a whole series of new records which have remained unbroken.

5 Bellini II, 1967, by Bonum III out of Belle de Jour III, won the prestigious Prix d'Amérique three times and was just as successful in front of the sulky as under the saddle.

6 Fakir de Vivier, 1971, by Sabi Pas out of Ua Uka, won numerous victories, and set new records both in France and Italy.

7 In some trotting races in France the horses are ridden, as in the Prix du Président de la République.

from his dam and grandmother. Bars I bequeathed this combination of traits to his descendants and became the founding sire of the Orlov Trotter breed — soon to be famous throughout Europe and for a long time unbeatable on the racecourse.

The French Trotter was not developed until about a century later. The breed traces back to five founding sires, of which the two most important were Conquérant and Normand, both descendants of Young Rattler, a Thoroughbred foaled in 1811, which played a leading role in the development of the Anglo-Norman breed. An English Norfolk Trotter stallion, Norfolk Phenomenon, was even more influential. This new breed of trotter from France soon proved itself to be markedly faster than the Orlov Trotter breed.

Today the American trotting breed, or Standardbred, is the most influential throughout the world. Many different breeds, including the Norfolk Trotter and the Narragansett Pacer, contributed to its development, but although Hambletonian 10 is considered to be the actual founding sire, the English Thoroughbred played by far the most important role, through Messenger, a stallion imported into America in 1788. Over ninety per cent of all Standardbreds trace their descent from him. Like the English Thoroughbred, the Standardbred's outstanding qualities are the result of a ruthlessly selective breeding programme. The American Trotter, which is somewhat smaller than the French, is not such an elegant animal and has on average less stamina over longer distances, but over shorter distances it is faster than any other breed.

The Russian Trotter was developed around the turn of the century as the result of crossing American Standardbreds with Orlov Trotters. In Europe, after World War Two, French and American trotters were crossed to produce the European Standard Trotter breed which is common today in most European countries.

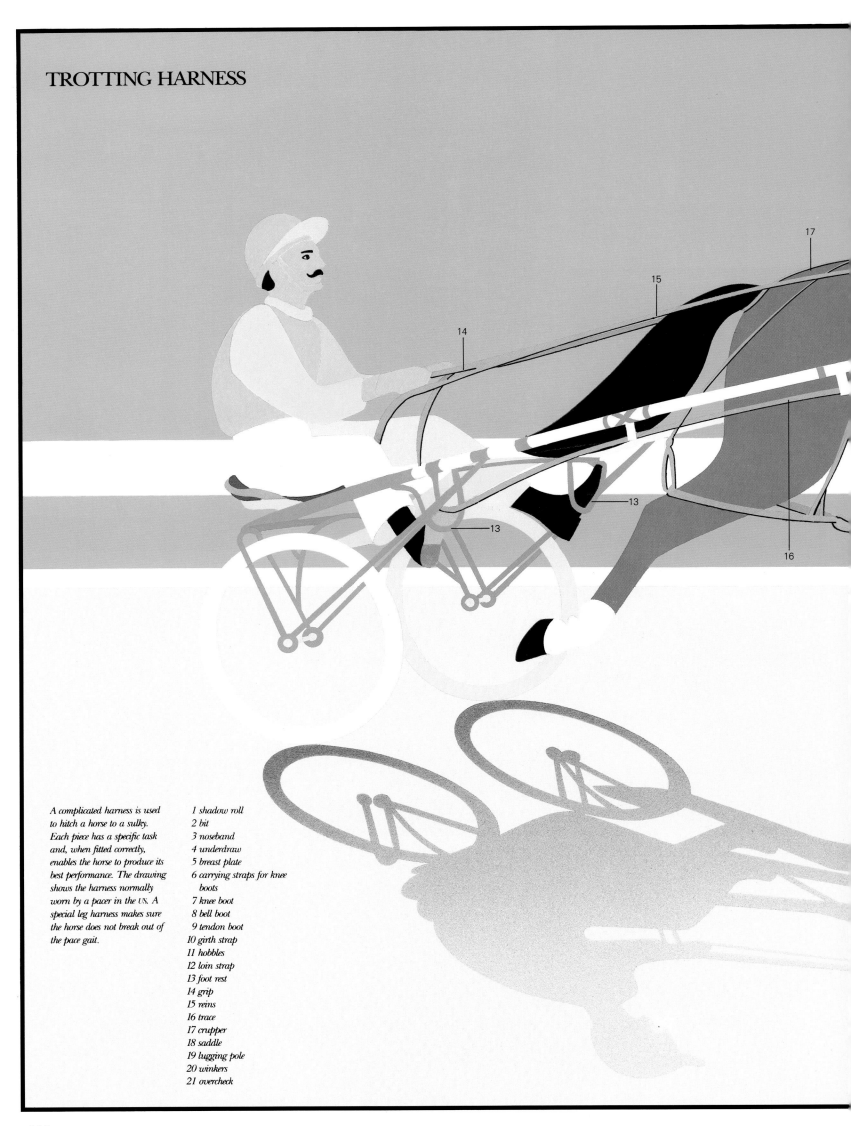

TROTTING HARNESS

A complicated harness is used to hitch a horse to a sulky. Each piece has a specific task and, when fitted correctly, enables the horse to produce its best performance. The drawing shows the harness normally worn by a pacer in the US. A special leg harness makes sure the horse does not break out of the pace gait.

1 shadow roll
2 bit
3 noseband
4 underdraw
5 breast plate
6 carrying straps for knee boots
7 knee boot
8 bell boot
9 tendon boot
10 girth strap
11 hobbles
12 loin strap
13 foot rest
14 grip
15 reins
16 trace
17 crupper
18 saddle
19 lugging pole
20 winkers
21 overcheck

Left: Colts on the broad meadows of Castleton Farm in Lexington.

1 Sometimes over 1700 horses are being bred on Hanover Shoe Farm in Pennsylvania, the largest trotting stud in the world.

2 Walnut Hall in Lexington is an outstanding trotting stud, with picturesque buildings typical of the Kentucky countryside.

3 Castleton Stud in Lexington.

The aptitude for the trot which the breeding programmes perpetuate does not, however, automatically produce racehorses, which are the product of an intensive and lengthy training process. This training relies on the use of various mechanical aids, including the complicated harness shown on pages 298-299. The trotting gait consists of such unnaturally long steps that the forelegs in particular must be protected against injury by the use of bell boots and various tendon and knee protectors. The overcheck is another unusual feature. This consists of straps fastened either to the overcheck snaffle or to nose straps, and then connected to the headcheck which goes over the head to the withers, while the underdraw or jump reins are joined to the strap which is put around the lower part of the chest. These two straps hold the horse's head and neck in the best position for trotting at speed. Opinion is divided on whether such aids are appropriate or inflict unnecessary suffering on the animals. The hobbles are only worn by pacers, and hold the legs in the pace gait. There are many harness variations. In addition a shoe is seldom simply a shoe, and experts differentiate between over two hundred types. They are forged individually to fit the hooves of each horse, and small metal plates are often screwed on to the wall of the hoof so that each foot has the right weight to achieve both perfect balance and the highest trotting speed.

In almost every country the breeding of racehorses for trotting is nowadays in the hands of small-scale breeders, who often train their horses themselves and drive them in the races. Very few larger trotting studs exist except in the Soviet Union, France and in the US. In North America, because the opportunities for winning large sums in trotting races are on a par with other types of racing, there are many large, well organized studs. That the outlay is justified is reflected in the prices fetched by promising yearlings, which often exceed a hundred thousand dollars.

229

DRESSAGE

Dressage was first included in an Olympic programme in the Stockholm Games in 1912. Instead of performing the piaffe and passage, however, the competitors had to jump over five obstacles, which ranged from 5 cm to 110 cm in height, and the last of which was a barrel which was rolled towards the horse.

Equestrian functions which included dressage trials were organized in various countries as early as 1806. Usually they were versatility competitions for army officers and consisted of a combination of dressage, cross-country and jumping events.

The origins of dressage riding stretch back almost two and a half millennia to the time of Xenophon, the Greek historian and equestrian instructor. The basic principles of his approach to training a horse in dressage are still valid.

The next important milestone in the history of dressage riding was not until the Renaissance in Italy. Xenophon's works had just been rediscovered, and were apparently carefully studied by Federico Grisone, a Neapolitan who ran a riding school which attracted noblemen from throughout Europe. It is worth noting that he also introduced trotting exercises into his training programmes. Señor Grisone was not exactly gentle with the horses and some of his teaching aids were veritable instruments of torture, including curb bits with levers up to forty centimetres long. His methods also required the use of force, such as hitting the animal between the ears.

Antoine de Pluvinel, on the other hand, employed a much more humane approach and never advocated the use of force. An outstanding riding instructor during the Baroque period, his most famous pupil was Louis XIII. During training, de Pluvinel preferred working the horses thoroughly by hand, often while they were tied between two posts, known as 'the pillars', the use of which was his own invention. He also included in his lessons 'airs above the ground', which are still performed today at the Spanish Riding School in Vienna.

The Duke of Newcastle was equally famous, but his methods were much criticized, and with justification for they showed no 'understanding for the horse'. Among other ridiculous precepts his lessons included instructions on how to teach a horse to gallop backwards!

The works of Robichon de la Guérinière, on the other hand, are an important milestone on the path to modern dressage riding. His talent, which is reminiscent of Pluvinel, is proven by his literary legacy which appeared in 1733 under the title *Ecole de la Cavalerie*. Guérinière was a driving force behind the development of dressage and to a large degree the modern sport is based on his teachings.

RIDING IN
THE ARENA

Training in dressage is fundamental to riding. It does not matter whether this training follows the classical European pattern or the radically different style of the American cattle-herders, which evolved from the ancient Spanish style of riding — whatever the purpose, a riding horse must trust humans implicitly. It must obey the rider's commands; it must be acquainted with the aids, that is, the language a rider uses to communicate his wishes; it must be fit so that even when carrying the additional weight of a rider it can remain relaxed and keep its natural balance. Only a horse which has been properly reared and trained is a useful horse.

The basic training prepares the horse for its future tasks, whether as an athlete or simply an ordinary riding horse. A foal may be left to its own devices for two and a half or even three years and then broken in, but such an approach can prove to be both difficult and dangerous. It is so much better for both parties to accustom a foal to human contact while still very young. Put a halter on it occasionally and lead it around so that it learns to trust and obey people as well as its dam. Accustom it gradually, almost as an afterthought, to the longe rein, to the saddle, and to performing various small tasks, so that when it is time for the formal task of schooling to begin it will seem almost a game and present no serious problems.

The basics of dressage are taught when the horse is between three and five years old. It learns to walk at an even tempo in a straight line, to relax the back muscles, to be supple in making the turns, and to make the transitions to trot and canter smoothly and evenly. It becomes familiar with the intricate geometry of the arena, learns to make the turns on the fore and hindquarters and to move sideways and backwards.

When the horse is about five years old and has completed this basic schooling it is usually possible to judge its potential

The figures:
2 *change of rein down centre line*
3 *circle*
4 *change of rein from circle to circle*
5 *change of rein through the circle*
6 *figure of eight*
7 *change of rein on the diagonal across the whole arena*
8 *change of rein on the diagonal across half the arena*
9 *volte*
10 *changing direction out of the corner*

1 The normal arena measures 20 x 40 metres and has points of reference which are designated with certain letters according to international ruling. These permit the movements to be performed with precision. The advanced tests take place in an arena which is 20 x 60 metres long.

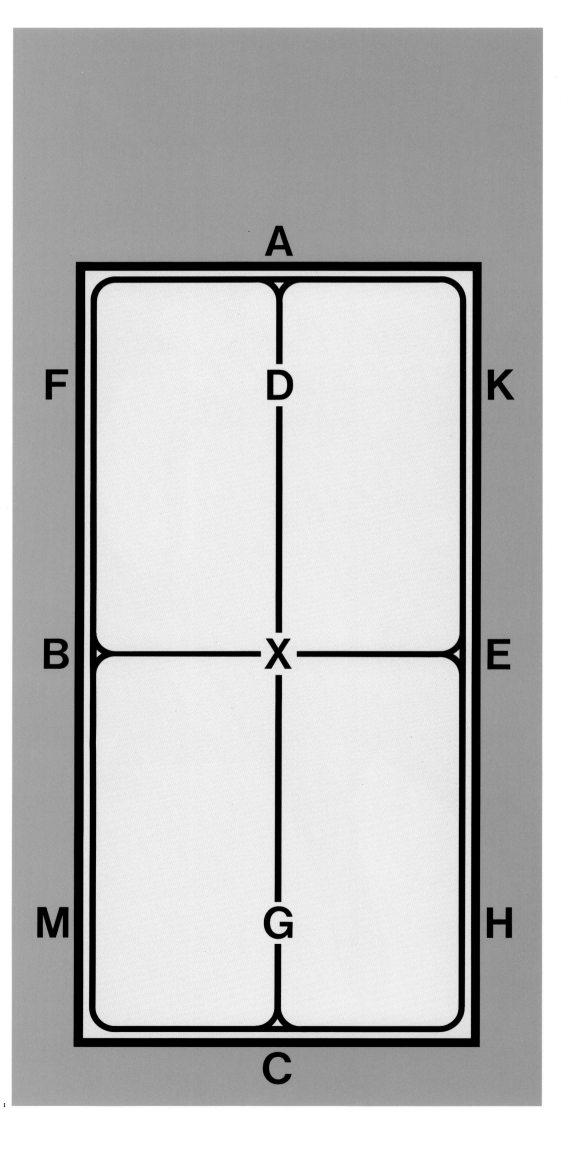

for this exacting sport and decide if it can be turned into a first class dressage performer. If not it may be more successful as perhaps a show-jumper or an eventer; or perhaps its qualities fit it to be 'just' a riding horse. Lineage will often provide some clues to the direction in which its talent lies. If an aptitude for dressage was present in the families of both parents, then it is very likely it will have inherited it — but not necessarily so. The horse may be bored by the repetitiveness of the dressage lessons and might be happier show-jumping or tackling a cross-country course. One fact is certain: a horse that has to be forced to perform dressage and shows no enjoyment of its tasks will have no chance of reaching the highest levels.

When both horse and rider are talented then dressage becomes a sport and an end in itself, and the wearisome period of preparing the horse for its great tasks can begin. This requires the greatest sensitivity and endless patience.

In many countries there are preliminary easier levels at which the beginner can test his progress and where the horse can get used to the competitive atmosphere. At international level the FEI (Fédération Equestre Internationale) has laid down the requirements for three events of increasing difficulty: the Prix St Georges, the Intermédiaire and the Grand Prix.

The Prix St Georges is considered to be an event of average difficulty. The horse is required to have mastered the halt and the rein back, as well as have the ability to perform the three basic gaits at varying speeds. All its movements must be distinct and evenly spaced. In addition it has to perform various arena figures such as the volte and serpentine, and the movements on two tracks (the most difficult task of all) both at the trot and the canter. Half-pirouettes are also included as well as flying changes of leg which must be made after each three strides at the canter.

The Prix St Georges consists of thirty-one different movements which have to be learnt by heart and ridden, in the correct sequence, in 9.30 minutes, in an arena which measures 20 x 60 metres.

The Intermédiaire is a more difficult intermediate stage, and a preparation for the Grand Prix, the highest level in the art of dressage.

TRAVERS, PIROUETTE, PIAFFE, PASSAGE

When it has completed the basic training which must be given to every riding horse, the future dressage horse begins its 'academy' training, and everything learnt up to this point is now refined to the highest possible degree of perfection. The horse is prepared both physically and temperamentally for the process of learning even the most difficult lessons in such a way that later it will be able to give a seemingly effortless performance.

Right: The counter-change of hand at the canter, which is ridden from the middle outwards in a zigzag pattern, is one of the most difficult exercises in the Grand Prix de Dressage. Each six strides in any direction must cover eleven metres of the arena.

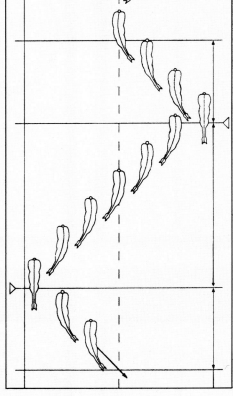

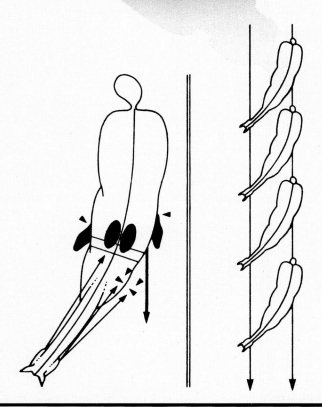

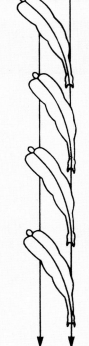

1 Shoulder-in. In this movement the horse's forehand is curved away from the direction in which it is moving. The inside legs pass and cross in front of the outside legs. The arrows indicate the rein and thigh aids which are required to produce this movement.

2 Travers. Here the horse's body is bent in the direction in which it is going; the head is kept facing forwards; the forelegs move along one line, and the hindlegs along a parallel one.

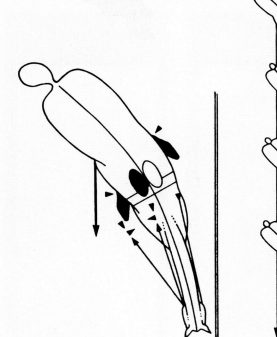

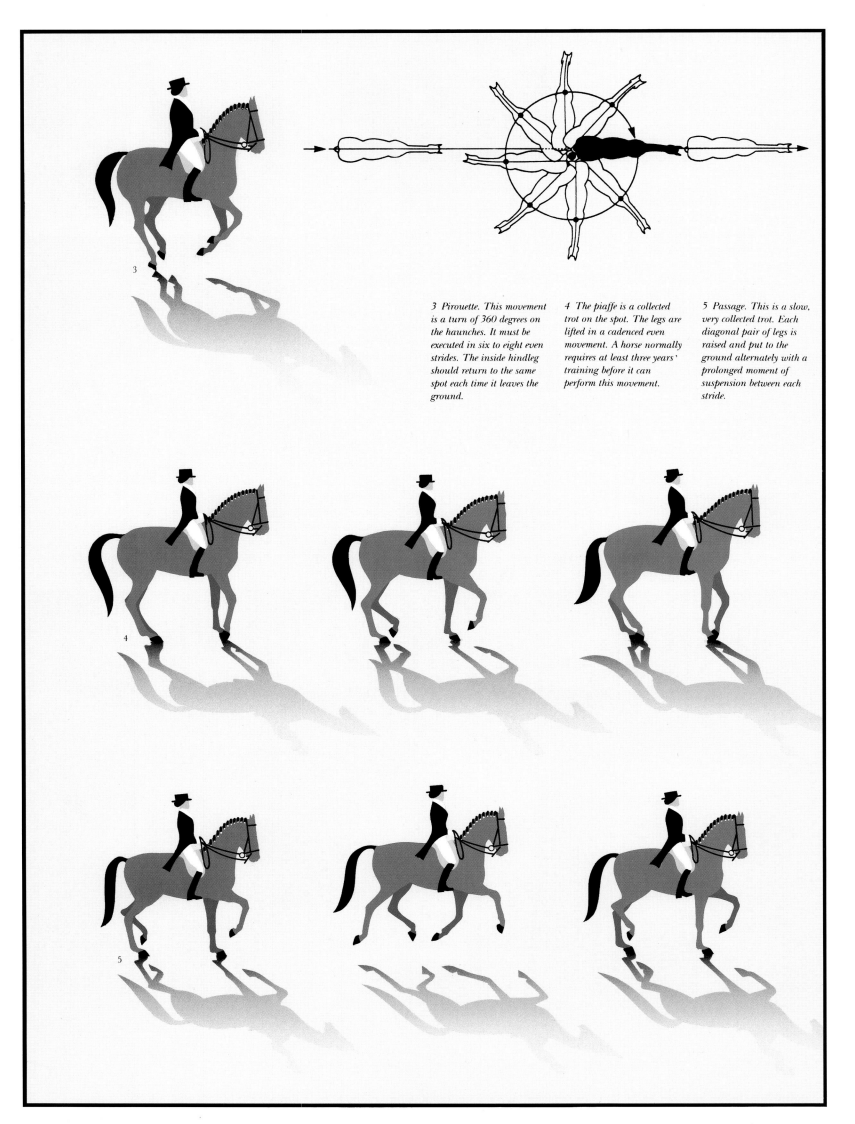

3 Pirouette. This movement is a turn of 360 degrees on the haunches. It must be executed in six to eight even strides. The inside hindleg should return to the same spot each time it leaves the ground.

4 The piaffe is a collected trot on the spot. The legs are lifted in a cadenced even movement. A horse normally requires at least three years' training before it can perform this movement.

5 Passage. This is a slow, very collected trot. Each diagonal pair of legs is raised and put to the ground alternately with a prolonged moment of suspension between each stride.

CELEBRITIES IN THE DRESSAGE SADDLE

The ideal dressage horse should present a thoroughly harmonious picture of grace and nobility. The head should be moderately long and straight with large, calm eyes, the neck long, and the shoulder sloping. The longish strong back should have good muscles, and the legs must be clean, correctly positioned, with tendons clearly visible. All movements should be powerful yet elegant. The horse should enjoy the work and the excitement of competition, but have a combination of calmness and sensitivity in its basic nature. There should be abundant energy, kept well under control.

To have a horse which approaches perfection as closely as possible — although the 'perfect' horse will probably never exist — is the wish of every dressage rider. Besides the many horses which correspond more or less to the ideal there have been a whole series of exceptions which have gained fame in the dressage arena.

The mare Afrika, for example, foaled on the Vornholz Stud in Westphalia in 1945, had a number of obvious blemishes. She had a stag neck and low withers (croup higher than the withers). She never learnt how to do a proper piaffe. She was far from even-tempered

and could only be ridden with a great deal of sensitivity. She also performed much better under equestriennes such as Baroness Ida von Nagel and Anneliese Küppers than under male riders. Yet despite these drawbacks the mare's verve and zest and her harmony of movement were so impressive that she was placed in seventy-four advanced dressage events and won two Grand Prix.

Although the English Thoroughbred's temperament is not ideal for a dressage horse, a number have achieved success. Pernod, foaled in 1939, also at Vornholz, was one of them. Initially a steeplechaser, at eight years old he was forced to give up the career because of a leg injury. The horse was not at all co-operative at the beginning of his dressage training, but in his saddle sat Willi Schultheis, one of the most talented of all dressage riders and trainers, and Pernod went on to win no less than seventy-five dressage events.

Schultheis rode another Thoroughbred — Chronist. Three years younger than Pernod, he also became famous and was placed in ninety-nine advanced dressage events, won thirty-one times, and gained three Grand Prix victories.

Brillant was perhaps the most amazing example of a Thoroughbred becoming

a first class dressage horse. Foaled in 1949, he was a flat-racing horse, and won the Ruhr Silver Ribbon twice and came third in the German Derby. In his second career, Brillant, also under Schultheis, twice became German Dressage Champion and gained 104 places in advanced dressage events.

Harry Boldt had at least two horses for which few would have prophesied a great future. Remus, foaled in 1955 in Westphalia, was one of them. He was a grey. He had a neck that was too short for an ideal dressage horse, a back that was also too short, and his forelegs were calf-kneed. There was very little expression in his movements and he was not much bigger than a large pony. During training, however, he developed to a quite amazing degree and was placed in 143 advanced events. Besides many other prizes, he gained the Olympic Silver Medal at Tokyo in 1964.

Golo IV, foaled in 1962 in Westphalia, was even more noticeably blemished. He was sway-backed, his hindlegs were bow-legged and his forelegs pigeon-toed. He also had a violent and almost uncontrollable temper. By chance he was brought into Harry Boldt's stable and three years later he became German Champion. In 1974 he won the Dressage Derby and came fourth in the World Championship. He was a Grand Prix winner five times and was placed 124 times in advanced dressage events.

Granat, one of the most successful dressage horses of recent years, is without doubt the most famous example of an 'unsuitable' horse. He drove his rider, Christine Stückelberger, and the trainer Georg Wahl, to distraction many times. A Holstein, foaled in 1965, he

actually looked more like a cart horse; only when ridden did he display his remarkable elegance. He was bought principally because he performed the gaits well and was a bargain, but he proved to have an extremely difficult nature. He was unpredictable, did what he wanted and threw the rider off when and where it suited him. The horse was therefore trained in simple dressage and then sold, but Georg Wahl continued as his trainer. Quite suddenly Granat showed a new side of himself. Even though he was still a heavy horse he easily assimilated all he was taught, so Christine Stückelberger bought him back and rode him in several tournaments. When he wanted to he could perform in a very impressive manner — but often he simply did not want to. Once again his owner put him up for sale but by this time no one wanted to buy. Christine Stückelberger and Georg Wahl continued to work with him and succeeded in tiring him before each competition to the extent that he no longer exploded, but yet was still fresh enough to perform well. Since then Granat has become a European Champion, an Olympic winner, and a World Champion.

For years the Federal Republic of Germany has dominated the sport of dressage, though the Swedes were prominent in the twenties and again in the fifties. For twenty years Switzerland and the Soviet Union have also been in the forefront. The French, who between the wars belonged to the world's élite, have not done so well since then, while Canada, the US and Britain continue to play an ever increasing role. In future the Netherlands will probably become more prominent.

Some of the most famous names of recent years are: Josef Neckermann on Mariano, Venetia and Van Eick; Reiner Klimke on Dux, Mehmed and Ahlerich; Harry Boldt on Woyceck; and Uwe Schulten-Baumer on Slibovitz. They are all from Germany.

Henri Chammartin, on Wolfdietrich and Woermann, was a notable Swiss rider who has found worthy successors in Christine Stückelberger on Granat and Urich Lehmann on Widin. Jennie Loriston is a first class rider from Great Britain who came third in the World Championship in 1978 on Dutch Courage. The American Hilda Gurney has a marvellous horse in Keen, another Thoroughbred. The best Canadian horse at present is Martyr ridden by Cynthia Neal. The Soviet Union produced its first world class combination in Sergie Filatov who on Absent was the surprise winner at the Rome Olympics of 1960. Ivan Kizimov on Ichor and Elena Petuschkova on Pepel followed in his footsteps, as has more recently Irina Karacheva on her dainty horse Said.

Left: Jumping was once almost exclusively the prerogative of the cavalry, but since World War Two it has become by far the most popular of the equestrian sports. For over two decades it has also exerted considerable influence on the breeding of warm-blood horses.

Right: The first official jumping competitions were organized in Ireland in 1864. They were basically aptitude tests for assessing hunters.

JUMPING

The Irish Royal Dublin Society held its first Horse Show in Dublin in 1864. Included in the programme were jumping competitions for hunters.

These contests consisted of three events, each of which had only one obstacle. The first was a high jump, made of gorse and with three poles. The second was a wide jump over some hurdles. A first prize of five pounds and a second of two were awarded in each of these events.

In the third event the riders had to jump a stone wall. The winner received a cup to the value of ten pounds and a whip worth five.

On the day before this last event competitors had to take part in a qualifying round in which they were required to jump a wooden obstacle. It is recorded that this was 135 centimetres high, but no records remain of the dimensions of any of the other jumps in these contests.

So far as we know this event was the first officially organized jumping competition, but show-jumping events gained rapidly in popularity and soon spread throughout England and then on to the continent as well. Although it is one of the most recently developed forms of equestrian sport, it has become one of the most popular of all. Not only is show-jumping now an integral part of rural life, in its most exacting form it has become a highly demanding sport where a centimetre, or fractions of a second can be vitally important. Nowadays considerable amounts of money are tied up in this sport, and top class

jumpers and their horses are fêted as celebrities.

Unfortunately this is also just the kind of sport where excessive ambition encourages the use of reprehensible methods. Only too often the desire to win as many laurels as possible in the shortest time, coupled with a lack of patience and little sympathy for the horse, results in young animals which display a talent for jumping being made to compete at too young an age. After one or two years the horse suffers incurable leg injuries and ends up in the knacker's yard.

Brutal methods are often used to train a show-jumper. Its training is directed solely to the one aim — jumping — whereas there should be a solid grounding in dressage first. As a result a show-jumping event often becomes an unpleasant duel between rider and horse. The rider's handling of the problem is then greeted with applause as if he or she had done something laudable, for the commentator naturally describes the horse as difficult, never as badly trained.

Slow and careful training which conserves the horse's energy and allows it to progress gradually is a much more worthwhile approach. Two of the most successful jumpers of all time prove this most conclusively. For over ten years Hans Günter Winkler's Halla was a top class horse, and Fritz Thiedemann's Meteor took part in no fewer than three Olympic Games.

ORIGINS AND THE ITALIAN SCHOOL

Just two years after the first show-jumping event in Dublin, a great Concours Hippique was held in Paris, to be followed by a great many more tournaments all over France. In 1875 show-jumping events were held in Vienna; a few years later they were also being held in Holland, Belgium and Italy; and at the end of the last century show-jumping had spread to Germany as well.

In 1900 the first International jumping trials were included in the World Exhibition in Paris. The next great International tournament was held in 1902 in Turin. This lasted for ten days, and 147 riders, representing six nations, took part. There the Italians proved themselves to be far superior. A certain Federico Caprilli, for example, set an amazing high jump record of 2.08 metres and a new long jump record of 7.40 metres. The German riders performed so badly that the German Emperor forbade any further participation in International competitions.

Federico Caprilli's superb achievements in Turin had started something. His superlative high jump on Melopo unleashed a fervent interest in high-jumping. In Italy, France, Belgium and the US in particular, horses were being specially trained as high-jumpers, and they provided the thrills which a fast growing public was demanding. In a very short period of time the Belgian Cavalry School is said to have had more than twenty horses which were capable of jumping two metres. In Paris in 1906 the Frenchman George Crousse jumped over 2.35 metres.

The most sensational report, however, came from the US. By 1902 Heatherbloom, a Thoroughbred, ridden by Dick Donelly, had jumped more than 2.40 metres. A later report stating that Heatherbloom had jumped 2.51 metres could not be confirmed, and the official record, which still stands, is 2.49 metres. It was set in 1949 in Chile by Alberto Larraguibel on Huaso.

The long jump was less spectacular and did not attract a great deal of public interest. For a long time the record remained at 7.50 metres. In 1948 the eight metre mark was first passed by Nogueras Marquez on Balcamo. The current record is 8.40 metres, set in Johannesburg by André Ferreira on Something.

Federico Caprilli's high jump was sensational, but it was his jumping style that made this officer from the Cavalry School of Pinerolo near Turin world

1 to 3 The Dublin Horse Show was first held in 1864. From the beginning it included show-jumping events for hunters in its programme.
These three pictures taken around the turn of the century give some idea of the atmosphere at this very popular event.

4 This is how a rider used to jump: he straightened his legs, leant backwards, held on tightly to the reins and successfully obstructed the horse's natural jumping trajectory. This photo is of Federico Caprilli, the Italian riding instructor who evolved the modern jumping style. It was called the Caprilli system and was soon in general use throughout the world.

5 At the turn of the century Italian officers were the outstanding show-jumpers. Just for fun they would attempt all kinds of obstacles.

240

6 In the Italian jumping style developed by Federico Caprilli shortly before the turn of the century, the rider adapts himself to the jumping trajectory of the horse.

7 In the early days of show-jumping many attempts were made to raise the current high jump record. Federico Caprilli was the first to set an official record when in 1902 on Melopo he jumped 2.08 metres. In the same year in the US, Heatherbloom, a Thoroughbred, ridden by Dick Donelly jumped 2.40 metres. The current world record was set in Chile in 1949 by Alberto Larraguibel who on Huaso jumped over 2.49 metres.

famous. His innovation transformed the entire Italian team into superb jumpers. After 1902 it became known as the 'Caprilli Revolution', and spread quickly through the whole show-jumping world.

When hunting and steeplechasing in Ireland and England the riders had always sat bolt upright in the saddle like dressage riders. When jumping they straightened their legs and leant backwards so that on landing they did not fly out of the saddle. They used the same approach when show-jumping. Caprilli was able to prove that this style interfered with the horse's natural jumping trajectory. As the horse jumped, the rider's weight shifted backwards, which had exactly the opposite effect from the one intended. On landing the rider fell on to the horse's back, jerking at the reins as he did so. Caprilli, therefore, buckled the stirrups shorter, leant forwards during the jump, raised his seat out of the saddle and adapted to the horse's movement. He loosened the reins so that the animal could stretch out its head and neck freely and thus maintain its equilibrium.

The successes of the Italian officers proved that the new style was intrinsically correct. The French and the Belgians were quick to adopt it and a little later the British, the Swedes and the Amer-icans followed suit. Admittedly the upper echelons of the German cavalry vehemently resisted the introduction of this new fashion from Italy, and after the failure of the German team in Turin in 1902 it was years before Rittmaster Arnold von Günther dared to experiment. But when he did so, in 1910, he very quickly became the most successful show-jumper in Germany.

At first, though, he was able to convert only a few, and when the army issued its new cavalry regulations in 1912 it persisted in advocating the upright seat. Not until after the Amsterdam Olympics of 1928, in which the Germans won both the Individual and the Team Gold in dressage, but were placed among the also-rans in show-jumping, did Gustav Rau, the famous hippologist, promote the standardized introduction of the new style. He also suggested the founding of a specialized riding school.

JUMPERS

The first 'show-jumpers' were hunters, which had been bred in Ireland for a long time before show-jumping existed as a sport. From autumn through into spring they were accustomed to having to cope with obstacles of all descriptions. They had plenty of stamina, which they certainly needed to keep going through an Irish hunt, which normally lasted a whole day, and still be fit for the following day's hunt. They had tremendous jumping ability as well as the courage to tackle the huge banks, ditches, hedges and stone walls which so often confronted them.

Even before the turn of the century this remarkable jumping ability meant that Irish horses were much sought after, both at home and abroad. Since then Ireland has produced more top class jumpers than any other country, a fact which is even more remarkable when one realizes that the Irish hunter is not even a specific breed, but a halfbred. It is the result of the crossing of two breeds. A Thoroughbred stallion is almost always the sire; the dam, a strong draught mare, is a warm-blood, not a cold-blood, breed of working horse. The products of such a mating are called heavy hunters, and they make excellent steeplechasers.

Heavy hunter mares are then mated with Thoroughbred stallions to produce the lighter hunter type. These horses are particularly well suited for show-jumping.

Connemara pony mares are often crossed with Thoroughbred stallions, a cross which produces the small hunter which is such an excellent hunting and sporting horse for older children and lightweight adults. Although less than 150 centimetres high, several of them have become top class sporting horses. One such is Stroller which, under Marion Coakes, won the Silver Medal at the Olympic Games in Mexico. Others are Dundrum, which easily jumped two-metre high obstacles, Little Blue Haven, Smokey Joy and Errigal, all of which made the best of the large horses tremble in their shoes!

Over the last two or three decades efforts have been made in all the European countries to breed versatile saddle horses with a strong aptitude for jumping. In Germany the Holsteins and Hanoverians are renowned for their jumping ability. The Holstein is a very ancient breed, and since World War Two English Thoroughbreds in particular have been used to upgrade it. The Polish Anglo-Arab, Ramzes, also contributed a great deal to the development of the breed's sporting qualities.

Holsteins played a role in the development of the Hanoverian, which traces its origins to the Provincial Stud at Celle in Lower Saxony which was founded in 1735. Along with other breeds, a great deal of Thoroughbred blood was once again infused to improve the strain. The Hanoverian has since been crossed with breeds produced in other German regions and in other countries.

The Anglo-Norman is also a very

successful sporting animal. This breed was developed in northern France from the ancient Norman horse by adding English Thoroughbred and halfbred blood. The Anglo-Normans, too, have been crossed with various other European breeds used for competitive sport.

The French Anglo-Arab from southern France is an outstanding riding horse; the Groningen and the other

Dutch warm-blood breeds are producing more and more first class horses; and the Swedish warm-bloods are excellent saddle horses with a particular aptitude for dressage.

The Malapolski, the Polish Anglo-Arab, is the main Polish breed with excellent jumping ability.

In all the other Eastern bloc countries, too, great efforts are now being made to breed versatile horses which perform well in competitive sports.

English Thoroughbreds are often outstanding jumpers. They are courageous, and willing to perform, but their temperaments can often make them difficult to control, and they require riders endowed with a great deal of sensitivity.

Top class jumpers are always well built horses, though they frequently have external blemishes. A poorly built horse may have a definite liking for overcoming obstacles, and with good muscle training can achieve amazing results, but it will never be a really top class performer. The ideal show-jumper has long lines, a long sloping shoulder, pronounced withers, a powerful sloping croup, clearly defined tendons, and correctly positioned legs with strong well-angled joints.

Movement is very important. It must walk well, have a lively trot, and a long

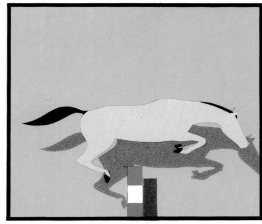

extended stride at the gallop. Equally important is the way it jumps. All movements must be even and balanced, and the total effect must be natural and relaxed. The legs must be well-angled and, when jumping, the body should form a convex arc from muzzle to dock. This is what is meant by the bascule.

A horse may have all these qualities, but they will be of little value without a natural love of jumping, the courage and ability to learn and perform, and the proper amount of caution.

1 The correct jumping trajectory.

2 A perfect jumping style.

3 Three of the most serious faults. On the left a jump without bascule, where the upper line of the horse's body has no curve. In the middle a very dangerous fault: the horse pulls its forelegs under its belly. On the right: the horse pulls its hindlegs under its belly.

4 Alfa, a Hanoverian, foaled in 1970 by Absatz out of Wolgaheldin. The ideal external appearance for a jumper.

CELEBRITIES IN THE JUMPING SADDLE

At its highest level the sport of show-jumping is about winning, and is as professional as other kinds of sport. Top class jumpers and their horses are fêted as celebrities and their appointment diaries are full both summer and winter.

1 The Brazilian Nelson Pessoa became famous on his incomparable grey, Gran Geste. Here he is riding Moët et Chandon Fan Rouge.

2 Raimondo d'Inzeo was born in 1925. Originally a military competitor, he was a member of the Italian Olympic team for the first time in 1948; in 1956 he was World Show-jumping Champion; and he is still an active competitor in top class events. He is pictured here on Posillipo.

3 Alwin Schockemöle on Warwick Rex in the individual event at Montreal 1976 where he won the Gold Medal.

4 Piero d'Inzeo, shown here on Easter Light, was always in his brother Raimondo's shadow, yet he too is one of the world's show-jumping élite. More than once he has finished a course as the better rider.

5 In 1978 during the Dublin Horse Show the Irishman Con Power set a stadium record when Rock Barton jumped clear, over the 220 cm high wall.

6 In the 1974 World Championship the American Frank Chapot was third equal with Simon. This picture was taken in 1966 when he won the Wiesbaden Casino Prize on San Lucas.

7 In 1970 Harvey Smith from England, on Sanyo San Mar, was placed third in the World Championships held at La Baule, France.

8 Englishwoman Marion Coakes on Stroller, an Irish pony which defeated much larger horses and elicited enthusiastic applause from every spectator.

9 The Italian V. Orlandi, on Fiorello, in the individual jumping event at Montreal in 1976.

10 David Broome from England was third in the individual event at Rome in 1960 and also at the 1968 Mexico Olympics. In France he came first in the 1970 World Championship. He is pictured here on Jägermeister.

11

12

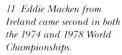
13

11 Eddie Macken from Ireland came second in both the 1974 and 1978 World Championships.

12 The Swiss Max Hauri on Woody Woodpecker; on Millview he came tenth at Tokyo in 1964.

13 The Englishwoman Caroline Bradley is considered to be one of the show-jumping élite. Here she is riding Marius.

14 Walter Gabathuler is a leading Swiss show-jumper. He has had several International successes on Harley.

15 Hubert Parot from France on Moët et Chandon.

16 The German Hartwig Steenken on Simona was placed fourth at Munich in 1972 and was World Champion in 1974 in England. This picture was taken in 1975 as he was jumping the Olympic Gate, on Erle, at the European Championships in Munich.

17 In 1978 Sönke Söksen on Kwept was Champion German Show-jumper.

18 In this photo, Jeff McVean, the popular Australian, is perched right over Copper Royal's neck.

14

15

13

16

17

18

19

20

19 Bad luck for the Austrian Hugo Simon when his grey, Lavandel, refused a jump at the opening of the 1977 season. In 1974 he was placed third in the World Championship on the same horse.

20 The German Hans Günter Winkler on Torphy. He was the Olympic winner at Stockholm in 1952 and World Champion in 1954 and 1955.

21 Graziano Mancinelli from Italy. In 1970 he was second in the World Championship in France, and in 1972 he won the individual event at Munich.

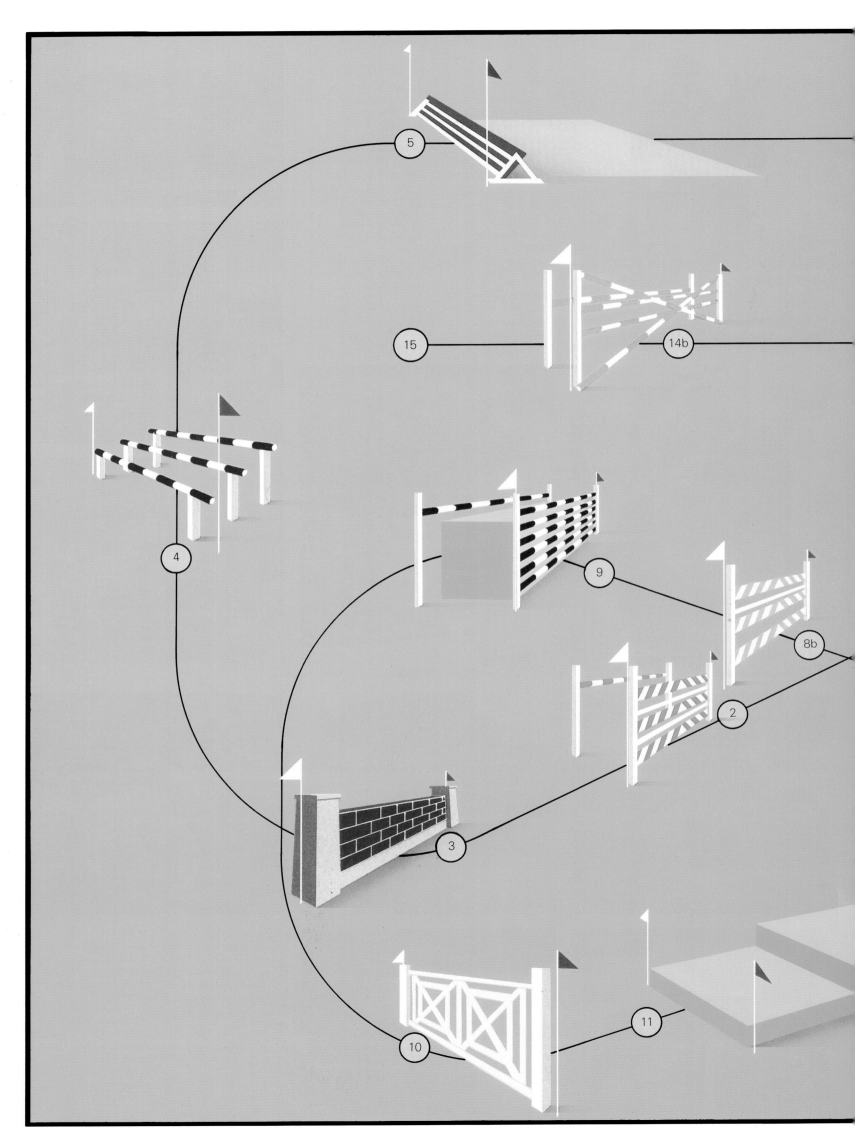

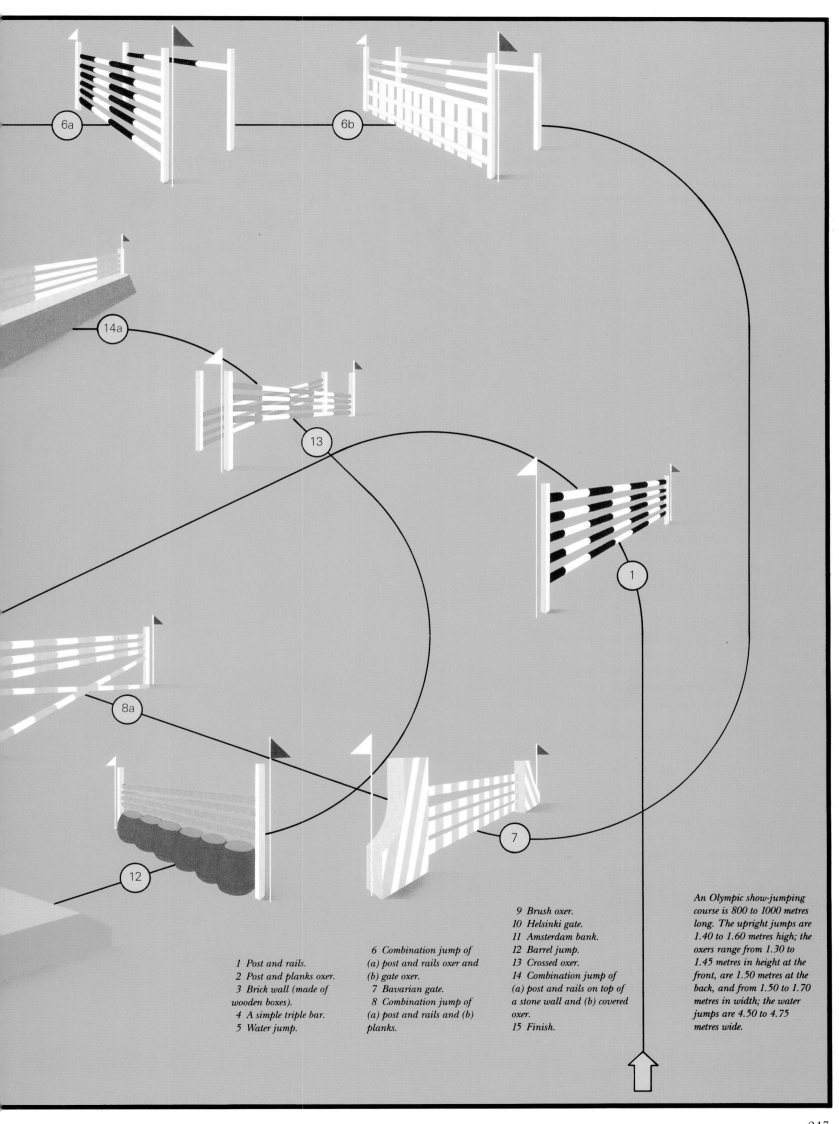

6a

6b

14a

13

1

8a

7

12

1 Post and rails.
2 Post and planks oxer.
3 Brick wall (made of wooden boxes).
4 A simple triple bar.
5 Water jump.

6 Combination jump of (a) post and rails oxer and (b) gate oxer.
7 Bavarian gate.
8 Combination jump of (a) post and rails and (b) planks.

9 Brush oxer.
10 Helsinki gate.
11 Amsterdam bank.
12 Barrel jump.
13 Crossed oxer.
14 Combination jump of (a) post and rails on top of a stone wall and (b) covered oxer.
15 Finish.

An Olympic show-jumping course is 800 to 1000 metres long. The upright jumps are 1.40 to 1.60 metres high; the oxers range from 1.30 to 1.45 metres in height at the front, are 1.50 metres at the back, and from 1.50 to 1.70 metres in width; the water jumps are 4.50 to 4.75 metres wide.

Below: The origins of the
Military can be traced back
to the contests organized by
many early equestrian people
to assess the worth of their
cavalry horses.

Military events in the
modern sense were first held
at the beginning of this
century. They remained
essentially the prerogative of
cavalry officers until after
World War Two.

Right: The Military, or
Combined Training, is now
a highly competitive sport. It
may have lost all its martial
connotations but it still
demands total commitment
from both rider and horse.

THE MILITARY —
COMBINED TRAINING

The three-day event, or the Military,
is possibly the most demanding and
rewarding of any equestrian activity.
The skill and versatility of both rider
and horse are tested to the limit and
both must be highly motivated and
competitive.

The Military proper — combined
training competition — is a
comprehensive test held on three
consecutive days. In the dressage
section, on the first day, the rider,
using finely co-ordinated aids, must
demonstrate that the horse is
obedient, yet able to perform
naturally and apparently without
effort. The speed and endurance
section on the second day is the
most arduous. It takes place across
roads and tracks and includes a
steeplechase gallop, and a cross-
country course which requires both
courage and skill. The final section,
on the third day, is a show-jumping
contest. Then both horses and
riders prove how well they have
coped with the strains and stresses
of the previous day.

FROM CAVALRY MOUNT
TO THREE-DAY EVENTER

The military or three-day event was originally a trial for cavalry mounts, and can be traced back to the various exercises used by the early equestrian peoples to improve the fitness of their cavalry horses, and to the contests they staged to test the results. Until after World War Two the military event was almost exclusively the prerogative of cavalry officers and their horses, even though these events had been part of the Olympic programme since 1912.

In the nineteenth century many cavalry schools included stretches of countryside on which riders and horses were taught how to overcome difficult obstacles. These were also used for local contests. The *Escuela de Equitacion militar* in Zarzuela near Madrid, for example, has a steep cliff which seems to pose an insuperable obstacle for a horse and rider. The first eleven metres of its fifteen-metre height are an almost vertical drop.

Both the famous cavalry schools of Pinerolo, near Turin, and the Tor di Quinto, near Rome, contain stretches of countryside with many different kinds of obstacles. Towards the end of the last century Rittmaster Federico Caprilli, in particular, placed the greatest emphasis on a horse's suitability for cross-country work. Other countries — Germany for instance — tended to concentrate on dressage.

In the last quarter of the nineteenth century the popular Concours Hippique included both show-jumping and dressage events; but on the European continent the competitors were almost exclusively from the military. Long-distance rides also enjoyed a growing popularity, and most of the officers who competed in the Concours events also took part in these tests of stamina.

Long-distance rides were no novelty in Russia. Although the distances were sometimes truly immense, again and again the noble Akhal Teké horses demonstrated their remarkable stamina.

What was probably the first long-distance ride to be held in Central Europe took place in 1892. One hundred and fifteen officers started from Berlin to Vienna, while, at the same time, ninety-three Austro-Hungarian officers set off on the same route from the opposite direction. The Austrian Count von Starhemberg was the first to complete the race, in a time of 71 hours and 26 minutes, but his horse collapsed with heart failure. The German von Reitzenstein took about one and a half hours longer. His horse also died of exhaustion, two days later. Only sixty-six Germans and thirty-six Austrians completed the six hundred-odd kilometres.

The ride from Brussels to Ostende which was held in 1902 also became famous. The total distance was 132 kilometres. In this race, too, the horses were insufficiently trained and were ridden at too fast a tempo. Of the sixty animals that started, thirty-one had to be withdrawn before the finish, and sixteen died of exhaustion.

Before this event, the various societies which campaigned against cruelty to animals had pleaded in vain for regulations to ensure that long-distance rides could be worthwhile events rather than a trip to the knacker's yard for the horses. After the Brussels-Ostende ride even the organizers began to realize that in their current form such events were pointless, and new regulations were drawn up before the next *Raid Militaire* with the aim of protecting the horses.

This race was about 230 kilometres long, from Paris to Deauville in Normandy. The first 130 kilometres, i.e., as far as Rouen, had to be ridden in a prescribed time; the riders were not permitted to cover the distance in less. This restriction was then relaxed for the second part, but on the day after the contest the condition of the horses was tested.

One of the participants in this ride was Paul Bausil. He seems to have been the first person to work out a precise fitness programme. He also adhered firmly to predetermined tactics. His findings were published in a book which was widely distributed, and had an important influence on distance riding.

Bausil also proposed that distance rides should no longer be restricted simply to races along roads, but should

1 and 2 Some of the cavalry schools had extremely difficult cross-country tests. This was particularly true of those in Mexico, Spain and Italy, and the steep slope at the Spanish Military School at Zarzuela near Madrid was without doubt the most hair-raising of them all. The cliff was fifteen metres high and the first eleven metres were an almost vertical drop. Anyone who sees this slope finds it hard to believe that a horse and rider could possibly make a safe descent.

3 The Caprilli slope was the most formidable of all the many cross-country obstacles at the Tor di Quinto Cavalry School near Rome. Here Lieutenant Acerbo (1902) is attacking it in perfect textbook manner.

4 In this picture taken at the Tor di Quinto, a horse and rider are using the slope as a take-off point. At the Italian Cavalry School, emphasis was on a horse's suitability for cross-country; dressage training was restricted to the absolute minimum.

3

4

be combined with cross-country trials. His suggestion was accepted, and the 1905 ride from Lyon to Aix included a cross-country stretch. This was to be ridden on the second day. It covered sixty-five kilometres and had a number of natural obstacles.

Later on, a gallop round a racetrack was also included in each ride, most of which now lasted three days. The average distance to be covered each day was about sixty-five kilometres. Other countries soon adopted these French fitness trials. Posts were set up along the routes where veterinarians tested the condition of the horses, and exhausted or lamed animals were eliminated from the contest.

The first true precursor of the modern three-day event took place in 1902 in Paris. It was called the *Championnat du Cheval d'Armes* and lasted two days. On the first day a dressage event was held. The programme was not specified and each rider could choose a routine that suited his own abilities. This was followed

by a steeplechase which had fourteen jumps and was four kilometres long. It had to be completed in a maximum of time of nine minutes. Finally there was a cross-country ride. This covered sixty kilometres and had a time limit of three hours and forty-five minutes.

On the second day there was a show-jumping contest. At this event most emphasis was still placed on dressage, but when the same competition was held the following year, the emphasis had shifted to the show-jumping. The cross-country did not come to the fore until later.

With the exception of the war years the Parisian *Championnat* was an annual event. Similar events were also being held in other countries.

At the *Military Internationale*, held in Brussels for the first time in 1905, there were thirty-seven competitors representing four countries. It consisted of a free dressage event, a cross-country over fifteen kilometres, then a show-jumping event. This was followed by another

cross-country ride over nine kilometres, another jumping event, and finally a gallop of 3500 metres round a racetrack.

The first competition based on this pattern was held in 1907 in Italy. (It did not include a dressage section.) It was organized on a national basis and was won by Federico Caprilli. By 1908 the Italian Military had attracted international interest, and one hundred and three officers, from Italy, France, Spain, Belgium, Rumania, Russia and the Argentine, took part.

CROSS-COUNTRY

The core of the three-day event is the cross-country, which forms part of the speed and endurance section held on the second day. On this course the horse needs to have great self-confidence in tackling completely new obstacles. Although a show-jumper in the arena is also faced with difficult obstacles, these are likely to be simply variations of jumps that are already familiar; usually post and rails, oxer, triple bars and water jumps.

The cross-country course in a three-day event is always made up of new and unfamiliar obstacles and combinations. And cross-country obstacles are almost always fixed. If the horse does not jump sufficiently high or wide, or if it gauges the distances incorrectly or no longer has sufficient strength for the jump, then it will hit its legs painfully or fall. No poles or wooden boxes will simply clatter to the ground behind it. Nor are these obstacles constructed on a smooth attractive show-jumping arena. They are scattered over open country, often in the middle of steep slopes or combined with banks or sand-pits. Sometimes the horse has to jump in and out of watercourses as well.

All these difficulties are compounded by the length of the course — about eight kilometres — and by the fact that the horses have just completed an endurance ride of sixteen to twenty-two kilometres, plus a steeplechase course of 3500 to 4000 metres which had to be ridden at the gallop.

The obstacles in a three-day event should be constructed so that they blend into the landscape and seem to have occurred naturally, though most of them are, of course, built expressly for the events. They often involve considerable expense, especially for major competitions. An obstacle can be a thick tree trunk lying on the ground or even a simple fence, but it may also be a tricky zigzag construction made from wooden poles. A rider must study such an object very carefully beforehand to work out exactly how to make the approach and the jump.

Many of the jumps in the major competitions are difficult; some are not safe. As well as being tests of the horse's jumping ability, they also require both horse and rider to prove their courage, skill and experience. But they are seldom as dangerous as the notorious concrete pipes at the Olympic Games in Rome in 1960. These were 1.15 metres high and 1.10 metres long. They were treacherous because they had to be jumped lengthwise, and the landing place was on a slope. This upset many of the horses at the last moment, so that they miscalculated the take-off point and knocked their

1 The cross-country course at Helsinki in 1952 was excellent. Here Piero d'Inzeo on Pagore is tackling a wide jump.

2 A jump into the water at the Alpine Cup in Rome in 1979. The Swiss, Ernst Baumann, seen here on Baron, was killed in a fall on the same horse at the World Championships in Luhmühlen in 1982.

3 Jump off a bank over a fixed fence on to a lower lying landing place at the Olympic cross-country at Munich. Up to that point Horst Karsten on Sioux, was leading, but he was one of the riders who fell there and had to retire.

4 The 'Theke', the final jump in the cross-country at the European Championships in 1979 at Luhmühlen.

5 A high jump at Walldorf.

legs on the sharp edges of the pipes. Military obstacles should, of course, be difficult but certainly should not be so unfair.

A trakehner ditch is also a difficult jump. This is a tall post and rails set in the bottom of a ditch, and the horse must judge its take-off and landing place exactly or it will fall into the ditch. At the Olympic Military in Stockholm in 1956 the Swedish horse Iller broke a leg when tackling a jump of this kind and had to be shot on the spot, although the obstacle itself was not treacherous and the distances had been worked out to match the horses' capabilities. Unless these proportions are worked out correctly, the obstacle will have an unacceptable degree of risk. At the European Championships held in 1973 at Kiev in the Soviet Union, the pole oxer in the ditch was built according to correct principles, but seventeen out of forty-three horses fell there, and it was only by great good fortune that there were no fatalities.

Every three-day event includes jumps into the water. They may look spectacular, but as a rule they are comparatively easy so long as the horse is not afraid of water — and eventers by definition are fearless. The Trout Hatchery on the excellent cross-country course at Burghley House in England is one of the most difficult watercourses. The horse has to jump over a post and rails as it goes into the water, and then over another as it comes out. Many riders are defeated here, but it cannot be described as dangerous. On the other hand, the water

6 A drop jump at Badminton where in 1976 Hugh Thomas came second.

7 The No. 2 jump at the 1973 European Championships in Kiev where 14 out of the 43 riders fell. It was one of the trickiest obstacles of all (see also 13).

8 Overgrown ditch with fence at the Olympic qualifying contest which was held at Warendorf in 1972. The rider is Otto Rothe on Trux von Kamax.

9 Princess Anne on Doublet at the Badminton Horse Trials.

10 A high spread jump which needed to be treated with respect. This picture of S. R. Schwarz on Power Game was taken at Walldorf in 1979. He was the winner in the advanced section.

crossing at the Olympic Games in Mexico in 1968 was highly dangerous. There the horses had to jump over rails into a stream which was about forty centimetres deep. It seemed quite harmless, but in the middle of the event a violent thunderstorm changed this peaceful stretch of water into a raging torrent which became almost impassable.

11 The Olympic trakehner ditch at Stockholm in 1956 where the Swedish horse Iller fell so badly that it had to be destroyed on the spot. Albert Hill's Countryman III is just managing to clear the obstacle, although he has had to leap up from too far down in the ditch.

12 A leap into space at Luhmühlen in 1968. The course was difficult but well constructed.

13 Horst Karsten on Sioux was one of the lucky riders who successfully negotiated Obstacle No. 2 at the European Championships in Kiev in 1973. This was a highly dangerous, covered ditch.

14 The concrete pipes on the cross-country course at Rome in 1960 achieved almost as much notoriety as Obstacle No. 2 at Kiev.

CELEBRITIES IN THE MILITARY SADDLE

Military events were originally almost exclusively restricted to army officers, although occasionally horsewomen were permitted to take part. Only one was really successful: Irmgard von Opel who, on Nanuk, won the Military at Vienna in 1932.

It was not until after World War Two that the rules were relaxed to allow civilian participation.

Forty-three officers and sixteen civilian riders took part in the three-day event at the 1952 Helsinki Games. There were nineteen complete teams, six of them made up of civilians. Two of these, Germany and the US, won the Team Silver and Bronze, behind the Swedish team.

Since then the Military has become a predominantly civilian sport. It is extremely tough, and understandably female riders are in the minority, but as the foremost among them, particularly the English women, have achieved first class results in all the major events, there is no doubt about their acceptance as the equals of their male colleagues.

To be successful, competitors must be outstanding riders, for, as well as having to compete in dressage, show-jumping and difficult cross-country events, they have to cope with temperamental horses. A good eventing horse must be aggressive, with a strong personality, to enable it to cope with the rigours of a cross-country course. First class eventers usually have a high proportion of noble blood in them. Some are pure Thoroughbreds; most have at least fifty per cent Thoroughbred blood.

High and Mighty, ridden by English-woman Sheila Wilcox, was one of the most amazing eventers of the post-war period, and between 1955 and 1958 he was the winner in seventeen difficult events. He came of mixed ancestry. (Such a combination would be almost unheard-of on the European continent, but it occurs quite frequently in England.) His sire was a Thoroughbred; his dam a halfbred pony, produced by the crossing of a Highland pony mare with an Arab stallion. High and Mighty inherited the pony's intelligence, skill and courage, the Arab's stamina, and the toughness and speed of the Thoroughbred. Although he was only 161 centimetres tall, he was never afraid of an obstacle and did not fall once in his whole career! When his eventing days were over, he spent the next eleven years as a first class hunter.

Our Solo was almost ten centimetres smaller. His Australian rider, Bill Roycroft, is an impressive 1.87 metres tall, and together they made rather an odd-looking couple. Despite his small stature Our Solo was a Thoroughbred. Although

intended to be a children's pony, he proved far too unruly, and Roycroft was able to buy him cheaply with the idea of using him as a polo pony.

Two years later, in 1957, Roycroft began to compete in three-day events. He was soon at the heels of the best of the Australians, and by 1960 he was a member of the Olympic team. Before the Olympics, he was the winner on Our Solo at the famous Badminton Horse Trials, rather to everyone's surprise.

At Rome he was a sensation. Our Solo fell at the notorious concrete pipes and Roycroft broke a collarbone, yet he finished the cross-country, riding with the use of only one hand. He was taken by helicopter to the hospital, but discharged himself the following morning. Although the doctors had forbidden him to ride, he completed a faultless round in the show-jumping event and thereby helped his team to win the Gold Medal.

Thoroughbreds can make good eventers, but they should be of the powerful, strong-limbed type which is mainly bred in Ireland. Doublet, ridden by HRH Princess Anne, however, was an exception and proved that the lighter weight, fine-limbed type can also be outstanding.

HRH Princess Anne also had an excellent horse in Goodwill, and over a period of seven years he successfully completed fourteen difficult three-day events. In 1975 he was second in the European Championships at Luh-mühlen.

The winner at that event was Lucinda Green (née Prior-Palmer), also English, on Be Fair. The same rider, on George, won the next European Championships at Burghley in 1977. Be Fair was a typical eventer who made life very difficult for his young rider, and in their early years together he threw her from the saddle many times. George was very different.

1 Bill Roycroft, an Australian, and one of the most striking personalities in the Military. He is as hard as iron and refuses to be defeated. Since Rome in 1960 he has taken part in numerous Olympics; the last time as a sixty-one-year-old, in 1976 at Montreal.

2 Since 1970 HRH Princess Anne has repeatedly proved her equestrian ability in the military saddle. She has won, and been placed, in many top class events. She was European Champion in 1971 and second in 1975.

3 Between 1955 and 1968 Sheila Wilcox was the leading British equestrienne. At Copenhagen in 1957 she won the first European Championship for Women, and she made Badminton history with her three consecutive wins: 1957, 1958 and 1959.

4 Since 1971, when she was a member of the team that won the junior Gold Medal at the European Championships, Lucinda Green (née Prior-Palmer) has ridden from success to success. She has won four times at Badminton (each time on a different horse), and she won two Gold Medals at the European Championships.

7

8

5 For years Otto Ammermann has been one of the German élite in the Military. He was twice German Champion.

6 In Germany Klaus Wagner is known as the Grand Old Man of the Military. Since the first post-war Military was held in 1950 he has competed in numerous events, including four Olympic Games.

7 Both Thierry (picture) and Jean-Yves Touzaint of France competed in the 1976 Olympic Games. The Team Gold at the Military Festival at Fontainebleau in 1980 has been their greatest success to date.

8 Karl Schultz, FRG, has been the victor at many international three-day events: at Wylye, twice at Walldorf, and three times at Achselschwang. He has also won several medals at the European Championships and at the Olympic Games, and been a World Champion.

9 Mark Phillips, Great Britain, has been successful in all the major events in England. He has won at Wylye, at Burghley, and three times at Badminton. He also won the Team Gold at the 1982 Olympic Games at Munich.

10 Horst Karsten is one of the most senior of the top class riders in Germany. In Tokyo in 1964 he won the Team Bronze Medal; then had further individual and team successes at Moscow, Munich, Kiev and Burghley.

11 Richard Meade, Great Britain, came second in the 1966 and 1970 World Championships. He was an individual and team winner in the 1972 Olympics and has been a dependable member of the British team for many years. With his help they have won numerous medals in the European and World Championships and at the Olympic Games.

12 Bruce Davidson, US. Pupil of the famous Le Goff. He was World Champion in 1974 and 1978.

13 Frank Weldon, Great Britain, is a technical delegate of the FEI, an International judge, and a course designer at Badminton. He was European Champion once and runner-up three times. At the 1956 Olympic Games in Stockholm he won the Individual Bronze and the Team Gold.

Anton Bühler, Switzerland, is much in demand worldwide both as a judge for three-day events and as a technical expert. He can look back on a long riding career. He was Swiss Champion five times, and was highly placed in the European Championships at Basle in 1954 and Windsor in 1955. He also competed in three Olympic Games. In Rome in 1960 he won the Individual Bronze and the Team Silver.

9

10

11

12

13

14

14 Herbert Blöcker, FRG, is small but tough. At the Olympic Games in Montreal he became a legend when, with only one stirrup strap, he managed a faultless round and helped his team to win the Silver Medal.

15 Michael Plumb is an outstanding rider in the American team. In five Olympic Games he has won a Team Gold, an Individual Silver, and three Team Silver Medals. He also won the Individual Silver and the Team Gold at the 1974 World Championships at Burghley. His most recent victory was at the CCI in Luhmühlen in 1980.

16 Nils Haagensen from Denmark competed in the 1976 Olympics in the dressage team and then changed to the military, where he had a meteoric rise to fame. He was European Champion in 1979 and winner at the Military Festival at Fontainebleau in 1980.

15

16

Lucinda Green described him as an 'English gentleman' in the very best sense of the word. He never resisted, but simply did everything that was required of him.

From a statistical point of view, Sioux, a Westphalian halfbred grey, is undoubtedly the most successful eventer. Between 1971 and 1977, under Horst Karsten, he was out in front again and again. Typically he was the most difficult horse that Karsten had ever ridden.

First class eventers, if they are well ridden, often show amazingly few signs of wear and tear despite the tough cross-country courses, which do cause frequent injuries. They continue to perform well into old age. Fortunat is one of the most famous. His rider Reiner Klimke referred to him as 'a sprightly old gentleman of thirty-five'.

255

EVENTING — THE FIRST DAY

A three-day event begins with the dressage test, performed in an arena twenty metres by sixty metres in area. The programme has twenty movements, and all three basic gaits are required, the most difficult movements being frequent changes of tempo and gait, the counter canter, and counter changes of hand at the trot.

At the conclusion of the programme, marks are allocated in regard to fluency and accuracy of performance, impulsion, lightness, and the rider's seat.

The time allowed is seven minutes, thirty seconds.

Points are deducted for exceeding the time limit or making mistakes in the programme.

The aim in the Military dressage is to have a horse that is easy to ride and that reacts to the slightest touch of the rider's aids. It must co-operate with all its energy and not resist the rider.

In the other sections of the Military, points are awarded solely in regard to mistakes and time. The dressage, on the other hand, is judged according to a human scale of values and therefore a certain degree of subjectivity is inevitable. A good presentation by horse and rider, even though it has nothing directly to do with the actual dressage performance, cannot fail to make a positive impression on even the most objective judge.

Who could remain unmoved by the sight of a horse with plaited mane, with its tail carefully combed, its coat shimmering like silk, its tack clean and polished and a rider in ceremonial tail coat and top hat, wearing a stock and white gloves?

Left: Lucinda Green (née Prior-Palmer) from England was twice European Champion in the Military. In the dressage test she and Be Fair are an impressive demonstration of complete harmony right from the start, yet in his early years this chestnut horse proved very difficult to control.

Right: No three-day event is won in the 20 x 60 m dressage arena, but a good result is encouraging. The purpose of the dressage in the Military is to provide an obedient horse that will be easy to ride in the cross-country.

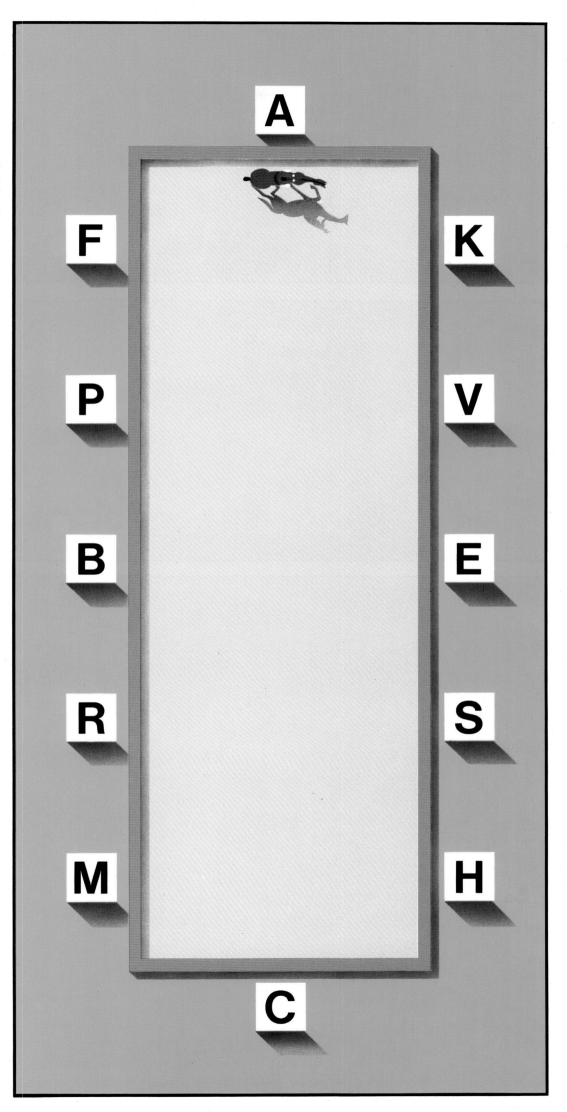

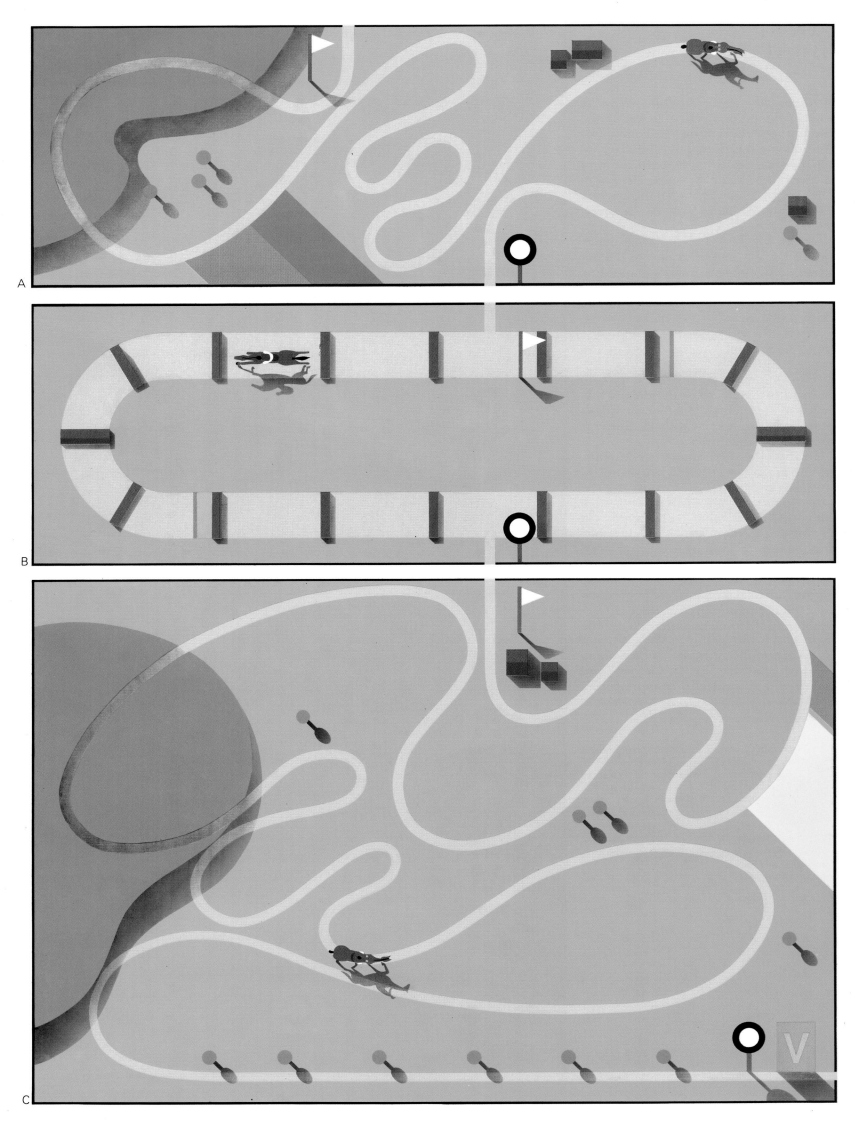

THE SECOND DAY

The speed and endurance test takes place on the second day. This is the core of the three-day event and is completely ruled by the clock. This is when the wheat is separated from the chaff, and the riders find out whether their preparations were sufficiently thorough.

Because of all the preparations in his stable, an experienced eventer already knows exactly what is about to follow. The horse knows that this time he will not have to be well-behaved and perform figures in shortened gaits, but can let loose. Even as his legs are being carefully bandaged he can barely stand still for excitement, and when he first feels the light saddle on his back he becomes difficult to restrain, for now everything starts in earnest.

The speed and endurance section is divided into four phases — A, B, C and D.

Phase A is a ride of four to six kilometres across roads and tracks, and must be ridden at a tempo of 240 metres per minute. There are no bonus points for riding any faster, but if the time limit is exceeded then the rider receives one minus point for each second.

Phases A and C, which are also called the trotting sections, usually take the rider through charming, rural countryside. The course at Badminton, for example, is set in the beautiful park owned by the the Duke of Beaufort and is dotted with magnificent trees, some of which are over a century old.

Maienfeld, in Switzerland, is also a very picturesque setting. The track winds high above the village through the middle of the vineyard-covered slopes, with the majestic Alps as a backdrop.

Phase A forms the prelude to the steeplechase, B, which follows immediately afterwards. In this stage, where the lie of the land — a verge perhaps — permits, the horse is often allowed to proceed at a slow gallop — as Ottokar Pohlmann, on Polarfuchs, is doing in the top picture on this page. Given the opportunity, some riders like to jump small obstacles so that their horse is best prepared for the steeplechase to come.

The steeplechase itself follows on immediately after Phase A. The track is 3500 to 4000 metres long and has to be ridden at a tempo of 690 m/min. Twelve obstacles are spread around the course. These may be up to 1.40 metres high, but the fixed part of the obstacle must not be higher than a metre, or more than four metres wide. Most of the horses know these obstacles so well that they 'sail' over them like experienced steeplechasers. Lucinda Green's horse, George, the Badminton and European Champion in 1977, showed no respect at all

Facing page: The speed and endurance tests — Phases A, B and C.

Left: Ottokar Pohlmann and his elegant chestnut gelding, Polarfuchs, were the winning combination in the 1958 International Military held at Harewood in England. This photo was taken during the roads and tracks section.

Below: At the veterinary control after the second roads and tracks section. Only horses which have clearly recovered during the ten-minute pause and show no signs of lameness are allowed to take part in the cross-country, the most difficult part of the whole event.

for the steeplechase obstacles and simply galloped through them. George was normally a very dependable jumper, but he caused his rider more anxious moments on the steeplechase course than afterwards on the cross-country itself.

During Phase B the rider's main task is to conserve the horse's energy so that it has enough in reserve for the cross-country course. It may even be worthwhile risking accumulating a few penalty points, and riding any faster than required would be an unnecessary waste of reserves as it does not earn any bonus points.

A reliable feeling for tempo is essential, and the three required speeds become second nature to an experienced event rider. These are 240 m/min for Phases A and C; 690 m/min for Phase B; and 570 m/min for Phase D.

The end of the steeplechase gallop is also the start of Phase C, which is a road and tracks course over twelve to sixteen kilometres. In this phase the well trained horse soon recovers from the effects of the fast steeplechase gallop while trotting and cantering slowly. Although this stretch allows no time for dawdling, riders still have time to go over the cross-country course once more in their minds. They will have already covered it several times on foot, but this is a good opportunity to review the obstacles and the difficulties of the course.

A ten-minute compulsory pause is included at the end of Phase C, when the horses are once again given a thorough examination by a veterinarian, and only those which pass this stringent test are allowed to go on to compete in Phase D.

In the time remaining, the sweating horse is washed, cooled down, dried, watered and its bandages and shoes are checked. Then begins Phase D, the cross-country, the ultimate test.

259

1 The first obstacle should not be too difficult or the horses will be wary of those that follow. The oxer over a small ditch has a wide front, is clearly marked, and well constructed.

2 The course leads through the garden of a farmyard: the entrance is over a wall or the garden gate; the exit over a hedge. A successful example of how an obstacle can be made to blend in with the natural surroundings.

3 The horses can jump over this two-metre wide wagon in two ways. They can either save time and take it in one jump or touch down briefly with their hind feet on the top of the load. The barn on the one side and the hedge on the other make an excellent frame.

4 Obstacle No. 13 at Horsens. After negotiating the steep slope through the forest on the right edge of the picture the horses have very little room to get up enough speed to clear the obstacle. This makes the jump over the wide ditch more difficult.

5 A birchwood staccionata at the top of a steep slope provided one of the trickiest problems in the 1981 European Championships. It was difficult for the rider, because he was approaching the jump after a longish slightly sloping stretch at the gallop and had to ensure the horse had enough momentum so that it would not refuse, yet he had to prevent it from jumping too far over the slope or he risked a fall.

1

2

3

4

5

CROSS-COUNTRY

The cross-country is the climax of the three-day event, the decisive phase where the qualities of both horse and rider are tested to the utmost.

The horse has just completed two stretches of roads and tracks plus a fast steeplechase gallop, but must still have the energy to tackle seven kilometres of demanding obstacles at the gallop. He must keep up an average speed of 570 metres a minute, through hilly countryside up and down steep, enervating slopes, through water and often over wet and heavy ground. And as if this were not enough he also has to cope with more than thirty obstacles, each one of which would probably make a beginner's heart sink into his boots. If a jump is misjudged, there are no loose poles, boards, or wooden boxes which simply clatter to the ground. A miscalculated jump results in a painful stumble or even a serious fall.

Cross-country competitors have to be courageous and extremely fit. During the ride they must also be continually aware of the horse's physical condition and state of mind. They must notice immediately if the horse's attention starts to waver or if it becomes irresolute and needs encouragement to keep going. They must be aware of all its moods, know how to detect and deal with them; know when the horse is giving its utmost and when it is just coasting along, and be able to distinguish whether this is due to laziness or incipient exhaustion. In the latter case wise and generous riders will always suppress their own ambitions and either retire immediately or ride the horse gently to the finish.

About the middle of the cross-country, an eventer very often goes through a difficult period, when it is inclined to slacken speed and tackles each obstacle with obvious effort. The experienced rider recognises these symptoms and slows down a bit. Usually the horse recovers very quickly and soon becomes its energetic lively self again, and even as it approaches the final jumps it will continue to display the courage, superb fitness and tremendous motivation that characterizes every first class eventer.

THE THIRD DAY

The show-jumping contest on the third day is in essence simply a test of condition and obedience.

The course is 750 to 900 metres long and has to be ridden at a tempo of 400 m/min. There are ten to twelve jumps. A maximum height of 1.20 metres is stipulated for high jumps; the high spread jumps may be no more than two metres wide; and the spread jumps may not exceed 3.50 metres in width.

Every event horse is basically an outstanding jumper, and when this is taken into consideration then the course seems less impressive. There are few faultless rides, however, because each horse is still affected to some degree by the exertions of the previous day.

The cross-country is the crucial part of the three-day event and quality is the determining factor. Even a good horse, of course, does have his bad days, but with all the luck in the world a horse that is basically lacking in ability cannot reach the topmost rungs in this sport. It may surpass itself in the cross-country and mobilize all its reserves, but afterwards it will be so totally exhausted that it will probably not pass the veterinary examination on the following morning, and consequently not be eligible to compete in the show-jumping. Even if it does pass, it probably will not be able to cope with the course.

Often, however, there is so little to choose between the leading horses at the end of the first phases, that the show-jumping becomes the decisive event. The 1975 European Championships, which were held in Luhmühlen in northern Germany, were a classic example of this. The cross-country course, although generally considered to be outstanding, had no obstacles tricky enough to separate out the good competitors from those who were less experienced. The overall standard was also extremely high. Out of fifty combinations who started, only seven did not finish the cross-

country, and forty horses were eligible to compete in the show-jumping. At the end of the cross-country, the team from Great Britain was in the lead, although Janet Hodgeson on Larkspur then retired. The remaining competitors in this all-women team were HRH Princess Anne, Lucinda Green (*née* Prior-Palmer) and Susan Hatherley, who all competed in the show-jumping on the following day. The teams from the Soviet Union and the FRG were behind the British.

HRH Princess Anne, on Goodwill, completed the show-jumping without problems. Everyone was convinced then that the Englishwomen would take home the Team Gold, but apparently Susan Hatherley's horse had not recovered from the strains of the previous day, and at the end of the show-jumping she had forty-two penalty points. All four of the Soviet riders completed the course without incurring any faults, to become the surprise Team winners in what was an exciting competition.

The British salvaged their country's honour in the individual awards. The young Lucinda Prior-Palmer, on Be Fair, won the Gold and HRH Princess Anne won the Silver. Third place was decided in the show-jumping. The Soviet rider Peter Gornuschko, on Gusar, won the Bronze Medal ahead of the German Helmut Rethemeier on Pauline. The team from the Federal Republic of Germany did win the Team Bronze.

In principle, the preparations for the show-jumping begin immediately after the cross-country. The horses need

plenty of care to ensure that they will not be hopelessly stiff and plagued by aching muscles on the following day, and all three-day event competitors have evolved their own system for dealing with this problem. The British use electrical massaging equipment, the American team take a professional masseur along to every major event, but most methods follow basically the same procedure.

First the horse is washed down with a mixture of lukewarm water and spirits, then wiped with the sweat scraper. Small wounds are treated with antiseptic spray; the veterinary surgeon is called in to deal with any more serious wounds. Then the horse is covered and led around at the walk for an hour to loosen up its muscles. The boots are removed, its legs are sprayed with cold water, given a few minutes' massage and finally wrapped in a sweat bandage which is changed every three hours. Only now is the horse allowed to drink and eat as much as it wants, though after all its exertions it will probably have very little appetite.

It is left in its stable to rest until the evening, when it is massaged for half an hour, and then led around at the walk for another half hour. Horses with very stiff muscles are sometimes kept on the move all night long.

On the following morning the horse is ridden for about two hours at the walk and then given another massage.

The veterinary examination is held about an hour before the beginning of the show-jumping. Any horse which is lame, seriously hurt or unusually exhausted is not allowed to compete.

A long warm-up ride, which includes some small jumps and usually two or three larger jumps at the end, is necessary before the actual event.

As all this indicates, a great deal of time and effort is required if a horse is to be able to tackle the show-jumping successfully.

Right: The horses have to undergo yet another stringent veterinary examination before they tackle the show-jumping, the final section of the Military.

THE SPORT OF DRIVING

The ancient Romans were avid racing fans, and contemporary historians report that up to 250,000 spectators would gather to watch the chariot races. Modern driving bears little resemblance to the contests waged by the fearless Roman charioteers — nowadays no one poisons their opponents' horses or has another driver treacherously murdered — but the sport still exerts considerable fascination on young and old. In both Western and Eastern countries enthusiastic spectators gather in their thousands at the major driving events.

The four-in-hand seems to attract most attention. Certainly the driver of a four-in-hand is always an impressive sight, and he seems to have more than merely manual skills as he puts his horses elegantly through their paces in the dressage arena, or drives them at a fast tempo along narrow pathways between the obstacles. How else could he guide his four animals from a distance using only his voice, whip and reins? The four-in-hand seems the perfect example of a united team in harmony.

DRIVING

Excavations made in the Near East suggest that horses were harnessed first, but not ridden until a later date, although this theory can probably never be proved conclusively. The earliest domesticated horses were harnessed either to war chariots or to carts used on ceremonial occasions.

Driving in the modern sense did not exist until shortly before the arrival of railways and the automobile. Before then the horses and carts which travelled along the dreadful roads were used predominantly for commercial purposes. They transported freight and the few passengers were incidental.

This changed when the streets were improved, for carriage owners then discovered that they actually enjoyed holding the reins themselves rather than being driven by a coachman. Anyone with social aspirations would like to show off his horses himself — on a drive in the park, at the hunt, or on the way to the office. From there it was only a small step to competing in long-distance drives and driving contests. Driving became a sport.

Inevitably the horse disappeared from the army, from transport and agriculture. Although the sport of riding suffered only a slight setback, driving on the other hand almost became a forgotten art.

Harness rooms that were once so well looked after became junk rooms; coach-houses were turned into garages for cars. After all, what part could the horse and cart play in modern traffic! Valuable harness was thrown away and classic carriages sold for ludicrously low prices or were even burnt.

But enthusiasts remained in a few places. They kept up the art of driving in the doldrum years and helped to bring about its renaissance when all seemed lost. The harness and carriages which had been kept were brought out, restored and re-equipped.

The first European Championships in driving fours were held in 1971 in Budapest. Driving became one of the equestrian sports officially recognized by the International Equestrian Federation (FEI). Championships were held at Kecskemet, Windsor, Zug and Apeldoorn. HRH Prince Philip, who was President of the FEI at the time, also competed in the events himself.

The way in which the reins are held follows a carefully worked out system. When driving a one-horse carriage (6) the driver holds one rein in his hand. One end is connected at the right hand side of the horse's mouth, the other at the left. Coupling reins are added when driving a pair (7) or more horses. This is a second, shorter rein which is buckled on to both the right and the left hand rein. Thus the driver, using just one rein, can control both horses at the same time. The rein can also be adjusted, which enables horses of different temperaments to be harnessed together. When driving three-in-hand (8) another coupling rein is simply buckled on. When driving four-in-hand (9) the driver holds two coupling reins in his hands; one for the wheelers, the other for the leaders.

Any discussion on driving must include the name of Benno von Achenbach (1861-1936). With typical German thoroughness he set about improving the English style of driving, although by general consensus it was already considered excellent. He made small alterations to harness and carriages with the aim of alleviating the hard lot of working horses which, around the turn of the century, were still a familiar sight in the streets. The system he devised for holding the reins has remained unsurpassed, and he worked out an excellent method for systematically increasing the number of reins that could be held.

Using the Achenbach system the driver has more control over the horses when they perform dressage movements. It produces successful results with either the single horse, the tandem, or the four-in-hand. Theoretically, it is possible to harness any number of horses to a carriage.

Driving is a far more time-consuming sport than riding, for not only do the horses have to be looked after and exercised daily, but the harness and carriage require constant attention as well. The leather must be oiled, the metal parts must be polished to a high shine and the beautifully varnished carriages have to be carefully washed down each time they are used.

Understandably, many people feel that far too much work is involved in preparing for a driving competition, and prefer simply to harness their horses and go for a drive without worrying about judges assessing their carriage and harness for cleanliness and quality. Enjoying a drive with family or friends across country is also driving for sport. Travelling at ten kilometres an hour allows plenty of time for appreciating the sights along the way, the colourful flower gardens and picturesque old houses which are so often overlooked. A horse and carriage passing by is a pleasant nostalgic sight for pedestrians too, which reminds older people of their youth, and gives the younger a taste of the good old days when life was less hectic.

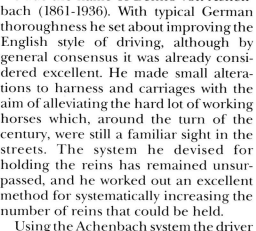

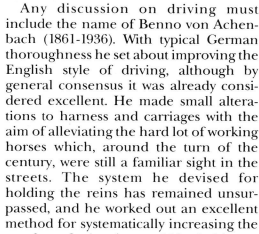

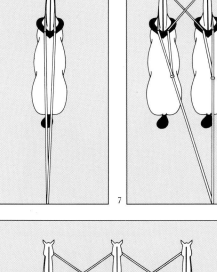

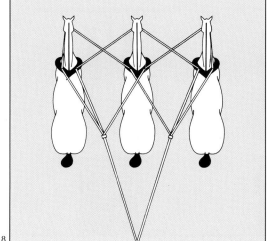

TYPES OF HARNESS

The method used to harness a horse to a carriage depends on the work the animal is expected to do. An eleven-in-hand (11) or even an eight-in-hand (12) can be regarded as frivolities, but all the other kinds of harnessing shown in these drawings did once serve a useful purpose.

A six-in-hand could be hitched up in two ways (13 and 14).

The five- (15), four- (16) and three-in-hand (17) were extremely practical; while the unicorn (18) was regarded as the poor man's four-in-hand.

Pairs (19) and singles (21) were the most widely used methods of harnessing.

The tandem (20) originated in England. This was the usual method of driving to the hunt and, on arrival, the leader was unharnessed and saddled up for hunting.

Multiple horses in harness are always welcome sights at equestrian events.

1 A team of seven elegant greys.

2 Six horses in English harness are drawing a coach belonging to the Swiss Cavalry School at Berne.

3 A horse harnessed to a phaeton in the classic English manner.

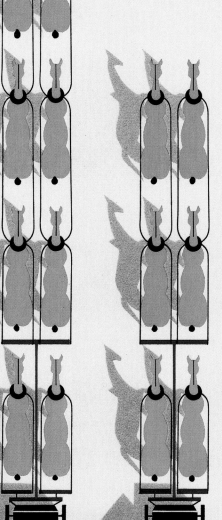

11 12 13 14 15

...ces involving teams of ...king horses are always a ...t attraction. Usually four ...es are harnessed to a farm

5 and 6 The tandem has two, and the randem has three horses, harnessed one in front of the other. Both require an excellent driving technique. The foremost horse must be very reliable as the rest are totally dependent on it.

7 Theoretically there are no limits to the number of horses that can be harnessed together; in practice the limits are set by the number of reins a driver can hold in his hands. In this picture thirteen horses were harnessed together for a celebratory birthday drive.

8 The Czechoslovakian Kladrub Stud often gives multiple team displays. This is a picture of a Kladrub team seen from the whip's point of view.

9 The Hungarian five-in-hand was the classic team. Two horses are harnessed to the shaft while three run in front.

10 Five mule teams, one behind the other, taking part in a religious festival in Andalusia.

16   17   18   19   20   21

ENGLISH HARNESS

The classic English harness was the most widely used for ceremonial or town carriages, and this method was improved to such a degree that it was almost a science. Over the decades a style was evolved which was perfectly suited to the excellent European roads.

The English harness consists of a collar, which is the towing mechanism, and a variety of curb bits. The English style also requires that only horses of a similar temperament are harnessed together. (The Hungarian, by comparision, frequently harnesses horses of different temperaments in the one team.)

Both carriages and harness are designed for maximum efficiency. The leather parts and buckles are strong where they are used for pulling and

stopping; less demands are made on the other parts of the harness, which are often of finer workmanship.

The same can be said of the carriages. A vehicle is of top quality when it is as light and yet as elegant as possible.

Left: The English style of driving had a tremendous influence in all the European countries, and princely carriages were fitted out according to its principles. In this picture a four-wheeled dog-cart is being drawn by a single horse.

Below: A variety of curb bits were used in the English harness. The bits shown here are a Liverpool; a jointed elbow bit (with snaffle effect); and a Buxton bit with side piece. In multiple harnessing, the side piece prevents the rein at the front from getting caught on the end of the bit (this is normally open at the bottom). The English worked out their method with almost scientific precision and every part is there for a practical reason. Their harness is extremely efficient.

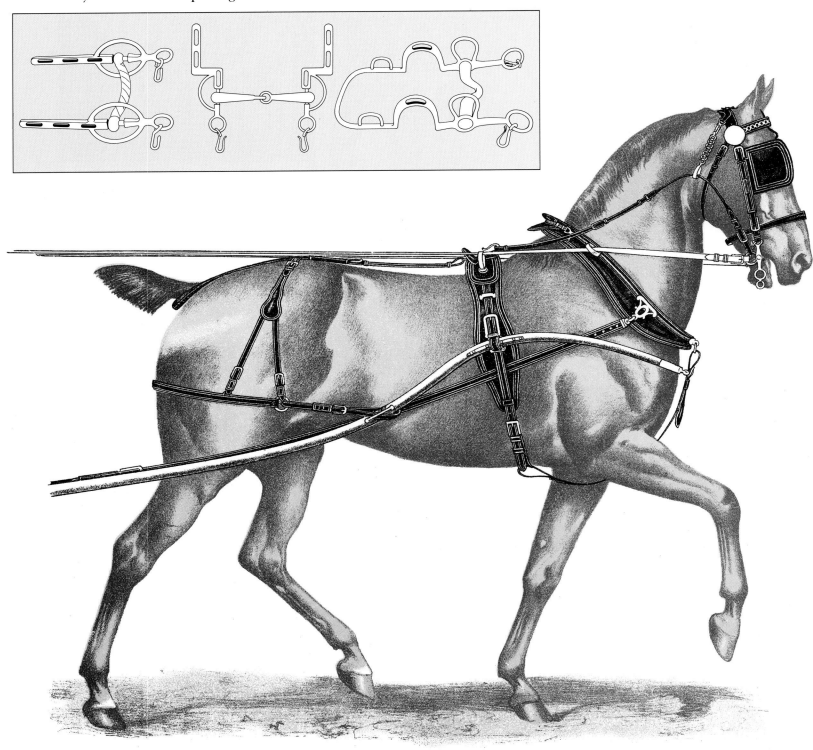

HUNGARIAN HARNESS

Next to the English, the Hungarian harness is the most widely used. The horses wear a breast band. In England the basics of driving were worked out with almost scientific precision; the Hungarian method reflects an intuitive empathy with nature.

The Magyars always harness several horses together when driving for sport. Horses are never driven singly, and they prefer a team of five. Frequently horses of quite different temperaments are harnessed together and a double ring snaffle bit is used to give a greater degree of control. The drivers hold the reins

Left: In Hungarian harnessing the costumes worn by the passengers enhance the colourful picture.

Below: The breast band and double-ringed snaffle bit are typical of the Hungarian harness. The harness is light and usually richly decorated. The nobly bred horses complete the picture of lightness and liveliness.

in both hands as this, too, gives better control over the temperamental horses.

Both pairs and teams of four are driven in this way; in each case the driver holds only two reins in his hands. The front

reins of the two leaders in a four-in-hand are buckled into the reins of the two wheelers. The whip is a straight stick with a long thong.

Colourful outfits worn by the passengers add to the generally picturesque effect. The Hungarian gala costume is not bound by any rules, but is left completely to personal choice. The harness, too, is richly decorated, and the fly fringe, or *schalanken*, in particular always attracts admiration. Intricate decorative patterns are usually worked into the leather straps. The harness includes a bell with a high-pitched ring, which adds to the overall impression of lightness and animation.

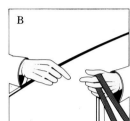
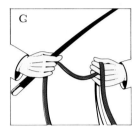
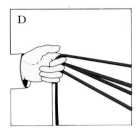

A How to hold the reins when driving a single or pair with coupling reins. The left (driving) hand is supported by the right hand.

B Basic position when using one hand to drive a single or pair with coupling reins.

C How to turn to the right when driving a single or pair with coupling reins.

D Basic position when using one hand to drive a team of four.

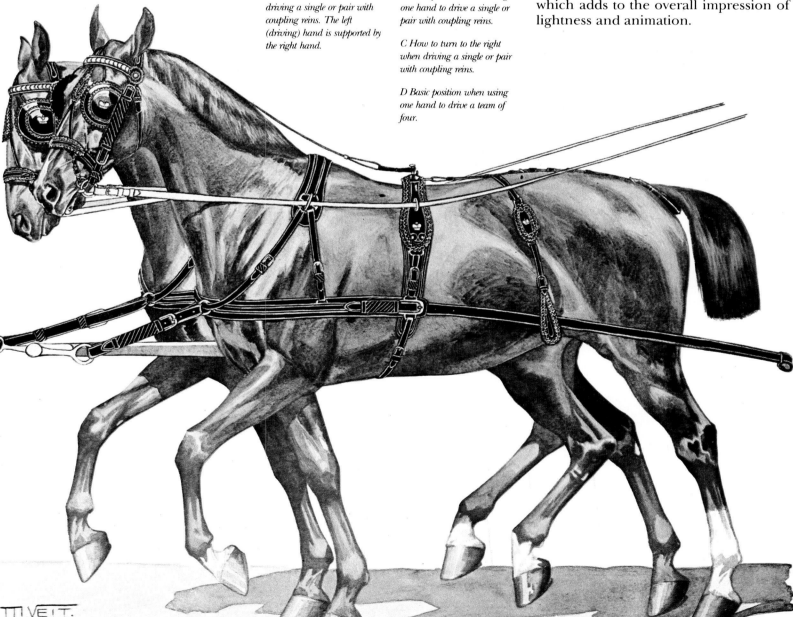

RUSSIAN HARNESS

Few have not heard of the Russian troika, where the middle horse trots and the other two horses gallop. These three horses harnessed abreast are considered to be typically Russian but, in fact, the one-horse carriage has a much wider distribution throughout this enormous country.

The Russian harness never gained a foothold outside its native land. One of its characteristics is the duga, the high wooden hoop which connects the shafts over the top of the horse's body. It is often richly decorated with metal.

Russian harnesses are just as sumptuously decorated. Originally they had few buckles because, in the low temperatures of winter, the frost caused the metal to ice up and this made harnessing and unharnessing extremely difficult. Russian carriages and sleighs are small and light.

The driver of a troika holds four separate reins in his hands. Two of these are connected to the middle horse; each of the other two is joined to the outer ring on the snaffle bit of one of the outer two horses. Another rein connects each of these two to the duga, so that the horses can then turn their heads to the side only as far as this connecting rein allows. The right hand horse gallops in left lead, the left hand one in right lead. The trotting horse in the middle is guided; the outer horses follow the pull of the connecting rein. The driver winds the reins around his hands and drives with his arms stretched out in front of him. He seldom lets his horses walk for a Russian prefers his team to be full of fire.

The Russian harness was most widely used only in Russia itself. It was always richly decorated with metal, which was an indication of the owner's wealth and position. The curved wood over the middle horse, known as the duga, was also used on a one-horse carriage.

GALA AND SEMI GALA

Harness for special occasions was required to comply with certain ritual requirements, and today a ceremonial or even a formal harness is rarely seen, except on official or ceremonial occasions at the few remaining royal courts. This type of harness included the two-, the four-, the six- or the eight-in-hand driven by a coachman on the box; or the eight-in-hand driven from the box with a postillion rider. Protocol was very strict in regard to the dress and accoutrements of both the postillion rider and the outrider who rode in front of the team. If the carriage was driven from the saddle, then the harness was referred to as *à la Daumont*.

Above: No other kind of harness had to follow such strict rules as the gala and semi-gala, and monarchs are as punctilious about etiquette as anyone else. This picture was taken at Ascot where every year Queen Elizabeth II, following an ancient tradition, is driven down the course in a landau, à la Daumont.

Above right: The buggy was the typical one-horse carriage in America. This type of vehicle was very soon mass-produced.

Below: The American harness was very lightweight. It was obviously strongly influenced by the trotting harness, but its English origins are still visible.

AMERICAN HARNESS

Although the American harness is very similar to the English, a typical American style does exist, to which both the town and the rural teams conform. Speed is the main criterion, and everything — horses, carriages and harness — is directed towards this end.

Western movies have made the stagecoaches familiar to all. It was possible to make these coaches very light in weight, thanks to the local hickory wood, and as efficiency, not beauty, was the main objective, the harness maker used few decorations on the delicate harness. Usually the single horse wears a breast band, while a collar is used for driving a pair. For a whip, an American uses a riding crop without a curve. The trotting influence is unmistakable.

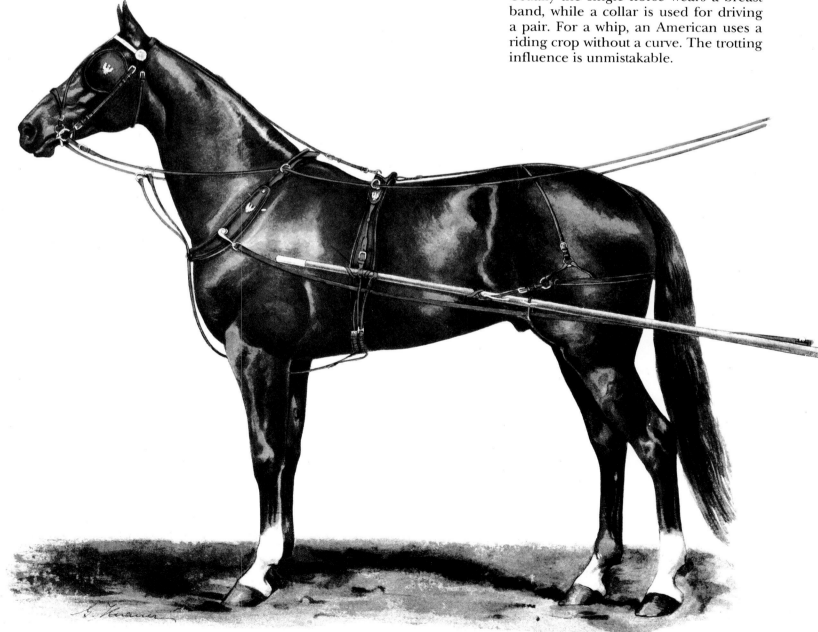

WORK HARNESSES

There are innumerable different methods of harnessing working and agricultural teams of horses. At one time the use of either the collar or the breast band varied from region to region, and to confuse matters even further the way in which the collar was made varied as well. There were good reasons for this, for every driver, whether a farmer or the owner of a horse and cart, made adjustments to the harness to lighten his horse's work load as much as possible. His reason was not entirely altruistic; he prolonged the economic usefulness of the animal and enabled it to transport heavier loads. Larger and stronger collars were made and breast bands were widened in order to spread the weight of the load over as much of the horse's body as possible. In the agricultural harness, luxury had to take second place to practicality, but the saddler still liked to make even working harnesses ornamental by the use of buckles and all kinds of decorative stitching.

The harness of working teams in the cities was usually very attractive. Mills and breweries in particular spared no expense and decked their teams out magnificently, and some of them have retained their horses as a tradition up till the present day. Other businesses, too, used horses for advertising, for a majestic horse and cart made an ideal notice board.

In the splendid leather harness which was kept for special occasions the horses were often almost hidden beneath the richly decorated leather straps and shining metal parts, and a great deal of care and effort was expended in making collar, buckles and bridle as handsome as possible.

Above: Breweries are still proud of their teams and spend a great deal of money on their upkeep. Economic usefulness is no longer a factor, and the magnificently outfitted horses and carts are simply regarded as ideal advertising media.

Below: No single type of working harness is predominant. In each region saddlers made the harness which worked best in practice. On the left is an advertising harness for a light two-in-hand. No expense was spared, for an elegant harness was a firm's display board. The picture on the right shows a heavy French work harness of the type used to pull a two-wheeled cart.

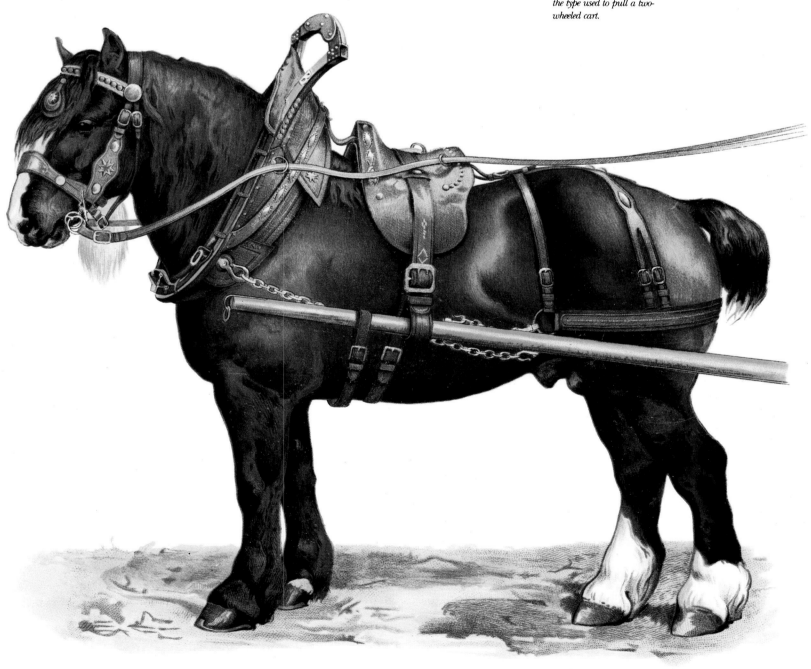

PRESENTATION

Presentation is the first part of a driving event. Shortly before the start, the beautifully lacquered carriages with their well oiled leather and gleaming metal parts are given a last minute dusting down and the horses are harnessed. By the time the ladies in their elegant clothes and wide-brimmed hats have taken their places in the carriages, the presentation is more like a scene from the 'good old days', and has none of the atmosphere of a modern driving competition.

All these preparations do have a purpose! The presentation is marked on a scale from nought (not performed) to ten (excellent), and points are awarded not only for the horses, the harness, carriage and the total impression, but also for the driver, grooms and passengers. Normally each individual team is evaluated by three judges, each standing at a different place. The average mark is calculated, and then included in the final score, which is out of a maximum of fifty points.

The 'man in the black bowler hat' assesses the horses on how well they are suited and whether they function as a team. He also judges their general condition, their shoes and whether they have been thoroughly groomed. It goes without saying that the harness will have been well cared for, but it must also be a perfect fit so that it does not chafe, press or hurt the animals. In addition, the judge's eagle eye will take note of how thoroughly horse and harness have been cleaned.

It is very difficult to judge a carriage objectively, but there are certain criteria which are taken into account in the

awarding of marks. Is the lacquer still in excellent condition or is it scratched and peeling? Does the carriage suit the size of the horses? Does it comply with traffic regulations? And are driver, passengers and grooms sitting comfortably? After having given his attention to all the details the judge then assesses the team as a whole. He must evaluate whether the horses, carriage, and passengers in front of him present an historically accurate picture, and then award marks accordingly.

First the teams are inspected. The judges do not appraise the team simply on appearance, but also take into account whether the harness fits well and thus alleviates the horse's work load. They must therefore be meticulous, regardless of whether the sun is shining, as it was at the four-in-hand

World Championships held in 1980 in Windsor (above) or raining, as it was at the 1978 Swiss Championships in Hünenbert (below). In this picture the former World and European Champion, Auguste Dubey (right) is inspecting the EMPFA team driven by Hermann Mast.

DRESSAGE

The dressage competition which follows the presentation differs quite considerably from dressage as we normally think of it, with a rider in the saddle. A driver cannot use either his thighs or his seat as aids, and the horse's centre of gravity is differently placed.

The judge will expect the animals to have a long-striding action and to perform the collected, extended and working trot.

This is the driver's opportunity to show how well he or she controls the four horses. Do they trust their master? Will they stand motionless at the halt, salute, and wait for the command to trot on? Can he drive them in a serpentine with five curves, a volte and a double volte? If the team is unsettled and shows signs of disharmony, then the driver's problems will really begin as he enters the dressage arena. The rein back reveals

Both driver and horses are tested in the dressage arena. As they perform the various movements they demonstrate the horses' level of training and the driver's style. In driving contests the teams perform in a dressage arena which is 100 metres long and 40 metres wide. The tests include the walk, various trotting gaits and a few basic figures. The white markings on the diagram on the right show: at A and C the two voltes of 30 metres in diameter; at A the double volte, each circle of which has a diameter of 20 metres; the semi-circles at B and E, each with a diameter of 20 metres. Horses of many different breeds, from cold-bloods through to noble warm-bloods, can be put in harness, and this makes it more difficult to award marks impartially. Points are given for the dressage movements

themselves, but they are also awarded for the total impression, as well as the gaits, and the horses' obedience, lightness and ease of movement. The whip's driving style is also assessed.

The Frenchman Frank Deplanche (above left) is driving his four Freibergers at the International tournament in Windsor in 1978. George Bowman from Great Britain with his Welsh Cobs (above right) is performing the double volte at the 1978 World Championships at Kecskemet (Hungary). Tjeerd Velstra the 1982 World Champion, is pictured driving two different teams. At the 1980 World Championships in Windsor (below left) he is driving Dutch warm-bloods; and (below right) he is driving a team of Friesians with Windsor Castle in the background.

a great deal about a team. The various movements in the programme show the judges the level of training which the horses have reached, as well as whether they are obedient and can perform the required gaits correctly.

The programme must be ridden from memory; the two grooms on the back seat are allowed to intervene only if there is any danger. As in the presentation, the marks are awarded on a scale from nought to ten. The horses are judged as a team, not individually. The driver is also assessed. Does he administer the aids too roughly, or allow the horses to pull so that voltes become oval instead of round?

MARATHON

On the second day of a driving competition the horses are harnessed for the cross-country event, also called the marathon, although it is not nearly so long as the historical forty-two kilometres.

At an international championship the marathon course is divided into five phases, which are comparable with the speed and endurance section of a three-day event.

This section makes the greatest demands on the horses. This is when the slow and careful fitness programme they have been put through in the preceding weeks is put to the test. If it was sufficiently thorough they will reach the finish safely and accumulate only a few penalty points.

For the drive to be successful, both driver and passengers have a role to play. The driver's skill is revealed in the way the obstacles are tackled. Only a practised eye, a confident grip on the reins, and lightning-fast decisions will achieve success. The driver must also ensure that the horses have enough strength to last to the end so that they do not arrive at the finish utterly exhausted.

The passengers' job is to help in achieving this. On the day before the event they, together with the driver, will measure out the entire course down to the last metre, and make a note of various points along the way. During the drive they will use these plans to check the time they have taken against the amount of ground they have covered. This is the only way they can keep to the specified time. Penalty points are given for driving too fast or too slowly.

The passengers have also another job to do. They must have excellent reflexes, for as the carriage encounters uneven patches or obstacles they have to ensure that it stays upright by changing the position of their weight. They must also let the driver know when the back wheels are safely past an obstacle. Besides all

Above: HRH *Prince Philip, the* FEI *President, has contributed a great deal to the growing popularity of the sport of driving, and has himself taken part in Championships, driving a team owned by the Queen.*

Series of pictures:
The obstacles are always the focal points of the speed and endurance section, for a driver will quite frequently take too many risks and overturn his vehicle.

Below: The marathon is made up of five sections: two are to be completed at the walk; two at a normal trotting tempo; and one has to be driven at a fast trot. Although the horses' fitness is being tested in each section, the obstacles are the real test of the driver's style and technique. The passengers also have a part to play. They help the driver to keep within the prescribed times, and quickly change their positions as required to ensure that the carriage stays upright in critical situations.

Right: A marathon course usually includes water obstacles and stream crossings; natural obstacles which quickly sort out the competitors. If they are to avoid upsets both driver and passengers must reconnoitre the course very carefully beforehand. To be successful, horses, driver and passengers must all work together as a team, and if the carriage does overturn they then have to set it on its wheels again.

this they have their hands full at the intermediary stops, when they have to water the horses and sponge them down.

Both carriage and harnesses have to be able to withstand the demands of a cross-country. Splendid antique harness and classic carriages — the creations of famous carriage builders — no longer feature in a modern marathon. The harness and carriages must be tough and practical, with parts which can be replaced very quickly. Leather straps have been replaced by man-made fibres which are stronger; wooden carriages are gradually being supplanted by lighter vehicles built of metal.

A referee sits next to the driver throughout the speed and endurance section to make sure that the horses keep to the prescribed gaits, and to take note of any offences incurring penalties, such as someone putting down the whip, dismounting at an obstacle or overturning the vehicle. The referee also makes a note of any incidental events that might cause the team to lose time during the drive.

OBSTACLE SPEED COMPETITION

The obstacle speed competition, which is the final section after presentation, dressage and marathon, is the ultimate test of the driver's skill and often upsets many temporary placings in the event.

In this he must successfully negotiate his team through a course containing a maximum of twenty obstacles. He may use his own discretion and drive at the walk, the trot, or even gallop, the aim being to complete the course without a mistake and within the required maximum time. The passageways are normally from thirty to sixty centimetres wider than the track width of the vehicle, and

The obstacle driving is the final section in a three-day driving tournament. Now the teams have to negotiate a course of about twenty gateways, where the obstacles are marked out by cones or poles. The distance between the pairs of cones is only a little greater than the track width of the vehicles. The aim of the obstacle event is to test whether the horses have recovered from the exertions of the previous day. If they are still tired and stiff, it will be difficult for the driver to negotiate the obstacles accurately.

Opposite page: The Hungarian competitors, with their manoeuvrable shorter-coupled teams are always in the top placings in the obstacle driving. This picture is of György Bardos and his team of four Lipizzaners. He has won both the World and European Championships several times.

ten penalties are added to the total if a horse or a wheel knocks over a cone. If the prescribed time is exceeded, then 0.5 penalty points are added for each additional second.

The obstacle driving reveals a great deal! The driver must have nerves of steel. Again and again drivers are disqualified for taking the wrong route, for the course must be driven from memory and the passengers are not allowed to help either by word or gesture. The horses' legs are probably still suffering from the effects of the marathon on the previous day, but if they have been well trained they will now show what they are made of. On the last day they will happily continue to move forward, always up to their bits, and wait attentively for the commands from their master in the coachman's seat.

Obstacle driving offers the spectators

the most variety. There is plenty of tension: will the cone fall, will it not? The course builder does much to make obstacle driving an exciting spectacle. An obstacle driving course does not need to be flat; a slight slope considerably increases the degree of difficulty and allows the driver to reveal his skill and his horses' obedience to the full. The course builder may also lay out the course in such a way that he tempts the drivers into taking risks, which definitely adds to its spectator appeal.

CROSS-COUNTRY ROUTE IN THE 1980 WORLD CHAMPIONSHIPS

The Fifth World Championships for four-in-hands was held on 11-14 September 1980, at Windsor, England. The marathon was laid out in the two thousand hectares of Windsor Great Park.

Forty-two teams from eleven nations were at the start. The course was 33.583 kilometres long and the crucial part was the ten kilometre long stretch which had to be covered at a fast trot. There were eight obstacles and the degree of difficulty was very high, even for a World Championship; besides which, this fast trot section came last, thus placing an additional burden on the competitors, several of whom were not yet equal to the demands of a World Championship.

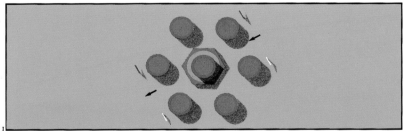

Above; The forty-two teams had to cover a good thirty-three kilometres in the marathon, both at the walk and the trot. First there was the 12 km trotting section, tempo 15 km/h (A — A); this was followed by 1167 m at the walk, tempo 7 km/h (B — B); 9.5 km trot, at tempo 15 km/h (E — E); and another 1050 m walk (D — D). Finally there was the 9866 metre fast trotting stretch (C — C) with tempo of 16 km/h and eight obstacles. At the Fifth World Championships the degree of difficulty of the obstacles was very high, and after the official viewing some of the eight obstacles had to be modified. Obstacle 1, 'The Grouse Barrel Garden' (1) was one of them, as it would have been impossible for even a pair to drive along the prescribed path.
The competitors needed plenty of time for the second obstacle, 'The Garden Seats' (2) where the path had to be found between trees and seats; and for 'Virginia Water' (3). The many

280

tall old trees in Windsor Great Park were very impressive. Their foliage was sparse at this time and they had developed quite amazing shapes. The fourth obstacle, 'The Obelisk Trees' (4) made use of this peculiarity. 'The Wood Yard' (5) also had to be modified. The path narrowed at the sixth obstacle, 'The Garden Pens' (6). Several paths seemed to open up but only one one was negotiable. Most of the retirements were at the second to last obstacle, 'The Sandpit' (7). The horses were nearly at the end of the course and already rather tired. The deep sand was very wearying. But those who mastered the sandpit had still not reached the finish; they still had to negotiate 'The Maze' (8). This labyrinth made out of wooden fences was the final test of the horses' fitness and whether after thirty-three kilometres they were still willing to obey their master's commands.

⊗ Flower bed

4

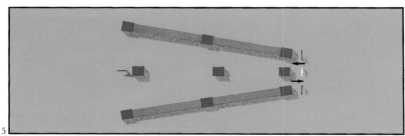

5

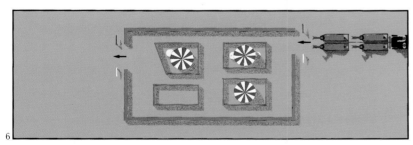

6

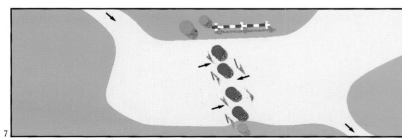

7

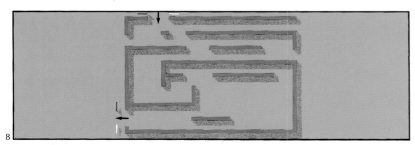

8

THE OBSTACLE RACE

The obstacle race on the fourth and final day of the tournament was held on Smith's Lawn, a large flat area of mown grass which was more like a large lawn than a field. Tents and grandstands were set up around this meadow, and there were covered stalls in the northern part of the grandstands. In between there were the booths selling snacks and cold drinks and tea, usually with a long queue of spectators waiting in front of them.

As on the previous day, the spectators came in their thousands, for HRH Prince Philip, driving a team owned by the Queen, was a member of the British team, which, after the dressage and the marathon, was in the lead. Only two teams did not take part in the obstacle course.

It was 670 metres long, with twenty gateways which had to be negotiated at an average speed of 200 metres a minute. The course, which was designed to allow for a smooth round, was full of variety with lavishly built obstacles and colourful flower beds. Five competitors had clear rounds. György Bardos from Hungary was, once again, one of the stars and successfully defended his title.

Above: The course was 670 metres long. The twenty gateways had been set up on Smith's Lawn, a smooth meadow of closely mown grass. The individual gateways were marked out by two cones, each pair placed only as far apart as the track width of the vehicle plus 30 cm. A bridge (obstacle 9) and 'The Castle', which was number 12, added variety to the simple cone obstacles. The three magnificent flower beds provided brightly coloured highlights.

HIGH SCHOOL

High school is the epitome of classical equitation; it is also the most exacting of the hippological disciplines. It is now practised at only two places in the world: the French Cavalry School in Saumur and the Spanish Riding School in Vienna.

The expression 'classical equitation' clearly implies that this approach to dealing with horses is a legacy from antiquity, and the historical section of this book has explained how the Greeks laid the foundations of this particular form of riding. Simon of Athens, who lived about 400 BC, seems to have been the first exponent of the art, and Xenophon, a riding instructor who wrote a series of philosophical and political works, recorded Simon's teachings and his own major discoveries in two important books. One of these, *Peri Hippikes*, contained the basis of classical dressage and made him the real founder of the science of hippology.

The writings were lost during the decline of Greek civilization and Xenophon's teachings were forgotten for almost two thousand years. His books were not rediscovered until shortly before the Renaissance.

At that time a certain Federico Grisone of Naples studied these works thoroughly, and, using them as a base, he then constructed his own theory of the art of riding. In one essential point he differed from his Greek models, for Grisone did not hesitate to use force; the Greeks' attitude is very clearly expressed in Simon's statement that 'you cannot teach a dancer to dance by using whip and spurs'.

In 1532 Grisone founded a riding academy for noblemen, where one of his leading pupils was Giovanni Pignatelli, who taught the Frenchman, Antoine de Pluvinel. It was de Pluvinel who considerably improved and humanized Grisone's methods for teaching dressage.

William Cavendish, Duke of Newcastle, became famous both for his riding school and for his important hippological treatise,

Left: High school — where the horse is required to perform the most difficult exercises, all based on its natural gaits. Here an officer from the Cadre Noir, *Saumur, is performing a capriole.*

Below: William Cavendish, Duke of Newcastle, also performing a capriole, a good three hundred years earlier.

which appeared in 1658. Although beautifully illustrated, in content this book is far inferior to de Pluvinel's work.

In Germany Georg Engelhard von Löhneyssen was the most famous master of the art of riding. His works appeared about the year 1600.

Louis Seeger, an instructor at the first private riding school in Berlin, and his pupil Gustav Steinbrecht, were two other great names. Both were vehemently opposed to the *Méthode d'équitation* which was published by the Frenchman, Francois Baucher, in 1842. Although as far as sales were concerned it was a very successful book, it contained numerous basic mistakes, as Baucher himself was later forced to admit. All the same, Baucher did invent the flying change of leg at every stride which nowadays is included in all top level dressage competitions.

Perhaps the most influential instructor of all was the Frenchman, Robichon de la Guérinière, who lived in the first half of the eighteenth century. His lucid insight enabled him to sift out the valid points in the methods which had been previously formulated, and he then evolved a precise method of training with the aim of achieving freedom and lightness of movement. Both the modern sport of dressage and high school equitation are based on his findings.

THE SPANISH RIDING SCHOOL

As far as is known, a *Spainischen Reithsall* (Spanish riding hall) is first mentioned in a document dated 1572.

The horses which were brought to the stables next to the Hofburg in Vienna came from Spain, and most of them were certainly Andalusians with a high proportion of Barb and probably Arab blood as well. They were noble animals with their distinctively rounded shape, powerful yet still elegant, and they moved with a dancer's grace. They were also endowed with the amazing ability to learn which was so much sought after throughout Europe during the Baroque period. Georg Englehard von Löhneyssen, who was a sixteenth century German riding instructor, described these horses as the 'cleverest, bravest and most generous of all'. The Spanish Riding School in Vienna was named after them, and not after the Spanish style of riding.

The Winter Riding School is considered to be one of Europe's most magnificent examples of Baroque architecture. Designed between the years 1729 and 1735 by Josef Fischer von Erlach, it conveys a profound impression of the splendour of the Austro-Hungarian empire, especially so when the snow-white stallions in their golden saddlery and their riders in ceremonial costume fill it with life. The hall is fifty-five metres long, eighteen metres wide, and seventeen metres high. The gallery is supported by forty-six columns. A stone tablet bears a Latin inscription which states the purpose of the arena:

'This Imperial Riding School was built in the year 1735 upon the order of the Emperor Charles VI, son of the late

Emperor Leopold I, under the supervision of Gundaker, Count Althann, the General Director of Buildings and Head of the Imperial Stables, for the education and training of noble youths and for the training of horses in classical equitation and for war.'

The hall was also used as a showplace on a number of splendid occasions, of which Maria Theresa's 'Ladies' Carousel' was probably the most famous. This was held on 2 January 1743. The programme consisted of two quadrilles, ridden by equestriennes of noble birth, and two displays driven in imposing silver phaetons. Maria Theresa herself led the first quadrille.

Festivals and exhibitions of all kinds were held there. These included important conferences, concerts, balls, tournaments which were reminiscent of the duels fought by knights in the Middle Ages, and the macabre 'Stab the Moor' in which artificial heads wrapped in turbans were spiked with lances or cut off with swords by riders on galloping horses.

Horses were not always part of the programme. The first Austrian Diet met there in 1848. Thirty years before then, the Swiss inventor Jakob Degen had demonstrated his flying apparatus with which he is said to have raised himself

1 Work on the long reins. They require tremendous sensitivity from the rider and the stallion must first be very highly trained.

2 Levade in hand in the park of the palace of Schönbrunn where the Spanish Riding School also gives performances.

3 The row of stalls in the Imperial stables at Vienna. This magnificent Renaissance building is open to the public daily from 2 to 4 o'clock in the afternoon.

4 School quadrille in the famous Baroque riding arena of the Spanish Riding School.

5 The School quadrille, performed by eight stallions and their riders, is the finale of the programme.

6 The young stallions are tied up in stalls, but the fully trained horses are allowed to move about freely in their boxes.

7 Capriole in hand.

8 Courbette in hand. When the horse is standing on its hindlegs in a levade, it must then make several forward jumps.

5

6

7

8

almost to the ceiling with thirty-four beats of his wings.

On 23 November 1814, the arena of the Spanish Riding School was the setting for the most glittering occasion of all. This was a carousel organized by the Emperor Francis I, which greatly impressed a large section of European nobility. Those invited included the Kings of Prussia, Bavaria, Württemburg and Denmark, as well as such statesmen as Metternich, Talleyrand, Hardenburg and Lord Castlereagh.

Up till the end of World War One the arena was the exclusive province of the nobility, and the performances were solely for the Emperor's guests. With the collapse of the Austro-Hungarian monarchy, the demise of the Spanish Riding School seemed imminent, and there was a fear that this unique cultural inheritance could disappear for ever. To prevent this, patrons were found who ensured that the institution remained and that it was able to maintain itself financially by giving performances and riding tuition.

Today high school equitation in its purest form is preserved there, and riders and horses continue to be trained in this art. In accordance with tradition there is always a bay horse among the white stallions, to demonstrate that not all Lipizzaners are greys. Every day visitors are allowed to watch the morning workout, which gives them some idea of the wearisome training process. Performances are held twice weekly, and in almost reverential silence both equine enthusiasts and the merely curious watch a unique programme.

First the young stallions, which have completed their first year of training, perform the *Pas de Deux*. This is a free dressage exercise performed by two riders in which the movements of each rider are a mirror reflection of the other. This is followed by a display of work in hand, and on the long reins, when the rider follows his horse on foot, holding the long reins in his hands; the airs above the ground; and finally the School quadrille, the 'ballet of the white stallions'.

Since 1920 the horses which are trained here have been brought from the State Stud at Piber. The Lipizzaner breed was developed in the small village of Lipica, in the Karst region, where the Austrian Archduke Charles founded an Imperial Stud in 1580. This is now part of modern Yugoslavia. In the turmoil of the wars the Lipizzaners had to be evacuated more than once, but since 1947 they have been bred once again in the old buildings of the original stud.

THE CAVALRY SCHOOL AT SAUMUR

Possibly only one other institution can bear comparison with the Spanish Riding School in Vienna: the French Cavalry School in Saumur, which is situated on the left bank of the Loire. Here on 20 June 1828, in honour of the Duchess de Berry, cavalry officers performed a school quadrille for the first time. It was a perfect example of high school equitation as taught by the French riding instructors of the Baroque period, though it did have a distinctly martial flavour.

The Cavalry School at Saumur dates back to 1763. As the pupil of de Pluvinel, Louis XIII (1610-1643) devoted himself to advanced dressage, and did not attach a great deal of importance to training his cavalry in the techniques of war, but his great-great-grandson Louis XV (1755-1774) was more concerned with producing a mobile, powerful, well organized cavalry. He had numerous schools built, the most important of which was the Cavalry School at Saumur, for it was there that the Royal *Corps des Carabiniers* was trained.

In the following decades the Royal Cavalry changed its training venue several times, and for a while it was even housed in the palace at Versailles, where there were also very large stables. In 1825 it was finally settled in Saumur. In the meantime Louis XVIII (1814-1824), in his coronation year, had opened a riding academy at Saumur.

The instructors at the French Cavalry Schools wore blue uniforms and were therefore known as the *Cadre Bleu*. In order that the Royal instructors at Saumur could be distinguished from the others, they were given a black coat with gold braid and gold embroidery, and a

black pill box hat called a *lampion*. Today they are world famous as the *Cadre Noir*.

In 1969 the French Cavalry School was turned into a training centre for armoured divisions, but the Cadre Noir continued to exist. It was separated from the Cavalry School and became the teaching staff at the National Equestrian Institute.

In 1972 this became the outstanding *Ecole nationale d'équitation*, the famous national riding school, and the Cadre Noir took over the training programme from the government Department for Youth and Sport. This includes teaching prospective dressage, show-jumping and military riders. They also retain their traditional task and preserve the dressage style of the former Royal Cavalry. Their brilliant performances of quadrilles in the ancient French style, and airs above

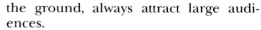

the ground, always attract large audiences.

The quadrille is performed by the *écuyers*, the *sous écuyers* and the *maîtres de manège* under the guidance of the *écuyer en chef*. The horses used are always of noble blood — the majority are Thoroughbreds — and they add their own distinctive flair to these quadrilles. The figures are ridden in the three basic gaits. Counter-changes of hand, where the horse's outer legs cross in front of its inner ones at each step, as it moves forwards and sideways at the same time, at the walk, trot or canter, are included in the quadrille.

The zigzag counter-changes of hand at the canter are performed with flying change of leg. The passage, which many experts also call the 'Spanish Step', is

1 The airs above the ground are included in the public performances given by the Cadre Noir at Saumur. The riders have no stirrups and sit in saddles with high backs, as was customary in the Baroque. At Saumur the movement shown here, where the standing horse energetically kicks out backwards on command, is called a croupade. In some other schools the word croupade refers to a different movement.

2 Saumur, with its 23,000 inhabitants, is pleasantly situated on the left bank of the Loire in western France. It is well known, not only for its Cadre Noir, but also for the castle which dates from the fourteenth century and for its white wine.

3 and 4 Most of the horses that perform the ballet-like quadrille at Saumur are Thoroughbreds.

5 The classical name for this movement is the pesade. At Saumur it is called the courbette. In the genuine courbette the horse, while in this position, leaps forward on its hindlegs several times. 5

considered to be the most difficult movement in the quadrille. This is a collected trot with regular, high, very cadenced leg movements. The second most difficult movement is the piaffe, which is an elegant trot on the spot in perfect time. Although this is required in the most advanced dressage competitions, it is not performed at Saumur.

The airs above the ground are particularly impressive. Other horses, the *sauteurs*, or jumpers, are trained to perform these movements. These horses are generally powerful, energetic Anglo-Normans. The riding instructors of the Baroque period originally developed the airs above the ground as part of classical dressage, but, until the introduction of firearms, cavalry horses were also trained in this art. It is easy to understand the

infantry's desire to keep out of the way of a horse that could, on command, rise up on its hindlegs, jump forwards, or kick out backwards both forcefully and accurately!

The pesade, levade, courbette, croupade, ballotade and capriole are all included in the airs above the ground which are performed at the Spanish Imperial Riding School in Vienna.

The *sauteurs* at Saumur salute the public with the pesade (there it is called the courbette). They rear up on their hindlegs with their bodies raised at an angle of more than forty-five degrees and their forelegs bent. In the levade, which is a more recent and more difficult variation of the same movement, the hindlegs are bent more sharply and the body is at an angle of less than forty-

five degrees. The courbette, where the horse rears up and then leaps forwards several times on its hindlegs, was developed from the levade or pesade. In the croupade the horse rears, then jumps vertically with its hindlegs drawn up towards its belly. In the ballotade it half rears, then jumps forward, drawing its hindlegs up below its quarters. The capriole is an extension of these jumps. As the horse jumps into the air it kicks out energetically with both hindlegs.

GLOSSARY OF EQUESTRIAN TERMS

A

ABORT
To miscarry, give birth to a premature foal. Most frequent causes are a twin pregnancy or a virus infection. The latter can be prevented by immunization.

ACCHETTA PONY
A breed of pony from Sardinia.

ACHENBACH
Benno von Achenbach (1861-1936) used the English driving system as a basis from which he evolved the modern international sport of driving.

ACHILLES TENDON
Attachment of the soleus and gastrocnemius muscles of the calf to the heel bone.

ACTION
The manner in which a horse moves. High knee action is particularly desirable in coach and show horses.

AFRICAN HORSE SICKNESS
Acute infectious disease carried by mosquitoes. Prevalent in Asia and Africa.

AGE
Depending on the breed, a horse is fully mature between 3 and 6 years. On average the large breeds live about 20 to 30 years. Northern ponies sometimes live to be 40. An expert can tell a horse's age by the extent to which its teeth are worn down.

AI
Abbreviation for Artificial Insemination.

AIDS
All the ways by which a rider or driver communicates his or her wishes to the horse — these include legs, hands and seat.

AIRS ABOVE THE GROUND
Any of the various high school airs performed with the legs off the ground: capriole, courbette, levade, pesade, ballotade, croupade.

AKHAL-TEKÉ
Very noble Russian breed, similar to the Thoroughbred.

ALBINO
Horses which are born with pink skin and white hair. True albinos have red eyes. Most albinos, however, have pale blue 'glass eyes'. Greys are born dark.

ALVEOLA
A small cavity, cell or pit on the surface of an organ.

AMAZONS
A race of equestrienne warriors in Greek mythology.

AMERICAN
Very light wagon driven one- or two-in-hand in special American harnessing.

AMERICAN SADDLE HORSE
An American riding horse which was formerly much in demand for the cavalry. Now degraded into a mere show horse.

AMMONIA VAPOUR
Gas which is released by decomposing horse dung. In badly ventilated stables it can seriously damage the horse's breathing passages.

ANAEMIA
Lack of red blood corpuscles.

ANATOMY
The science dealing with the structure of an animal's body.

ANCESTRY
The horse's parentage as shown on a genealogical tree; with its sire and dam, then their respective sires and dams back through several generations.

ANDALUSIAN
Elegant breed of horse from southern Spain.

ANGLO-ARAB
Very noble breed obtained by crossing Arab pure-bred and English Thoroughbred. Bred mainly in southern France, Poland and Hungary.

ANGLO-NORMAN
French breed developed by crossing English breeds with the 'Norman horse'. A strong horse suited to competitive sports.

APPALOOSA
Excellent Western horse, bred in various distinctive spotted patterns.

ARAB
Long established breed from the Middle East. Has had a considerable influence on horse breeding throughout the world, particularly on the English Thoroughbred.

ARENA
Large area marked off either in the open air or in a hall. Usually 20 x 40 or 20 x 60 metres.

ASSATEAGUE PONY
Ponies which live in the wild on the island of Assateague off the coast of Virginia, US. Probably descended from Spanish horses.

ASSYRIANS
First military power to use troops of cavalry as well as war chariots in battle.

AZOTURIA
Black water, or 'Monday morning disease'. Reveals itself in muscle cramps in the small of the back and a stiff, wobbly gait. It is normally the result of eating feed which is too rich in protein on rest days, and appears when a horse starts work again after an idle period. Move the animal as little as possible, cover and keep warm. Call vet immediately.

B

BABOLNA
Hungarian State Stud, famous for the breeding of Arabs.

BACK
To accustom the unbroken horse to the saddle and the weight of a rider.

BADEN-BADEN
Home of the Iffezheim racecourse, an international racing venue.

BADMINTON
The home of the Duke of Beaufort in Gloucestershire, England, is the setting for the Badminton Three-Day Horse Trials, an important international fixture.

BALD FACE
White markings which cover the whole of the front of the horse's face.

BALLOTADE
An 'air above the ground' (q.v.).

BANDAGE
To put protective bandages on the horse's legs.

BANK
Natural or artificial obstacle in show-jumping or on a cross-country course.

BARB
Lightly built, noble warm-blood breed from North Africa. Immensely hardy, the foundation stock of the Andalusian breed and through it of all the major European breeds during the Baroque period.

BARGE-HORSE
A horse used to tow boats along the canals.

BARREL
The part of the horse directly under the rider.

BARREL RACING
A very popular equestrian sport in the US.

BASCULE
The desired curve of the horse's neck and back while jumping.

BASUTO PONY
A breed of pony from South Africa.

BAY
Horses with a blackish to light-brown coat; mane, tail and legs are always black.

BEAGLE
A small hound formerly much used for hunting hares.

BEARING IN (OR OUT)
Changing direction towards the inner (or outer) part of the track.

BEARING REIN
Fixed rein between the bit and the saddle by which a horse's head is held up and its neck made to arch.

BEHAVIOUR PATTERNS
Natural reaction to certain stimuli according to an inherited pattern of behaviour. Social behaviour is very important as the way horses are handled is based on it, e.g., herd instinct, pecking order. Knowledge of mating behaviour is important for the breeder; as is the way an animal behaves when it encounters danger or an enemy

BELGIAN HEAVY DRAUGHT
A strong, heavy, cold-blood breed which can weigh over 1000 kg.

BELL
In jumping: rung to interrupt or cut short a ride.
In racing: the signal that the race is starting and no more bets will be accepted.

BELL BOOTS
Bell-shaped, rubber protective boots which are put on over the wall of the hoof to protect the coronary band. Used mainly on trotters and jumpers.

BELLEROPHON
In Greek mythology Bellerophon tamed Pegasus, the winged horse and killed the Chimaera, a dragonlike monster. He aspired to become one of the gods on Olympus; but Zeus sent a gadfly to sting Pegasus, whereupon the horse threw his rider and Bellerophon was crippled.

BELORUSSIAN
Very light, small cold-blood breed.

BERBER
From Barbary, Africa; Barb (q.v.).

BIGA
In Greek and Roman times, a cart drawn by two horses abreast. See also Quadriga and Triga.

BIT
The part of the bridle that goes in the horse's mouth.

BITE
Collective term for the horse's teeth.

BLACK
A horse with a black coat, mane and tail with no other colour present except possibly white markings.

BLANKET PATTERN
One of the pattern variations of the Appaloosa horse.

BLAZE
A broad white marking or stripe covering almost all the horse's forehead.

BLIND STAGGERS
Incurable brain infection. Upsets the sense of balance and causes mental disturbances, sometimes bouts of madness.

BLINKERS
A device fixed to the bridle which prevents the horse from looking anywhere other than in front. Mainly used on draught horses but sometimes on racehorses. (Also called winkers.)

BLOODSTOCK
Collective term for pure-bred horses.

BLOOD TEST
Used:
1. To determine a horse's blood group for proof of parentage.
2. To diagnose an illness.
3. As a pregnancy test.

BOLT
When a horse flees in panic while being ridden or driven. Usually caused by fright or shock at an unknown object or an unusual noise.

BOOKMAKER
A professional betting man who is licensed to accept the bets placed by others at racecourses.

BOOTS
Protective covering for the legs or feet.

BOREDOM
Horses are by nature sociable creatures; if they are kept on their own for too long they suffer from boredom, and often develop stable 'vices' as a result.

BOSAL
The piece of braided rawhide which forms part of a hackamore bridle. It is most common in Western style riding and is used when breaking in a horse.

BOSNIAN PONY
Tough, undemanding mountain breed from Yugoslavia.

BOULONNAIS
A cold-blood breed from northern France which has become very rare.

BOW-LEGGED
Faulty position of the hindlegs — shaped like a bow.

BOX
The coachman's raised seat on a carriage.

BOX STALL
A compartment in the stable where the horse does not have to be tied up as it does in a stall.

BRAN
The inner husks of corn which often form part of a mixed feed.

BRAND
1. A mark used as a means of identification, imprinted with a specially shaped red-hot iron on the horse's neck, flank or saddle region. It testifies that the horse has been entered in the register of its breed. Stud and owner brands are also common.
2. To apply the brand mark.

BRANDENBURG
Warm-blood breed descended from the Hanoverian.

BREAK IN
To tame and school a young horse. Term derives from the time when this process involved the use of force.

BREAST BAND
A short wide strap that is placed around the neck in front of the withers. It is attached to the saddle to prevent the latter from slipping back.

BREEDING REGISTER
Register of a breeding association in which mares, after passing certain tests, are entered and officially allowed to breed.

BREEDING SELECTION
Choice of a horse suitable for breeding.

BREEZING
Working a horse fast over a short distance before a race.

BRETON
Cold-blood breed from Brittany. There are three distinct types.

BRIDLE
1. To put a bridle on.
2. The part of the horse's tack which is placed about its head.

BRONCHITIS
A frequent infection of the respiratory organs.

BRONCO
A term use to describe feral horses in North America, i.e., domestic horses which have turned wild.

BRUISED SOLE
A bruise in the soft tissue underlying the horny sole of the foot which causes it to bleed and often leads to temporary lameness.

BRUMBY
Australian feral horse.

BRUSHING
One foot knocks against the other leg as the horse moves.

BRUSHING BOOTS
Protective covering for the limbs; usually made out of leather or felt.

BUCEPHALUS
Alexander the Great's famous war-horse. Alexander built the city of Bucephala (Jalalpur) in northern India to honour the stallion.

BUCK
When the horse leaps into the air with all four legs off the ground and its back arched. Can develop into a dangerous vice.

BUCKSKIN
Term used in the US to describe a greyish-yellow-coloured horse.

BUDYONNY
Noble warm-blood breed from the Soviet Union. Named after a famous cavalry general.

BUGGY
In America a one-horse four-wheeled light vehicle.

BUILD
Bodily structure; horse's exterior.

BYERLEY TURK
One of the three founding sires of the English Thoroughbred breed.

C

CAB
A public carriage or taxi which used to be horse-drawn in Britain and the US.

CABRIOLET
A light two-wheeled carriage.

CADRE NOIR
Elite riders belonging to the French Cavalry School at Saumur, so-called because of their black uniforms.

CAIO
Abbreviation for: Concours d'attelage international officiel = official international driving tournament.

CALIBRE
Relationship of body height to weight.

CALKIN
A pointed piece on a horseshoe to give extra grip.

CAMARGUE PONY
Small grey-coloured breed from the Rhone delta.

CANNON BONE
Supports the limb from the hock to the fetlock.

CANTER
A pace in three-time; a slow gallop.

CAPARISON
A large rectangular cloth placed under the saddle.

CAPRILLI
The Italian, Federico Caprilli, was the originator of the 'forward seat' in jumping.

CAPRIOLE
An 'air above the ground' (q.v.) in classical equitation.

CARPAL JOINT
The joint of the foreleg which is often wrongly described as the horse's knee.

CARRIAGE HORSE
Any warm-blood breed used to draw coaches. Usually strong but elegant.

CART
Two-wheeled vehicle drawn by one horse.

CARTER
Driver of a working team of horses.

CART HORSE
Cold-blood horses are often called cart horses. Warm-bloods in harness are known as carriage horses.

CASTRATION
Removal of the testicles of a stallion, making it into a gelding.

CATARACT
Painless diseased clouding of the eye lens.

CAVALETTI
Wooden cross-pieces so joined that a pole can be laid across at different heights by turning them over. Frequently used to teach jumping.

CAVALRY
Horse-soldiers; a troop of horsemen.

CAVESSON
A specially constructed noseband on to which is set a metal plate. This is fitted with three rings to which the longe rein is connected. Particularly recommended for early schooling exercises.

CCIO
Abbreviation for: Concours complet international officiel = official international three-day event.

CDIO
Abbreviation for: Concours de dressage international officiel = official international dressage tournament.

CENTAUR
A mythical monster with the head, trunk and arms of a man, and the body and legs of a horse.

CHAISE
A light two-wheeled carriage.

CHARIOT RACING
Probably known in pre-Greek civilization. Very popular in Greece and Rome and still a favourite pastime in rural areas.

CHEEK-PIECE
Side pieces of a bit to which the reins are attached.

CHECK
To slow the horse down by use of the reins.

CHESTNUT
1. Horny projection on the inside of the leg. Vestige of the first or second toe.
2. Light reddish to dark brown-coloured coat; mane and tail are either the same or a lighter tone.

CHINA PONY
Collective term for various breeds which originated in China.

CHIO
Abbreviation for: Concours hippique international officiel = equestrian tournament.

CHUCK WAGON
A supply wagon from the period of the American pioneers.

CHUKKA
Period of play in a game of polo.

CIRCLE
A circular figure performed in the arena.

CIRCUS
Equestrian routines with or without riders were popular entertainments in antiquity. In the nineteenth century the equestrian circus performers had their heyday.

CLASSICAL EQUITATION
The basic principles of classical dressage riding were laid down by the Greek Xenophon about 2400 years ago, refined in the Baroque period, and preserved today at the Spanish Riding School in Vienna and at the Cavalry School at Saumur.

CLASSIC RACES
One of any of the five chief English flat-races: One Thousand Guineas, Two Thousand Guineas, the Oaks, St Leger and the Derby.

CLEAN
Noble horses have clean limbs and a clean head, i.e., tendons and bones can be clearly seen through the skin and are not covered by fatty layers.

CLEVELAND BAY
Excellent warm-blood breed from England; always bay-coloured.

CLOSE-BREEDING
The mating of closely related individuals, such as brother and sister, sire and dam, or son and dam.

CLUBFOOT
Defective shape of hoof; angle is too sharp.

CLYDESDALE
Large cold-blood breed from Scotland.

COACH
A large closed four-wheeled carriage driven two or more in hand.

COACH HORSE
Medium heavy to light weight horse used in harness. Heavier horses are called draught horses.

COB
A short-legged strong horse.

COLD-BLOOD
Powerful to very heavy breeds with a phlegmatic temperament. These draught horses are descended from the primitive breeds. The term cold-blood has nothing to do with the temperature of the animal's blood.

COLIC
Sharp abdominal pains. Call the vet immediately! Until he arrives lead the horse around in a circle. Do not let it lie down.

COLLAPSE
When the horse loses the correct posture desired in the European style of riding.

COLLAR
Construction made out of padded wood which is placed around the horse's neck for pulling a wagon or plough.

COLLAR HARNESSING
Method of harnessing developed in England, using the collar instead of the breast band.

COLLECTED CANTER
The slowest of the dressage canters.

COLLECTED TROT
The slowest of the dressage trots.

COLLECTED WALK
The slowest of the dressage walks.

COLLECTING RING
The area on a show-ground where the competitors assemble.

COLLECTION
A horse is collected when it is completely controlled, when it is ridden up to its bit at every pace and ready and willing to obey the rider's aids.

COLOSTRUM
The mare's first milk after foaling. It is very important for the foal as it provides it with immunity against some diseases.

COLOURS
1. Hair colours of the horse. 2. Jockeys and harness drivers wear the registered colour combinations of the horses' owners.

COLT
A male foal.

COMBINATION OBSTACLE
In show-jumping, an obstacle consisting of two or more separate jumps laid down at a distance of 6.5 to 12 metres from each other. They are judged as one obstacle.

COMBINED TRAINING COMPETITION
A comprehensive test consisting of dressage, cross-country and show-jumping. In driving it includes presentation and dressage, a marathon and an obstacle speed competition.

COMPETITIVE TRAIL RIDES
Competitive rides over a distance of from 50 to 160 km under veterinary control. Penalty points are given for exceeding the prescribed time limit, but no extra points are awarded for completing the course in less.

COMTOIS
A light cold-blood breed from France.

CONCAVE
Profile of the nose curved inwards as in Arabs.

CONCENTRATED FEED
Feed with a high nutritional value, e.g., oats or concentrated feed pellets.

CONDE
Frederick the Great's favourite horse. This fleabitten grey from England lived to be 42 years old.

CONDITION
State of health. A horse is in good condition when, as the result of correct training and careful feeding, it has been enabled to attain its sporting potential.

CONNEMARA PONY
Excellent breed for riding, from Ireland.

CONSTITUTION
The inherited condition of the body.

CONTACT
Continuous connection between the bit in the horse's mouth and the reins in the rider's hand. This is desirable in the European style of riding, but not necessarily so in the American.

CONTRACTED HEELS
A condition in which the foot becomes smaller at the ground surface than at the coronary band. Needs a corrective orthopaedic shoe.

CONVEX
The profile of the nose is curved outwards, as in a ram's head.

COPENHAGEN
The Duke of Wellington's horse which took part in the Battle of Waterloo; a grandson of Eclipse.

CORRECTIVE SHOE
Special shoe to correct positional defects or protect an injured hoof.

COSSACKS
Formerly an independent people; later organized into cavalry troops in the Czar's army. Outstanding horsemen.

COSTENO PONY
Extremely hardy breed found in the Andes. Descended from Spanish horses.

COUGH
Often an indication that the respiratory organs are infected. Should always be taken seriously as can have various causes.

COUNTER-CANTER
Dressage movement in which the horse canters in a circle with the outer rather than the inner leg leading.

COUPE
A closed four-wheeled carriage.

COUPLING REINS
The pair of lines (reins) of a two-in-hand joined together.

COURBETTE
An 'air above the ground' (q.v.).

COURSING
Using greyhounds to hunt hares.

COVER
The act of mating. A mare is covered by the stallion.

COWBOY
Mounted cattle-herder in the US.

COW-HOCKED
Faulty conformation of the hindlegs.

COW PONY
The specially trained horse which a cowboy rides when working cattle.

CRIB-BITING
Not an illness but a vice, caused mainly by boredom. The horse sets its incisor teeth against its manger, tenses its muscles and sucks air. It can be prevented by a neck halter.

CRIOLLO
An Argentinian breed with great stamina. It is descended from Spanish horses.

CROSS-COUNTRY
The course which forms part of the speed and endurance section, i.e., the second day, of the three-day event.

CROSS-COUNTRY RIDE
Ride in the open air as a leisure pursuit.

CROUP
The region around the pelvis.

CROUPADE
One of the 'airs above the ground' (q.v.).

CRUPPER
A strap which passes from the saddle under the horse's tail to prevent the saddle from sliding forwards. It is necessary in animals which have hardly any withers, e.g., many ponies.

CSIKOS
Mounted Hungarian herdsman.

CSIO
Abbreviation for: Concours de saut international officiel = official international show-jumping tournament.

CUPS
Depressions in the incisor teeth from which an expert can deduce a horse's age.

CURB
Swelling in the hollow outside the hock. Usually considered to be a blemish.

CURB BIT
Bit with longish shanks. Because of the shanks' action, it requires more sensitivity in the rider than does a snaffle bit.

CURB CHAIN
Thin chain which is fitted underneath the curb bit.

CURRAGH
A famous racecourse in Ireland.

CURRICLE
A two-wheeled open chaise drawn by two horses abreast.

CYST
A bubble-like growth on a mare's ovary.

D

DANUBIAN
Very strong warm-blood horse. Bred in Bulgaria, Yugoslavia, Hungary and Czechoslovakia.

DAPPLE-GREY
A grey horse with dark round flecks, most noticeably on the croup.

DARLEY ARABIAN
The most important of the three Oriental founding sires of the English Thoroughbred breed. Eclipse was one of his most famous descendants.

DARTMOOR PONY
A small breed of pony often described as the ideal children's pony. Lives in a half-wild state on Dartmoor in south-western England.

DEAD HEAT
The result of a heat or race in which two or more horses cross the finishing line at exactly the same moment.

DEEP-LITTER METHOD
In an open stall, fresh straw is usually just added daily on top. Every few months the whole stall is completely cleared out.

DEEP THROUGH THE GIRTH
Distance from the withers to the breastbone is generous.

DEER NECK
Undesirable curve of the neck.

DEFECTS
These are laid down by law and include any traits which drastically reduce a horse's performance or make it unsuitable as a saddle horse. If a major defect is recognized within fourteen days of a sale the seller is required to take the horse back.

DENERVING
Operation carried out in certain infections of the foot. By cutting through the nerves in the foot, the infection, although not healed, runs its course painlessly. Such horses can usually continue to work for a couple of years. Experts disagree on the necessity for such an operation.

DE PLUVINEL
Antoine de Pluvinel (1555-1620), Louis XIII's riding instructor who founded a famous riding school in Paris.

DEPTH
The distance between the withers and the girth.

DERBY
Classic flat-race, instituted by the 12th Earl of Derby in 1780 in England. Nowadays the expression is also used for trotting races and show-jumping competitions.

DESCENT
A horse's parentage which is proved by its genealogical tree over several generations. Outstanding stallions which are prepotent can found valuable pedigrees. Prepotent mares found distaff families.

DISH-FACED
Facial contour is slightly concave; desired shape in Arabs and Arab types.

DISQUALIFICATION
Exclusion from a competition because of an infringement of the rules.

DISTAFF SIDE
In a pedigree, the female line of descent traced through the dam.

DITCH
A depression with or without water which acts as an obstacle.

DOCK
1. Shortening of the tail root by an operation. Formerly a widespread practice with cold-blood breeds. Nowadays forbidden by law in many countries.
2. The bony part of the horse's tail.

DOG CART
A two-wheeled horse-drawn vehicle with seats back to back.

DOLE
Small light cold-blood breed from Norway.

DOMESTICATE
To tame wild animals.

DON
Hardy, medium-sized warm-blood breed from Russia. Made famous by the Don Cossacks.

DOPE
To administer drugs to a horse. It is an illegal practice.

DORMEUSE
A large four-wheeled travelling coach fitted out for sleeping.

DOUBLE
In show-jumping, a combination obstacle consisting of two separate fences.

DOUBLE NOTE
A sharp staccato note blown on the horn to indicate the beginning of the hunt.

DOUBLE RIG
See Ridgeling.

DOURINE
An infection which is transmitted during mating. Often fatal, but rare nowadays.

DRAG HUNT
In countries where hunting on horseback after live game is forbidden, an artificial trail is laid across country with, e.g., aniseed to simulate a game animal's track. Hounds and riders then follow this trail. The artificial hunt can be just as demanding for riders and horses as a hunt after live game.

DRAUGHT HORSE
Horse used for pulling heavy loads.

DRESS
To come into line; the formation of straight columns in 'display' riding.

DRESSAGE
1. The art of schooling an unbroken horse into an obedient riding animal.
2. A competitive sport.
3. Training in classical equitation.
4. Training of circus horses to perform tricks usually without a rider. Known as free dressage.

DRESSAGE ARENA
An area 20 x 40 m or 20 x 60 m for schooling the horse and rider in dressage movements.

DRESSAGE SADDLE
Saddle specially developed for dressage riding.

DROP
An obstacle where the landing point is lower than the take-off point. Found in hunting, steeplechasing and particularly in three-day events. The most famous drop is Becher's Brook in the Grand National Steeplechase, held at Aintree, near Liverpool.

DROSHKY
A four-wheeled cab drawn by horses.

DUGA
High wooden hoop which connects the two shafts of a wagon above the horse's withers. Common in Russian method of harnessing.

DÜLMEN
A primitive breed of pony which has been allowed to remain wild. From the Merfelder Bruch region of North Rhine Westphalia.

DUN
A horse with a yellowish or greyish brown coat (mouse-dun), black legs, black mane and tail, often with a dark eel-stripe along its back and a hint of light zebra striping on its legs.

DUTCH WARM-BLOOD
Modern warm-blood breed. Very versatile and an excellent sporting horse.

E

EAST BULGARIAN
Very noble warm-blood breed.

EAST FRIESIAN
Ancient warm-blood breed. Originally heavy, nowadays a medium-sized horse.

ECLIPSE
One of the greatest Thoroughbred sires of all time. Foaled in England in 1764, was never beaten in a race, sired 335 champion horses, and appears in about ninety per cent of Thoroughbreds' pedigrees.

ECOLE DE CAVALERIE
French Cavalry School at Saumur.

EEL-STRIPE
Dark stripe lengthwise along the back. A distinguishing mark of wild horses. Also occurs frequently in Isabella and dun-coloured horses.

ELIMINATION
Exclusion from taking any further part in a competition because of making a certain number of mistakes.

ENDURANCE RIDING
The winner is the fastest fit horse over the distance. The greatest race of this kind was the Great American Horse Race which was run in 1976 from New York to California. It covered about 6000 km and took three months.

ENGLISH HARNESS
The different varieties of harness, including the collar, which originated in England and which form the basis of that used in the modern sport of combined driving.

ENGLISH THOROUGHBRED
Since 1793 a pure-bred breed. It is supreme in flat-racing and indispensable for the breeding of all warm-blood breeds. Nowadays bred throughout the world.

ENTIRE
A stallion.

EOPHIPPUS
Another name for Hyracotherium, *the oldest known horse-like animal; an Eocene fossil.*

EPONA
Celtic goddess, protector of horses and cavalry.

EPSOM
Famous venue for the English Derby.

EQUESTRIAN CIRCUS ACTS
Gymnastics performed on the back of a moving horse, sometimes on a longe rein, in a circle about 14 m in diameter. Instead of a saddle, a circus horse has a band with two hand grips.

EQUESTRIENNE
A female rider or performer on horseback.

EQUIDAE
A family of ungulate mammals consisting of the genus Equus (horse, ass, zebra) and various fossil forms.

EQUINE INFECTIOUS ANAEMIA
Infectious viral disease (swamp fever).

EQUINE VIRAL RHINOPHEUMONITIS
Infection of the respiratory passages. Often causes a viral abortion (miscarriage of the foal). Recommended that a mare be immunized before mating.

EQUIPAGE
Term used to describe the carriage and attendants belonging to a person of noble rank.

ETHOLOGY
The scientific study of the function and evolution of animal behaviour.

EUROPEAN TROTTER
A trotting breed developed from French, American and Russian trotting breeds, particularly Orlov Trotters. Now bred in several European countries.

EVOLUTION
The theory first described by Charles Darwin according to which higher forms of life have gradually arisen out of lower. This is how the different species of plants and animals evolved.

EXACTA
In horse racing, bets are placed on the sequence in which the first two horses cross the line.

EX AEQUO
This Latin expression means 'equally'. When two or more horses gain the same number of points in a competition they are said to be ex aequo.

EXMOOR PONY
The most primitive breed of pony. It still lives in a half-wild state on Exmoor in south-western England.

EXTENDED CANTER
Fastest dressage canter.

EXTENDED TROT
Fastest dressage trot.

EXTENDED WALK
Fastest dressage walk.

EXTERIOR
The horse's external appearance.

F

FALABELLA PONY
The smallest breed of pony in the world, often only 60 cm high. Developed in Argentina from Shetland ponies.

FANTASIA
A North African equestrian sport.

FAVOURITE
The horse which is expected to win in a competition.

FEATHER
Long silky hair which grows on the fetlock region. Particularly luxuriant in cold-blood breeds; sparse or non-existent in noble warm-bloods or pure-breds.

FEI
Abbreviation for Fédération Equestre Internationale = *International Equestrian Federation.*

FELL PONY
Large, strong pony breed from the north of England; unfortunately very rare nowadays.

FERAL HORSES
Domestic horses which have become wild, as are all the horses which live in the wild today, e.g., in North and South America, Australia, New Zealand and Asia. They are not genuine wild horses.

FERTILITY
Ability of the mare or stallion to produce foals. Traditional horse-breeding methods achieve a fertility rate of only about sixty per cent; in herds living in the wild it is over ninety per cent.

FETLOCK
Another term for feather (q.v.).

FIACRE
A hackney coach, a cab.

FIELD
All participants in a hunt, race or similar event.

FIGURE OF EIGHT
Dressage movement consisting of two circles.

FILLY
A female foal.

FINISH
1. The sequence in which racehorses cross the finishing line.
2. The end of a race or hunt.
3. The final spurt to the finishing line.

FINNISH KLEPPER
Small sturdy versatile breed from Finland.

FISH EYES
Glass eyes (q.v.).

FIVE-GAITED HORSE
Term used in America to describe those show horses which can perform five gait variations, e.g., American Saddle Horse, Tennessee Walking Horse.

FJORD HUZULE PONY
A more recently developed breed. Norwegian Fjord ponies were crossed with Huzule ponies from the Carpathian mountain region.

FJORD PONY
A large strong breed of pony from Norway with distinctive cold-blood qualities.

FLAT-RACING
Racing over a flat track where there are no obstacles for the horses to jump.

FLEABITTEN
Having small patches of reddish hair.

FLEHMEN RESPONSE
The upper lip is curled back, giving the appearance of a careful tasting of smell. Can be observed in all horses, but particularly in stallions near mares in oestrus.

FLOATING THE TEETH
The teeth are often worn down unevenly and chisel-like surfaces develop which are often very painful. They can cause a loss in appetite and must then be filed down (floated).

FLEXOR TENDONS
Tendons that bend the joints of the fore- and hindlegs. They are easily damaged, particularly when the horse is jumping.

FLY FRINGE
The schalanken which decorates the head collar of a Hungarian harness. Consists of fine strips of leather which also serve to protect the eyes from flies.

FLYING CHANGE
The horse changes from left to right lead 'in the air', in a single stride while cantering.

FOAL
1. To give birth to a foal.
2. A young horse. After its first year it is called a yearling, after its second a two-year-old.

FOAL HEAT
A mare comes into season seven to ten days after foaling. She is usually covered at this time.

FOALING STALL
A loose box where the mare can foal. It must have easy access for thorough cleaning, be light, dry, roomy and secluded, with adequate lighting.

FOREHAND
The part of the horse which is in front of the rider; i.e., the head, neck, shoulders and forelegs.

FORMAT
Bodily shape as defined by length and height.

FOUR-IN-HAND
A coach drawn by four horses harnessed two by two.

FOXHOUND
A hound used for chasing foxes when hunting on horseback. In Britain foxhounds are never referred to as dogs.

FOXHUNT
Genuine or simulated hunting of the fox, on horseback.

FOX-TROT
A gait variation common in America.

FRACTURE
Breaking of a bone.

FRAME
Size of the horse in relation to the average size of horses of the same breed. Normally large-framed horses are much sought after.

FREDERIKSBORG
Formerly parade horses at the Danish court; developed from Spanish breeds, nowadays bred as a sporting horse.

FREE DRESSAGE
Training a horse to perform tricks without a rider, mainly in the circus.

FREE JUMPING
Jumping exercises without a rider.

FREIBERGER
Small, medium weight cold-blood breed from Switzerland.

FRENCH TROTTER
A trotting breed from northern France; has tremendous stamina.

FRESH
Temperamentally eager to get going; particularly a horse which has been standing for a long time in its stall.

FRIESIAN
Ancient Dutch breed. Formerly in great demand for cross-breeding.

FROG
V-shaped horny pad on the sole of a horse's foot.

FURIOSO
Versatile Hungarian warm-blood breed whose founding sires were two English Thoroughbreds: Furioso and North Star.

G

GAG SNAFFLE
Special bit which works more strongly on the corners of the horse's mouth.

GAITS
The horse has three basic gaits: walk, trot and gallop. In addition it has about ten gait variations, e.g., pace, tölt, rack, fox-trot.

GALL
A sore produced by saddlery or harness rubbing on parts of the body.

GALLOP
The fastest of the horse's three basic gaits.

GALLOP UP
Cause a horse to gallop by use of aids.

GALLOWAY HACK
In Australia, a pony of 140 to 150 cm height.

GALLOWAY PONY
Large, fast, Scottish breed of pony. Contributed a great deal to the development of the English Thoroughbred. No longer extant.

GARDIEN
Mounted cattle-herder in the Camargue, southern France.

GARRON
Also known as the Highland pony. From Scotland. The largest of the British pony breeds.

GAUCHO
Mounted cattle-herder of the South American pampas.

GEE UP
Command used to set a team in motion.

GELDERLAND
Very versatile Dutch breed.

GELDING
A male horse which has been castrated. Stallions which are not suitable for stud purposes are gelded to make them easier to manage.

GENEALOGICAL TREE
Horse's genealogy; its pedigree.

GENERAL STUD BOOK
Register of all Thoroughbreds foaled in England and Ireland. First published in 1793 and since then at varying intervals.

GENETIC PROGRESS
Selective breeding based on obtaining certain desired traits.

GÉRICAULT
Théodore Gericault (1791-1824) was a famous painter of equestrian scenes. He was killed in a fall from a horse.

GIDRAN ARABIAN
Hungarian breed of Anglo-Arab type.

GIG
Light two-wheeled carriage for two people.

GLAND
A cell or organ in a plant or animal which produces a secretion.

GLANDERS
A malignant contagious disease which affects horses, other domestic animals, and man. Usually incurable in horses. Nowadays virtually under control. One of the major defects.

GLASS EYES
Pale blue eyes which occur mainly in albinos and dappled horses. Also called fish eyes.

GODOLPHIN BARB
Often incorrectly called Godolphin Arabian. A Barb stallion from Morocco, foaled about 1724. He became one of the three founding sires of the English Thoroughbred breed.

GOES WELL
Used to describe a horse which naturally has a lively high-stepping action.

GOTLAND PONY
Native breed from the Swedish island of Gotland. About 120 cm tall. Nowadays bred in many countries as an excellent children's pony.

GRADE UP
Use a superior quality stallion to improve lesser breeds. Usually an English Thoroughbred or an Arab pure-bred.

GRADITZ
Thoroughbred stud founded in 1686. Now in East Germany.

GRAND NATIONAL STEEPLECHASE
Held annually since 1839 at Aintree near Liverpool; the most arduous of all steeplechases.

GRAND PARDUBICE
A very difficult steeplechase course inaugurated in 1875, in Czechoslovakia.

GRAND PRIX
Means Grand Prize.
1. Race for first class horses.
2. The highest level of the international dressage trials.

GRASS BELLY
A noticeably rounded belly, the result of eating too much raw food. Particularly common in small ponies.

GREASE
An infection of the skin near the fetlock's flexor tendon.

GREEN
A young horse or pony is said to be green when it is broken but not trained.

GREEN MEAT
Basic feed consisting of hay, grass and straw.

GREY
Horse with white hair on a darker pigmented skin. Greys are born dark and only turn white at 8 to 10 years, unlike albinos which are much rarer and have a lighter unpigmented skin.

GREYHOUND GUTTED
Tightly drawn-in stomach, usually caused by undernourishment and too little ballast stuff in feed. Sometimes occurs in racehorses when in training.

GRIP
To hold tight with the knees to the side of the saddle; especially important when jumping.

GRISONE
Federico Grisone, born about 1550, founded a riding school in Naples based on the classical riding system of the Greeks. He often used cruel methods.

GRONINGEN
Heavy Dutch warm-blood breed.

GROOM
Someone who has charge of the horses, or wears a livery and accompanies a carriage.

GROSBOIS
A splendid training venue for trotters near Paris.

GROUND LINE
The distance in front of an obstacle where the horse begins its jump.

GROUND SHY
A horse which has an abnormal fear of anything lying on the ground in front of it.

GUÉRINIÈRE
Francois Robichon de la Guérinière was born about the middle of the eighteenth century. He was the founder of present day dressage. He perfected the teachings of de Pluvinel and wrote the Ecole de Cavalerie.

GUMMY LEGS
Soft fatty parts which are the opposite of clean bone. Caused either by overfeeding when the horse is not being given sufficient muscle work, or by a natural tendency as in cold-bloods.

GYMNASTIC WORK
The very important muscle training which makes the horse first and foremost a beast of burden; also fitness programmes and other physical exercises.

H

HACK
1. Well-schooled horse for a riding pupil.
2. Term used to describe a worn-out or poor horse.

HACKAMORE
A bitless bridle which originated in America. It has a rope loop instead of a bit and works on the nose and chin. The genuine hackamore is made out of rope and leather; the so-called mechanical hackamore has metal shanks and a chin chain similar to the curb bit.

HACKNEY
A horse bred in England to draw light carriages. Has a very pronounced high-stepping action, which is often obtained by cruel methods.

HACKNEY PONY
The Hackney pony was developed by crossing a Hackney stallion with a pony mare. It is about 130 cm tall and is used as a show pony in front of a light carriage.

HAFLINGER
Mountain horse from the Tyrol. By size it is a pony — about 135 to 145 cm; by type it is a light cold-blood. It is a favourite horse for leisure pursuits.

HAIR
Slender filaments growing from the animal's skin, and covering the whole body. The animal's mane and tail are called its long hair. Its summer covering is fine and short, its winter one becomes thicker and longer, like fur, especially when animals are kept in an open stable. It is particularly luxuriant in northern pony breeds.

HAIR COLOURS
Wild horses are yellowish to brown or mouse grey in colour, with black mane and tail, and usually a dark eel-stripe along their backs. Domestic horses may be dun-coloured, but they are also black, bay, chestnut, grey, skewbald, spotted, albino and numerous in-between shadings.

HALFBRED
A warm-blood horse or pony which has one parent, usually the sire, which is an English or Arab pure-bred.

HALF HALT
In show-jumping a horse is halted momentarily in front of an obstacle so that it can then pick up speed and better prepare for the jump.

HALF PASS
As the horse moves forward diagonally, only its front or back feet cross over.

HALF-SCHOOLED
A saddle horse which obeys the aids willingly and has had some schooling.

HALLA
First class jumper ridden by Hans Günter Winkler in the 1950s and 1960s.

HALTER
1. Head gear made out of leather, cotton or nylon.
2. A rope used for tying up or holding a horse.

HAMBLETONIAN 10
Grandson of Messenger. A Thoroughbred that was one of the most important founding sires of the American Trotting breed. In 27 years he sired 1300 foals.

HAND
A measure of the hand's breadth, four inches, or ten centimetres.

HANDICAP
A method of evening out the odds in galloping and trotting. In trotting, distance allowances are made according to the horse's previous performances. In galloping, weights are assigned to each horse so that all have an equal chance of winning.

HANGING PARTITION
Used to mark off the stalls between horses in a stable.

HANOVERIAN
Large, versatile breed of saddle horse which has produced numerous first class jumpers.

HANOVERIAN RIDING HALTER
A method of bridling developed in Germany.

HARAS
French term for stud farm.

HARDDRAVER
Dutch word for trotters.

HARNESS TYPES
Different methods of harnessing horses to vehicles, e.g., English, Russian, American, Hungarian.

HARRIER
Dog used for hunting hares.

HAUNCHES
Collective term for the hip, knee and hock joints of hindlegs.

HAY-RACK
A container for hay usually fixed on to the wall of the stall. It is constructed in such a way that the horse can pull the hay out through the gaps between the slats.

HEART ROOM
Circumference of the chest. Sufficient depth means there is plenty of room for the lungs and heart to operate efficiently.

HEAT
The period when the mare is sexually responsive to the stallion; occurs about every 21 days.

HEAVE LINE
A lengthways depression on the horse's flank. It is caused by the abdominal muscles having to give an extra squeeze to force the intestines against the diaphragm so that air is forced out of the lungs.

HEAVES or BROKEN WIND
Chronic incurable respiratory infection. Occurs frequently. Main cause is said to be poorly ventilated stables, for it seldom occurs in horses kept in open stalls. As the illness progresses the animal becomes more and more short of breath.

HEAVY-FRONTED
Shape of the chest is very broad. Undesirable in riding animals but desirable in cold-bloods.

HEAVY HORSE
Any horse belonging to one of the breeds of large draught horses.

HEIGHT
Height of a horse is measured with a measuring stick from the ground to the highest point of the withers. If a tape measure is used, the measurement is taken along the curve of the body and is therefore greater.

HEREDITARY DEFECTS
Physical defects or undesirable characteristics which are hereditary.

HERNIA
Protrusion of any internal organ through the wall that contains it. The most common is congenital umbilical hernia which occurs in foals. A horse can suffer from various other internal ruptures, including scrotal hernia.

HERPES
An infection which can be transmitted during mating; usually runs its course harmlessly.

HESSIAN
Versatile saddle horse very like the Hanoverian or Trakehner.

HIGH SCHOOL
The classical art of equitation well known through the Spanish Riding School in Vienna, the Cavalry School in Saumur, and the circus.

HIGHLAND PONY
Also known as the Garron. Large pony from Scotland with excellent qualities.

HINNY
The offspring of a stallion and a she-ass.

HIPPODROME
Term used in antiquity for a racecourse where chariot races were held.

HIPPOLOGY
The study of horses. People who have a great deal of theoretical and practical knowledge about horses are called hippologists.

HIPPOSANDALS
Hoof protectors made out of iron and leather and used by the Romans before shoes were invented.

HITCH UP
Harness a horse or horses to be driven.

HOLD
When a mare becomes pregnant after mating she is said to have 'held' to the service.

HOLSTEIN
A versatile, rather heavy saddle horse developed from the heavy native breed under the strong influence of pure-breds. Outstanding representatives are Granat, ridden by Christine Stückelberger, and Meteor, ridden by Fritz Thiedemann.

HOME STRAIGHT
The straight to the finish in a race.

HOOF
The insensitive horny covering which protects the sensitive parts of the horse's foot.

HOOF BEAT
The sound made by the horse's hooves.

HOOF PICK
A metal instrument used to clean out the horse's hoof.

HOPPEGARTEN COUGH
An infectious disease of the upper respiratory tract.

HORIZONTAL CRACK
Horizontal fissure in the hoof wall. Often a long drawn-out, wearying infection.

HORSE ARMOUR
Chain or iron armour worn by war horses in the Middle Ages.

HORSE BRASS
Ornamental hinge or clasp on a horse's harness.

HORSEPOWER
Unit of power in machines. The power a horse can exert, i.e., the power to lift 75 kg one metre high in one second. In reality a horse is about ten to thirteen times stronger.

HORSE SACRIFICE
In many ancient civilizations horses were sacrificed to the gods, or killed when their owners died and put into the grave with them.

HORSESHOE
Curved piece of iron which is the same shape as the hoof. It is fitted over the hoof to prevent it from being worn down. Apparently invented by the Celts about two thousand years ago.

HUNGARIAN HARNESS
Trace or breast band harness. A light carriage harness without a collar.

HUNT
Pursuit of wild game on horseback with dogs; sometimes an artificial trail is laid.

HUNTER
Riding horse bred in England and Ireland. Usually the result of crossing a strong, heavy warm-blood mare with a Thoroughbred stallion. Excellent jumping ability and tremendous stamina.

HURDLE RACING
Horse races over a course of hurdles.

HUZULE PONY
Hardy, agile pony breed from the Carpathian mountains; grows to about 130 cm tall.

HYBRID
Product of a cross between two different, but closely related animal species. In the Equidae family, hybrids are not normally capable of reproducing. The most well known hybrids are mules and hinnies. Artificial crossings, e.g., those between zebra and horse and zebra and ass are called zebroids.

I

ICELANDIC PONY
Strong, hardy breed from Iceland, which remained pure-bred for about a thousand years. Grows to about 130 cm. Nowadays a very popular breed for leisure pursuits.

IMPULSION
Natural long, striding, forward movement that is expected from a good horse.

INDIAN PONY
Small, hardy breed descended from Spanish horses. In exceptional cases it is carefully bred (Appaloosa).

INDIGENOUS
Term used for breeds which have remained in their original homelands for long periods of time without being cross-bred with other breeds.

INFIELD
That part of a racecourse which is divided off and where the actual races are run.

INFLUENZA
Hoppegarten coughing; very contagious disease of the respiratory organs.

INOCULATION
Preventive protection against various infections such as joint ill, influenza, tetanus, viral abortion, rabies.

INSPECTION
Selecting a stallion for stud on the basis of its external appearance. Often a performance test is included.

INTELLIGENCE
As a typical herd animal which relies on speed to escape from danger, the horse has 'much feeling but little understanding'. This means that it is guided by instinct and that thought plays very little part in its actions. A horse is therefore less intelligent than a dog, though it does have an excellent memory.

INTERMÉDIAIRE
A level below the Grand Prix in advanced dressage.

IRISH DRAUGHT
Strong heavy warm-blood breed. It is often the female basis used for the breeding of Irish Hunters.

IRISH HUNTER
Strong halfbred Irish horse usually with a Thoroughbred sire. Has outstanding jumping ability.

IRON
Brand-iron used to put on the brand mark.

ISABELLA
Hair colour, not a breed. Yellowish brown, golden yellow, chestnut, or bay to grey but always with a light-coloured mane and tail. If it has a golden-coloured coat with a silvery mane and tail it is called a Palomino.

ITALIAN JUMPING STYLE
Developed by Federico Caprilli about the turn of the century. Today its principles of the 'forward seat' are universally accepted in show-jumping.

J

JOCKEY
Person engaged to ride a horse in a race. In many countries riders have to pass certain tests before they qualify to be called jockeys.

JOCKEY CLUB
Association located in Newmarket, England, which controls all aspects of flat-racing.

JODHPURS
Riding trousers which originated in India. The legs fit the calf of the leg tightly and reach to the ankles. They are worn with short boots.

JOINT ILL
An infectious disease affecting newborn animals. Can be prevented if the newborn foal is inoculated within its first twenty-four hours.

JOWL
Term used to describe the rear part of the horse's lower jaw.

JUCKER
Light elegant horse used in front of carriages in Hungary.

JUCKER CARRIAGE
Light four-wheeled vehicle originally driven by its owner, not by a coachman.

JUCKER HARNESS
Light, often richly decorated, breast band harness, particularly common in Hungary.

JUMP
A show-jumping obstacle.

JUMPER
Any horse trained to jump.

JUMPING LANE
A long, narrow, fenced-in area where young horses are taught to jump without a rider.

JUMP-OFF
In some show-jumping competitions, if a number of competitors gain the same number of points in the first round, another round is held to decide the winner. The obstacles are usually raised higher but their number is reduced.

JUTLAND
Strong, medium-sized cold-blood breed from southern Denmark.

K

KABARDIN
An important warm-blood breed in Russia.

KARABAIR
Warm-blood breed from the region to the south of the Aral Sea. Bred in three types.

KARABAKH
Rare warm-blood breed from the eastern Caucasus. Small build, very noble and temperamental.

KENNELS
The buildings and yard where a pack of hounds is kept.

KENTUCKY SADDLE HORSE
Another name for the American Saddle Horse.

KICK
A movement made with the hindlegs against a (supposed) enemy. Kicking is an extremely dangerous vice which is caused by bad handling.

KINCSEM
The 'wonder mare' from Hungary. Between 1876 and 1879 she ran in 54 races in five countries and won them all.

KLADRUBER
Large impressive carriage horse of Spanish origin. Used at the Austrian Court. Still exists at the Kladrub Stud in Czechoslovakia.

KNABSTRUP
Coloured type of ancient Frederiksborg breed from Denmark; leopard-spotted pattern on its coat; rare today.

KNEE ROLL
Padding on the saddle flaps to support the knees.

KNOCK OFF
If a rider knocks off parts of an obstacle and thereby alters the height or width of it he is given four penalty points.

KONIC
Slavic word meaning small horse. Breed from Poland which is very similar to the Tarpan.

KUHAYLAN
The masculine type of the pure-bred Arab.

KUMISS
Drink made in Mongolia from fermented mare's milk.

KUSTANAI
Beautiful small warm-blood breed from Kazakhstan. Bred in a strong draught and a fast riding type.

L

LAMINITIS
Inflammation of the inner hoof wall. Usually produced by an excess of protein in the feed, e.g., a change from hay to spring grass. Symptoms are lameness and the horse standing with its forelegs stretched out in front. Call the vet immediately.

LANDAU
A four-seater carriage with a folding top. Originated in Landau in the Pfalz, Germany, at the beginning of the nineteenth century.

LARGE PONY
Pony with a shoulder height of over 135 cm. Nowadays usually described as a small horse.

LASSO
A long rope with a running noose used by mounted cattle-herders for catching cattle or wild horses.

LATERAL MOVEMENTS
Dressage movements in which the horse's body is facing away from the direction in which it is moving, e.g., shoulder-in, travers.

LATVIAN
Strong warm-blood breed from Latvia. Most suitable as a carriage horse.

LEAD ANIMAL
Highest ranking stallion or mare in the herd.

LEADING SIRE
A stud stallion with first class qualities.

LEADING STUD
A stud which produces outstanding stallions.

LEAP
Jump up to a raised obstacle, e.g., a bank.

LEG BRACER
The tendons are rubbed with a medicament which produces warmth to prevent damage to the tendons.

LEG PROTECTORS
Protective casing for the leg joints. These include hock boots and knee caps.

LEG YIELD
A sideways gait in which the horse responds to light pressure from one thigh.

LENGTH
Measurement of distance between one horse and another as it crosses the finishing line; can be by a nose, by a neck, by a half, whole or several lengths.

LEOPARD-SPOTTED
Horse or pony with a light-coloured coat and numerous round black or brown spots.

LEVADE
A high school movement in which the horse rears up on its hindlegs.

LIGHT HORSE
Any horse, except a Thoroughbred, used or suitable for riding.

LIGHT IN HAND
Term used to describe a horse whose neck and back muscles remain relaxed when the bridle is being put on and which does not resist the bit.

LIGHTNESS
Horse is completely relaxed and willing to pay attention to the rider's aids.

LINEAL DESCENT
The table of the male descendants of a particular stallion.

LINE-BREEDING
Breeding related animals to keep offspring closely related to an outstanding ancestor.

LINES
Driving reins for carriage horses.

LIPIZZANER
Warm-blood breed originated in Lipizza (Lipica) in modern Yugoslavia. Founding sires were mostly Spanish horses. Predominantly greys. Provide the horses for the Spanish Riding School in Vienna and are popular circus horses. In Eastern Europe they are also used to work the land.

LOCK-JAW
See Tetanus.

LOKAI
Robust breed from the Aral Sea region. Originally very similar to Prjevalsky's horse, upgraded by cross-breeding, mainly with Arabs.

LONGE (or LUNGE) REIN
A long rope about eight metres long, at the end of which the horse is lunged, i.e., made to go round in a circle without a rider. In European riding this forms a very important part in preparing young horses for their actual schooling.

LOOSE-BOX
A large stall in a stable where horses can move around freely.

LOP NECK
Very thick neck with a mane which hangs to one side. Occurs mainly in stallions of cold-blood breeds.

LOW WITHER
Used to describe a horse whose croup is higher than its withers. Occurs frequently in young horses and in trotters.

LUNGE REIN
See Longe rein.

LUSITANO
Ancient Portuguese warm-blood breed; very elegant, similar to the Andalusian.

M

MACEDONIAN PONY
Hardy mountain pony from southern Yugoslavia.

MAIDEN MARE
A mare which has not had a foal, though she may be carrying one.

MAIDEN RACE
Race for horses which have never won a race.

MAIL COACH
A conveyance that carries the public mail.

MALAPOLSKI
The Polish Anglo-Arab breed.

MANE
The long hair which grows on top of the horse's neck along the crest.

MANÈGE
A defined area in the open air or in a hall where horses and riders are schooled and where competitions are held.

MAN O'WAR
A Thoroughbred stallion foaled in the US in 1917. Outstanding both as a racehorse and as a stud stallion.

MARATHON
Cross-country part of a combined driving event. Usually over 25 to 40 km of difficult terrain.

MARE
The female horse.

MARENGO
Napoleon's most famous horse; a grey Arab stallion.

MARKINGS
Those white hairs on the horse's head and legs which are permanent and are therefore entered in its pedigree papers as distinguishing marks. White hairs which grow on the scars of wounds, e.g., where the saddle has pressed, do not constitute markings.

MARTINGALE
Straps used to prevent the horse from raising its head higher than desired.

MASH
A soft crushed feed consisting mostly of cooked linseed and bran. Valuable food for sick or exhausted animals.

MASTER
'Master of Foxhounds' (MFH) is a respected title in Great Britain and Ireland. Has overall responsibility for the running and organization of all aspects of the hunt.

MATURITY
Though they reach puberty much earlier, usually stallions are physically mature at two and a half to three years, mares at three years, northern ponies and other late maturing breeds at four to five years.

MEALY MUZZLE
Lighter coloured hair around the muzzle and nostrils of a bay horse. A characteristic marking of Exmoor ponies.

MECHANICS
The way the animal's body works, particularly how the limbs function when in motion. A horse with a free-stepping, lively gait has excellent mechanics.

MECKLENBURGER
A warm-blood breed similar to the Hanoverian.

MECONIUM
Blackish contents of the intestine of the newborn foal; its first faeces.

MESSENGER
Famous Thoroughbred. Notable as the principal founding sire of the American trotting breed.

METEOR
Highly successful German jumper ridden by Fritz Thiedemann, 1943-1966.

MEZŐHEGYES
Ancient large Hungarian stud.

MILITARY
Versatility test consisting of dressage, speed and endurance trials, and show-jumping. Often called the 'crown of riding'.

MING HORSES
Small porcelain horses in various typical poses from the time of the Ming dynasty (1368-1644) in China.

MIOHIPPUS
A fossil horse.

MISSOURI FOX-TROTTER
Small, compact warm-blood breed from the state of Missouri, US. Often performs a specialized gait variation known as the fox-trot.

MIXED FEED
Strengthening mixture consisting of several types of feed stuff to supplement hay or grass.

MOBILE GATE
Car or truck with a wide, foldable gate attached to it, behind which trotters line up at the start of a race.

MORGAN
Noble, rather small, American warm-blood breed. Outstanding saddle horse.

MORT
Horn signal or yell which signifies the death at the end of a hunt.

MOUNT
In mating, the stallion mounts the mare.

MOUNTIES
Royal Canadian Mounted Police.

MULE
Offspring of an ass and mare. Usually larger than a hinny.

MUNIQI
One of the classical types of the Arab breed.

MUSTANG
Feral horses of Spanish origin in the western part of the US.

N

NAIL BLIND
A wound in the sole of the hoof caused by a shoe nail being driven in.

NAP
A horse is said to 'nap' if it will not obey the aids.

NATIONAL SIRE
A state-owned stud stallion.

NATIONAL STUD
A state-owned stud farm.

NATIONS' CUP
Competition in which teams from different nations compete against each other as teams.

NATIVE PONIES
The ancient breeds of moorland and mountain ponies in Great Britain.

NAVICULAR BONE
Small residual toe bone in the hoof.

NAVICULAR DISEASE
An inflammation of the navicular bone and surrounding tissue. Develops as a result of too much strain on the forelegs at an early age. The deep flexor tendon, where it crosses over between the navicular bone and the plantar cushion, becomes rubbed and causes a painful, often chronic inflammation. The infection can only be cured in its very early stages. Occurs frequently in show-jumpers.

NEAPOLITAN
Ancient warm-blood breed similar to the Andalusian; no longer extant.

NEARSIDE HORSE
The left-hand horse in a pair. The right-hand horse is called the offside horse.

NECK
Length, shape and muscle formation of the neck, plus the angle it forms with the back, are important not only for the total impression, but also as an indication of how the horse will perform.

NERVE
Horses with 'nerve' are temperamental but not nervous, have a great deal of courage and are excellent achievers.

NEWCASTLE
William Cavendish (1592-1676), Duke of Newcastle, was an English nobleman who opened a riding academy in Antwerp in the seventeenth century. He compiled A new method to dress horses and A general system of horsemanship.

NEW FOREST PONY
Half-wild breed which lives in the New Forest, a forested area in the south of England. Arabs and English Thoroughbreds contributed to its development.

NEWMARKET
Seat of the English Jockey Club, of numerous Thoroughbred studs, and one of the largest training centres for racehorses in the world.

NIBBLE
Mutual grooming by nibbling, particularly in the shoulder area, is part of the horse's social behaviour.

NICK
The muscle tendons which pull the tail downwards are cut to obtain a higher position for the tail, e.g., in Hackneys, American Saddle Horses, Tennessee Walking Horses. One of the numerous stupidities practised in show business.

NOBLE
Arab and English pure-breds are described as noble. Also used to describe any horses which bear the distinctive characteristics of these two breeds.

NONIUS
A warm-blood breed originated about 150 years ago in Hungary. Bred in two types: a large carriage horse, and an agile saddle horse.

NORFOLK TROTTER
Formerly used as a carriage horse in England. A popular breed for cross-breeding.

NORIKER
A South German medium-sized, cold-blood breed, also called Pinzgauer, or Oberländer. Sometimes occurs as leopard-spotted.

NORTH SWEDISH
Comparatively light, agile cold-blood breed.

NOSEBAG
A canvas food bag filled with feed which is fastened on to the horse's head so that it can eat while it is out working.

NOSEBAND
Part of the bridle which lies across the horse's nose.

NOVOKIRGHIZ
A rather small breed of saddle horse which was developed about forty years ago in Kirghiz, in the Soviet Union, by introducing Thoroughbred blood. Has excellent qualities.

NUMNAH
A cloth or pad placed under the saddle to prevent chafing.

O

OAKS
A famous English race for three-year-old fillies, held over 2400 metres. Inaugurated in 1779.

OBSTACLE
Natural or artificial raised barrier in the countryside, or in a jumping event, which must be jumped by horse and rider. Also known as a jump. It is called a chicane in a driving competition.

OCCIDENTAL HORSE
Term formerly used to describe cold-blood breeds.

ODDS
Ratio of probability used as the basis of a bet.

OFFSIDE HORSE
The right-hand horse in a pair.

OLDENBURG
Originally bred as a carriage horse, now a versatile saddle horse.

OLEANDER
A Thoroughbred stallion foaled in 1924 on the Schlenderhan Stud; one of Germany's greatest racing and stud horses.

OLYMPICS
Various kinds of horse races were part of the Olympic Games held in ancient Greece. The modern Olympic Games were first held in 1894. Since 1912 (Stockholm) equestrian sports, i.e., dressage, show-jumping and military (combined training) events, have been included.

ONAGER
The wild ass of Central Asia.

ONE-HORSE CARRIAGE
Carriage drawn by one horse.

ONE THOUSAND GUINEAS
One of the English classic races.

ON THE BIT
The horse has his neck at the correct angle, the reins are correctly positioned and it is mouthing the bit properly.

OPEN-FRONT SHELTER
A shelter which is open on one or two sides. It should face away from the prevailing winds. From the horse's point of view it is the most pleasant way to be housed.

ORDINARY CANTER
Average cantering tempo.

ORDINARY TROT
Average trotting tempo.

ORDINARY WALK
Average walking tempo.

ORLOV TROTTER
Bred in Russia. For a long time it was the fastest trotting breed; nowadays has been superseded by other breeds.

OROHIPPUS
A fossil horse.

OUTSIDER
A racehorse which is thought to have little chance of winning a race.

OVERREACH
When the hindfoot hits the forefoot as the horse moves.

OX
OX is written after the name of a pure-bred Arab. An English Thoroughbred has XX after its name.

OXER
A high spread fence in show-jumping.

P

PACE
1. A lateral gait in which the hindleg and foreleg on the same side move forwards together.
2. The speed in a race. Good jockeys are tacticians and try to keep to a tempo which will leave them with something in reserve.

PACER
The American trotting breed (Standardbred) is divided into trotters and pacers.

PACK
1. A group of foxhounds, beagles or hunting hounds. The pack is counted in couples.
2. A number of animals kept together for hunting.

PADDLING
Abnormal outward curving of the forelegs when moving.

PAINT HORSE
In the US nowadays skewbald or piebald Thoroughbreds or Quarter Horses are always called Paint Horses. Piebald horses of other breeds are called Pintos.

PAIR
Two horses harnessed together side by side.

PAIR CLASSES
Show-jumping competitions in which each participant has to ride two horses, one after the other, through the course. The time taken for saddling up is included.

PAIR JUMPING
Show-jumping event in which two riders go through the course side by side.

PALOMINO
Beautiful noble Western horse. Golden coat with a silver white mane and tail; excellent nature. Still not a consolidated breed as only about fifty per cent of the progeny have the desired palomino colouring.

PARCOURS
Show-jumping or driving course.

PARIMUTUEL
United States and Continental equivalent of the totalisator.

PAS DE DEUX
Dressage display by two riders.

PASO
South American breed of pace trotters (pacers). Also called Peruvian Paso and Paso Fino.

PASSAGE
A dressage movement. A trot which has a distinct period of suspension, when one diagonal pair of legs remains in the air at each step.

PASTERN
The part of the horse's foot from the fetlock to the hoof.

PASTURE
Fresh pasture is the best guarantee for healthy nourishment and for raising healthy foals. Outdoor exercise on soft grass is excellent therapy for any horse.

PATH
The (invisible) lines along which the horse goes on a racetrack.

PATO
Argentinian equestrian sport.

PECK
When the horse stumbles, but does not fall at a jump.

PEDIGREE
Record of ancestry.

PEDIGREE PAPERS
A document certified as correct by the breeding association. On it are entered the horse's pedigree, its sex, date of birth, colour and markings, its breeder and any subsequent changes of ownership.

PEGASUS
Winged horse of Greek mythology.

PELHAM BIT
Bit designed to produce the combined effect of the snaffle and the curb.

PERCHERON
Powerful, but still very agile, cold-blood breed from northern France (Perche).

PERFORMANCE TESTING
Many breeders use performance as an indication of the quality of the stallions selected for breeding, i.e., performance on the racetrack, and that of any progeny.

PERIODIC OPHTHALMIA
One of the major defects. A cloudy or inflamed condition of the eye which disappears and recurs at intervals of 4 to 6 weeks. Also called moon-blindness.

PESADE
A figure in high school equitation in which a horse rears up on its hindlegs without forward movement.

PHAETON
Numerous types of open four-wheeled carriages for one or two horses.

PHOTO FINISH
Racehorses are photographed as they cross the finishing line, so that even the smallest distance between them can be determined.

PIAFFE
In dressage, a slow cadenced elevated trot on the spot.

PIBER
Austrian Lipizzaner Stud which supplies the stallions for the Spanish Riding School in Vienna.

PIGNATELLI
A follower of Grisone; founded a famous riding school in Naples at the beginning of the sixteenth century.

PILLARS
Two wooden columns to which the horse is attached by reins so that it can be taught high school movements.

PINCER BITE
The perpendicular position of the incisors in a young horse.

PINCERS
Another term for the front incisor teeth.

PINEROLO
Italian riding school visited by cavalry officers of many nationalities between 1900 and 1932.

PINFIRING
Veterinary procedure used in certain infections of the tendon. The tiny burns remain very painful for several days and have the desired effect — the horse spares the leg and the healing process is hastened.

PINTO
Piebald or skewbald American Western horse of Spanish origins.

PINZGAUER
Another name for Noriker or Oberländer. A South German medium-sized, cold-blood breed.

PIROUETTE
In dressage, a 360 degree turn within the horse's length, i.e., with the inner hindfoot staying as close to one spot as possible.

PIT PONY
Ponies used for haulage in the mines. Often never saw daylight for years on end.

PLEASURE HORSE
Horse or pony with an undemanding nature that can easily be ridden by adults or children.

PLIOHIPPUS
A fossil horse.

PODHAJSKY
Alois Podhajsky was the Director of the Spanish Riding School in Vienna. He died in 1973.

POINTS
The most important external visible characteristics of the horse.

POINT TO POINT
Race across country with obstacles. About 3 to 6 km long. Very popular in Britain.

POISONOUS PLANTS
Horses usually avoid these, though not always. Yew is particularly harmful; others include meadow saffron, daphne, box, deadly nightshade, spurge, buttercup, lupin, foxglove, horsetail, snowdrop and leaves of the potato.

POITOU ASS
A large ass which originated in France. Much sought after for breeding mules and hinnies.

POLES
Poles placed around a racetrack at measured distances as markers.

POLING
Various constructions, including an iron which hits the horse's leg while it is jumping, used to make a horse jump higher. This dubious method is now forbidden in tournaments, but is often used 'behind the scenes'.

POLO
An ancient equestrian sport which originated in Persia; probably the oldest goal game.

PONY EXPRESS
A mail delivery service first organized in 1860 in the US for carrying news over some two thousand miles. Ponies were ridden at the gallop and changed every twelve miles or so.

PONY OF THE AMERICAS (POA)
Outstanding American breed of pony with the patterned coat of the Appaloosa horse.

PORT
The high curve of the mouth-piece of a curb bit, which allows the tongue a certain freedom of movement.

POST AND RAILS
A show-jumping obstacle of upright posts with horizontal posts laid between them.

POSTBOY
A boy who rode post-horses, or who carried letters.

POSTIER BRETON
The lighter type of the Breton cold-blood breed.

POULTICE BOOT
A specially constructed shoe to hold a dressing in place on an injury to the sole of the hoof.

PRACTISE JUMPS
At show-jumping competitions these are put up for the riders to use when warming up.

PREGNANCY
The average length of a mare's pregnancy is 340 days.

PREMATURE BIRTH
A foal which is born between the 300th and 325th day of pregnancy.

PRICKING
Injury to the hoof caused by driving a nail too close to the sensitive laminae.

PRIMITIVE BREEDS
The breeds of horse which existed in the wild and from which the domestic horse is descended. Only Prjevalsky's horse still exists today in a pure-blooded form, and only in captivity.

PRIX DES NATIONS
The lowest or first of the four levels of advanced dressage tests; followed by the Intermédiaire and the Grand Prix I and II.

PRJEVALSKY'S HORSE
The last breed of wild horse, probably only survives now in zoos.

PROFESSIONAL RIDING INSTRUCTOR
Must have passed the requisite examinations and attained the qualifications laid down by the British Horse Society.

PUISSANCE
A show-jumping competition with a few high jumps which are raised higher for each round. Even if points are still equal there are at most only three jump-offs.

PULL
Mane and tail of show horses are made thinner by removing a few hairs at each grooming.

PULLER
A horse which takes the bit between its teeth and pulls against the rider's hands.

PUR SANG
French for Thoroughbred.

PUSH BALL
Equestrian game between two groups in which the horses push an enormous ball.

Q

QUADRIGA
In Greek and Roman times, a two-wheeled cart drawn by four horses abreast. See also Triga and Biga.

QUADRILLE
Equestrian dance performed by groups of eight or twelve with musical accompaniment. Ranges from simple movement displays in a riding school to the graceful performances of classical equitation.

QUAGGA
An extinct South African wild ass.

QUARTERS
This term refers to all that part of the horse which lies 'behind the hand' of the rider.

QUICKSILVER S
A Dutch trotter which won 145 trotting races before retiring from the racetrack in 1966, aged 17.

QUOTA
The ratio between the total amount received in bets and the winning sum which has been paid out. Calculated by the totalisator after the race.

R

RACE
A competitive trial of speed. The most important horse races are either flat-races, steeplechases, hunt races, harness races, or cross-country.

RACECOURSE
A track specially constructed for racing with all the relevant facilities such as grandstands, paddocks, totalisator booths, weighing rooms.

RACEHORSE
A horse bred for speed and endurance. The English Thoroughbred is the prime example. The Arab is unbeatable in distance races; and in the United States a Quarter Horse can beat a Thoroughbred over a short distance. Halfbreds are bred for arduous hunts.

RACING SADDLE
Very small, light saddle with the stirrups buckled short.

RACK
Gait between a trot and a gallop.

RALLY
A competition to test skill and ability to follow an unknown route on a map. Usually 15 to 20 km long.

RAMENER
The horse's head is carried correctly; in European style this must be caused by the advance of the body towards the head. Often done unprofessionally, so that the neck is bent rather than curved.

RAM'S HEAD
Head in which the line of the profile is curved outwards.

RANDEM
Two-wheeled vehicle with three horses harnessed one behind the other.

RAU
Gustav Rau (1880-1954), famous German hippologist.

REAR
The horse rises up on its hindlegs. Typical stallion behaviour. The basis for high school airs and some circus routines.

REARING
Care of young horses when they are growing up, when specialized attention is very important.

RECTANGULAR CONFORMATION
A horse which, in the relationship of its length to its height, gives the impression of being rectangular.

REFORM COLUMNS
Change from a wide to a narrower formation, e.g., change from four to two columns.

REIN IN
Bring the horse down to a slower pace by pulling on the reins.

REINS
Long, narrow straps made out of leather or woven textile, attached to the bit or bridle, and used by the rider or driver to guide and control the horse.

REJECT
1. Refusal of the stallion by a mare not on heat.
2. Driving away of the foal by a mare which is pregnant again.

REJONEADOR
Mounted Spanish bullfighter.

REMOUNT
A fresh horse, or supply of horses, for army use.

RESIST
Horse which refuses to obey the aids.

RESISTANCE
A horse normally reacts to a dangerous situation by running away as fast as possible, but stallions, and mares with foals, are prepared to defend themselves by biting and by kicking with their hooves.

RESPIRATORY DISORDERS
Various acute or chronic infections of the breathing passages, which often require a long convalescence or leave permanent damage.

RETRAINING
Correction of a badly trained horse. Can be a much more wearying task than the initial training.

RHINELAND HEAVY DRAUGHT
Powerful cold-blood breed, weighs up to 1000 kg.

RIBOT
One of the greatest racehorses and stallions of all time. Bred by Tesio in Italy in 1952. He sired winner after winner.

RICKETS
A bone disease in foals caused by deficiency of phosphorus and/or calcium and vitamin D.

RIDGELING (RIG)
Stallion in which one or both testicles do not descend. It is usually less fertile.

RIDINGER
Johann Elias Ridinger (1698-1767), famous painter of horses and equestrian scenes.

RIDING GEAR
In Europe the usual attire for riding consists of knee-length boots, riding breeches, coat and hard riding hat. For equestrian events, regulations often stipulate what is to be worn. For social riding in the Western saddle, jeans and short boots are the accepted gear.

RIDING SCHOOL
An establishment where people are taught to ride. Used to be predominantly military institutions, nowadays mainly civilian.

RIDING STYLE
European style of riding is based on classical dressage; American Western style evolved from a working style. Dressage, jumping and hunting each have their own individual style.

RIG
Another name for a ridgeling (q.v.).

RINGBONE
Chronic infection of the pastern joint. Can lead to lameness.

RISING SEAT
Rising out of the saddle at the gallop. When jumping the rider stands firmly in the stirrups and holds on with knees and calves. The opposite is 'sitting seat'.

ROACH BACK
Back which is curved upwards in front of the croup, and therefore unsuitable for riding.

ROAN
Coat with an admixture of white hairs which modify the colour.

ROARING
Chronic infection of the windpipe. The affected vocal cords vibrate, causing a roaring sound. A major defect.

RODEO
Equestrian sport from the United States. An exhibition of cowboys' skills developed from their various working tasks. Also popular in Australia and New Zealand.

ROGUE
Term for a bad-tempered horse. This behaviour is usually the result of mishandling.

ROPE HORSE
A cowboy's horse trained to work actively with the rider when he is using the lasso to rope cattle.

ROSINANTE
Don Quixote's horse.

ROTTALER
Bavarian warm-blood breed from the Rott valley.

ROUND-UP
A driving together of half-wild cattle, horse or pony herds.

RUGS
Used to protect the horse against the cold, wet and insects. Horses can develop weak constitutions if they are constantly rugged up.

RUINED
Term used to describe a horse that refuses to obey the aids, or does so unwillingly as the result of being ridden badly when young.

RUNABOUT
An American light four-wheeled vehicle.

RUNNING WALK
One of the gait variations taught, often by cruel methods, to the Tennessee Walking Horse.

RUN OUT
To leave the track or go around the side of an obstacle instead of jumping it.

RUSSIAN HEAVY DRAUGHT
Strong, very small cold-blood breed from the Ukraine.

RUSSIAN TROTTER
A trotting breed developed by crossing Orlov Trotters with American Standardbreds.

S

SADDLE CLOTH
Blanket put underneath the saddle to protect the saddle and the horse's back.

SADDLE GIRTH
Straps that go round the front of the horse's chest and fasten on to the front of the saddle to prevent it slipping to the rear.

SADDLE HORSE
A horse which is sold under this description must have mastered simple dressage lessons, be able to jump low obstacles, be safe in the country and in traffic, and be no problem to handle. The riding horse is usually a warm-blood.

SADDLE SHAPE
Saddles vary in shape according to their purpose. They include dressage, jumping, utility, racing, military, as well as various working saddles, e.g., American Western saddle.

SADDLE SHY
An almost neurotic fear in young horses, usually the result of saddles which are unprofessionally made. Can only be cured by a great deal of patience and sensitivity.

SADDLE SORE
Skin infection caused by a badly fitting saddle or folds in the blanket on saddle cloth. Often takes a long time to heal and leaves permanent white patches on the coat.

SAINT GEORGE
Since AD 300, the patron saint of horsemen.

SAINT HUBERT
Since AD 700, the patron saint of huntsmen.

SAINT SIMON
Foaled in 1881, one of the greatest of all Thoroughbreds, and one of the most prepotent of all sires.

SALIVA TEST
Occasionally saliva tests are taken during tests for doping.

SALT CRACK
A vertical split in the wall of the hoof, down from the head. Treatment is similar to that given for horizontal split.

SALT LICK
Hard salt block given to horses and cattle. It is often enriched with additional minerals.

SANDCUTTER
Another term for a jucker or light four-wheeled carriage.

SAQLAWI
One of the types of the Arab pure-bred.

SARDINIAN PONY
Acchetta, a small breed from Sardinia.

SAUMUR
Place where the French Cavalry School was founded in 1763.

SCHALANKEN
Fly fringe (q.v.) on Hungarian harness.

SCHLESWIG HEAVY DRAUGHT
Ancient cold-blood breed, basically the same as the Jutland. Medium-sized, weighing up to 900 kg.

SCHOOLED
Term used for a well trained horse which responds to the aids without resistance.

SCHWARZGOLD
A mare foaled in 1937 at the Schlenderhan Stud. Often described as the finest German Thoroughbred.

SCHWARZWALDER
Small, agile, cold-blood breed from the upper regions of the Black Forest.

SCORING
Preliminary warm-up ride before the start of a competition.

SEAT
The way the rider sits on the horse, or his or her ability to stay on a horse which is bucking and unruly.

SECOND HORSE
Horse taken along as a spare on a hunt.

SELECTION
In natural selection, i.e., in horses living in the wild, weak and sick animals died so that only the healthy could reproduce. In artificial selection the breeder chooses the fastest, strongest or most beautiful animals to breed from, castrates the less valuable stallions, and leaves the less valuable mares uncovered.

SELECTION ON THE TURF
English Thoroughbred race-horses, trotters, some Arabs and some other breeds are selected for breeding on the basis of their performance on the Turf.

SELECTIVE BREEDING AREA
Region to which a breed from another area is brought so that it can continue to be kept pure-bred.

SERVICE
Mating; a female is serviced by the male.

SEYDLITZ
Friedrich Wilhelm Baron von Seydlitz (1721-1773) was a famous Prussian cavalry general.

SHAFTS
The poles of a carriage on either side of the horse.

SHAGYA
Noble warm-blood breed from Hungary. Closely related to the pure-bred Arab.

SHANDERIDAN
A four-wheeled vehicle usually harnessed to a pair.

SHANDRYDAN
A light two-wheeled cart on springs, from Ireland.

SHELL HARNESS
In Arabian countries, in the Tyrol and in the Netherlands the harness is decorated with shells on festive occasions.

SHETLAND PONY
Small ponies often under 100 cm tall, from the Scottish Shetland Isles. A popular children's pony.

SHIRE HORSE
World's largest breed of horse. Originated in England. A stallion can have a withers height of over 2 metres and weigh up to 1300 kg.

SHOE
1. Act of shoeing a horse.
2. Rim of iron nailed to the horse's hoof.

SHOULDER-IN
The first basic lesson when beginning to work on two tracks in dressage.

SHOW-JUMPING
A competition in which riders have to jump a succession of obstacles. First held only a century ago, and now a popular equestrian sport in many countries.

SHOW-JUMPING DERBY
An international show-jumping competition first held in 1920 in Hamburg.

SHOW-JUMPING SADDLE
Saddle with padded knee rolls on the panel, which support the rider's thighs and give the knees a good grip.

SHY
Swerve aside suddenly at an unexpected noise or moving object. An instinctive behaviour. It is more common in Thoroughbreds and young horses than in older more experienced animals or in cold-bloods.

SIDEBONES
A common infection in show-jumpers.

SIDE REINS
Reins used when schooling to help the horse get on the bit and obtain the correct neck and head position.

SIDE SADDLE
Saddle designed for women, on which the rider sits with both feet at the same side. In common usage from the Baroque up till the nineteenth century.

SIMULATOR
A device used to simulate driving conditions for teaching the handgrips without a horse.

SINGLE-TOED
All members of the zoological family of the horse have only one toe.

SITTING SEAT
Opposite of rising seat. The rider remains sitting deeply in the saddle even when the horse is trotting.

SIX-IN-HAND
Six horses harnessed in pairs, one in front of the other.

SKELETON BRAKE
A four-wheeled carriage with no superstructure apart from the coachman's seat. Harnessed two-in-hand.

SKIJORING
The sport of being towed on skis by a horse or motor vehicle.

SKOGRUSS
Another name for the Swedish Gotland pony.

SLANT
The horse does not naturally walk quite straight; its body is slightly curved in what is called the natural slant.

SLIP
Premature birth or expulsion of a foal which is too under-developed to survive.

SLOAN
Tod Sloan, an American jockey who, about 1897, developed his 'acey deucey' style of riding with one stirrup shorter than the other.

SLOPING CROUP
A croup that slopes and tapers from the hips to the buttocks.

SMALL HORSE
Technical term to describe a pony which is over 130 cm tall.

SNAFFLE
1. Bit consisting of a single bar with a ring at each end to which one pair of reins is attached.
2. To fit a snaffle.

SNIP
A small white marking between nostrils and upper lip.

SOCIABLE
A low-slung, four-wheeled open carriage in which four people sit facing each other.

SOCIAL RIDING
Riding as a leisure pursuit with no great sporting or competitive ambitions.

SOUR
Term used to describe a horse which has been ruined by bad handling.

SOVIET HEAVY DRAUGHT
Heavy, medium-sized cold-blood breed developed about 1940 on a basis of Belgian Heavy Draught stallions and other European breeds.

SPANISH RIDING SCHOOL
A riding institution opened in Vienna in 1735 in a stately Baroque building. Today it still preserves the art of classical equitation, using Lipizzaner stallions.

SPAVIN
Inflammation or bony enlargement of the hock. Caused by over-demands. Can be cured in its early stages. Occurs mainly in dressage horses and in trotters.

SPEED SHOW-JUMPING
Competition in which the course has to be completed within a specified time.

SPEED AND ENDURANCE SECTION
The second part of the three-day event.

SPLINT
A bony growth usually occurring on the inside of the cannon or splint bones area of the foreleg. Various causes. Can result in only a blemish or be more serious and cause lameness.

SPLINT BONE
A thin bone which runs along the length of the upper two-thirds of the long bone on all four limbs. Also known as small metacarpal and small metatarsal bones.

SPLIT UP BEHIND
A croup with a lengthwise hollow. Typical sign of a cold-blood horse.

SPOTTED
A horse with a spotted coat.

SPREAD JUMP
Usually a jump over a wide sunken trough of water.

SPRINTER
A racehorse which is very fast over shorter distances, but does not have the powers of endurance needed for longer ones. Opposite of a stayer.

SPUR
A pointed device strapped on to the heel of the rider's boot, and used to urge the horse onwards.

SQUARE CONFORMATION
A horse which, in the relationship of its height to its length, gives the impression of being square.

STABLE
A collection of horses belonging to one owner.

STABLE COLOURS
Each racing stable has its own colours, or silks, which the jockeys wear when racing.

STABLE VICES
Horses living on their own or those with too little to do get bored. This can lead to the development of bad habits.

STACCIONATA
A show-jumping obstacle similar to a fence.

STAGECOACH
A large heavy travelling coach.

STAG HOUND
The Scottish deer hound used for stag hunting on horseback.

STAG HUNTING
Hunting stags, usually on horseback. A stag is a male deer, especially a red deer over four years old.

STAIRCASE
A series of obstacles in a cross-country event.

STAKES
A race for which money is staked or contributed.

STALE
To urinate.

STALL
The place where a horse is tied up in a stable.

STALLION
An ungelded male horse.

STANCE
The proper position or conformation of the limbs which is requisite to correct movement.

STANDARDBRED
American Standard Trotter, the fastest trotting breed.

STANDS UNDER
Faulty position of the forelegs.

STAR
White marking on the forehead.

STAR APPEAL
A Thoroughbred stallion foaled in 1970 on the German Stud of Röttgen. Earned the record sum of DM 1.5 million.

STAR GAZER
Head held awkwardly. Pokes its nose with face upturned. Often because of damage to the horse's back through being badly ridden, and therefore very difficult to control.

STARTING FEE
The sum which has to be paid in addition to the nominating fee before a race.

STARTING GATE
A group of stalls into which horses are shut before a race. When the starter presses a button all the gates open simultaneously.

STATE COACH
A large, closed four-wheeled carriage, especially one used on state occasions.

STATE STUD
Stud farm owned by a federal state.

STAYER
A racehorse with great powers of endurance, as opposed to the very fast sprinter which is suitable only for short stretches.

STEEP CROUP
The slope of the croup is too short and steep. A blemish, but not necessarily a disadvantage.

STEEPLECHASE
A race over a specified distance on which there are a number of obstacles to be jumped.

STIRRUP IRON
A metal or wooden device, suspended from the saddle by straps, which serves as a support for the rider's foot.

STOCK SADDLE
A saddle which has a raised pommel and cantle. Very suitable as a pack and trekking saddle. Most frequently used in Asia, Spain, Latin America and the western states of the US.

STRAIGHT PASTERN
Very straight position of hoof and pastern. Can be hereditary or develop as the result of the tendon shortening. Hereditary straight pastern in a foal can be cured. The acquired straight pastern of the tendon is often incurable.

STRANGLES
Feared contagious disease easily transmitted by bacteria. Attacks animals of all ages, but most common in young stock and others after a change in climate. The symptoms are a high fever, swelling of the glands under the jaw. Usually speedy recovery once the glands have opened and discharged pus. Sometimes lymph glands on internal organs are affected, which is often fatal. Affected animals must be strictly quarantined. Animals require several weeks of convalescence to prevent the development of chronic complications.

STRAW
Used for bedding material in the stable. Usually wheat straw, sometimes wood shavings or peat.

STROLLER
An Irish pony ridden by Marion Coakes, an Englishwoman. Exceptionally successful against top world class show-jumpers. Won the Silver Medal at the Mexico Olympics in 1968.

STUD
1. Private or state-owned establishment for breeding horses.
2. Stallion kept for breeding.

STUD BOOK
A record of horses' pedigrees.

STUD FEE
Amount which the mare's owner must pay to the owner of the stallion.

SUBSTANCE
When judging a horse, the overall impression, which is more important than the evaluation of the individual exterior parts.

SUCKLING
An unweaned foal.

SUFFOLK PUNCH
Immensely powerful, short-legged cold-blood breed from Suffolk, England. Very compact, weighs 1000 kg or more.

SULKY
A light two-wheeled vehicle used in trotting races.

SUMMERHAYS
R. S. Summerhays, born 1881. British hippologist and author of numerous books on horses.

SWAMP FEVER
Equine Infectious Anaemia (q.v.).

SWAN-NECKED
Neck too long and thin.

SWAYBACK
A concave or sagging back. Can be hereditary or can be caused by a rider who is too heavy for a young horse. May occur in young mares as a result of pregnancy.

SWEAT SCRAPER
A knife-shaped instrument used to remove sweat or for scraping off surplus water after washing.

SWEDISH ARDENNES
Cold-blood breed developed about a hundred years ago by crossing Swedish Draught and Ardennais. Still has a widespread distribution.

SWEDISH WARM-BLOOD
Noble, versatile modern riding horse with a special aptitude for dressage.

SWEEPSTAKE
A method of gambling. Each participant's stake is pooled and numbers, horses, etc., are assigned by lot. The Irish Sweepstake which is financed from many countries is one example. The profits go to Irish hospitals.

SWEET ITCH
A dermatitis which occurs mainly in summer. Northern ponies frequently suffer from it. Causes intense irritation.

SYNDICATE
In the United States in particular, groups of about forty people often put a certain amount of money into a pool to buy valuable Thoroughbred stallions. Group ownership.

T

TACK
Equipment used in riding and driving horses.

TACT
The rhythmic beat of foot-falls in all gaits. The aim is for these to be as regular as possible.

TANDEM
Two-wheeled carriage with two horses harnessed singly, one behind the other.

TAPE MEASURE
Perpendicular measurement from the ground to the withers along the curve of the horse's body. Usually the withers height is measured with a measuring stick.

TARPAN
Extinct European wild horse. Occurred in two types: forest, and plains or steppe.

TATTERSALLS
A famous London horse mart and auction house.

TEAM
1. Set of animals harnessed together.
2. Vehicle with horses harnessed to it.

TEASER
A stallion or rig used to test the response of a mare prior to breeding, or used to determine whether the mare is on heat and ready to breed.

TEETH
When fully mouthed the horse has 40 teeth: 12 incisors, 6 in each jaw; 4 canines, 1 on each side of the upper and lower jaw; and 24 molars, 6 above and 6 below on each side. Females have no canines. An expert can tell the age of a horse by the amount of wear on its teeth.

TEMPERAMENT
Disposition. Cold-bloods are normally calm and phlegmatic. Thoroughbreds can often be highly excitable.

TENDON DAMAGE
Damage to the leg tendon. Usually a wearisome business to cure. Particularly frequent in jumping and dressage horses.

TENNESSEE WALKING HORSE
Originally a horse used for work on the plantations. Possesses great stamina. Today almost exclusively degraded into a show horse. Dubious and often painful methods are used to teach it unnatural gaits.

TERSKY
A warm-blood breed from the Soviet Union. Bred as a saddle horse in a type very similar to the Arab and in a stronger draught horse type.

TETANUS
Infectious, often fatal disease caused by the tetanus bacillus entering a horse's body through wounds. Recommended that horses be vaccinated.

THERAPEUTIC RIDING
A form of therapy for those with cerebral damage, with the help of trained personnel. The horses and ponies used have to be quiet and absolutely dependable. Very successful physical and emotional results have been obtained.

THIGH AIDS
Orders are given to the horse by pressing the thigh against its side.

THILLS
The shafts of a carriage.

THOROUGHBRED
Term used to describe Arabs or English Thoroughbreds or horses which have been noticeably influenced by these breeds. Also used to describe particularly elegant, fast and spirited horses and ponies.

THOROUGHBRED BREED
A horse which traces its descent from any of three Arabian stallions of the early eighteenth century.

THRUSH
An inflammation in a horse's frog. Can be avoided by proper care of its feet. Usually easily cured.

TICK TACK
Bookmaker's telegraphy by arm signals. Used in Britain and Ireland.

TICINO
Outstanding Thoroughbred stallion foaled in 1939 on the Erlenhof stud.

TIERCÉ
French for trifecta, i.e., the first three horses across the finishing line, given in the correct order.

TIGHTEN THE GIRTH
Fasten the saddle girth more tightly after riding for a while.

TILBURY
Dutch two-wheeled carriage with a leather hood.

TILTING AT THE RING
Ancient equestrian sport. At full gallop a rider uses a lance to thread a ring suspended on a gallows.

TIME ALLOWED
The prescribed period of time in which a competitor must complete a show-jumping course. Jumping errors are often deducted in seconds.

TOES OUT
Faulty position of the feet.

TÖLT
A fairly fast gait which is very comfortable for the rider. In many countries it is taught to ponies, horses and donkeys. It is particularly well known through Icelandic ponies, whose normal gait it is.

TONGUE DEFECTS
Horses which lay their tongues over the bar of the bit, or let them hang out the side of their mouths, make it impossible to use the reins correctly. Can be corrected with the use of spoon bits or other aids.

TOR DI QUINTO
Cavalry school opened in Rome in 1891. Made famous by Federico Caprilli, who evolved the modern style of show-jumping. Has been closed since World War Two.

TORIC
A warm-blood breed developed in Estonia, now part of the Soviet Union. Bred in a riding type similar to the Arab, and a carriage type which is slightly heavier.

TOTALISATOR
A system of betting developed in France. Nowadays used in most countries. The total amount staked (minus tax) is divided among the winners in proportion to the size of their individual stake.

TOURNAMENT
A military sport of the Middle Ages. Nowadays dressage, show-jumping and three-day events are all called tournaments.

TRACTIVE POWER
The pulling power of a horse; about 1000 kg.

TRAIL RIDING
An equestrian sport popular in the US. Riding along trails across country, often with tests of skill en route.

TRAINER
The professional trainer must be able to ride unbroken horses, and school novices in dressage and show-jumping up to Stage I level.

TRAINING
*1. The preparation of a young horse for its future tasks as a riding or draught horse; requires an expert.
2. The schooling of the future rider or driver.*

TRAIN OFF
Over-train a horse so that its performance deteriorates.

TRAIT DU NORD
French cold-blood breed similar to the Ardennais and the Belgian Heavy Draught.

TRAKEHNER
Outstanding breed of saddle horse which originated at the Trakehnen Stud, founded in 1732 in East Prussia. Also bred in Poland and West Germany. Those bred in Poland are called Wielkopolski.

TRAKEHNER DITCH
Popular, very demanding obstacle; often found in the cross-country section of the three-day event.

TRANQUILIZER
A sedative given to nervous dressage and event horses before a competition. Some tranquilizers are covered by the doping regulations and are not permitted in competitive events.

TRANSITIONS
Movements from one gait to another. In dressage these must always be made progressively, in a smooth and precise manner.

TRAVERS
A dressage movement on two tracks.

TREAD
Wound on the coronet.

TREBLE
In show-jumping, a combination of three separate obstacles which are counted as one jump.

TREE
The framework of the saddle, which was traditionally made from wood. Nowadays it is also made of plastic or fibreglass, and reinforced with steel.

TREKKING
Long-distance riding purely for pleasure, with no competitive element involved.

TRIGA
In Greek and Roman times, a two-wheeled cart, usually a war chariot, drawn by three horses abreast. See also Biga and Quadriga.

TRIM
Before a horse is shod, the part of the hoof wall which has grown must be trimmed to make it even. Horses and ponies which are unshod must also have their hooves trimmed occasionally.

TRIPLE BAR
In show-jumping, a high spread fence consisting of three sets of posts and rails, built in staircase fashion with the highest at the back.

TRIPLE CROWN
Accorded to the racehorse that wins the three classic races: in England, the Two Thousand Guineas, Derby and St Leger; in the United States, the Kentucky Derby, Preakness and Belmont Stakes.

TROIKA
A Russian vehicle for three horses harnessed abreast. The middle horse trots under the arch of the duga; the two outer horses gallop.

TROPILLA
A gaucho's herd of horses.

TROT
One of the horse's three basic gaits.

TROTTER
*1. Breed of horses which show outstanding traits at the trot.
2. The American trotting breed (Standardbred) is divided into trotters which trot normally (diagonally) and pacers, which trot laterally.*

TROTTING LIGHT
Rising out of the saddle at every second trotting step.

TROTTING RACES
Trotting or pacing races between specially bred horses harnessed to sulkies. In France also ridden under the saddle.

TURF
Any course over which horse racing is conducted. The Turf = horse racing and betting.

TUSH
Also called pointed, gelding or stallion tooth. Appears in male horses at about four years in the gap between the incisors and the molars.

TWITCH
A piece of cord fastened to a fairly short piece of stick, which is placed around the horse's nostrils, and then twisted tight to make the horse stand still. Used to distract the animal when treating a wound, or on the mare during mating.

TWINS
Healthy, normally developed twins occur in about one out of every 1500 live births. Usually they are aborted at an early stage. If they are carried to full term they are often both too small to be capable of developing normally.

TWO THOUSAND GUINEAS
One of the English classic races.

U

UKRAINIAN WARM-BLOOD
Modern, noble warm-blood breed strongly influenced by Thoroughbred, Trakehner and Hanoverian stallions.

UNDERPINNING
Term used to describe the horse's legs; sometimes includes the skeleton as well.

UNHARNESS
Remove the harness.

UNHITCH
Unfasten a horse from a vehicle.

UNMADE
Young horse ready to be schooled.

UPRIGHT MANE
A mane which falls down both sides of the neck. Common in northern ponies and cold-blood breeds.

UPRIGHT SHOULDER
Undesirable feature. Reduces the stride and increases the impact so the horse strikes the ground harder.

URINE TEST
Urine tests are taken to discover whether drugs have been given to horses which are entered in a competition; to test for pregnancy in mares which have been covered; and to diagnose an infection.

UTILITY SADDLE
A saddle which is designed for general purpose use and can be used for most forms of equitation.

V

VAQUERO
Mexican herdsman, usually on horseback.

VESTLANDHEST
Norwegian name for the Fjord pony.

VETERINARY SURGEON
Someone skilled in the diagnosis and treatment of diseases of domestic animals.

VICES
Any of the many bad habits that a horse may acquire. Not hereditary faults, but the result of faulty or unprofessional handling. Some of the stable vices are cribbing, wood-chewing, pawing. Others are being excessively fearful, resisting saddle or bit, throwing the head up, rearing, biting, kicking. Stable vices often develop because the horse is bored, kept on its own, with too little to occupy it. These vices are almost unknown in horses which live in groups in an open stall. Other vices develop as the result of being pampered when a foal, or when too many demands are made during breaking in, or because of badly fitting bridles or saddles.

VICTORIA
An open four-wheeled carriage for two people. Has a folding hood.

VIRAL ABORTION
Expulsion of a foetus before it is fully developed. Caused by a viral infection. Can be vaccinated against.

VIS-À-VIS
A light, four-wheeled carriage with seats facing each other.

VIZIR
One of Napoleon's grey Arab stallions.

VLADIMIR HEAVY DRAUGHT
Powerful draught horse, first bred about a hundred years ago in the region east of Moscow. Used for agricultural work.

VOLTE
In dressage, a full turn on the haunches in a circle of 6 to 8 metres diameter.

VOLVULUS
Condition in which the intestines are twisted, i.e., the bowel itself, or the membranes supporting it, thus cutting off the blood supply and causing severe pain.

W

WAGON FORTIFICATION
Defensive position made up of wagons placed one behind the other in a circle.

WALER
Noble warm-blood breed developed in Australia from English halfbreds and Arabs.

WALK
The slowest of the three basic gaits.

WALK ON
Set the horse in motion by the use of aids.

WARENDORF
State stud in North Rhine Westphalia.

WAR HORSE
Strong but agile horse, which had to be capable of carrying a knight in full armour into battle.

WARM-BLOOD
All noble breeds of saddle horses and all lighter carriage horses. They are all influenced to a greater or lesser degree by English Thoroughbreds or Arabs. Halfbreds, of which one parent is an Arab or English Thoroughbred, are also warm-bloods.

WARRANTY
In many countries the seller of a horse is legally responsible for any defects, as recognized in law, which were not evident when the horse was purchased. Normally the warranty lasts up to fourteen days after purchase.

WATERING PLACE
A place where animals go to drink or bathe.

WATER JUMP
Natural or artificial obstacle.

WEAN
A foal is often taken away from its dam when it is only four to six months old, which can result in physical and emotional disturbance. Mares in free-roaming herds, depending on whether they are pregnant, 'wean' their foals at ten months or even later.

WEATHERBY
In 1791 the first of Weatherby's General Stud Books appeared. This English firm has continued to publish this annual register of English Thoroughbreds.

WEAVING
A stable vice caused by boredom. A weaving horse rocks from side to side. Frequently copied by neighbouring horses.

WEEDON
British Cavalry School. The Royal Household Cavalry is trained there.

WEIGHT
1. Racehorses must carry a specified weight. To obtain this, lead weights are inserted in a weight cloth in the saddle. 2. In Britain and Ireland hunters are divided into classes according to weight.

WELSH PONY
Outstanding breed from Wales. Bred in five distinct types or sections.

WESTERN HORSE
Those breeds of horse, including those of Spanish origin, which are found in the American West, e.g., Mustang, Quarter Horse, Appaloosa, Pinto, Palomino.

WESTERN SADDLE
A very comfortable saddle developed to meet the requirements of cowboys who had to spend all day on horseback. Very suitable for social riding and for many equestrian sports.

WESTERN STYLE
A riding style developed by cowboys herding cattle. Most striking characteristics are the long reins and the fact that the legs are kept almost straight. Very suitable style for leisure time pursuits, for trekking, and for many equestrian sports.

WEST FRIESIAN
Ancient cold-blood breed very like a warm-blood in appearance.

WESTPHALIAN
Versatile warm-blood breed of the same type as the Hanoverian.

WHEELER
The horse at the back when four or more horses are hitched up.

WHINNY
The horse's contact call, which carries for a great distance.

WHITE MUZZLE
White markings covering both lips up to the nostrils.

WHITE STOCKING
White marking on the legs which extends up to or over the ankle joint.

WIELKOPOLSKI
A breed developed in Poland after World War Two from what was left of the Trakehner breed. The Polish Trakehner.

WIND GALLS
Swellings form on the joint or sheaths of the tendons. They can sometimes cause lameness, but usually only result in a blemish. Galls can develop as the result of over-exertion or an excess of protein in the diet.

WINDSOR GREYS
The greys which are harnessed on ceremonial occasions for the British Royal Family. Originally a present from the Dutch Queen Wilhelmina.

WINKERS
Blinkers (q.v.).

WINTER SHOEING
Horseshoes with calkins as protection against sliding.

WITHERS
The highest part of a horse's back; the area at the base of the neck between the shoulder blades.

WOOD-CHEWING
A vice, the result of boredom, nutritional inadequacies or stress.

WOOD TAR
Oily substance used to protect the hooves from mouldy straw.

WORMS
There are about 70 varieties of parasitic worms which can infect the horse. A virulent attack of worms can weaken the animal and often cause a fatal infection. Modern medicaments are, however, effective against all varieties and can be administered twice yearly in the feed.

WORONESH
Light, agile cold-blood breed from Russia.

WOUWERMANS
Philip Wouwermans (1619-1668). Dutch painter famous for his paintings of horses.

WÜRTTEMBERG
Very noble warm-blood breed similar to the Trakehner.

X

X
X after a horse's name indicates that it is a pure-bred Anglo-Arab; its ancestors were all English Thoroughbreds or pure-bred Arabs.

XX
XX after a horse's name indicates that it is an English Thoroughbred; OX indicates it is a pure-bred Arab.

XENOPHON
A Greek historian about 430-354 BC. Author, among other books, of comprehensive works on the art or riding. Some of his observations are still valid today.

Y

YEARLING
Colt or filly aged one year.

YORKSHIRE COACH HORSE
Very noble breed of carriage horses descended from Cleveland Bays with a high proportion of Thoroughbred blood. Have been used to improve many other breeds. Also make excellent saddle horses.

Z

ZEBRA
Any of a group of striped, horse-like animals of the genus Equus. All are found only on the African continent.

ZEBROID
Offspring of a male zebra and a female ass. These hybrids are normally sterile.

ZWEIBRÜCKER
Noble warm-blood breed from the Zweibrücken stud in the Pfalz. Stongly influenced by Arabs and Thoroughbreds.

INDEX

ACKNOWLEDGEMENTS

All the photographs were taken by Hans D. Dossenbach, except for the following:

All Sport House Morden, England 35; 196/197; 200/201; 202; 213; 84/85; 214/1,2,3; 215/4,5; 216/217
M.E. Ammann 252/1,2,4,5; 253/9,10; 254/3,4,6; 255/11,12,13A,13B,14,16; 256
Archiv für Kunst und Geschichte, Berlin 98/3; 102a; 103/a; 105/4; 106/2; 14/1; 115; 120/1; 121/7; 123/3, 5; 126/4; 128/3; 130/3; 132/2; 133/3,5; 134/1,2; 35/4,7; 136/1; 140/1; 184/1; 185 a,b; 264/2; 265/5
M. Baumann, Schaffhausen, 83 ra; 107/6
Bavaria Bildagentur; 141/4; Interfoto 130/3; R. Jungblut 264/3; 265/4; M. Pedone 103/3; S. Sammer 132/1; D.H. Teuffen 131/4
BBC Hulton Picture Library 190/1, 2, 3, 6; 192/5; 193/8; 194/2; 195/6,8; 198/1,4,5,6; 199/10,11,12
Agence P. Bertrand et Fils 225/5,6,7
Bild + News Photoservice, Zurich 236/1; 245/12,14, 16, 19, 20, 21
British Museum London 92/1,2,3; 93/4-7; 94/1; 95/4; 96/2,3; 97/4-12; 98/2; 99/5,7; 106/1,3,4; 108/1; 109/5,6,7; 110/2; 111/4,5,7; 116/117/1-7; 131/5; 133/4; 137/5
The British Race Horse 195/7
M. Bruggmann 88/1,2; 89/3; 172/1-4; 173/5,7
Editions du Cercle d'Art, Paris 104/1,2; 105/7
Gerry Cranham Colour Library 201 b; 253/9
F. Davidson 245/15; 276/b (Bildserie)
A.E. Derkson 169/1-8
Direktorium für Vollblotzucht und Rennen e. V 203/3, 4, 5
Escuela d'Equitacion 250
W. Ernst 230/231; 236/3,4; 237/5-9; 244/3, 9; 253/13; 254/2;
Agence Jacana-Explorer 84/85; Dubois 174/3; J. Joffre 175; 176/177; P. Lorner 156/2; Ph. Masse 90/1; Michel 83/4; R. Sidney 82/1; 83/5
H. Farkas 25/2
K.D. Francke 174/1,2
Film- und Lichtbildstelle des Bundesministeriums für Land- und Forstwirtschaft Wien 161/4; 284/1-4; 285/5-8
Fotostudio 61/Office du livre 149
Archiv T. Frei 268-273b
T. Frei 152/153/14-27; 262/263; 268 a: 271 ar; 272 a; 274-279
Editions les Garennes 282; 286/1-4; 287/5
A. Gebs 162/163
G. Gerster, Dr. 9
F. Hack 165 a; 173/6
F. Hemelrijk 244/10
Holle Bildarchiv 80/81; 95/5,7; 99/4; 101/5; 104/3; 107/7,8; 108/3; 111/6; 112/2; 125/3; 230 al
M.Byron-Moore 34
Hughes Photograph 299

Internationale Bildagentur Oberengstringen (IBA) 114-145 (illustrations for the margins); M. Müller 144
The Irish Horse Board 187/3; 240/1,2,3
Keeneland Library Kentucky 266/4-6; 207/7-10; 208/3, 5, 6; 269/8,9; 212/1, 2, 4, 5
Kienzer 30/2
Ch. Küenzi 146/147
Kunitsch, Dr 10/11
L. Lane 244/4
Foto Löbl-Schreyer 100/1; 108/4; 120/2
H. Mäder 2/3; 86/87; 158/159; 178/179
T. Mayer 187
H.P. Meier 157/5
W. Menzendorf 161/3; 252/3; 253/8; 255/8, 11; 259/a; 261
J. Metzger, Tages-Anzeigers, Zürich 266/3
W.I. Nikiforow, Albert Müller Verlag 29/13; 32/25; 180; 181
New York Racing Ass. 203/1, 2; 266/6, 7, 8; 267/13; 212/2
Sammlung der Universität Solo 116/9; 117/14,17,18
Okapia Frankfurt 273 ar
J. Piekalkiewicz, Südwest Verlag 145
R. Rogers, Ashbourne, Ireland 187/3
Ringier Dokumentationszentrum, Zürich 236/2; 244/6
Santa Anita Park 206/9; 208/1; 212/1
Bildarchiv Sammer 125/4
Shostal 21/9; 82/2; 110/1
Instituto Scala, Florence 95/8; 96 a; 102/2; 103/4, 5; 109/8; 120/1; 124/1,2; 125/5; 128/1,2; 129/6; 183 r; 184/2,3; 263 r; 264/1
Silvester/Rapho 62/63; 76/77
Skyviews, New York 209/7; 212/3
R. von Siebenthal 267/6,9
Schultze-Naumburg, Dr. 186/2
Bildarchiv K.H. Schuster 157/3; Hirschmann 189; Kanne 98/1; Reisel 99/6; Zeitler 273 al
Staatliches Historisches Museum Stockholm 116/8 10,11,12,13; 117/15,16
Studio Tavera, Pinerolo 251
S.A. Thompson, Albert Müller Verlag 29/9; 32/24; 224/2, 270 a
H. Weber 94/2
H. Wettstein Uster 161/5; 266/1; 267/7
Zefa: K.E. Deckart 273 am; G. Heil 91/5; K. Helbig 94/3; 95/8; 102/1; T.Schneiders 112/1; 113; 121/6; 160/2; Dr F. Sauer 83/3; H. Sunak 127/5; Starfoto 108/2; E. Weiland 70/71
N. Zalis, Dr. 32/26; 267/8
b: below; m: middle; a: above; l: left; r: right